# Capital Punishment
## Global Issues and Prospects

# The Waterside Press Criminal Policy Series

**Volume I**

*Transforming Criminal Policy*

**Volume II**

*Capital Punishment: Global Issues and Prospects*

**In preparation (working titles)**

*Drugs and Criminal Policy*

*The Scottish Criminal Justice Process*

*Golden Threads: Questions for the Law of Evidence*

# Capital Punishment
## Global Issues and Prospects

Edited by

## Peter Hodgkinson
## Andrew Rutherford

**Waterside Press Criminal Policy Series** Volume II
**Series Editor** Andrew Rutherford

# Capital Punishment Global Issues and Prospects

**Published** 1996 by
WATERSIDE PRESS
Domum Road
Winchester SO23 9NN
Telephone or Fax 01962 855567

**ISBN** Paperback 1 872870 32 5

**Cataloguing-in-publication data** A catalogue record for this book can be obtained from the British Library.

**Criminal Policy Series** Volume II.

**Cover design** by John Good Holbrook Ltd, Coventry

**Printing and binding** by Antony Rowe Ltd, Chippenham

# Acknowledgements

We are most grateful to the individual contributors who worked under extraordinary time constraints and for their ready agreement that royalties be used to support the work of the Centre for Capital Punishment Studies at the University of Westminster. We are confident that this collection of original essays will further enhance the reputation of the Centre among scholars, policy makers and practitioners. The students associated with the Centre provided the raison d'être and inspiration for this book.

Our gratitude extends to Bryan Gibson, publisher at the Waterside Press, who has displayed fortitide and patience at all stages of the project. Gaynor Dunmall, researcher to the Centre for Capital Punishment Studies, merits a very special note of appreciation for the numerous tasks she has undertaken and, in particular, for her work in preparing the index. We also gratefully acknowledge the financial support provided by the Universities of Southampton and Westminster, and a grant awarded by the Barrow and Geraldine S. Cadbury Trust

On a personal note, AR acknowledges the loving support of Judith and Max. PH thanks Sue, Katie and Hannah for their understanding and encouragement, and for the constant reminding that it was possible to turn off the television!

**Peter Hodgkinson**
**Andrew Rutherford**

February 1996

# The contributors

**HUGO ADAM BEDAU** is Austin Fletcher Professor of Philosophy, Tufts University and visiting professor and on the Advisory Board of the Centre for Capital Punishment Studies, University of Westminster. His publications include *The Death Penalty in America* (fourth edition forthcoming) and *In Spite of Innocence* with Constance Putnam and Michael Radelet. He is the past chair of the National Coalition for the Abolition of the Death Penalty.

**SIMON COLDHAM** is a Senior Lecturer in Law at the Department of Law, School of Oriental and African Studies, University of London. Formerly he was a Lecturer in Law at the University of Nairobi (1973-1975) and at the University of Birmingham (1975-1978). He has published extensively on a wide range of issues relating to the laws of Commonwealth African countries and has been co-editor of the *Journal of African Law* since 1983.

**EDWARD FITZGERALD** QC is a practising barrister based in London who specialises in criminal appeals and international human rights law. He has represented death row prisoners before the Judicial Committee of the Privy Council in cases from Jamaica, Belize and Trinidad. He is a member of JUSTICE.

**STANISLAW FRANKOWSKI** studied at Warsaw University, Poland where he also taught for many years before joining St. Louis University School of Law, Missouri in 1983. He received an LL.M at New York University School of Law and was a Fellow at the Max Planck Institute in Frieburg. His publications include *Abortion and the Protection of the Human Foetus* (co-edited with George Cole), *Preventive Detention* (co-edited with Dinah Shelton) and *Legal Reform in post-communist Europe* (co-edited with Paul B. Stephan III).

**JOHN HATCHARD** is a Senior Fellow at the British Institute of International and Comparative Law. He has taught law at universities in Zambia, Zimbabwe, the United States and the United Kingdom. He has written widely on criminal law, criminal justice and evidence, with particular reference to southern Africa. He is joint editor of the *Journal of African Law*.

**PETER HODGKINSON** is the Director of the Centre for Capital Punishment Studies at the School of Law, University of Westminster, a project he founded in 1993. Prior to joining Westminster in 1989 he was with the Inner London Probation Service for 15 years where he developed an expertise in life-sentenced and mentally disordered offenders. He is a member of the Council of the Howard League for Penal Reform, chair of DEATH WATCH (a European abolitionist group) and a member of the Management Council of 'Hands Off Cain' (an international group campaigning for the abolition of the death penalty). He is a former Honorary Secretary of the British Society of Criminology and is a one-time member of the editorial board of the *Journal of Criminal Behaviour and Mental Health*.

**MICHAEL PALMER** is Senior Lecturer and formerly head of the Department of Law, School of Oriental and African Studies, University of London. He is also Academic Director of the Practical Training Scheme for Young Chinese (PRC) Lawyers, Honorary Senior Research Fellow, China Research Unit, City University, London and an advisor on Chinese law to the Attorney General of Hong Kong.

**MICHAEL L. RADELET** is Professor of Sociology, University of Florida. He holds a Ph.D from Purdue University, and spent two years doing post-doctoral work in Psychiatry at the University of Wisconsin. From 1979-1987 he taught the required course in Medical Ethics at the University of Florida Medical School. In recent years his interests have shifted to capital punishment. He has now written four books and three dozen scholarly papers on various aspects of the death penalty. In addition he has testified in four dozen capital trials throughout the United States, and worked closely with death row inmates and their families, particularly around the time of executions, in Florida. He is visiting professor and a member of the Advisory Board of the Centre for Capital Punishment Studies at the University of Westminster.

**ANDREW RUTHERFORD** is Professor in Law at Southampton University. He is the author *of Prisons and the Process of Justice, Growing Out of Crime: The New Era, Criminal Justice and the Pursuit of Decency* and *Transforming Criminal Policy*. He is visiting professor at the University of Westminster and a member of the Advisory Board of the Centre for Capital Punishment Studies. Since 1984 he has been chair of the Howard League for Penal Reform.

**WILLIAM A. SCHABAS** is Professor and Chair, Départment des Sciences Juridiques, Université du Québèc à Montréal. He is a member of the Advisory Board, Centre for Capital Punishment Studies, University of Westminster, editor of the *International Yearbook on Capital Punishment* produced by the Centre and author of *The Abolition of the Death Penalty in International Law*.

**GER PIETER VAN DEN BERG** is Senior University Docent for East European Law in the Institute of East European Law and Russian Studies at the University of Leiden, Netherlands. His doctoral dissertation was on 'The Government of Russia and the Soviet Union'. He is associate editor of the *Review of Socialist Law* and of the *Review of Central and East European Law*. His publications include *The Soviet System of Justice: Figures and Policy*, *Sovjet Staat en Recht in Begweging* and *A Comment on the Constitution of the Russian Federation* (forthcoming).

# Capital Punishment
## Global Issues and Prospects

CONTENTS

CHAPTER

WATERSIDE PRESS

WINCHESTER

# CHAPTER 1

# Introduction

## Peter Hodgkinson and Andrew Rutherford

The gallows is not only a machine of death, but a symbol. It is the symbol of terror, cruelty and irreverence for life; the common denominator of primitive savagery, mediaeval fanaticism and modern totalitarianism. It stands for everything that mankind must reject, if mankind is to survive its present crisis. (Arthur Koestler, who 18 years before he wrote these words, had spent three months under sentence of death, witnessing the executions of his fellow prisoners in a Spanish prison and awaiting his own).[1]

Every person shall have the right to life. If not, the killer unwittingly achieves a final and perverse moral victory by making the state a killer too, thus reducing social abhorrence at the conscious extinction of human beings. (Justice Albie Sachs, delivering the eleventh and final opinion of the Constitutional Court of the Republic of South Africa which, on 6 June 1995, unanimously declared the death penalty for murder to be unconstitutional).[2]

Across much of the world capital punishment remains a remarkably resilient instrument and symbol of public policy. As the third millennium approaches, the dividing line between states on the issue of the death penalty is becoming increasingly sharp. Virtually outlawed within the European Union, the right of the state under its domestic law to put certain people to death is aggressively defended in such otherwise disparate political systems as the United States of America, the People's Republic of China and many Islamic states. While the question of capital punishment has always interested students of criminology and penal policy, it has also long been recognised as spanning the spectrum of political philosophy. The issue of capital punishment is at the heart of defining the kind of society sought by its citizens.

The purpose of this volume is to place the death penalty and the resort to capital punishment within an historical and contemporary social and political context in order to illuminate and assess current issues and emerging developments. Undertaking this project, we were challenged by Roger Hood's observation as to the sparseness of research (and sometimes even quite basic data) outside the USA.[3] Indeed, as Hugo Bedau has noted, more has been published about the death penalty in the USA than in the rest of the world combined. There is, of course material on the USA here (and not only in the chapter written by Professor Bedau), but the book breaks new ground by including chapters on regions of the world that have been all but ignored in the literature on the death penalty.

The need for a global view is underlined by the gathering pace of international human rights law with its implied mission of restricting, if not abolishing, the death penalty under all circumstances. As William Schabus observes in the next chapter, while certain basic norms which restrict the application of capital punishment have become relatively well accepted, the issue of abolition has become increasingly controversial within fora such as the General Assembly of the United Nations. We are hopeful that this volume will contribute to the debates at global and regional meetings attended by national representatives .

Global perspectives allow opportunities to trace the presence of the death penalty and the application of capital punishment with respect to the transition from traditional to modern societies. For example, Michael Palmer comments in Chapter 5 that the Chinese criminal justice system, with its unambiguous reliance upon the death penalty, bears the imprint of many traditional Chinese legal norms and values. Furthermore, in much of Commonwealth Africa, for example, the death penalty structure more closely reflects both the colonial past and traditional societies than the status of recently gained independent statehood. Account has to be taken of the growth of Islam which is briefly addressed in this volume. A further exploration would need to compare those states driven by a religious imperative with those which focus upon a particular interpretation of *chari'a*. A rather different comparison would be between those countries, such as Egypt, which rely upon secular legislation and others, such as the Sudan, which apply the principles of Islamic *faqih*. This latter distinction was stressed by Professor Aly Fahmi at an international conference held in Tunis during 1995; he went on to note that the special tribunals which exist in some Islamic countries are particularly oblivious to international law and conventions.[4]

Several themes recur in the chapters which follow. First, there is a definitional issue of some importance which arises with reference to the mostly uncertain relationship between the death penalty and the actual application of capital punishment. While the death penalty and capital punishment are not synonymous, however the terms are conventionally interchanged. There are circumstances where a precise distinction is essential. In some states, for example, the death penalty may exist but with no expectation or intent that capital punishment ever be carried out. This describes the situation in Belgium where, as noted in Chapter 8, no attempt has been made in recent years to disturb this state of *de facto* abolition. Even in situations where death sentences are regularly imposed, only a tiny proportion of the total are actually carried out. As noted in Chapter 4, for example, in Russia the death penalty, as opposed to capital punishment, is defended on the grounds that it acts as a deterrent. A somewhat similar situation exists in the USA with some fifty or sixty executions a year against the background of more than 3000 persons held on death rows across the country. The unwritten policy presumption appears to be that only a small number of people from a much larger pool of candidates need be put to death. But how is this number derived and what criteria determine which people are selected for execution?

A rather different situation exists where the scope of the death penalty is widened against the background of a declining number of executions. This second theme, which is a scene all too familiar to historians of eighteenth century England and is described by John Hatchard and Simon Coldham in Chapter 7. As the authors comment, in spite of a trend to extend death penalty offences in Commonwealth Africa it is unusual for executions to be carried out in most states. In this connection, mention should be made of the converse phenomenon of executions taking place without imposition of the death penalty. Extrajudicial executions, which receive only slight attention in this volume, continue to be widely reported in many parts of the world. Amnesty International and other human rights organizations have drawn regular attention to these abuses, including 'disappearances', which serve, at least implicitly, the purposes of the state. Indeed, regular killings of this sort are by no means unusual in some states where the death penalty has been formally dispensed with, as is the case in some parts of central and south America.

A third theme that emerges is the role of the death penalty within the broader framework of criminal policy. The availability of the death penalty (even when only rarely carried out) may have the effect of escalating the overall range of criminal penalties. One aspect of this linkage of capital punishment to penalty as a whole is the impact upon the discourse regarding alternatives. In the USA, for example, little consideration has been given to options which fall short of life imprisonment without the possibility of parole. While abolitionists may argue, and with some justification, that it is not for them to propose alternatives to phenomena as intrinsically evil as slavery or the burning of witches, the death penalty cannot easily be divorced from the wider structure of penalties or other problems of penal policy and practice.

Fourth, and connected to the preceding theme, there is the resonance of the death penalty issue as a commodity to be traded in the market places of the mass media and politics.[5] Once again this is especially evident in the USA where, with very few exceptions, even liberal Democrat politicians tend to conceal whatever personal abhorrence they may have for capital punishment. On the other hand, in the aftermath of abolition the death penalty as a political issue tends to recede rapidly. For example, despite the emergence of crime and punishment as a domestic political topic in Britain the death penalty itself has been largely eclipsed. However, as described in Chapter 8, the British government has done little or nothing to encourage the development of international law in this area.

The final theme is the problematic location of the death penalty within a general human rights framework. As is evident from the chapters which follow there are quite distinct approaches to this issue. For some commentators, the logic of human rights unequivocally leads to abolition. In sharp contrast, some supporters of the death penalty argue that combating crime is to be regarded as an aspect of the humanisation of criminal law. In Chapter 4, Ger Pieter van den Berg quotes a well known Russian jurist as insisting that 'humanism cannot be one-sided'. More than once in this volume the question is also raised as to whether an agenda based upon rights of the offender necessarily contributes to abolition of the death penalty. For example, progress towards a procedurally flawless legal process, at least in terms of appearances, may best serve the cause of retentionists. Similarly, if the complaint is one of undue delay, on death row the preferred solution may be for the state to find ways of speeding up the process leading to execution. Unintended and often unforeseen consequences of this sort which arise from creative litigation and progressive jurisprudence are constant features of the various struggles against capital punishment.

The volume identifies several current and emerging issues which seem likely to shape the international discourse and national policy debates on the death penalty as the new century unfolds. The status of the offender's victim, the role of the victim's family and the burgeoning variety of victim groups prompt a number of complex questions which are reviewed in these pages, including the proper place for victim impact statements and the degree of legitimacy to be afforded to organizations which purport to speak for victims in death penalty cases. There are also those issues arising from the involvement of medical personnel in the sentencing and execution processes, highlighted in the penultimate chapter by Michael Radelet. For example, he asks whether the mentally incompetent ought to be treated and thereby declared fit for execution. Radelet also draws attention to the minutely detailed display of the dissected remains of an executed man made available to subscribers on the Internet, and to the growing international market in organs removed from executed people.

The prospects for abolition are far from encouraging in many parts of the world, notably China, the USA, and some Islamic states. However, certain developments elsewhere continue to offer hope. The unanimous decision to strike down the death penalty by the new constitutional court of South Africa in June 1995 deserves special mention in this respect. But it also important to stress that future prospects for the death penalty do not depend, for the most part, on crusades by moral élites, organized lobbying of the legislature or upon the law-making activities of the courts. Time and again throughout this volume, the reader is reminded of the extraordinary spectrum of events and other external circumstances which continually shape the historical, social and political contexts, which in turn ultimately determine the fate of capital punishment.

• • •

The essays can be said to fall into five loose sections. In the following chapter, William Schabas notes that capital punishment 'sits squarely within those issues which are fundamentally matters of domestic policy and in which international human rights have been increasingly assertive'. He is impressed by the logic of international law which points towards abolition, and observes that 'the limitation of the death penalty is a central theme in the development of international human rights law.' He notes that while half the world's states currently apply the death penalty, some forty-seven have abolished it (at least with regard to peacetime offences). The next three chapters address the status of the death penalty within states which place heavy reliance on the existence of the death penalty, namely China, the USA and Russia (consideration is also given here to other parts of the former USSR). Chapters 6 and 7 deal with two regions of the world where a mixed pattern is evident, namely Commonwealth Africa and the Caribbean. Chapters 8 and 9 consider western and eastern Europe, where by the early 1990s the death penalty had essentially vanished. Finally, some general issues are raised in terms of the role of the medical profession in the process of capital punishment; the volume concludes with a comparative study of two abolitionist struggles.

# ENDNOTES

1. Arthur Koestler, *Reflections on Hanging* (New York, Macmillan, 1957), 170.

2. Opinion of Sachs J., *The State v. T. Makwanyane and M Mchunu*, Constitutional Court of the Republic of South Africa , Case No. CCT/3/94. Delivered on 6 June 1995.

3. Roger Hood, *The Death Penalty. A World-Wide Perspective* (Oxford, Oxford University Press, revised edition, 1990), 4.

4. See 'The death penalty in international law and in the legislations of the Arab countries.' Report of the proceedings of the Tunis Conference organized by the Arab Institute of Human Rights and Hands Off Cain, October 1995.

5. On the contemporary usages of aspects of criminal policy as a 'commodity' see Thomas Mathiesen, ' Driving Forces Behind Prison Growth' (paper to the International Conference on Prison Growth, Oslo, April 1995), 9-10.

# CHAPTER 2

# International Legal Aspects

## William A. Schabas

International law is, at least historically, a law of sovereign states. It establishes their reciprocal rights and obligations and it is premised on a mutual respect for the territorial integrity and the *domaine réservé* of each equal partner in the world community. From a criminal law standpoint, these principles are evidenced in notions of jurisdiction, by which states accept the fact that their internal criminal law systems may only exercise authority where there is a nexus, be it territorial or personal, with the crime.[1] How states deal with criminals within their own borders is, in principle, a matter that concerns them and them alone.

But this classic view of international law has evolved dramatically in the twentieth century. International law no longer inhibits itself to the rights and obligations of states between themselves, it now encompasses rights and obligations that states undertake to respect vis-à-vis individuals.[2] International law's focus on individual human rights began rather modestly, following the First World War, with the creation of the International Labour Organization and the guarantees of minority rights in the post-war treaties concerning the remnants of the Austro-Hungarian, Russian and Ottoman empires. Since 1945, human rights has become one of the overarching themes of international law. It embodies a dialectic that pervades the *United Nations Charter*, confronting the protection of the human rights of individuals with the troublesome undertaking, found in article 2(7) of the *Charter*, that the United Nations will not 'intervene in matters which are essentially within the domestic jurisdiction of any state'.

The use of the death penalty sits squarely within those issues which are fundamentally matters of domestic criminal policy and in which international human rights law has been increasingly assertive. This takes a number of forms. First, conventional and customary human rights norms address the issue directly, positing that the death penalty may not be imposed under certain circumstances, and with respect to certain individuals. This is the 'minimal' position, although a large number of states have sought to go further, and proclaim the abolition of the death penalty as a norm of international human rights law. Second, the death penalty arises in areas of international legal cooperation, with many states now refusing to extradite individuals if they will be subjected to capital punishment. Third, with a renewed interest in prosecution for international crimes by international tribunals, it becomes essential to establish the appropriate sanction. Here, the

17

international community has shifted from a position that virtually assumes the death penalty to be the only appropriate response, in the post-Second World War crimes trials, to the contemporary view which holds it to be an inhuman punishment, no matter how heinous the crime. Finally, these developments on an international level impact upon domestic legal systems, compelling national courts to adjust their jurisprudence in the light of developments elsewhere.

## INTERNATIONAL LEGAL NORMS

The death penalty is associated with two fundamental human rights norms, the right to life and the protection against cruel, inhuman and degrading punishments. Both norms can trace their roots to the great instruments of Anglo-American constitutional law. The guarantee against 'cruel and unusual punishments' was set out in the English Bill of Rights of 1689.[3] It was aimed at some of the more barbaric accompaniments of execution that characterized Stuart England: drawing and quartering, disembowelling while alive, amputation, and so on. The 'right to life' was immortalized by the words of Thomas Jefferson, in the Declaration of Independence of 1776. The American revolutionaries sought to protect the right not to be deprived of life 'without due process of law', a not so tacit recognition of the legitimacy of capital punishment.[4] Yet in their more modern formulation, both of these rights have served to restrict and in some cases prohibit the death penalty.

### The Right to Life
The drafters of the *Universal Declaration of Human Rights*[5] of 1948 looked to domestic constitutions[6] for inspiration in preparing a document that they termed 'a common standard of achievement for all peoples and all nations'. Most of these constitutions were inspired to a greater or lesser extent by the principles of the English *Bill of Rights*, the American *Declaration of Independence* and *Bill of Rights*, and the French *Déclaration des droits de l'homme et du citoyen*. High on the list of this new international catalogue of human rights was the 'right to life' (article 3 of the *Universal Declaration*). However, the scope of this right was considerably different, and broader, than it had been when it was first announced in the eighteenth century, as many participants in the drafting process took pains to point out.

As such, the *Universal Declaration* makes no mention of the death penalty. But in distinction with the domestic constitutions from which it is derived, nor does the *Declaration* explicitly refer to the death penalty as an exception to the right to life. Indeed, unlike the case of the American *Bill of Rights*, it cannot be said that the drafters of the *Universal Declaration* sought to preserve the death penalty as an implicit limit on the right to life. The debates in the General Assembly's Third Committee during the autumn of 1948 make this quite clear.

The original draft of the *Universal Declaration*, prepared by John P. Humphrey in early 1947, recognized a right to life that 'can be denied only to persons who have been convicted under general law of some crime to which the death penalty is attached'.[7] But Eleanor Roosevelt, who chaired the Drafting Committee, cited movement underway in some states to abolish the death penalty, and suggested that it might be better not to make any explicit mention of the matter.[8] René Cassin reworked Humphrey's draft and removed any reference to the death penalty.[9] Cassin's proposal found its way, virtually unchanged, into the final version of the *Declaration*, despite some subsequent attempts to return to the original proposal.[10] It is clear from the *travaux préparatoires* that the death penalty was considered to be incompatible with the right to life, and that its abolition, although not immediately realizable, should be the goal of Member states.[11] Subsequent interpretations, by General Assembly and Economic and Social Council resolutions, support this conclusion.[12]

The *Universal Declaration* was not intended to establish binding treaty obligations. However, it provided the normative framework for the *International Covenant on Civil and Political Rights*[13] and the three major regional human rights treaties. A chronological perspective on the adoption of these treaty provisions shows that although the death penalty was maintained as an exception or limitation on the right to life, it has been progressively limited.

The first off the mark was the Council of Europe, adopting the *European Convention of Human Rights*[14] in November, 1950, less than two years after the *Universal Declaration*. Article 2 of the *Convention* recognizes the right to life, 'save in the execution of a sentence of a court following his conviction of a crime for which this penalty is provided by law'. It reflects the post-war context in Europe, when war crimes trials (and the resulting executions) were still fresh in the collective memory. Yet as a provision, it was almost immediately anachronistic. There have been only a handful of executions within Member states of the Council of Europe since 1950. In 1989, the European Court of Human Rights observed that capital punishment has been abolished *de facto* in the Contracting states of the *European Convention*.[15] By the early 1970s, the Council of Europe had begun work on a protocol to the Convention, which was adopted in 1983,[16] that modifies article 2 by abolishing the death penalty in peacetime.[17]

Negotiation of a human rights treaty took considerably more time in the United Nations than in the Council of Europe. Although drafting work was already underway as early as 1947, it was not until 1966 that the treaty intended to accompany the *Universal Declaration* - the *International Covenant on Civil and Political Rights*[18] - was adopted. It took yet another ten years before the instrument had obtained the necessary thirty-five ratifications for it to come into force.[19] The 'right to life' provision, article 6, was drafted during the 1957 session of the Third Committee of the General Assembly. Although only seven years younger than the corresponding text in the *European Convention*, it already shows the remarkable and rapid evolution of international law respecting the death penalty. Although article 6 of the *Covenant* also admits the death penalty as an exception to the right to life, it lists detailed safeguards and restrictions on its implementation. The death penalty may only be imposed for the 'most serious crimes', it cannot be pronounced unless rigorous procedural rules are respected, and it may not be applied to pregnant women or to individuals for crimes committed while under the age of eighteen. Furthermore, article 6 of the *Covenant* clearly points to abolition as a human rights objective, and implies that states that have already abolished the death penalty may not reintroduce it.[20] It too has been completed with an additional protocol, adopted in 1989, proclaiming the death penalty to be abolished in time of peace and war.[21]

The second major regional human rights treaty is the *American Convention on Human Rights*, adopted in 1969 and in force only since 1978.[22] Here also, the progress is evident. Taking article 6 of the *International Covenant* as a model, the *American Convention* tightens the restrictions on use of the death penalty, and affirms explicitly that states may not reintroduce capital punishment once they have abolished it.[23] This renders the *American Convention* an abolitionist instrument, to the extent that ratifying states that have already abolished the death penalty are now bound as a question of international law not to use the death penalty. In 1990, the *American Convention* was completed with an abolitionist protocol patterned generally on the *Second Optional Protocol.*[24]

The third major regional treaty is the *African Charter of Human and Peoples' Rights,*[25] adopted in 1981 and in force since 1986. It enshrines the right to life but, unlike the European, American and universal instruments, it makes no mention of capital punishment as an exception or limitation to this right. There is little interpretative material to assist in construing the *African Charter*'s right to life provision. Some scholars point to African practice, where a majority of states still employs the death penalty, in concluding that the *Charter* in no way forbids capital punishment.[26] Nevertheless, the *Charter* is to be interpreted in light of other international human rights instruments, including 'the Universal Declaration of Human Rights [and] other instruments adopted by the United Nations'.[27] At the very least, then, the restrictions and limitations on the death penalty found in the *International Covenant* must apply. Several African states have already abolished the death penalty,[28] the most recent being South Africa,[29] and this will surely influence future interpretation of the *Charter*.

The recent *Arab Charter of Human Rights*, adopted September 15, 1994 but not yet ratified by any members of the League of Arab States, proclaims the right to life. Three distinct provisions, articles 10, 11 and 12, recognize the legitimacy of the death penalty in the case of 'serious violations of general law', prohibit the death penalty for political crimes,[30] and exclude capital punishment for crimes committed under the age of eighteen and for both pregnant women and nursing mothers, for a period of up to two years following childbirth.[31] In international *fora* such as the United Nations, Arab (and more generally, Islamic) nations have been among the most aggressive advocates of retention of the death penalty, defending its use in the name of obedience to Islamic law and the strictures of the *chari'a.*[32]

20

Observers sometimes cite the right to life provisions of the *International Covenant on Civil and Political Rights* and those of the regional treaties, which allow the death penalty as a limitation or exception on the right, in defence of the affirmation that abolition of the death penalty is not an international norm.[33] In fact, with the adoption of the three protocols, abolition is indeed an international norm, although not a universal one. As of 1995, forty-nine states were abolitionist from the standpoint of international law, having ratified either one of the three protocols or the *American Convention of Human Rights*, which expressly prohibits reintroduction of the death penalty once it has been abolished.[34]

The notion that fundamental rights are subject to limitations is well accepted in human rights law. Generally, such limits exist as a counterbalance to individual rights, and express the collective rights concerns of the community as a whole. Thus, for example, prohibitions on hate propaganda constitute limits on freedom of expression that are not only authorized but required by international law.[35] As we have seen, in several instruments, the death penalty is expressed as a limitation to the right to life. But it is a unique limitation, born of political compromise rather than respect for collective rights, and couched in terms that express the desirability of its abolition.

## The Prohibition of Cruel, Inhuman and Degrading Punishment

The same international legal instruments that protect the right to life also affirm the prohibition of torture and cruel, inhuman and degrading treatment or punishment.[36] The *travaux préparatoires* of these instruments indicate that their drafters considered that the issue of death penalty fell within the context of the right to life, and that it was not an issue raised by the prohibition of torture or cruel punishment. The two norms co-exist in human rights law, but to the extent that the formulation of the right to life appears to authorize the death penalty, there is an essential and inevitable tension with a norm that, at least potentially, may prohibit it. 'Cruel' punishment is obviously not a static notion; it reflects the 'evolving standards of decency that mark the progress of a maturing society'.[37] International tribunals recognize that human rights norms must be interpreted in a evolutive or dynamic manner.[38] Even if the death penalty was not deemed 'cruel' in 1948, or 1957, or 1969, it may well be today or at some future date.

In 1989, a majority of the European Court of Human Rights stopped short of concluding that the death penalty constituted cruel, inhuman and degrading punishment, prohibited by article 3 of the *European Convention*. The Court looked to subsequent state practice for elements that would assist in interpretation.[39] The members of the Council of Europe had chosen, in the 1980s, to present abolition of the death penalty in the form of an optional or additional protocol to the *Convention*, and not a mandatory or amending protocol. Therefore, the Court concluded, it was going too far to suggest that the *Convention* now prohibited the death penalty, despite the terms of article 2 (the right to life provision). Judge Jan de Meyer was alone in adopting a more radical and dynamic view of the *Convention*:

21

The second sentence of Article 2§1 of the Convention [which permits the death penalty as an exception to the right to life] was adopted nearly forty years ago, in particular historical circumstances, shortly after the Second World War. In so far as it still may seem to permit, under certain conditions, capital punishment in time of peace, it does not reflect the contemporary situation, and is now overridden by the development of legal conscience and practice.[40]

Still, the Court found a way to apply the prohibition of cruel, inhuman and degrading punishment to the death penalty. The case involved the threat of extradition to the United States from the United Kingdom of an individual charged with murder, and therefore subject to execution by lethal injection in the State of Virginia. It was not the death penalty itself that the Court found offensive to the *Convention*, but rather the 'death row phenomenon', the years-long wait for the scaffold under gruesome conditions, both physical and psychological.[41]

The Human Rights Committee has been more conservative in its application of the corresponding norm in the *International Covenant*. The Committee has taken a different view than the European Court, holding that delay in and of itself in implementation of the death penalty following sentence cannot be termed cruel, inhuman and degrading treatment or punishment.[42] This view appears to be altering, perhaps because of the result of a growing weight of authority from domestic tribunals that have examined the same question,[43] as well as a consequence of the changing composition of the Committee.[44] As for the death penalty itself, the Committee shares the view of the European Court that the death penalty cannot be deemed 'cruel' and therefore contrary to article 7 of the *Covenant*, precisely because it is authorized as an exception to the right to life in article 6.[45]

Methods of execution may themselves be cruel, inhuman and degrading. The Human Rights Committee has affirmed that the use of the gas chamber in the State of California involves excessive and gratuitous suffering, and that it is therefore contrary to article 7 of the *International Covenant*.[46] But this puts human rights bodies in the uncomfortable and inappropriate position of ruling on what is the more humane way to kill an individual.[47] The Committee has since concluded that execution by lethal injection is not cruel, inhuman and degrading, despite uncontested evidence tendered before it showing that this more modern and fashionable method of execution also may involve terrible suffering.[48]

Serious issues of cultural relativism arise in the interpretation of the norm against 'cruel, inhuman and degrading punishment'. The scope of the three adjectives obviously depends upon value judgements, and these will vary depending on social and cultural conditions. When Commission on Human Rights rapporteur Gaspar Biro suggested in February, 1994 that the death penalty as imposed in the Sudan was contrary to articles 6 and 7 of the *Covenant*,[49] his 'blasphemy' in attacking 'Islamic punishments' was condemned.[50] In fact, however, enthusiasm for the death penalty appears to cross cultural lines: its most aggressive defenders on the international plane are the United States, China, Singapore and the Sudan!

## Customary norms

It is of course not possible to assert that abolition is a customary norm of international law. The interest in identifying a norm as being customary is that states are bound by it, regardless of whether they have ratified one or more of the relevant treaties. Customary international law exists when there is evidence of state practice accompanied by unequivocal manifestations of policy or *opinio juris*,[51] and with roughly half of the world's states still employing the death penalty, this is clearly not the case. However, a strong argument can be made that some or all of the limitations on use of the death penalty enumerated in article 6 of the *International Covenant* have attained the status of customary law.

The requirement that strict procedural safeguards accompany any capital trial undoubtedly belongs to this category of customary law. The universal condemnation of summary executions within the human rights bodies of the United Nations shows there is unanimity on this point. Moreover, common article 3 of the *Geneva Conventions*, often cited as the lowest common denominator of humane behaviour, proscribes

> the passing of sentences and the carrying out of executions without previous judgment pronounced by a regularly constituted court affording all the judicial guarantees which are recognized as indispensable by civilized peoples.[52]

The International Court of Justice has held that common article 3 codifies a customary rule.[53]

Another customary principle is the prohibition on executions for crimes committed by young persons. This rule respects an undisputed principle of criminal law, that children have diminished criminal liability due to their immaturity. The Inter-American Commission on Human Rights has stated that there is a customary norm prohibiting executions of juvenile offenders, although it has stopped short of fixing the cut-off age at eighteen.[54] The Commission was only prepared to conclude that a norm setting the age at eighteen was 'emerging'. More recently, the Human Rights Committee has suggested a corresponding hesitation in its recent General Comment on reservations, which affirmed that the execution of 'children' (and pregnant women) was contrary to customary norms, but without specifying the precise age.[55] Yet both the *International Covenant* and the *American Convention of Human Rights*, as well as the *Convention on the Rights of the Child*,[56] the fourth *Geneva Convention* and its two additional protocols,[57] specify eighteen as the minimum age.

When the United States of America ratified the *International Covenant* in 1992, it included a reservation to the provision concerning juvenile executions.[58] Several European states objected that the reservation was incompatible with the object and purpose of the *Covenant*, and therefore invalid.[59] The Human Rights Committee, in its consideration of the initial report by the United States pursuant to article 40 of the *Covenant*, in March and April 1995, has also concluded that the reservation is inadmissible.[60] This argues strongly for the position that there is a customary norm prohibiting executions for crimes committed while under eighteen.

## The death penalty in wartime

Most domestic legislation establishes distinct rules concerning the death penalty in time of war, when it is employed more frequently and with less concern for procedural safeguards. This distinction has been carried over into the abolitionist protocols. In the case of *Protocol No. 6* to the *European Convention of Human Rights*,[61] execution in wartime is simply excluded from its scope. The *Protocol* prohibits the death penalty only in time of peace, allowing, in article 2, that '(a) state may make provision in its law for the death penalty in respect of acts committed in time of war or of imminent threat of war'. This compromise in the drafting process of the first abolitionist treaty reflected the fact that many European states had abolished capital punishment in time of peace only.[62] Increasingly, however, European states have abolished the death penalty altogether. The Steering Committee for Human Rights of the Council of Europe is studying the possibility of a draft protocol to the *European Convention* which would abolish the death penalty in war as well as peace.[63]

The protocol to the *International Covenant* takes a different approach, outlawing capital punishment in all circumstances, but allowing states to make a reservation if they seek to preserve the possibility of imposing the death penalty in wartime for serious crimes of a military nature.[64] Only two states are party to the *Protocol*, Spain and Malta have formulated such a reservation.[65]

The humanitarian law treaties provide specific rules concerning the death penalty in wartime. Two groups of individuals are contemplated by the legal rules concerning the death penalty in time of war, combatants taken prisoner and non-combatant civilians in the hands of a belligerent. The protection of prisoners of war is governed principally by the third *Geneva Convention* of 1949.[66] According to the *Convention*, prisoners of war are subject to the laws, regulations, and orders in effect in the armed forces of the detaining power.[67] If the death penalty is applicable in the laws of the detaining power, then a prisoner of war may be exposed to the threat of capital punishment. The *Geneva Convention* specifically envisages this possibility in two articles whose aim is to mitigate the rigours of the death penalty and encourage commutation or even exchange of prisoners.[68] These provisions are a more extensive version of an article in the earlier 1929 *Geneva Convention* that protected prisoners of war facing the death penalty.[69]

Civilians in the hands of belligerent forces were slower to receive comprehensive protection in the international humanitarian conventions,[70] but

24

the grave abuses of capital punishment, mainly by the Nazi occupying forces during the Second World War, compelled the elaboration of specific norms in the fourth *Geneva Convention.*[71] The *Convention* limits the nature of capital crimes *ratione materiae*, prohibits the execution of persons for crimes committed while under the age of eighteen, and establishes a six-month moratorium on execution after sentencing. It also provides that an occupying power may never impose the death penalty if this has been abolished under the laws of the occupied state prior to the hostilities. The norms in the fourth *Convention* have been expanded somewhat by *Protocol Additional I to the 1949 Geneva Conventions and Relating to The Protection of Victims of International Armed Conflicts,*[72] which prohibits the death penalty for offences related to the armed conflict in the case of pregnant women or mothers having dependent infants, and for offenders under the age of eighteen at the time of the crime. The death penalty provisions in *Protocol Additional II,*[73] which deals with non-international armed conflicts, largely repeat the norms found in article 6 of the *International Covenant*, and reflect the human rights scope of the *Protocol*.

# INTERNATIONAL LAW AND DOMESTIC COURTS

The classic weakness of international human rights law is in its means of implementation. However, international human rights law is increasingly applicable before domestic courts, and this contributes immensely to its effectiveness. In some countries, it is given primacy over incompatible domestic legislation. In others, it has been used by courts to assist in interpreting the scope of constitutional norms which have usually been inspired by the international instruments. Death penalty jurisprudence provides one of the most dramatic examples of this synergy between international and domestic human rights law.

Courts of several states, including South Africa,[74] Zimbabwe,[75] Canada[76] and the United Kingdom[77] have found international law to be particularly helpful in the interpretation of such notions as the right to life and cruel, inhuman and degrading punishment. In the recent judgement of the South African Constitutional Court, which found capital punishment to be incompatible with the right to life and the protection against cruel, inhuman and degrading punishment, President Arthur Chaskalson wrote:

> The international and foreign authorities are of value because they analyse arguments for and against the death sentence and show how courts of other jurisdictions have dealt with this vexed issue. For that reason alone they require our attention.[78]

He provides a detailed analysis of the international instruments as well as the case law of such bodies as the Human Rights Committee and the European Court of Human Rights.

# OTHER INTERNATIONAL INITIATIVES

As an important human rights issue, the death penalty has been the object of initiatives within several international organizations, including the United Nations, the Organization for Security and Cooperation in Europe and the European Union. Although this activity has not resulted in the creation of positive legal norms, it is a source of 'soft law' as well as a significant reference in the evolution of international custom.

## The United Nations

In parallel with the drafting of international legal norms found in the *Universal Declaration of Human Rights* and the *International Covenant on Civil and Political Rights*, different bodies of the United Nations have been involved in a variety of initiatives aimed at limiting and eventually abolishing the death penalty. As a general rule, these have originated in the Commission on Human Rights and its Sub-Commission and, where there was sufficient unanimity, resulted in resolutions in the Economic and Social Council and the General Assembly.[79]

An early resolution, presented at the 1968 session of the Commission on Human Rights, observed that 'the major trend among experts and practitioners in the field is towards the abolition of capital punishment'.[80] It cited a series of safeguards respecting appeal, pardon and reprieve, and delay of execution until the exhaustion of such procedures. It invited governments to provide for a six-month moratorium before implementing the death penalty.[81] In the General Assembly, even many retentionist states supported the draft resolution, noting that it confined itself to the 'humanitarian' aspect of the question,[82] although more militant abolitionist states criticized its timidity, saying it would not 'induce Governments to abolish the death penalty'.[83] The Commission's resolution, with some minor amendments, was then adopted by the General Assembly.[84] A few years later, an Assembly resolution declared that 'the main objective to be pursued is that of progressively restricting the number of offences for which capital punishment may be imposed with a view to the desirability of abolishing the punishment in all countries'.[85] In 1994, at the forty-ninth session, a draft General Assembly resolution called for a moratorium on the death penalty, 'with a view to ensuring that the principle that no state should dispose of the life of any human being be affirmed in every part of the world by the year 2000'.[86] However, a retentionist state, Singapore, proposed an 'amendment' that in effect distorted the original purpose of the resolution, by adding the following preambular paragraph: 'Affirming the sovereign right of states to determine the legal measures and penalties which are appropriate in their societies to combat serious crimes effectively'.[87] By a close vote, seventy-one to sixty-five, with twenty-one abstentions, the amendment was adopted. Those voting in favour of the amendment were retentionist states, essentially from Africa, Asia and the Caribbean. In the vote on the entire resolution, which then included the amendment, most of the abolitionist states abstained (a total of seventy-four), while the retentionist states tended to divide; thirty-six voted in favour and forty-four voted against.[88]

The United Nations Congress on Crime Prevention and Control, held every five years, has also provided a forum for debate on the death penalty. In 1975, the Congress successfully resisted attempts by non-governmental organizations[89] to raise the issue of capital punishment at its Geneva session, because the issue was not on the agenda.[90] At the Sixth United Nations Congress on the Prevention of Crime and the Treatment of Offenders, held in 1980 in Caracas, more time was devoted to the issue of capital punishment than to any other question.[91] A draft resolution called for restriction and eventual abolition of the death penalty and added that abolition would be 'a significant contribution to the strengthening of human rights, in particular the right to life'.[92] A controversial provision urged states which had not abolished capital punishment to 'consider establishing a moratorium in its application, or creating other conditions under which capital punishment is not imposed or is not executed, so as to permit those states to study the effects of abolition on a provisional basis'. But faced with some stiff opposition and inadequate time to complete the discussions, the sponsors withdrew the revised draft resolution.[93] At the 1990 Congress, held in Havana, a resolution on capital punishment was proposed that returned to the idea of a moratorium on the death penalty, 'at least on a three year basis'. The resolution was adopted in Committee by forty votes to twenty-one, with sixteen abstentions, but was rejected in plenary session because it failed to obtain a two-thirds majority.[94]

The 'Safeguards Guaranteeing Protection of the Rights of those Facing the Death Penalty' were drafted by the Committee on Crime Prevention and Control (now the 'Commission'),[95] at its March, 1984 session.[96] The 'Safeguards' expand upon the restrictions on use of the death penalty found in article 6 of the *International Covenant*. They specify that use of capital punishment must be confined to 'intentional crimes, with lethal or other extremely grave consequences'. With respect to categories of persons excluded from the death penalty, they add 'new mothers' and 'persons who have become insane' to juvenile offenders and pregnant women, who were already expressly protected by article 6 para. 5 of the *Covenant*. The death penalty can only be imposed 'when the guilt of the person charged is based upon clear and convincing evidence leaving no room for an alternative explanation of the facts'. The 'Safeguards' were later endorsed in resolutions by the Economic and Social Council,[97] the General Assembly[98] and the Seventh United Nations Congress on the Prevention of Crime and the Treatment of Offenders, held in Milan in 1985.[99]

## Organization for Security and Cooperation in Europe

European states have brought the death penalty debate to the Organization (formerly the Conference) on Security and Cooperation in Europe, but with only modest results. This is explained by the presence of retentionist states within the organization, the Russian Federation, to the east, and even more

27

important, the United States, to the west, and the fact that O.S.C.E. documents are adopted by consensus. In 1989, in the concluding document of the Vienna Follow-up Meeting, the participating states simply 'note' that capital punishment has been abolished 'in a number of them'. Those where it has not been abolished are reminded that they must respect general international norms on the matter.[100] The issue has arisen within the context of O.S.C.E. initiatives on the human dimension. A year later, at the Copenhagen Meeting on the human dimension, the concluding document cited the *Second Optional Protocol*, article 6 of the *International Covenant* and *Protocol No. 6 to the European Convention*. Participating states tamely agreed to 'exchange information'.[101] Similar pronouncements appear in the document of the 1991 Moscow Meeting on the Human Dimension.

The issue of the death penalty was discussed at the Implementation Meeting on the Human Dimension, held at Warsaw, September 25 to October 15, 1993, under the agenda item: 'Exchange of information on the question of the abolition of the death penalty'. It was also on the agenda of the Budapest Review meeting, Working Group III, November 1994, and the matter is addressed summarily in the concluding document.

**European Union**

Death penalty issues have frequently been raised within the European Parliament, which has generated a number of resolutions over the years.[102] In 1989, the European Parliament adopted the 'Declaration of Fundamental Rights and Freedoms', which proclaims the abolition of the death penalty.[103] Death penalty practice has also been a factor in assessing human rights within states whose recognition is being considered by the European Union. In its 'opinion' on recognition of Slovenia, the Arbitration Commission took note of the abolition of the death penalty in the Constitution of Slovenia.[104]

# INTERNATIONAL CRIMINAL LAW

Death penalty issues also arise within international criminal law, both in the context of international criminal prosecutions and international judicial cooperation. In both areas, there are recent and important developments that promote abolition of the death penalty. These have the added interest of setting an example that influences the debate within domestic legal systems.

**International tribunals**

In recent years, there has been increasing recognition that human rights law must have a punitive component. Where massive violations of human rights are not punished, an unacceptable climate of impunity is created. Human rights lawyers and activists have found themselves on unfamiliar ground, prosecuting rather than defending. The issue of appropriate punishment arises and this, inexorably, has led to debate about capital punishment.

28

At Nuremberg and Tokyo, crimes against humanity committed during the Second World War were generally punished with death.[105] During drafting of the *Charter of the Nuremberg Tribunal*, when Uruguay objected to including the death penalty, it was actually accused of having Nazi sympathies.[106] At its first session, the General Assembly endorsed the *Charter of the Nuremberg Tribunal*, which provided for execution as the supreme penalty for war criminals.[107]

A sign of changing values, it is now virtually unthinkable that a United Nations-sponsored tribunal employ the death penalty. The 1993 *Statute of the International Tribunal for the Former Yugoslavia*, which is an annex to a Security Council Resolution, declares that the maximum sentence shall be life imprisonment.[108] The International Law Commission's draft statute for a permanent international criminal court, which is to have jurisdiction over serious violations of humanitarian law, crimes against humanity, including genocide, and certain narcotics-related and terrorist crimes, also excludes the death penalty.[109]

However, when the *ad hoc* tribunal for war crimes in Rwanda was proposed, in autumn, 1994, controversy erupted. Rwanda, which by pure chance was itself a member of the Council at the time, opposed the prohibition on capital punishment, which it still retained in its own domestic legislation.[110] It claimed there would be a fundamental injustice in exposing criminals tried by its domestic courts to execution if those tried by the international tribunal - presumably the masterminds of the genocide - would only be subject to life imprisonment.[111]

But even here, Rwanda's position on the death penalty is far from unequivocal. The death penalty has not been imposed in Rwanda since the early 1980s, and the programme of the Rwandese Patriotic Front, which won military victory in July, 1994, calls for its abolition. The current Minister of Justice, Alphonse-Marie Nkubito, is a committed abolitionist. Furthermore, in the 1993 Arusha peace accords, which have constitutional force in Rwanda, the government undertook to ratify the *Second Optional Protocol*, although it has not yet formally taken this step.[112]

### Extradition

Many states insist upon treaty provisions that permit them to refuse extradition if the accused person will be subjected to the death penalty.[113] Such clauses appear in international law as early as 1889, in the *South American Convention*, in the 1892 extradition treaty between the United Kingdom and Portugal, in the 1908 extradition treaty between the United States and Portugal, and the 1912 model treaty prepared by the International Commission of Jurists.[114] European states now systematically refuse to extradite where there is a threat of the death penalty,[115] although the argument that there is a customary rule prohibiting extradition in such cases has been rejected.[116] Although the Human Rights Committee agrees that the *International Covenant* applies where breaches are only threatened if extradition is to be effected, in three troublesome Canadian cases concerning extradition to the United States, it has refused to find that the *Covenant* is violated by extradition for a capital offence. [117]

The European Court of Human Rights, in the 1989 case of *Soering* v. *United Kingdom*, [118] ruled that extradition to Virginia breached the *European Convention's* guarantee against cruel, inhuman and degrading treatment or punishment not because of capital punishment *per se*, but because of the 'death row phenomenon'. It has yet to deal with a case where the applicant invokes capital punishment directly. [119]

# CONCLUSION

The limitation and abolition of the death penalty is a central theme in the development of international human rights law. The number of states that choose to bind themselves, as a matter of international law, to the abolition of the death penalty continues to grow. Those that have not yet accepted the abolitionist norms are subject to a number of specific rules limiting use of the death penalty, of both convention and customary origin.

Norms limiting the death penalty to serious crimes and excluding specific categories of individuals from its scope, such as juveniles and pregnant women, have been relatively well accepted. Recent resolutions in the General Assembly and other international fora suggest that these principles, earlier recognized in provisions of the *International Covenant*, now enjoy the status of international custom. But remarkably, controversy surrounding the issue of abolition has actually grown with time. [120] This is plainly a result of the growing number of abolitionist states, and their increasingly assertive posture. In opposition, mainly Islamic states have aggressively defended capital punishment within the United Nations.

The presence of international norms has helped to advance the debate in many countries that are anxious to demonstrate their conformity with the most progressive human rights norms. In Brazil, for example, recent attempts to reintroduce the death penalty have been blocked because of that country's desire for international respectability as it seeks a permanent seat on the Security Council. The Rwandese judicial system is confronted with the fact that individuals condemned by the International Tribunal for genocide will not be executed, although those convicted of the same crime in the domestic system remain subject to the death penalty. Therefore capital punishment within Rwanda appears unfair, and this serves to promote abolition.

Even the United States, whose seemingly undying enthusiasm for the noose leaves it standing virtually alone in the developed world, is increasingly challenged by international developments. How else can we explain the belated ratification of the *International Covenant on Civil and Political Rights*, albeit with reservations to the death penalty provisions? The United States was well aware when it ratified the *Covenant* of the risk that its controversial reservations might be deemed inadmissible. Following the recent conclusion by the Human Rights Committee that the reservations concerning the juvenile death penalty are inadmissible, the United States finds itself bound at international law by norms with which its legislation, as well as the case law of the Supreme Court, are incompatible. The result is of immense political importance.

The existence of international norms, such as the prohibition on juvenile executions, provides persuasive arguments to progressive legislators and jurists within the United States. The same arguments that compelled the Senate to authorize ratification of the *Covenant* - namely, a desire for international human rights legitimacy - must also favour amendment of death penalty statutes. On the judicial plane, perhaps the United States Supreme Court will eventually feel compelled to assess the 'evolving standards of decency' that serve as interpretative guidelines for the Eighth Amendment not only in light of American legislative policy but also with an eye to the international context.

## ENDNOTES

1. *The S.S. Lotus (France v. Turkey)*, (1927) P.C.I.J. Ser. A., No. 10.

2. *Barcelona Traction, Light and Power Company, Limited*, [1970] I.C.J. Reports 3, 32.

3. 1 Wm. & Mary, 2d Sess. (1689), c. 2. See: Anthony F. Granucci, "'Nor Cruel and Unusual Punishments Inflicted": The Original Meaning', (1969) 57 *California L. Rev.* 839.

4. *Gregg* v. *Georgia*, 428 U.S. 153, 177, 96 S.Ct. 2909, 2927, 49 L.Ed.2d (1976) (Stewart J.); *Callins* v. *Collins*, 114 S.Ct. 1127, 1127 (1994) (Scalia J.).

5. G.A. Res. 217 A (III), U.N. Doc. A/810 (1948). For academic comment on article 3 of the *Declaration*, see: Lilly E. Landerer, 'Capital Punishment as a Human Rights Issue Before the United Nations', (1971) 4 *H.R.J.* 511; Alfred Verdoot, *Naissance et signification de la déclaration universelle des droits de l'homme*, Louvain, Paris: Nauwelaerts, 1963, at 99-100; William A. Schabas, *The Abolition of the Death Penalty in International Law*, Cambridge: Cambridge University Press (Grotius Publications), 1993, at 30-45.

6. U.N. Doc. E/CN.4/AC.1/3/Add.1

7. *Ibid.*; reprinted in U.N. Doc. E/CN.4/21, Annex A.

8. U.N. Doc. E/ CN.4/AC.1/SR.2, 10.

9. U.N. Doc. E/CN.4/AC.1/W.2/Rev.1; U.N. Doc. E/CN. 4/AC. 1/W. 2/Rev. 2.

10. U.N. Doc. E/CN.4/82/Add.2; U.N. Doc. E/CN.4/82/Add.12, 24.

11. A Soviet amendment calling for addition of a paragraph providing for the abolition of the death penalty in time of peace (U.N. Doc. A/C.3/265) was deemed premature, and was rejected by twenty-one votes to nine, with eighteen abstentions (U.N. Doc. A/C.3/SR.107, p. 4). The vote can in no way be interpreted as a gesture favourable to the death penalty, however.

12. G.A. Res. 2393(XXIII); G.A. Res. 2857(XXVI); G.A. Res. 32/61; G.A. Res. 44/128; E.S.C. Res. 1745(LIV); E.S.C. Res. 1930(LVIII). See also the Secretary General's report on the death penalty: U.N. Doc. E/5242 (1973), para. 11.

13. *International Covenant on Civil and Political Rights*, (1976) 999 U.N.T.S. 171.

14. *Convention for the Protection of Human Rights and Fundamental Freedoms*, (1955) 213 U.N.T.S. 221, E.T.S. 5.

15. *Soering* v. *United Kingdom and Germany*, Series A, Vol. 161, 11 E.H.R.R. 439, para 102; see also: *Çinar* v. *Turkey* (App. no. 17864/91), (1994) 79-A D.R. 5, at p. 9. Nevertheless, in recent years it has been pronounced (although not imposed) in Turkey, Poland and Belgium.

16. *Protocol No. 6 to the Convention for the Protection of Human Rights and Fundamental Freedoms Concerning the Abolition of the Death Penalty*, E.T.S. no. 114.

17. Alphonse Spielman, 'La Convention européenne des droits de l'homme et la peine de mort', in *Présence du droit public et les droits de l'homme, Mélanges offerts à Jacques Vélu*, Brussels: Bruylant, 1992, p. 1503; A Adinolfi, 'Premier instrument international sur l'abolition de la peine de mort', (1987) 58 *Revue internationale de droit pénal* 321; Peter Leuprecht, 'The First International Instrument for the Abolition of the Death Penalty', (1983) 2 *Forum* 2; Erik Harremoes, 'The Council of Europe and Its Efforts to Promote the Abolition of the Death Penalty', (1986) 12-13 *Crime Prevention and Criminal Justice Newsletter* 62; Gilbert Guillaume, 'Protocole no 6 à la Convention de sauvegarde des droits de l'homme et des libertés

fondamentales concernant l'abolition de la peine de mort', in L. E. Pettiti, E. Decaux, P. H. Imbert, *La Convention européenne des droits de l'homme*, Paris: Economica, 1995, 143-154.

18. *Supra* note 13. Article 6 states:

> 1. Every human being has the inherent right to life. This right shall be protected by law. No one shall be arbitrarily deprived of his life.
> 2. In countries which have not abolished the death penalty, sentence of death may be imposed only for the most serious crimes in accordance with the law in force at the time of the commission of the crime and not contrary to the provisions of the present Covenant and to the Convention on the Prevention and Punishment of the Crime of Genocide. This penalty can only be carried out pursuant to a final judgement rendered by a competent court.
> 3. When deprivation of life constitutes the crime of genocide , it is understood that nothing in this article shall authorize any State Party to the present Covenant to derogate in any way from any obligation assumed under the provisions of the Convention on the Prevention and Punishment of the Crime of Genocide.
> 4. Anyone sentenced to death shall have the right to seek pardon or commutation of the sentence. Amnesty, pardon or commutation of the sentence of death may be granted in all cases.
> 5. Sentence of death shall not be imposed for crimes committed by persons below eighteen years of age and shall not be carried out on pregnant women.
> 6. Nothing in this article shall be invoked to delay or to prevent the abolition of capital punishment by any State Party to the present Covenant.

19. It is now ratified by approximately 130 States: Jean-Bernard MARIE, 'International Instruments Relating to Human Rights', (1995) 16 *H.R.L.J.* 75.

20. See the dissenting opinion of Bertil Wennergren in *Kindler* v. *Canada* (no. 470/1991), U.N. Doc. CCPR/C/48/D/470/1991, 14 *H.R.L.J.* 307, 6 *R.U.D.H.* 165: 'What article 6, paragraph 2, does not, in my view, is to permit States parties that have abolished the death penalty to reintroduce it at a later stage'.

21. *Second Optional Protocol to the International Covenant on Civil and Political Rights Aimed at Abolition of the Death Penalty*, G.A. Res. 44/128, (1990) 29 I.L.M. 1464.

22. *American Convention on Human Rights*, (1979) 1144 U.N.T.S. 123, O.A.S.T.S. 36.

23. The Inter-American Court of Human Rights has issued two advisory opinions that interpret this provision: *Restrictions to the Death Penalty (articles 4(2) and 4(4) American Convention on Human Rights)*, Advisory Opinion OC-3/83 of September 8, 1983, Series A No. 3, 4 *H.R.L.J.* 352, 70 I.L.R. 449; *International Responsibility for the Promulgation and Enforcement of Laws in Violation of the Convention (articles 1 and 2 of the American Convention on Human Rights)*, Advisory Opinion OC-14/94 of December 9, 1994.

24. *Additional Protocol to the American Convention on Human Rights to Abolish the Death Penalty*, O.A.S.T.S. 73, 29 I.L.M. 1447.

25. *African Charter on Human and People's Rights*, O.A.U. Doc. CAB/LEG/67/3 rev. 5, 4 E.H.R.R. 417, 21 I.L.M. 58. For a comment on the right to life provision in the *African Charter*, see Johannes G. C. Van Aggelen, *Le rôle des organisations internationales dans la protection du droit à la vie*, Brussels: E. Story-Scientia, 1986, at 41.

26. Etienne-Richard Mbaya, 'À la recherche du noyau intangible dans la Charte africaine', in *Le noyau intangible des droits de l'homme*, Fribourg: Éditions universitaires Fribourg Suisse, 1991, 207-226, at p. 221. See also: Keba Mbaya, *Les droits de l'homme en Afrique*, Paris: Pedone, 1992, at 197.

27. *African Charter on Human and People's Rights*, *supra* note 25, art. 60.

28. John Hatchard, 'Capital Punishment in Southern Africa: Some Recent Developments', (1994) 43 *I.C.L.Q.* 923.

29. *Makwanyane and Mchunu* v. *The State*, Case No. CCT/3/94, judgement of June 6, 1995. See: William A. Schabas, 'South Africa's New Constitutional Court Abolishes the Death Penalty', (1995) 16 *H.R.L.J.* 133.

30. Reynaldo Galindo Pohl, special *rapporteur* of the Commission on Human Rights on Iran, has observed that '. . . there are groups of Islamic legal scholars and practitioners who recommend the abolition of the death penalty for political crimes on the ground that it is contrary to Islamic law': U.N. Doc. E/CN.4/1989/26, para. 36.

31. *Charte arabe des droits de l'homme*, (1995) 7 *R.U.D.H.* 212.

32. For example, during debate at the 1994 session of the General Assembly, the Sudanese delegate noted that '. . . capital punishment was a divine right according to some religions, in particular Islam . . . [C]apital punishment was enshrined in the Koran and millions of inhabitants of the Muslim world believed that it was a teaching of God' (U.N.Doc. A/BUR/49/SR.5, para 13). On capital punishment in Islamic law, see: Frédéric Sudre, *Droit international et européen des droits de l'homme*, Paris: Presses universitaires de France, 1989, at 85-87; A. Wazir, 'Quelques aspects de la peine de mort en droit pénal islamique', (1987) 58 *Revue internationale de droit pénal* 421; Centre des Études de Sécurité (Arabie Saudite), 'L'égalité et commodité de la peine de mort en droit musulman', (1987) 58 *Revue internationale de droit pénal* 431; N. Hosni 'La peine de mort en droit égyptien et en droit islamique', (1987) 58 *Revue internationale de droit pénal* 407.

33. See, for example, the remarks of President Arthur Chaskalson, of the Constitutional Court of South Africa, in *Makwanyane* and *Mchunu* v. *The State*, *supra* note 29, at para. 36. According to President Chaskalson, 'Capital punishment is not prohibited by public international law, and this is a factor that has to be taken into account in deciding whether it is cruel, inhuman or degrading punishment within the meaning of section 11(2) [of the interim constitution of South Africa].' It would have been more accurate to say the opposite, namely, that capital punishment is now prohibited by conventional norms that have been ratified by nearly fifty States, and that this suggests an evolution of standards towards its being considered cruel, inhuman or degrading punishment.

34. Jean-Bernard Marie, *supra* note 19.

35. *International Covenant on Civil and Political Rights*, *supra* note 13, art. 20(2); *International Convention on the Elimination of All Forms of Racial Discrimination*, (1969) 660 U.N.T.S. 195, art. 4(*a*).

36. *Universal Declaration of Human Rights*, *supra* note 5, art. 5; *International Covenant on Civil and Political Rights*, *supra* note 13, art. 7; *European Convention of Human Rights*, *supra* note 14, art. 3; *American Convention of Human Rights*, *supra* note 22, art. 5(2); *African Charter of Human and Peoples' Rights*, *supra* note 25, art. 5.

37. The phrase is borrowed from Chief Justice Earl Warren of the United States Supreme Court in *Trop* v. *Dulles*, 356 U.S. 86, 101, 78 S.Ct. 590, 598, 2 L.Ed.2d 630 (1958).

38. *Loizidou* v. *Turkey (Preliminary objections)*, Series A, No.310, paras. 71-72.

39. As authorized by art. 31(3)(*b*) of the *Vienna Convention on the Law of Treaties*, (1979) 1155 U.N.T.S. 331.

40. *Soering* v. *United Kingdom, supra* note 15, at p. 51.

41. On the *Soering* case, see: W. Ganshof Van der Meerch, 'L'extradition et la Convention européenne des droits de l'homme. L'affaire Soering', (1990) *Revue trimestrielle des droits de l'homme* 5; Frédéric Sudre, 'Extradition et peine de mort - arrêt Soering de la Cour européenne des droits de l'homme du 7 juillet 1989', (1990) *Revue générale de droit international public* 103; Michael O'Boyle, 'Extradition and Expulsion under the European Convention on Human Rights, Reflections on the *Soering* Case', in James O'Reilly, ed., *Human Rights and Constitutional Law, Essays in Honour of Brian Walsh*, Dublin: The Round Hall Press, 1992, p. 93; Ann Sherlock, 'Extradition, Death Row and the Convention', (1990) 15 *European L. Rev.* 87; David L. Gappa, 'European Court of Human Rights - Extradition - Inhuman or Degrading Treatment or Punishment, Soering Case, 161 Eur. Ct. H.R. (Ser.A) 1989)', (1990) 20 *Georgia J. Int'l Comp. L.* 463; H. Wattendorf, E. du Perron, 'Human Rights v. Extradition: the *Soering* case', (1989-90) 11 *Michigan J. Int'l L.* 845; C. Warbrick, 'Coherence and the European Court of Human Rights: the Adjudicative Background to the Soering case', (1989-90) 11 *Michigan J. Int'l L.* 1073; J. Quigley, J. Shank, 'Death Row as a Violation of Human Rights: Is it Illegal to Extradite to Virginia?', (1989) 30 *Virginia Int'l L. J.* 251; Richard B. Lillich, 'The *Soering* case', (1991) 85 *A.J.I.L.* 128; Christine Van den Wyngaert, 'Applying the European Convention on Human Rights to Extradition: Opening Pandora's Box?', (1990) 39 *I.C.L.Q.* 757; Susan Marks, 'Yes, Virginia, Extradition May Breach the European Convention on Human Rights', (1990) 49 *Cambridge L. J.* 194; Henri Labayle, 'Droits de l'homme, traitement inhumain et peine capitale: Réflexions sur l'édification d'un ordre public européen en matière d'extradition par la Cour européenne des droits de l'homme', (1990) 64 *Semaine juridique* 3452; L. E. Pettiti, 'Arrêt Soering c./Grande-Bretagne du 8 juillet 1989', [1989] *Revue de science criminelle et de droit pénal comparé* 786.

42. *Pratt and Morgan.* v. *Jamaica* (nos. 210/1986, 225/1987), U.N. Doc. A/44/40, p. 222, para. 13.6; *Reid* v. *Jamaica* (no. 250/1987), U.N. Doc. A/45/40, Vol. II, p. 97, 11 *H.R.L.J.* 319, para. 11.6; *Barrett and Sutcliffe* v. *Jamaica* (no. 271/1988), U.N. Doc. CCPR/C/44/D/1988 and 271/1988, para. 8.4; *Martin* v. *Jamaica* (no. 317/1988), U.N. Doc.

36

CCPR/C/47/D/317/1988, para. 12.1; *Kindler* v. *Canada* (no. 470/1991), *supra* note 20, para. 15.2; *Cox* v. *Canada* (no. 539/1993), U.N. Doc. CCPR/C/52/D/539/1993 (1994), §17.2.

43. *Pratt et al.* v. *Attorney General for Jamaica et al.*, [1993] 4 All.E.R. 769 (P.C.), 14 *H.R.L.J.* 338, 33 I.L.M. 364; *Catholic Commission for Justice and Peace in Zimbabwe* v. *Attorney-General et al.*, (1993) 1 Z.L.R. 242 (S), 4 S.A. 239 (Z.S.C.), 14 *H.R.L.J.* 323.

44. *Cox* v. *Canada* (no. 539/1993), *supra* note 42, para. 17.2. See also the individual views of Committee members Herndl, Sadi, Tamar Ban and Wennergren.

45. *General Comment 20(44)*, U.N. Doc. CCPR/C/21/Rev/1/Add.3.

46. *Ng* v. *Canada* (no. 469/1991), U.N. Doc. CCPR/C/49/D/469/1991 (1994). For an American view on the question, see: *Gomez* v. *U.S. Dist. Court for N.D. of Cal.*, 112 S.Ct. 1682, 1685 (1992) (Stevens J., dissenting).

47. As dissenting member Christine Chanet pointed out in *Ng* v. *Canada*, *ibid.*

48. *Cox* v. *Canada* (no. 539/1993), *supra* note 42.

49. U.N. Doc. E/CN.4/1994/48.

50. Statement by H. E. Mr Abdelaziz Shiddo, Minister of Justice and Attorney-General of the Republic of the Sudan and Leader of Sudan Delegation to the 50th Session of the Commission on Human Rights, Commenting on the report of Dr. Gaspar Biro, Special Rapporteur on Human Rights situation in the Sudan under agenda item (12), Geneva, February 25, 1994. See also: U.N. Doc. E/CN.4/1994/122, para. 58-64.

51. *Statute of the International Court of Justice*, art. 38.

52. *Geneva Conventions of 12 August 1949* , (1950) 75 U.N.T.S. 135.

53. *Military and Paramilitary Activities in and Against Nicaragua (Nicaragua* v. *United States)*, [1986] I.C.J. Reports 14, paras. 218, 255, 292(9).

54. *Case 9647 (United States)* (1987), Inter-Am. Comm. H.R. Res. No. 3/87, *Annual Report of the Inter-American Commission on Human Rights: 1986-1987*,

OEA/Ser.L/V/II.71 Doc.9 rev.1 (1987) 147, *Inter-American Y.B. on Human Rights, 1987* (Dordrecht/Boston/London: Martinus Nijhoff, 1990) at 328, 8 *H.R.L.J.* 345, para. 60.

55. 'General Comment No. 24 (52)', U.N. Doc. CCPR/C/21/Rev.1/Add.6, para 3.

56. G. A. Res. 44/25, 28 I.L.M. 1448, art. 37(1). But not, surprisingly, the *African Charter of Rights of the Child*, CAB/LEG/153/Rev.2; however, article 46 states that the *African Charter* is to be interpreted with an eye to the universal *Convention on the Rights of the Child*.

57. *Geneva Convention of 12 August 1949 Relative to the Protection of Civilians*, (1950) 75 U.N.T.S. 135, art. 68(4); *Protocol Additional I to the 1949 Geneva Conventions and Relating to The Protection of Victims of International Armed Conflicts*, (1979) 1125 U.N.T.S. 3, art. 77(5); *Protocol Additional II to the 1949 Geneva Conventions and Relating to the Protection of Victims of Non-International Armed Conflicts*, (1979) 1125 U.N.T.S. 609, art. 6(4).

58. 'Multilateral Treaties', U.N. Doc. ST/LEG/SER.E/11 (1993), p. 132.

59. *Ibid*. On the debate concerning the United States' reservation, see: William A. Schabas, 'Les réserves des États-Unis d'Amérique aux articles 6 et 7 du *Pacte international relatif aux droits civils et politiques*' (1994) 6 *R.U.D.H.* 137; David P. Stewart, 'U.S. Ratification of the Covenant on Civil and Political Rights: The Significance of the Reservations, Understandings and Declarations' (1993) 14 *H.R.L.J.* 77; V. P. Nanda, 'The U.S. Reservation to the Ban on the Death Penalty for Juvenile Offenders: An Appraisal under the International Covenant on Civil and Political Rights', (1993) 42 *Depaul L. Rev.* 1311; E. F. Sherman., 'The U.S. Death Penalty Reservation to the International Covenant on Civil and Political Rights - Exposing the Limitations of the Flexible System Governing Treaty Formation', (1994) 29 *Texas Int'l L.J.* 69; John Quigley, 'Criminal Law and Human Rights: Implications of the United States Ratification of the International Covenant on Civil and Political Rights', (1993) 6 *Harvard Human Rights J.* 59; Louis Henkin, 'U.S. Ratification of Human Rights Conventions: The Ghost of Senator Bricker', (1995) 89 *A.J.I.L.* 341; J. Green, *The 'Matrioshka' Strategy: U.S. Evasion of the International Covenant on Civil and Political Rights*, (1994) 10 *South African J. Human Rights* 357.

60. 'Consideration of reports submitted by states parties under article 40 of the Covenant, Comments of the Human Rights Committee', U.N. Doc. CCPR/C/79/Add.50 (1995), para. 14. See: William A. Schabas, 'Invalid

Reservations to the International Covenant on Civil and Political Rights: Is the United States Still a Party?', (1995) 21 *Brooklyn J. Int'l L.* 277.

61. *Supra* note 16.

62. Gilbert Guillaume, *supra* note 17.

63. See: Parliamentary Assembly Recommendation 1246 (1994).

64. The *Protocol* to the *American Convention, supra* note 24, adopts the same approach.

65. U.N. Doc. CCPR/C/2/Rev.3, p. 101.

66. *Geneva Convention of 12 August 1949 Relative to the Treatment of Prisoners of War*, (1950) 75 U.N.T.S. 135.

67. *Ibid.*, art. 82.

68. *Ibid.*, arts 100, 101.

69. *International Convention Relative to the Treatment of Prisoners of War*, (1932-33) 118 L.N.T.S. 343.

70. Some norms protecting civilians appear in the *Hague Regulations*, although none address the death penalty: *Convention Regulating the Laws and Customs of Land Warfare (Hague Convention No. IV), Regulations Concerning the Laws and Customs of Land War*, 3 Martens (3rd) 461, 2 A.J.I.L. Supp. 20, arts. 23, 25, 27, 28, 42-56.

71. *Geneva Convention of August 12, 1949 Relative to the Protection of Civilians, supra* note 57, arts. 68, 75.

72. *Supra* note 57.

73. *Protocol Additional II to the 1949 Geneva Conventions and Relating to The Protection of Victims of Non-International Armed Conflicts, supra* note 57.

74. *Makwanyane* and *Mchunu* v. *The State, supra* note 29

75. *Catholic Commission for Justice and Peace in Zimbabwe* v. *Attorney-General et al., supra* note 43.

76. *Kindler* v. *Canada*, [1991] 2 S.C.R. 779, 67 C.C.C. (3d) 1, 84 D.L.R. (4th) 438, 6 C.R.R. (2d) 193.

77. *Pratt et al.* v. *Attorney General for Jamaica et al.*, *supra* note 43.

78. *Makwanyane* and *Mchunu* v. *The State*, *supra* note 29, para. 34.

79. G.A. Res. 1396(XIV), G.A. Res. 2392(XXIII), G. A. Res. 2857(XXVI), G.A. Res. 3011(XXVII), G.A. Res. 32/61, G.A. Res. 36/59, G.A. Res. 37/192, G.A. Res. 39/127; E.S.C. Res. 934(XXXV), E.S.C. Res. 1574(L), E.S.C. Res. 1656(LII), E.S.C. Res. 1745(LIV), E.S.C. Res. 1930(LVIII).

80. U.N. Doc. E/CN.4/SR.990 (1968), p. 267.

81. U.N. Doc. E/4475 (1968), U.N. Doc. E/CN.4/972 (1968), at 134-136, 162-164.

82. U.N. Doc. A/C.3/SR.1557 (1968), para. 17 (China); U.N. Doc. A/C.3/SR.1558 (1968), para. 10 (France).

83. U.N. Doc. A/C.3/SR.1558 (1968), para. 2 (Austria).

84. G.A. Res. 2393(XXIII). U.N. Doc. A/PV.1727 (1968), by ninety-four votes to zero, with three abstentions. Adoption in the Third Committee: U.N. Doc. A/C.3/SR.1559 (1968), para 34.

85. G.A. Res. 2857(XXVI).

86. U.N. Doc. A/49/234 and Add. 1 and Add. 2 (1994), later revised by U.N. Doc. A/C.3/49/L.32/Rev.1 (1994). The resolution originated from a newly-formed non-governmental organization, 'Hands Off Cain - the International League for Abolition of the Death Penalty Before the Year 2000'.

87. U.N. Doc. A/C.3/49/L.73 (1994).

88. U.N. Doc. A/C.3/49/SR.61 (1994).

89. Amnesty International, *The Death Penalty*, London: Amnesty International, 1979, at 33.

90. U.N. Doc. A/CONF.56/1/Rev.1 (1975). Capital punishment had been discussed in the African Regional Preparatory Meeting, where it was noted that there was still 'widespread reliance on capital punishment': 'Report on the African Regional Preparatory meeting of Experts on the Prevention of Crime and the Treatment of Offenders', U.N. Doc. A/CONF.56/BP/4 (1975), para. 33.

91. See comments of the Chief, Crime Prevention and Criminal Justice Branch, U.N. Doc. A/C.3/35/SR.74 (1980), para. 40.

92. U.N. Doc. A/CONF.87/C.1/L.1 (1980). Sponsored by Austria, Ecuador, the Federal Republic of Germany, Sweden. The resolution is reproduced as an Annex to the Congress Report (U.N. Doc. A/CONF.87/14/Rev.1 (1980), at 58-60.

93. U.N. Doc. A/CONF.87/14/Rev.1 (1980), para 111. See: Roger S. Clark, 'Human Rights and the U.N. Committee on Crime Prevention and Control', (1989) 506 *Annals of the American Association of Political and Social Science* 68, at 75.

94. U.N. Doc. A/CONF.144/C.2/L.7; U.N. Doc. A/CONF.144/28/Rev. 1, paras. 350, 358. See: Roger S. Clark, 'The Eighth United Nations Congress on the Prevention of Crime and the Treatment of Offenders, Havana, Cuba, August 27-September 7, 1990', (1990) 1 *Criminal Law Forum* 513, at 518-519

95. Roger S. Clark, *The United Nations Crime Prevention and Criminal Justice Program, Formulation of Standards and Efforts at Their Implementation,* Philadelphia: University of Pennsylvania Press, 1994, at 58-62.

96. 'Draft resolution VII', U.N. Doc. E/1984/16 (1984), U.N. Doc. E/AC.57/1984/18 (1984).

97. E.S.C. Res. 1984/50, adopted without a vote.

98. G.A. Res. 39/118, U.N. Doc. A/PV.101 (1984), para. 79, without a vote.

99. U.N. Doc. A/CONF.121/22/Rev.1 (1985), 83-84, 131-132. See also, for follow-up on the 'Safeguards', 'Implementation of the Safeguards Guaranteeing Protection of the Rights of Those Facing the Death Penalty', E.S.C. Res. 1989/64, adopted without a vote.

41

100. 'A Frame Work for Europe's Future', concluding document of the Vienna Follow-up Meeting, 1989, para. 24.

101. *Document of the Copenhagen Meeting of the Conference on the Human Dimension of the C.S.C.E.*, (1990) 8 *Netherlands Q.H.R.* 302, 29 I.L.M. 1306, art. 17.

102. E.C. Doc. 1-20/80, March 13, 1980; E.C. Doc. 1-65/81; *Official Journal of the European Communities, Debates of the European Parliament*, No. 1-272, Annex, 116-129; the Irish extremist Ian Paisley spoke against the proposal, as did some Greek members. The Report was adopted on June 18, 1981: *Official Journal of the European Communities, Debates of the European Parliament*, No. 1-272, Annex, 225-228; E.C. Doc. A 2-167/85, Doc. B 2-220/85; *Official Journal of the European Communities, Debates of the European Parliament*, No. 2-334, Annex, 300-303.

103. *Official Journal of the European Communities, Debates of the European Parliament*, Annex, No. 2-377, 56-58, 74-79, 151-155; E.C. Doc. A 2-3/89.

104. (1992) 31 I.L.M. 1512, p. 1516, para. 3(*a*)i).

105. *Charter of the Nuremberg Tribunal*, (1951) 82 U.N.T.S. 279, art. 27. On the debate about use of the death penalty for war crimes, see: Claude Pilloud, 'La protection pénale des conventions humanitaires internationales', [1953] *Revue internationale de la croix rouge* 842, at 862-863.

106. U.N. Doc. A/C.3/SR.811 (1957), §28.

107. 'Affirmation of the Principles of International Law recognized by the Charter of the Nuremberg Tribunal', G. A. Res. 95(I).

108. 'Statute of the International Tribunal for the Former Yugoslavia', S/RES/827 (1993), annex, art. 24(1).

109. U.N. Doc. A/49/10 (1994), art. 47.

110. Despite Rwanda's opposition, the *Statute* of the Tribunal, like its counterpart for the former Yugoslavia, excludes capital punishment: 'Statute of the International Tribunal for Rwanda', S/RES/955 (1994) annex, art. 23(1).

111. U.N. Doc. S/PV.3453, 16.

42

112. 'Protocole d'Accord entre le Gouvernement de la République Rwandaise et le Front Patriotique Rwandais portant sur les questions diverses et dispositions finales signé à Arusha', 3 August 1993, *Journal officiel*, Year 32, no. 16, August 15, 1993, 1430, art. 15.

113. Usually, they are based on model extradition treaties: *European Convention on Extradition*, (1960) 359 U.N.T.S. 273, E.T.S. 24, art. 11; *Inter-American Convention on Extradition*, (1981) 20 *I.L.M.* 723, art. 9. The 'Model Treaty on Extradition' proposed by the Eighth United Nations Congress on the Prevention of Crime and Treatment of Offenders, 1990, contains the following: 'Article 4. Extradition may be refused in any of the following circumstances: . . . (c) If the offence for which extradition is requested carries the death penalty under the law of the requesting State, unless that State gives such assurance as the requested State considers sufficient that the death penalty will not be imposed or, if imposed, will not be carried out' (U.N. Doc. A/CONF.14/28/Rev.1 (1990), 68).

114. J. S. Reeves, 'Extradition Treaties and the Death Penalty', (1924) 18 *A.J.I.L.* 290; 'American Institute of International Law, Project No. 17', (1926) 20 *A.J.I.L. Supplement* 331; 'Harvard Law School Draft Extradition Treaty', (1935) 29 *A.J.I.L.* 228.

115. *Dame Joy Davis-Aylor*, C.E., req. no 144590, 15/10/93, D. 1993, IR, 238; J. C. P. 1993, Actualités no 43, [1993] *Revue française de droit administratif* 1166, conclusions C. Vigoreux; *Short* v. *Netherlands*, (1990) 76 Rechtspraak van de Week 358, 29 I.L.M. 1378,.[1991] *Netherlands Yearbook of International Law* 432.

116. *Re Cuillier, Ciamborrani and Vallon*, (1988) 78 I.L.R. 93 (Constitutional Court, Italy).

117. *Kindler* v. *Canada, supra* note 20; *Ng* v. *Canada, supra* note 46; *Cox* v. *Canada, supra* note 42. The cases arose after the Supreme Court of Canada declined to overrule the Justice Minister's refusal to seek an assurance from the United States that the death penalty would not be imposed, despite a provision authorizing this in the extradition treaty: *Kindler* v. *Canada, supra* note 20; see also: See also: Sharon A. Williams, 'Extradition and the Death Penalty Exception in Canada: Resolving the Ng and Kindler Cases', (1991) 13 *Loyola L.A. Int'l Comp. L. J.* 799; Sharon A. Williams, 'Extradition to a State that Imposes the Death Penalty', [1990] *Canadian Yearbook I.L.* 117; Sharon A. Williams: Striking the Balance', (1992) 3 *Criminal Law Forum* 191; Donald K. Piragoff, Marcia V. J. Kran, 'The

43

Impact of Human Rights Principles on Extradition from Canada and the United States: The Role of National Courts', (1992) 3 *Criminal Law Forum* 191; John Pak, 'Canadian Extradition and the Death Penalty: Seeking a Constitutional Assurance of Life', (1993) 26 *Cornell Int'l L. J.* 239; William A. Schabas, 'Extradition et la peine de mort: le Canada renvoie deux fugitifs au couloir de la mort', (1992) 4 *R.U.D.H.* 65; William A. Schabas, '*Kindler* v. *Canada*', (1993) 87 *A.J.I.L.* 128.

118. *Supra* note 15.

119. Several such cases have been declared inadmissible by the European Commission of Human Rights, and as a result have not come before the Court. Of the most recent, see: *Aylor-Davis* v. *France* (No. 22742/93), (1994) 76-A D.R. 164; *H.* v. *Sweden* (App. no. 22408/93/91), (1994) 79-A D.R. 85.

120. Joan Fitzpatrick, Alice Miller, 'International Standards on the Death Penalty: Shifting Discourse', (1993) 19 *Brooklyn J. Int'l L.*, 273.

CHAPTER 3

# The United States

## Hugo Adam Bedau[*]

The United States of America has no uniform, nation-wide criminal justice system. Instead, each of the fifty states, the District of Columbia, and the federal government has its own criminal and penal code. Of course, there is considerable agreement among these jurisdictions on general features of the system, partly for historical reasons and partly because the national constitution as interpreted by the Supreme Court is the final court of appeal on many matters affecting criminal justice. Nevertheless, the diversity that results from having so many jurisdictions each with its own system must be kept in mind as one attempts to assess national trends and other generalizations about a given law, practice, or policy. As a case in point, the story of the death penalty in the United States is exceedingly complex and constantly under greater or lesser change at any given moment in any of several jurisdictions. This has never been more true than at present, for reasons that will emerge in due course.

## CURRENT STATUS OF THE DEATH PENALTY

As of mid-1995, some 3,000 persons were under death sentence in the United States; all but 48 were men.[1] In 1995, fifty-six people were executed and an average of 27 were executed each year between 1990 and 1994. Between 1977 and 1994, thirty-eight of the fifty states have meted out at least one death sentence and 24 have carried out at least one execution. To be sure, some jurisdictions - during 1994 there were 15 - administer a penal code devoid of capital statutes, and so mete out no death sentences and carry out no executions. But these jurisdictions are and always have been the exception, and two of them - Kansas in 1994 and New York in 1995 - have recently ended their experiments with abolition by re-enacting the death penalty.

The current situation in the United States concerning the death penalty, succinctly described above, has undergone considerable change during the past half a century. After a peak of executions nationally in the mid-1930s (199 in 1935), the number of executions steadily declined and in the late 1960s ended altogether. This decline was largely a consequence of litigation in the federal courts that challenged capital punishment on several constitutional grounds.

Variations on three basic constitutional themes were argued in the federal courts against the death penalty: It violated 'due process of law' and 'equal protection of the laws,' and - above all else - it was a 'cruel and unusual punishment.'[2] In 1972, in the landmark decision in *Furman v. Georgia,* a narrow majority of the Supreme Court agreed that the death penalty statutes as then administered did indeed violate constitutional protections. More than six hundred death row prisoners were resentenced to imprisonment on the strength of that decision.[3]

However, the chief response by the state legislatures to this ruling was to redraft their capital statutes in order to satisfy the Supreme Court that they had eliminated the arbitrariness and discrimination in application that was the basis for constitutional complaint.[4] In 1976 the Supreme Court ruled in three related cases (*Gregg v. Georgia, Jurek v. Texas, Proffitt v. Florida*) that the death penalty was not per se a 'cruel and unusual punishment,' and that many of the new death penalty statutes enacted in the wake of *Furman* had indeed addressed and solved the problems of arbitrariness and discrimination, at least in principle. On the other hand, the Court also ruled that mandatory death sentences - leaving no discretion in sentencing once the defendant had been convicted of a capital crime - was unconstitutional on the ground that it ruled out 'individualized sentencing' (*S. Roberts v. Louisiana, Woodson v. North Carolina*). The following year the Court ruled that the death sentence for rape (commonly the law in southern states - as a legacy of slavery and its aftermath - and used mainly to punish blacks convicted of raping white women[5]) was excessive and unconstitutional (*Coker v. Georgia*). The same argument was used to rule that the death penalty for kidnapping was unconstitutional (*Eberhart v. Georgia,* 1977).

The Court found no objections, however, to the new system of capital punishment created by statute in Georgia, Texas, and Florida, whose principal features were three: a bifurcated trial, first on the issue of guilt and then on the issue of sentence; guidance for the trial court in exercising its sentencing discretion provided by a statutory list of aggravating circumstances and another list of mitigating circumstances, with the sentencer to decide on the basis of evidence which of these condition, if any, applied to the defendant in question and then to sentence accordingly; and automatic review of the conviction and sentence by a state appellate court.

These decisions inaugurated the current era of death penalty law and practice was established. The first execution under the new laws was held in Utah in 1977, by the end of 1995, 313 executions in twenty-four states had been carried out.[6]

# LAWFUL METHODS OF EXECUTION

Legislatures in death penalty jurisdictions currently may enact any of five constitutionally permitted methods of execution (*Table 1*). Historically in the United States, hanging was the usual method of carrying out a death penalty;

it remains in the law only of three states. Executions under military law were often administered by a firing squad, and two states permit its use for executions under civil law. The electric chair (an American invention) was introduced in New York a century ago and widely adopted as a method superior to hanging; it is used in a dozen states. In the 1920s, the lethal gas chamber was invented and deemed a humane improvement over both hanging and electrocution; eight states use the gas chamber. With the resumption of executions in 1977, after a nine-year de jure moratorium, death by lethal injection was introduced and is now the most widely used method of execution (25 states).[7]

Lethal injection is generally regarded as the most 'civilized' way to carry out a death sentence among the five methods. Probably the least painful of the five,[8] it is certainly the least disfiguring and least distressing to observe. However, death by lethal injection - not least because of its unsavoury historic echoes of Nazi medical experiments - has aroused considerable opposition in medical circles (for a full discussion of this issue, see Chapter 10 of this work by Michael L. Radelet). And like the other methods of execution, this one in actual practice has its history of botched attempts and improper administration.[9]


## DEATH ROW

Prisoners on death row at present are predominantly male (about 98%), and a large plurality is white (about 49%). African Americans account for most (40%) of the rest; about 7% are Latino, 2% native American, and less than 1% ethnically Asian. Among the death row prisoners executed since 1977, 55% were white, 38% black, and 6% Latino. Although about half of all murder victims in the United States during the 1990s are non-white, the vast bulk of all executions (85%) since 1977 have been of defendants found guilty of murdering a white victim.[10]

A defendant's minimum age at the time of a crime making him eligible for a death sentence varies among the states (*Table 2*). Nine states specify no minimum age; one specifies a minimum age of 14 (Arkansas), two specify the age of 15 (Louisiana, Virginia), nine specify the age of 16, four specify the age of 17, and the remaining dozen states (including the federal government) set 18 as the minimum age for liability to the death penalty. Among those on death row at the end of 1994, forty were sentenced in a dozen different states for a crime committed when they were 17 or younger; nine others aged 17 at the time of the crime have already been executed between 1985 and 1993.[11]

The criminal history of current death row prisoners presents the following picture: 68% had some record of prior felony conviction, including 240 (9%) with a prior conviction of some form of criminal homicide (first-degree murder, second-degree murder, voluntary manslaughter).[12] Whether these data show that the current death penalty system effectively winnows out the worst criminals from among the bad is difficult to say. One would need to examine the criminal history of all convicted murderers who were not sentenced to death and then compare the prior felony records of two groups, and no such research has been undertaken.[13]

Conditions of confinement for prisoners under sentence of death vary from jurisdiction to jurisdiction; no uniform practice prevails across the nation. Typically, prisoners under sentence of death are housed under special security conditions or even in a special prison unit. As the average time spent under sentence of death prior to execution is now about nine years,[14] time lies heavy on the prisoners' hands. Little opportunity for exercise or productive labour is the lot of the vast majority of these convicts; their chief diversion is television, and their chief preoccupation is the status of their legal case on appeal for review of their convictions or death sentences. Not a few of these prisoners are virtually abandoned by family and friends; except for visits from their lawyers (and many prisoners have no lawyers at one or another stage of their confinement) or the prison chaplain, their lives are truly isolated and lonely.[15] Attempts by attorneys to argue on behalf of their death row clients that conditions on death row violate constitutional prohibitions of 'cruel and unusual punishment' have so far been unsuccessful.[16]

## MURDER, DEATH SENTENCES, EXECUTIONS, AND PENAL POLICY

The United States is said to have the highest violent crime rate, highest criminal homicide rate, and greatest use of guns in the commission of violent crimes of any western nation.[17] The country also has more persons currently on death row and more persons in prison for crimes of all sorts than any other western nation. These facts about crime and punishment are not disconnected, and they bear on the current status of the death penalty.

The death penalty in the United States is essentially confined to the crime of murder. So far in the 1990s, the Federal Bureau of Investigation has reported in its annual *Uniform Crime Reports* about 24,000 criminal homicides each year, which yields an average annual rate of about 9.5 per 100,000, of the general population. The arrest ('clearance') rate for criminal homicide is about 65%, and about 90% of those arrested for this crime are prosecuted for it. The average annual number of convictions is considerably less, about 10,000 annually.[18] Only a small fraction of all these convictions involve defendants who might be sentenced to death (so-called 'death eligible defendants').

For nearly two centuries in the United States, the death penalty for murder has been limited to those convicted of 'first-degree murder' - wilful, deliberate, premeditated killing of another person - as well as felony-murder: any homicide committed in the course of another felony, such as rape, robbery, burglary, or arson. It has been estimated that no more than two to four thousand convicted murderers each year are death-eligible.[19] The volume of death sentencing, however, is at best a tenth of those eligible: around 250

48

per year.[20] The story of capital punishment in the United States today is largely the story of this extraordinary attrition - 24,000 criminal homicides, 18,000 arrests, 10,000 convictions, 2-4,000 death eligibles, and 250 death sentences (and two dozen or so executions each year). Two questions in particular arise from these figures: Are they to be read as a successful winnowing of the worst cases from the rest, or are the resulting death sentences far more arbitrary than that? What functional role - deterrence, incapacitation, retribution (rather than a mainly symbolic one) - can the death penalty really play in a society when 24,000 criminal homicides are punished with death in only 1% of the cases?

Many have observed that the death penalty in the United States is not evenly distributed across the nation. Rather, it is largely confined to the South and West (*Table 4*). The homicide rates in these states are generally higher than in states with few or no death sentences[21] - and defenders of the death penalty would argue the unverifiable proposition that without the death penalty, the rates would be even higher.

Also unpredictable and without evident pattern is whether a given death sentence will culminate in the defendant's execution (*Table 5*). Of nearly 5,000 persons who were sentenced to death between 1973 and 1993, nearly 60% remained on death row at the end of 1993, less than 5% having been executed, and the rest - about a third - were removed from death row for various reasons.

One of these reasons - exercise of clemency power by the chief executive or pardon board to commute a death sentence to life in prison - has lost most of its historic influence. In the 1990s, the clemency power has ceased to exist as an option for all but the rarest death row prisoner.[22] Once we eliminate those commutations awarded on purely technical grounds (e.g. in response to an appellate court order overturning a death sentence), what remains are the few prisoners who leave death row by commutation on humanitarian grounds. Their number - an average of about two per year - is the same as those who leave death row by suicide.[23]

But the real scandal is the travesty of justice that unfolds all too often in the trial of a defendant charged with murder and where, if there is a conviction, the judge or the jury (depending on the plea and on the sentencing law) must decide the punishment. Underpaid, overworked, inexperienced, incompetent defence counsel; failure to submit any, or any adequate, evidence of mitigation during the penalty phase of the trial; indifferent judicial conduct of the trial; improper and misunderstood instructions to the jury; confusion, brow-beating, and impatience among the sequestered jurors - these deplorable features of actual capital trials have been cited again and again by knowledgeable observers.[24] As one commentator has noted, a death sentence more often than not is handed down 'not for the worst crime but for the worst lawyer.'[25]

49

# PUBLIC OPINION

Public opinion on the death penalty, if one can trust the survey research reports published over the past two decades, is solidly in favour of the death penalty (*Figure 2*). When asked, 'Do you favour the death penalty for murder?' 80 percent or so of Americans will answer in the affirmative; few are undecided. It is now commonplace for the media to report this widespread support, thereby perhaps helping to sustain it. Polls have also shown that deterrence and incapacitation are not the governing considerations in this support; rather, it is retribution - 'a life for a life' - or even revenge that dominates the public's thinking on the subject. [26]

Closer analysis of this support, however, has shown that public attitudes on the death penalty are more complex than these figures reveal. Research published in 1990 showed that in California, for example, while it was true that some 82% of the sample surveyed professed to support the death penalty, support plummeted to 26% if respondents were given the opportunity to choose between death and the alternative punishment of life in prison without any possibility of parole plus some form of restitution by the offender to surviving family members of the victim. In the years since, such a falling off of support for the death penalty when given the alternative of 'LWOP plus R' has been confirmed by further research. Thus, while one must concede the undeniable public 'acceptance' of the death penalty in principle, it is clearly possible to argue that this does not imply any general public 'preference' for that penalty in practice. [27] So far, however, there has been no success in translating these revealed attitudes into repeal of death penalty statutes in favour of statutes providing for LWOP plus R. Perhaps as the costs of the death penalty system mount,[28] requiring taxpayers to underfund schools, pensions, highways and other public goods in order to pay for a death penalty system that executes only a handful, the public preference for long-term imprisonment may some day persuade politicians to legislate accordingly.

If one seeks to explain public support for the death penalty, one discovers very little relevant research. No doubt the public's anger at criminals, fear of victimization, and frustration over government's inability at all levels to alleviate the perceived causes of this anger, fear, and frustration play important roles. Electoral political campaigns in recent years have exploited these emotions and have re-inforced the association between a government official's opposition to the death penalty, on the one hand, and his or her indifference to the public welfare and apparent sympathy for criminals rather than for their victims, on the other. It is now widely assumed that no political candidate in the United States can hope to run for president, governor, or other high elective office if he or she can successfully be targeted as 'soft on crime'; the candidate's position on the death penalty has become the litmus test. [29]

So long as these facts prevail, there is little likelihood of further success in abolishing the death penalty under state or federal law in the United States. Worse than that, considerable political effort is being directed toward expansion of the death penalty to cover additional crimes, to reduce support

50

for publicly funded defence and appellate counsel in capital cases, and to undertake major reform of procedural aspects of the death penalty perceived to be the cause of unconscionable delays in carrying out sentences and of raising the dollar costs of a death penalty system. [30] None of this bodes well for those who had thought in the late 1960s or early 1970s that there was a good chance the death penalty in the United States would be completely abolished by the year 2000. [31]

## CONSTITUTIONAL ISSUES

Since 1976, when the Supreme Court ruled that the death penalty as such was not an unconstitutionally 'cruel and unusual punishment', a constant flow of litigation on lesser constitutional issues has transpired. Virtually every year sees one or more new decisions that shape the legal processes involved in administration of the death penalty. The result is that 20 years of post-*Furman* and post-*Gregg* rulings by the Supreme Court have built an enormously complex legal structure surrounding this punishment. Here is a sketch of the most important Supreme Court rulings:

*1978.* Mitigating circumstances are not confined to those mentioned by statute; the capital jury must be allowed to consider 'any aspect of the defendant's character or record and any of the circumstances of the offense that the defendant professes as a basis for a sentence less than death.': *Lockett v. Ohio.*

*1979.* A death sentence is invalid if it is imposed by a jury that failed to specify any statutory aggravating circumstance during the penalty phase of the trial: *Presnell v. Georgia.*

*1980.* The aggravating circumstance defined by statute as 'outrageously or wantonly vile , horrible or inhuman in that it involved torture, depravity of mind or an aggravated battery to the victim', is too vague to be constitutionally permissible: *Godfrey v. Georgia.* (This ruling was virtually overturned in 1990 by the holding in *Walton v. Arizona* to the effect that the statutory aggravating circumstance of a murder 'especially heinous, cruel or depraved' was not too vague.)

*1982.* The death penalty is disproportionately severe if imposed on a defendant convicted of aiding and abetting a murder but who himself did not kill, attempt to kill, or intend to kill the victim: *Enmund v. Florida.* (Modified in 1987 in *Tison v. Arizona,* holding that a defendant who assists in the crime of murder and whose 'mental state is one of reckless indifference to the value of human life' may be sentenced to death.)

51

*1983*. Psychiatric testimony regarding the future dangerousness of a defendant, placed before the jury by the prosecution during the sentencing phase of the trial, is admissible even though the testimony is not based on any interview with the defendant: *Barefoot v. Estelle*.

*1984*. Establishing that a death sentence was fairly imposed by comparing it with other cases in which death was (and was not) imposed in the same jurisdiction (so-called 'proportionality review') is not a constitutional requirement of a death sentencing procedure: *Pulley v. Harris*.

*1984*. A statute allowing the trial judge to impose a death sentence despite the jury's unanimous recommendation of a life sentence is not unconstitutional: *Spaziano v. Florida*.

*1986*. Execution of the insane is unconstitutional, and state procedures must accommodate the condemned person's right to submit evidence of insanity: *Ford v. Wainwright*.

*1987*. A mandatory death penalty for a defendant who murders while serving a life prison term for a prior murder is unconstitutional: *Sumner v. Shuman*.

*1987*. Victim impact evidence, showing the pain and suffering of surviving relatives and friends of a murder victim and offered in support of the prosecution's argument for the death penalty during the penalty phase of a capital trial, may not be introduced: *Booth v. Maryland*. (Overruled in 1991, *Payne v. Tennessee*.)

*1987*. Even if racism infects the administration of a state's death penalty system (in particular, if race of victim and defendant serve as significant predictors of sentencing decisions in capital cases), there is no constitutional violation of 'equal protection of the laws' so long as there is no evidence of intentional racial discrimination against a particular defendant: *McCleskey v. Kemp*.

*1988*. A statute that permits execution of a juvenile defendant under the age of 16 at the time of the crime is unconstitutional: *Thompson v. Oklahoma*. (It is not a 'cruel and unusual punishment' to sentence to death a juvenile who is 16 or older at the time of the crime. 1989, *Stanford v. Kentucky*.)

*1989*. There is no constitutional objection as such to the execution of a mentally retarded defendant. However, mental retardation is a mitigating circumstance, and the jury is entitled to hear evidence on the point during the sentencing phase of the trial: *Penry v. Lynaugh*.

*1989.* States are not required to provide counsel for indigent defendants on death row who seek post-conviction relief in state courts beyond the automatic appeal of their conviction and sentence: *Murray v. Giarrantano.* (In federal courts, however, such counsel must be provided. 1994, *McFarland v. Texas.*)

*1990.* A death sentence imposed under a quasi-mandatory capital statute (requiring the jury to mete out a death sentence if it finds even one aggravating circumstance, whether or not it has also received any evidence from defence counsel concerning mitigating circumstances) is not unconstitutional: *Blystone v. Pennsylvania; Boyde v. California.*

*1990.* Despite the sentencing jury's reliance on an unconstitutional aggravating circumstance in deciding to sentence the defendant to death, the state appellate court may re-evaluate the evidence heard during the penalty phase of the trial and sustain the death sentence without returning the case to the trial court for a new sentencing hearing: *Clemons v. Mississippi.*

*1991.* A death row prisoner who has already litigated claims through a federal habeas corpus petition will not be granted another such opportunity (a 'successor habeas corpus petition') unless the prisoner can demonstrate 'cause and prejudice' for the failure to raise this new claim in his original petition: *McClesky v. Zant.*

*1991.* Defendant counsel's failure to file a timely notice of appeal in state court does not excuse such 'procedural default' even in the case of a death row prisoner: *Coleman v. Thompson.*

*1993.* A death row prisoner convicted under state law has no right to a hearing in federal courts on grounds of newly discovered evidence purporting to show the defendant is innocent if the evidence is belated under a state statute, unless the defendant can present a 'truly persuasive demonstration' of his innocence such that had the trial jury heard this evidence he would have been acquitted or not sentenced to death: *Herrera v. Collins.*

Taken all together, these decisions (and others to be mentioned below) establish several fundamental conclusions concerning the substantive and procedural law affecting the death penalty. First, there is at present no constitutional objection to the death penalty as such, as a majority of the recent and current members of the Supreme Court interprets the Constitution. Second, there is a strong presumption against any mandatory death penalty, no matter what the crime. Third, the death penalty will probably remain confined to crimes involving homicide in some way or other; the most likely exception is the possibility that a few persons convicted of large-scale drug trafficking ('drug kingpins') will be sentenced to death under recent federal statutes and actually executed.[32]

Procedurally, the Supreme Court seems to have lost interest in controlling and regulating state criminal procedures as they affect the death penalty, except where intervention has the effect of allowing more rather than fewer death sentences to survive review.

A prominent recent example illustrating this point concerns the Texas law on death sentencing.[33] Under Texas law enacted in 1974 and upheld by the Supreme Court in *Jurek* (1976), if a defendant convicted of murder is to receive a death sentence, the sentencer must find that the defendant is and will continue to be 'dangerous' to others. In 1989 the Court ruled in *Penry* that a defendant's mental retardation was relevant mitigating evidence even if it was a 'double-edged sword' (because it might convince the jury that the defendant was and always would be 'dangerous' to others, since mental retardation is a lifelong, irreversible condition). *Penry* left open whether youth or drug addiction or other conditions might also be relevantly mitigating. Defence counsel argued that *Penry* permitted introducing such factors, too; prosecutors argued that such a broad interpretation of *Penry* would lead to every death row murderer in Texas getting a new trial (there were some 300 inmates on Texas's death row at the time). In 1992 the Court ruled (*Graham v. Collins*) - and in 1993 reinforced that ruling (*Johnson v. Texas*) - that all these other potentially mitigating conditions were irrelevant unless they could be shown to be the cause of the defendant's committing the crime in the first place - obviously a difficult standard to meet in most cases. In 1994 the Court refused to grant certiorari and to review these 1993 rulings, with the result that - as one defence attorney said - '*Penry* now means nothing.' As the executive director of the Texas Resource Center (which coordinates capital defence litigation in Texas) observed, 'Johnny Penry himself could not find relief under the current state of the law.'

The story in this series of Texas cases illustrates what one commentator several years ago called the Supreme Court's 'deregulation' of death,[34] allowing each state great latitude in the administration and interpretation of its capital laws. The chief result of this attitude is that little has truly been accomplished over the past two decades to produce death sentencing systems in state criminal procedure that are free from arbitrariness in deciding which murder convicts are to be sentenced to death and which to life in prison. Ample evidence supports this conclusion.[35]

This was also the conclusion stated recently by Justice Harry A. Blackman. After three decades on the federal bench, during which he had voted to sustain the constitutionality of the death penalty in several major cases, he dissented in *Callins v. Collins* (1994), arguing that: '[T]he death penalty remains fraught with arbitrariness, discrimination, caprice, and mistake . . . Experience has taught us that the constitutional goal of eliminating arbitrariness and discrimination from the administration of death . . . can never be achieved without compromising an equally essential component of fundamental fairness - individualized sentencing . . . From this day forward, I no longer shall tinker with the machinery of death . . . I feel morally and intellectually obligated simply to concede that the death penalty experiment has failed.' In reaching this conclusion, however, Justice Blackman wrote in splendid isolation; none of his eight colleagues currently sitting on the Court has so far seen fit to join him in judging the Court's death penalty jurisprudence a failure.

# LEGISLATION

In September 1994, President Clinton signed into law the Violent Crime Control and Law Enforcement Act, part of which - the Federal Death Penalty Act - created a whole range of new federal death penalties.[36] One effect of this legislation is to pre-empt state authority to try these offences. As a result, the federal government may now prosecute a given crime as capitally punishable even though it occurred in a state jurisdiction that did not authorize the death penalty for that crime. This pre-emptive federal legislation has made the death penalty into a punishment of nation-wide application for the first time in history.

To some extent, these new federal capital offences are window-dressing, since in most cases the new laws simply make explicit a special kind of criminal homicide (e.g. a drive-by shooting where death results) in order to attach a death penalty to it, when such a crime was already explicitly or implicitly prohibited by existing state laws against criminal homicide in general and punishable by death. With the exception of a death penalty for espionage, treason, persons who traffic in large quantities of drugs, and persons who attempt to kill witnesses, jurors or others involved in the prosecution of a 'continuing criminal enterprise,' all these new capital offences were created by expanding the felony-murder rule, so that any death caused in the course of committing some other crime (e.g. sexual abuse, hostage taking) now subjects the offender to prosecution for a capital offence.

Disappointing as the enactment of this legislation was to opponents of the death penalty, the refusal of Congress to include the Racial Justice Act was an especially bitter blow to them. Since 1987, when the Supreme Court decided *McKleskey v. Kemp* (by a vote of five to four) and refused to consider the racially disparate patterns of death sentencing as a sufficient ground to revise the administration of capital sentencing, efforts were made to persuade Congress to enact a statutory remedy for racial discrimination: the Racial Justice Act. This Act would prohibit a state from imposing the death penalty if the defendant could present suitable statistical evidence of racial disparities in death sentences within that state.[37] In refusing to enact this proposed legislation, Congress in 1994 followed the path carved out by the Supreme Court in 1987: No general overhaul of the death sentencing system in the United States will be undertaken by the federal government in order to remedy the impact of race on who gets sentenced to death and who does not - despite the long history of close association between the death penalty and American racism.[38]

The bombing of a federal building in Oklahoma City, Oklahoma, in April 1995 predictably led to agitation for new federal legislation aimed at deterring and punishing terrorism as an especially heinous act (despite the lack of any evidence that such legislation was needed or would be an effective counter-terrorist measure, and despite the fact that the crime was already punishable as a capital offence under Oklahoma law).[39] President Clinton immediately demanded the death penalty for this crime and Congress promptly responded with the Comprehensive Terrorism Prevention Act (a Senate bill) and the Effective Death Penalty Act (a House bill). If these bills are enacted into law, their immediate effect on the death penalty will be a radical revision in habeas corpus remedies with no relevance whatever to the crime or the punishment of terrorism.[40]

Federal habeas corpus is a long-standing statutory (not constitutional) writ that empowers a state prisoner to appeal to the federal courts to review his conviction or sentence on the ground that it violates fundamental federal constitutional protections.[41] Under the proposed new laws (their details vary), a death row prisoner will be allowed no more than one year from the end of post-conviction review by state appellate courts in which to file for review by the federal courts - and once that review is concluded, no further review would be allowed, except when a defendant claims he is factually innocent of the crime and that claim can be supported by newly discovered 'clear and convincing evidence' that could not have been discovered earlier by 'due diligence.'[42]

Thus it appears that one of the chief aims of those who favour the death penalty and deplore what they regard as the inordinate delay in carrying it out - the use (they would say 'abuse') by death row prisoners of the statutory writ of federal habeas corpus to obtain a hearing on the constitutional merits of their cases, despite earlier review in state courts - will finally have been achieved.

Two results of this attack on federal habeas corpus can safely be predicted. First, as its supporters insist, it will probably decrease the time in carrying out death sentences (unless, of course, far more convicts are sentenced to death in the first place, thereby placing even heavier demands on the appellate system). Second, as its supporters ignore, it will increase the likelihood of miscarriages of justice in capital cases - the execution of prisoners who are factually innocent or who are victims of procedural violations, but who were unable to establish these violations within the allowed time, not only in past decades but throughout the post-*Furman* era)[43] and charges that innocent persons are on death row continue to be aired, severely limiting this avenue of review and relief is a major retrograde development. It is particularly troubling when evidence shows that during the 1980s federal habeas corpus litigation of state-imposed death sentences resulted in 'as many as half of all death sentences being overturned' for procedural violations.[44]

56

Legislation affecting the death penalty also occurs at the state level, and in recent years virtually every state in the nation has had one or more bills in its legislature to enact, modify, expand, narrow, or abolish the death penalty. In 1994, for example, an attempt in North Carolina to exclude the mentally retarded from a death sentence died in committee; a bill in Louisiana to require all death sentences to be carried out within five years died in committee; in Virginia a bill to limit the number of surviving family members of a murder victim to witness the execution of the murderer died on the state senate floor.[45]

In 1995, for example, New York re-introduced the death penalty for murder;[46] bills to stage executions in public died in Arkansas and Mississippi; a bill to prohibit execution of the mentally retarded died in committee in Mississippi; bills to re-introduce the death penalty in Iowa, West Virginia and North Dakota were defeated.[47] Many other bills affecting the death penalty are still pending, and others will surely be filed in future legislative sessions. Most will die pigeon-holed in some legislative committee.

## ORGANIZED OPPOSITION TO THE DEATH PENALTY

Despite the public acceptance of the nation's current death penalty system, opposition to the death penalty is vocal, pronounced, and unrelenting in many quarters. Leading the parade is the National Coalition to Abolish the Death Penalty (NCADP), organized in 1977 in response to the Supreme Court's decision in *Gregg* and allied cases. With headquarters in Washington, D.C., the NCADP consists of several dozen national, state, and local organizations. Chief among these constituent organizations are the American Civil Liberties Union and the NAACP Legal Defence and Educational Fund, Inc., both of which have had policy opposition to the death penalty dating to the early 1960s. A third stalwart is of course Amnesty International U.S.A. Even in these organizations, however, one encounters members and supporters who give only lukewarm opposition to the death penalty.

For decades, organized religion - the major Catholic, Jewish, and Protestant denominations - have voiced opposition to capital punishment,[48] but it is obvious that the leadership of these groups do not speak for all or even most of their parishioners. Meanwhile, other Protestant groups, such as the Moral Majority and the Christian Coalition, as well as fundamentalist churches nationwide (but especially in the South, Midwest, and West), avidly support the death penalty, as do the Mormons.[49] Even though Pope John Paul II's the recent encyclical, *The Gospel of Life* (1995), strongly condemns the death penalty and thus may help enlist more support for abolition among church-going American Catholics, it is not likely to have much impact in the nation's religious communities generally.

# THE DEATH PENALTY IN THE MEDIA

For several decades, major American newspapers, such as *The New York Times, The Washington Post,* and *The Boston Globe* have editorially opposed the death penalty. Editorials, op-ed essays, news reports, and in-depth investigative reporting have kept the issue before the public. (Ever since the moratorium on the death penalty ended in 1977, *The New York Times* has published some sort of article, even if only a paragraph, on every execution in the nation.) Books and articles, especially research publications in professional journals, flow steadily from the presses - virtually all of it opposed to current policy on the death penalty.[50] Television often broadcasts debate or panel discussion on the pros and cons of capital punishment, although the 'sound-bite' remarks characteristic of these programs do little to inform and persuade viewers. Occasionally, a documentary or movie appears in which issues surrounding the death penalty are presented with skill and sensitivity. Nevertheless, investigations to determine just how much the public knows about the death penalty show that the public is quite misinformed and generally ignorant of even the basic facts about capital punishment in their own jurisdiction.

News reports as well as regular entertainment on television, however, portray a violent society, with crimes against the person being committed at every turn. Although television news and other shows rarely urge the death penalty as the solution to the problem of criminal violence, they do tend to foster a climate in which only extreme measures can be expected to protect the public. And every major urban area now has its radio or television talk show host who gives regular vocal support to the death penalty.

A recurring issue is whether actual executions ought to be filmed and shown 'live' on television.[51] Public executions in the United States officially ended in the mid-1930s, and since that time photographers have generally been excluded from the execution chamber. The print media, however, have always had their representatives present. In Texas in 1976, when that state's first execution seemed imminent, a television reporter argued in federal court that barring his cameraman from photographing and broadcasting the execution was unfair and unconstitutional. The reporter appealed both to the 'free press' clause and the 'equal protection of the laws' clause in the federal Constitution. The federal trial court ruled against the reporter; further litigation was mooted when the execution was indefinitely postponed.

The controversy was revived in 1984 when a Texas death row prisoner himself sought to get his execution televised. The Texas Board of Corrections unanimously refused to honour the request, the Board chairman arguing that 'propriety and decency,' as well as unspecified 'effects on the death penalty,' justified the denial.

In 1990, when California was getting ready to carry out its first execution in a quarter century, the controversy erupted again. Debate raged back and forth between those who thought such a television show should be lawful but that it was in poor taste (and on that ground should be ignored by any

58

responsible television station), those who thought such a show would be in the public interest (whether the effect was to deepen support for or opposition to the death penalty), and those who thought that such a show should continue to be prohibited on grounds of harming the public interest. The State of California argued that it was a bad idea because of the unpredictable effects watching an execution would have on the more than 300 other prisoners on California's death row, each of whom had a television set in his cell. As in Texas, the California court ruled that if prison regulations excluded television crews from the execution chamber, there was no ground for the courts to intervene on behalf of the disgruntled media. There the matter stands.[52]

## VICTIMS MOVEMENT

Agitation to preserve and expand the death penalty is not an organized movement. Supporters (like their opponents) range across the whole spectrum of American society. In recent years, however, the death penalty controversy has increasingly involved surviving family members of murder victims. It is now not uncommon for such family members to be permitted (indeed, invited) to witness the execution of the prisoner who murdered their loved one(s). Television news reporters frequently interview family members for their views about the impending execution of such a murderer; occasionally, family members will take the opportunity of a television interview to posture before the public, shrieking for revenge from the criminal justice system.

At present, surviving family members of murder victims can be found in one or both of two national organizations. 'Parents of Murdered Children, Inc.' has its headquarters in Cincinnati, Ohio. Although the organization takes no position on the death penalty as such, it is evident from its newsletter, *Survivor*, that many (perhaps most) of its members strongly support capital punishment. The other organization, 'Murder Victims Families for Reconciliation,' is strongly opposed to the death penalty; its headquarters is in Portage, Indiana.[53] Neither organization enrols more than a tiny fraction of the hundred thousand surviving family members of murder victims created each year by the more than 20,000 criminal homicides annually in the nation.

## INTERNATIONAL COVENANTS AND INFLUENCE

Death row prisoners in the United States - Sacco and Vanzetti in the 1920s[54] and the Rosenbergs in the 1950s,[55] to cite but two of the most famous - have occasionally aroused international interest and protest. More than once the Vatican has protested the impending execution of an American convict - for example, in the case of Caryl Chessman, executed in California in 1960.[56] Today, the worldwide membership of Amnesty International can be counted on to protest virtually every execution in America.[57]

The effects of such international attention, however, are hard to gauge. Americans (like others) are not easily persuaded of the vulnerability to criticism on moral grounds of any of their policies or practices by foreigners. And interfering outsiders who volunteer unsought criticism are rarely welcome anywhere. This indifference, not to say hostility, to foreign persuasion and agitation over the death penalty is most disturbing where it concerns the American response to international law and covenants. [58]

In 1968, the United States supported a draft resoluton in which the death penalty was declared to be in violation of both article 3 (recognizng the 'right to life') and article 5 (prohibiting 'cruel, inhumane, or degrading treatment or punishment') of the Universal Declaration of Human Rights. This action came at a time when the Attorney General of the United States had declared that the government was in favour of abolishing the death penalty[59] - a position that was promptly abandoned by his successor after the general election later that year.

In 1976 the International Covenant on Civil and Political Rights came into effect; it was ratified belatedly by the United States in 1992, under President Bush. The United States was one of three nations to express reservations concerning the right to life and article 6, with its general provisions for constraining the death penalty and encouraging its abolition. In what one commentator has described as 'by far the most extensive reservation to the capital punishment provisions of any international human rights treaty',[60] the United States flatly declared that it 'reserves the right, subject to its Constitutional constraints, to impose capital punishment on any person (other than a pregnant woman) duly convicted under existing or future laws permitting the imposition of capital punishment on persons below eighteen years of age.'

The Second Optional Protocol to the International Covenant, aimed expressly at abolition of the death penalty, took force in 1991. During the discussion stage in 1980, the United States insisted that it could not ratify such a document, but it did not actively resist formulation and adoption of the Protocol. In the General Assembly, which approved the Protocol in 1989, the United States voted against adoption.

The United States government has also refused to ratify the American Convention on Human Rights, with its provision of a nonderogable 'right to life.' Created in 1969 by a dozen American nations under the general auspices of the Organization of American States, the Convention was submitted to the U. S. Senate in 1977, as required by the constitution, for its ratification; but a draft reservation accompanied the submission, noting that the right to life provisions as they concern the death penalty may be in question.

In litigation, the United States has also resisted compliance with international norms. In *Roach and Pinkerton v. United States* (1985) the petitioners argued that, as they were under 18 at the time of the crimes for which they had been convicted, customary international law forbade their execution and that a proper interpretation of article 1 of the American Declaration of the Rights and Duties of Man (recognizing 'the right to life') so provided. The United States disagreed, holding that there was no rule of customary law to this effect. Concurrently, Roach and Pinkerton appealed to the United Nation's Commission on Human Rights; the Commission's request for a stay of execution pending study of the petitions as filed was denied, and the defendants were executed.

In *Soering v. United Kingdom et al.* (1989), the European Court of Human Rights considered whether extradition on a charge of first-degree murder to the United States of an American citizen under detention by the United Kingdom could proceed without the defendant first receiving assurances that he would not be liable to the death penalty, given that the death penalty constituted 'cruel, inhumane, or degrading treatment of punishment.' The Court ruled against the American contention that the extradition order should be enforced forthwith. In Washington, D.C., the Senate replied by introducing its 'Soering reservations' to the Convention Against Torture and the International Covenant on Civil and Political Rights, both then pending in the Senate. The reservations declared that in interpreting the 'cruel, inhumane, or degrading treatment or punishment' clause of these instruments, the United States would treat the clause as meaning exactly what the 'cruel and unusual punishment' clause of the eighth amendment to the U.S. Constitution means. Since the Supreme Court had clearly interpreted this provision of American constitutional law to be consistent with capital punishment, the Senate reservation effectively nullified any significance in American law of the international prohibition against 'cruel, inhumane, or degrading treatment or punishment' - so far as that prohibition affects the death penalty.

In *Short v. Kingdom of the Netherlands* (1990),[61] the issue was whether an American airman, serving with NATO forces in Holland and arrested by the Dutch authorities in connection with the murder of his wife and then so charged, should be remanded to the United States for trial under the Uniform Code of Military Justice (UCMJ), with its provisions for the death penalty, given that the Dutch had ratified the Sixth Protocol of the European Convention, whose first article prohibited the death penalty. Disruptive conflict between the Netherlands and the United States was avoided when the American military prosecutor informed the Dutch authorities that Short did not meet the criteria for death eligibility under the UCMJ, thereby freeing the Dutch to remand Short to the American authorities without having breached either the dike protecting guest nation authority under the NATO Status of Forces Agreement or the dike against Dutch complicity in a violation of article 1 of the Sixth Protocol.

## CONCLUSION

For more than two centuries, reformers have endeavoured to limit, nullify, and abolish the death penalty in the United States. It is in this country (in the state of Michigan, since 1847) where the death penalty for murder has been continuously abolished longer than in any other jurisdiction in the world. More has been investigated, researched, written, litigated, and publicly argued against the death penalty in America (especially but not wholly during the most recent half-century) than in the rest of the world combined. The history of the death penalty in this country is the history of novel modifications in administering the law so that fewer persons liable to this punishment would be actually executed: the distinction between degrees of murder, confining eligibility for death only to those convicted of first-degree murder; ending public executions; granting the jury the power to decide whether to sentence a convicted capital felon to death or to life; steadily reducing the variety of crimes punishable by death; experimenting with total abolition (*Table 6*); seeking less brutal and disgusting methods of carrying out the death penalty.

Yet it can also be argued that each of these reforms tended to entrench yet deeper what remained of the death penalty. The result is that tearing out the root has become more and more difficult, not least because abolition efforts in a given jurisdiction often have had little or no effect on a neighbouring jurisdiction. Mounting a national campaign to abolish the death penalty has in fact never been undertaken; the resources in money, people, and opportunity have never been available. The sole attempt to abolish the death penalty nationally, by persuading the Supreme Court to rule it out on constitutional grounds, failed (despite its notable achievements).

As the century comes to a close, the prospects for complete abolition in the United States are not encouraging; the death penalty has become part of partisan political campaigning in a manner impossible to have predicted a generation ago. And while there is evidence that very few Americans want large numbers of executions, there seems to be little discontent with two dozen or so a year. Yet the evidence from every direction supports the argument for abolition. There is no way to reduce the risk of executing the innocent, except by abolishing the death penalty. There is no foreseeable way to avoid the tendency of the death penalty to be used on the poor, the outcast, racial minorities, and others vulnerable to public hostility, anger, and fear. Short of severely restricting, if not virtually abolishing, the constitutional rights of the criminal defendant, there is no way to speed up the process from indictment to final disposition in capital cases except by abolishing the death penalty. There is no ideally humane method of inflicting the death penalty. Neither general deterrence nor incapacitation requires a policy of executions.

These are the conclusions one must reach if one studies the literature on the subject patiently accumulated over the past generation.[62] One can only hope that in due course the inhumanity of the death penalty, the way it mocks our moral pretentions as a civilized nation, will become so evident that responsible citizens will realize they do not need it and do not want it.


ENDNOTES See page 69

## Table 1: Method of Execution, by State, 1993

| Lethal injection | Electrocution | Lethal gas | Hanging | Firing squad |
|---|---|---|---|---|
| Arizona[a, f] | Alabama | Arizona[a] | Montana[a] | Idaho[a] |
| Arkansas[a, b] | Arkansas[a, b] | California[a] | New Hampshire[a, d] | Utah[a] |
| California[a] | Connecticut | Colorado[a, c] | Washington[a] | |
| Colorado[a, c] | Florida | Maryland | | |
| Delaware | Georgia | Mississippi[a, e] | | |
| Idaho[a] | Indiana | Missouri[a] | | |
| Illinois | Kentucky | North Carolina[a] | | |
| Louisiana | Nebraska | Wyoming[a, f] | | |
| Mississippi[a, e] | Ohio[a] | | | |
| Missouri[a] | South Carolina | | | |
| Montana[a] | Tennessee | | | |
| Nevada | Virginia | | | |
| New Hampshire[a, d] | | | | |
| New Jersey | | | | |
| New Mexico | | | | |
| North Carolina[a] | | | | |
| Ohio[a] | | | | |
| Oklahoma | | | | |
| Oregon | | | | |
| Pennsylvania | | | | |
| South Dakota | | | | |
| Texas | | | | |
| Utah[a] | | | | |
| Washington[a] | | | | |
| Wyoming[a, g] | | | | |

Note: Effective 2/18/93, federal executions are to be carried out by lethal injection. [a]Authorises two methods of execution. [b]Arkansas authorises lethal injection for those whose capital offence occurred after 7/4/83; for those whose offence occurred before that date, the condemned prisoner may select lethal injection or electrocution. [c]Colorado authorises lethal gas for those whose crimes occurred before 7/1/88 and lethal injection for those crimes which occurred on or after 7/1/88. [d]New Hampshire authorises hanging only if lethal injection cannot be given. [e]Mississippi authorises lethal injection for those convicted after 7/1/84; execution of those convicted prior to that date is to be carried out with lethal gas. [f]Arizona authorises lethal injection for persons whose capital sentence was received after 11/15/92; for those who were sentenced before that date, the condemned prisoner may select lethal injection or lethal gas. [g]Wyoming authorises lethal gas, if lethal injection is ever held unconstitutional.

Source: Bureau of Justice Statistics, *Capital Punishment 1993* p.4, Table 2.

## Table 2: Minimum Age of Persons Subject to Capital Punishment, by Jurisdiction, 1993

| Age less than 18 | Age 18 | None specified |
|---|---|---|
| Alabama (16) | California | Arizona |
| Arkansas (14) [a] | Colorado | Florida |
| Delaware (16) | Connecticut [b] | Idaho |
| Georgia (17) | Federal system | Montana |
| Indiana (16) | Illinois | Pennsylvania |
| Kentucky (16) | Maryland | South Carolina |
| Louisiana (15) | Nebraska | South Dakota[e] |
| Mississippi (16) [c] | New Jersey | Utah |
| Missouri (16) | New Mexico | Washington |
| Nevada (16) | Ohio | |
| New Hampshire (17) | Oregon | |
| North Carolina (17) [d] | Tennessee | |
| Oklahoma (16) | | |
| Texas (17) | | |
| Virginia (15) | | |
| Wyoming (16) | | |

Note: Reporting by states reflects interpretations by state attorney general offices and may differ from previously reported ages. [a]See Arkansas Code Ann. 9-27-318(b)(1)(Repl. 1991). [b]See Conn. Gen. Stat. 53a-46a(g)(1). [c]Minimum age defined by statute is 13, but effective age is 16 based on an interpretation of US Supreme Court decisions by the state attorney general's office. [d] Age required is 17 unless the murderer was incarcerated for murder when a subsequent murder occurred; the age may then be 14. [e]Juveniles may be transferred to adult court. Age may be a mitigating circumstance.

Source: Bureau of Justice Statistics, *Capital Punishment 1993*, Table 3. p.6.

## Table 3: Criminal History Profile of Persons Under Sentence of Death, by Type of Offense and Race, 1993

| | Prisoners under sentence of death | | | | | | | |
|---|---|---|---|---|---|---|---|---|
| | Number | | | | Percent[a] | | | |
| | All races[b] | White | Black | Hispanic | All races[b] | White | Black | Hispanic |
| US Total | 2,716 | 1,566 | 1,109 | 206 | 100% | 100% | 100% | 100% |
| **Prior felony convictions** | | | | | | | | |
| Yes | 1,740 | 963 | 760 | 120 | 67.9% | 64.8% | 73.2% | 60.9% |
| No | 822 | 522 | 278 | 77 | 32.1 | 35.2 | 26.8 | 39.1 |
| Not reported | 154 | 81 | 71 | 9 | | | | |
| **Prior homicide convictions** | | | | | | | | |
| Yes | 240 | 128 | 110 | 18 | 9.1% | 8.4% | 10.2% | 9.0% |
| No | 2,403 | 1,399 | 966 | 183 | 90.9 | 91.6 | 89.8 | 91.0 |
| Not reported | 73 | 39 | 33 | 5 | | | | |
| **Legal status at time of capital offense** | | | | | | | | |
| Charges pending | 167 | 101 | 61 | 10 | 6.9% | 7.3% | 6.3% | 5.5% |
| Probation | 230 | 130 | 98 | 16 | 9.5 | 9.2 | 10.1 | 8.8 |
| Parole | 491 | 255 | 232 | 51 | 20.3 | 18.1 | 23.7 | 28.0 |
| Prison escapee | 42 | 28 | 13 | 3 | 1.7 | 2.0 | 1.3 | 1.6 |
| Prison inmate | 60 | 33 | 27 | 4 | 2.5 | 2.3 | 2.8 | 2.2 |
| Other status[c] | 33 | 17 | 15 | 1 | 1.4 | 1.2 | 1.5 | 0.6 |
| None | 1,395 | 841 | 529 | 97 | 57.7 | 59.9 | 54.3 | 53.3 |
| Not reported | 298 | 161 | 134 | 24 | ... | ... | ... | ... |

[a]Percentages are based on those offenders for whom data were reported. [b]Includes whites, blacks, Hispanics, and persons of other races. [c]Includes 9 persons on work release, 4 persons on mandatory conditional release, 4 persons on bail, 1 person on temporary leave, 2 persons on halfway house, 1 absconder from bail, 1 person on accelerated rehabilitation, 1 person AWOL from the US Army, 1 person on work furlough, 2 persons in jail, 1 person under house arrest, 1 person in a pre-release treatment centre, 1 person in a community diversion program, 1 person in a supervised road gang, 2 persons in a community diversion program, and 1 person on conditional release. ... Not applicable.

Source: Bureau of Justice Statistics, *Capital Punishment 1993*, Table 8. p.10.

**Table 4: Number and Percent of Death Sentences Carried Out in 17 Selected Jurisdictions, by Rank Order of Death Sentences, 1977-1993**

| Jurisdiction | Death Sentences | Executions | Percent Executed |
|---|---|---|---|
| Florida | 542 | 32 | 5.9 |
| California | 493 | 2 | 0.4 |
| Texas | 468 | 71 | 15.2 |
| Alabama | 217 | 10 | 4.6 |
| Illinois | 209 | 1 | 0.5 |
| North Carolina | 206 | 5 | 2.4 |
| Pennsylvania | 201 | 0 | 0.0 |
| Oklahoma | 174 | 3 | 1.7 |
| Ohio | 173 | 0 | 0.0 |
| Arizona | 169 | 3 | 1.8 |
| Georgia | 151 | 17 | 11.2 |
| Tennessee | 139 | 0 | 0.0 |
| Missouri | 107 | 11 | 10.3 |
| Nevada | 94 | 5 | 5.3 |
| Virginia | 88 | 22 | 25.0 |
| Mississippi | 87 | 4 | 4.5 |
| Louisiana | 61 | 21 | 34.4 |

Note: Only states with more than 100 death sentences or more than 3 executions are included.

Source: Bureau of Justice Statistics, *Capital Punishment 1993* Appendix Table 4, p.15, and prior issues for years 1982-1992; the National Prisoner Statistics, *Capital Punishment 1981,* Table 11. p. 24. and prior issues for years 1977-1980.

## Table 5: Prisoners on Death Row, by Type of Removal, Annually, 1973–1993

| Year of sentence | Number sentenced to death | Execution | Other death | Appeal or higher courts overturned | | | Sentence commuted | Other or unknown reason | Under sentence of death 12/31/93 |
|---|---|---|---|---|---|---|---|---|---|
| | | | | Death penalty statute | Conviction | Sentence | | | |
| 1973 | 42 | 2 | 0 | 14 | 9 | 8 | 9 | 0 | 0 |
| 1974 | 150 | 9 | 4 | 65 | 16 | 29 | 22 | 1 | 4 |
| 1975 | 299 | 5 | 4 | 171 | 24 | 65 | 20 | 3 | 7 |
| 1976 | 234 | 11 | 5 | 137 | 16 | 42 | 15 | 0 | 8 |
| 1977 | 138 | 16 | 2 | 40 | 26 | 32 | 7 | 0 | 15 |
| 1978 | 187 | 27 | 3 | 21 | 35 | 60 | 8 | 1 | 33 |
| 1979 | 157 | 14 | 8 | 2 | 29 | 57 | 6 | 0 | 40 |
| 1980 | 183 | 18 | 11 | 3 | 32 | 46 | 6 | 1 | 67 |
| 1981 | 235 | 24 | 9 | 0 | 41 | 65 | 4 | 1 | 91 |
| 1982 | 272 | 29 | 11 | 0 | 26 | 61 | 6 | 0 | 139 |
| 1983 | 254 | 23 | 10 | 1 | 20 | 48 | 4 | 2 | 146 |
| 1984 | 285 | 20 | 10 | 2 | 33 | 55 | 4 | 4 | 157 |
| 1985 | 280 | 5 | 3 | 1 | 29 | 64 | 3 | 0 | 175 |
| 1986 | 308 | 8 | 10 | 0 | 38 | 49 | 4 | 5 | 194 |
| 1987 | 291 | 2 | 4 | 2 | 32 | 47 | 1 | 6 | 197 |
| 1988 | 298 | 5 | 6 | 0 | 25 | 37 | 1 | 0 | 224 |
| 1989 | 266 | 3 | 4 | 0 | 19 | 46 | 2 | 0 | 192 |
| 1990 | 263 | 2 | 2 | 0 | 24 | 16 | 0 | 0 | 219 |
| 1991 | 279 | 1 | 3 | 0 | 12 | 9 | 0 | 0 | 254 |
| 1992 | 281 | 2 | 0 | 0 | 2 | 2 | 0 | 0 | 275 |
| 1993 | 282 | 0 | 3 | 0 | 0 | 0 | 0 | 0 | 279 |
| Total 1973–1993 | 4,984 | 226 | 112 | 459 | 488 | 836 | 122 | 23 | 2,716 |

Note: Table based on most recent death sentence received. Source: Bureau of Justice Statistics, *Capital Punishment 1993*, Appendix Table 1, p. 12.

## Table 6: Abolition, Partial; Abolition and Restoration of the Death Penalty, by Jurisdiction, 1846-1995

| Jurisdiction | Year of Partial Abolition | Year of Complete Abolition | Year of Restoration | Year of Reabolition |
|---|---|---|---|---|
| Alaska | | 1957 | | |
| Arizona | 1916[a] | | 1918 | |
| Colorado | | 1897 | 1901 | |
| Delaware | | 1958 | 1961 | |
| D.C. | | 1973 | | |
| Hawaii | | 1957 | | |
| Iowa | | 1872 | 1878 | 1965 |
| Kansas | | 1907,1973 | 1935,1994 | |
| Maine | | 1876 | 1883 | 1887 |
| Massachusetts | | 1984 | | |
| Michigan | 1847[a] | 1963 | | |
| Minnesota | | 1911 | | |
| Missouri | | 1917 | 1919 | |
| New Mexico | 1969[b, c] | | | |
| New York | 1969[b, d] | | 1995 | |
| North Dakota | | 1915 | | |
| Oregon | | 1914,1964 | 1920,1984 | |
| Rhode Island | 1852[d] | | | |
| South Dakota | | 1915, 1977 | 1939,1979 | |
| Tennessee | 1915[e] | | 1919 | |
| Vermont | 1965[b, c] | | | |
| Washington | | 1913 | 1919 | |
| West Virginia | | 1965 | | |
| Wisconsin | | 1853 | | |

[a]death retained for treason
[b]death retained for killing a law officer on duty
[c]death retained for a second offense of murder
[d]death retained for murder of a guard by a life term prisoner
[e]death retained for rape

Sources: Bureau of Justice Statistics, *Capital Punishment 1982*, pp. 10-11; *Capital Punishment 1984*, p.4; NCADP, *Lifelines*, Jan.-Mar. 1994, p.3; *N. Y. Times*, 8 March 1995, p.1.

# ENDNOTES

*I wish to thank Constance Putnam, Michael L. Radelet, and Henry Schwarzschild for their assistance in putting this chapter into final form. They are to be excused for whatever errors or omissions remain.

1. This paragraph is based on NAACP Legal Defense and Educational Fund, Inc., 'Death Row, U.S.A.,' Winter 1994, and *N. Y. Times*, 30 Dec 1995, 28.

2. For a full discussion of this legal campaign, see Michael Meltsner, *Cruel and Unusual: The Supreme Court and Capital Punishment*, New York, Random House, 1973.

3. Research later showed that four of these death row prisoners were innocent and that seven others were convicted of a second murder (all but one of which occurred in prison). James W. Marquart and Jonathan R. Sorenson, 'A National Study of the Furman-Commuted Inmates: Assessing the Threat to Society From Capital Offenders,' 23 *Loyola of L. A. L. Rev.* 5 (1989).

4. For an account of the slip-shod procedures followed in Florida as its legislature rushed to become the first jurisdiction to re-enact death penalty statutes, see Charles W. Ehrhardt and L. Harold Levinson, 'Florida's Legislative Response to Furman: An Exercise in Futility?' 64 *J. of Crim. L. and Criminology* 10 (1973).

5. See Marvin E. Wolfgang and Marc Reidel, 'Race, Judicial Decision, and the Death Penalty,' 407 *The Annals of The American Academy of Political and Social Science* 119 (1973), and 'Rape, Racial Discrimination, and the Death Penalty,' in H. A. Bedau and Chester M. Pierce, eds., *Capital Punishment in the United States*, New York, 1976, 99-121.

6. 'Death Row, U.S.A.,' 4-8; *N. Y. Times*, 30 Dec 1995, 28.

7. U. S. Bureau of Justice Statistics, 'Capital Punishment 1993,' 4.

8. See Harold Hillman, 'The possible pain experienced during executions by different methods,' 22 *Perception* 745 (1993).

9. Herb Haines, 'Flawed Executions, the Anti-Death Penalty Movement, and the Politics of Capital Punishment,' 39 *Social Problems* 125 (1992), at 128.

10. 'Death Row, U.S.A.,' 1, 13.

11. Victor Streib, 'The Juvenile Death Penalty Today' (1995); in general, see Streib, *Death Penalty for Juveniles*, Bloomington, Ind., Indiana University Press, 1987.

12. 'Capital Punishment 1993,' 8, table 8.

13. For evidence suggesting that there are little or no differences between these two populations of convicted murderers, see Ursula Bentele, 'The Death Penalty in Georgia: Still Arbitrary,' 62 *Washington U. L. Q.* 573 (1985) and Vivian Berger, 'Rolling the Dice to Decide Who Dies,' *N. Y. State Bar J.*, October 1988, 32-37.

14. 'Capital Punishment 1993,' 11, table 2.

15. See, for example, David von Drehle, *Among the Lowest of the Dead: The Culture of Death Row*, New York, Random House, 1995; and Sam Howe Verhovek, 'A Double-Murder is Life on Death Row,' *N. Y. Times*, 13 Jan. 1995, B1.

16. See Robert Johnson, *Condemned to Die: Life Under Sentence of Death*, New York, Elsevier, 1981, and my review in 28 *Crime and Delinquency* 382 (1982). See also Robert Johnson and John L. Carroll, 'Litigating Death Row Conditions: The Case for Reform,' in Ira P. Robbins, ed., *Prisoners and the Law*, New York, Clark Boardman, 1987, 8-3 to 8-33. At present (mid-1995) the U. S. Supreme Court is considering the argument of Clarence Lackey that his seventeen years on Texas's death row is a 'cruel and unusual punishment.' Amnesty International U.S.A., 'Death Penalty Newsletter,' June-September 1995, 5.

17. Dane Archer and Rosemary Gartner, *Violence and Crime in Cross-National Perspective*, New Haven, Conn., Yale University Press, 1984.

18. F.B.I., *Crime in the United States 1993*, 58.

19. David C. Baldus, George Woodworth, and Charles A. Pulaski, Jr., *Equal Justice and the Death Penalty: A Legal and Empirical Analysis*, Boston, Northeastern University Press, 1989, 235; also Glenn L. Pierce and Michael L. Radelet, 'The Role and Consequences of the Death Penalty in American Politics,' 18 *N. Y. U. Rev. of L. & Social Change* (1990-91) 711-28.

20. 'Capital Punishment 1993,' 10.

21. *Crime in the United States 1993*, 60-67.

22. Michael L. Radelet and Barbara A. Zsembik, 'Executive Clemency in Post Furman Capital Cases,' 27 *U. Richmond L. Rev.* (1993) 289; H. A.

Bedau, 'The Decline of Executive Clemency in Capital Cases,' 18 *N. Y. U. Rev. of L. & Social Change* (1990-91) 255.

23. Radelet and Zsembik report 41 'humanitarian' commutations of death row prisoners between 1973 and 1992; 'Death Row, U.S.A.' reports 41 suicides on death row between 1973 and 1994.

24. See 'Symposium: The Capital Jury Project,' 70 *Indiana L. J.* (Fall 1995) 1033-1270.

25. Stephen B. Bright, 'Counsel for the Poor: The Death Sentence Not for the Worst Crime but for the Worst Lawyer,' 103 *Yale L. J.* 1835 (1994). See also Ronald Smothers, 'Court-Appointed Defense Offers the Poor a Lawyer, But the Cost May be High,' *N. Y. Times,* 14 Feb. 1994, A12; Ronald Smothers, 'A Shortage of Lawyers to Help the Condemned,' *N. Y. Times,* 4 June 1993, A21; Marcia Coyle, Fred Strasser, and Marianne Lavell, 'Fatal Defense,' *National L. J.,* 11 June 1990, pp. 30-44; Theodore Eisenberg and Martin T. Wells, 'Deadly Confusion: Juror Instructions in Capital Cases,' 79 *Cornell L. Rev.* 1 (1993); Susie Cho, 'Capital Confusion: The Effect of Jury Instructions on the Decision to Impose Death,' 85 *J. Crim. L. & Criminology* 532 (1994);

26. See in general Phoebe C. Ellsworth and Samuel R. Gross, 'Hardening of the Attitudes: Americans' Views on the Death Penalty,' 50 *J. of Social Issues* (1994) 19.

27. William J. Bowers, Margaret Vandiver, and Patricia H. Dugan, 'A New Look at Public Opinion on Capital Punishment: What Citizens and Legislators Prefer,' 22 *Amer. J. Crim. L.* (1994) 77; also Richard C. Dieter, *Sentencing for Life: Americans Embrace Alternatives to the Death Penalty,* Washington, D.C., Death Penalty Information Center, 1993.

28. See Richard C. Dieter, *Millions Misspent: What Politicians Don't Say About the High Costs of the Death Penalty,* Washington D.C., Death Penalty Information Center, 1994, rev. ed.

29. See, e.g., Norman Redlich et al., 'Politics and the Death Penalty: Can Rational Discourse and Due Process Survive the Perceived Political Pressure?' 21 *Fordam Urban L. J.* (1994) 239; Kenneth Bresler, 'Seeking Justice, Seeking Election, and Seeking the Death Penalty: The Ethics of Prosecutorial Candidates's Campaigning on Capital Convictions,' 7 *Georgetown J. of Legal Ethics* 941 (1994); Marshall Frady, 'Death in Arkansas,' *New Yorker,* 22 Feb. 1993, 105- 118, 120-26, 128-30; and Pierce and Radelet, op. cit. note 19.

30. See National Coalition to Abolish the Death Penalty, 1994 Survey of State Legislation, NCADP, Washington D.C., and earlier issues.

31. E.g., H. A. Bedau, *The Courts, the Constitution, and Capital Punishment,* Lexington, Mass., 1976, 90 ('we will not see another execution in this nation in this century').

32. 'Federal Courts Set to Resume Executions,' *N. Y. Times,* 14 March 1995, A26; and see Sandra R. Acosta, 'Imposing the Death Penalty Upon Drug Kingpins,' 27 *Harvard J. of Legislation,* 596 (1990).

33. The following account is based on Mark Ballard, 'Cert Denials Stun Capital Bar: "Penry Now Means Nothing,"' *Texas Lawyer,* 7 Nov. 1994, p. 1. See also Debora W. Denno, 'Testing Penry and Its Progeny,' 22 *Amer. J. Crim. L.* 1 (1994).

34. Robert Weisberg, 'Deregulating Death,' 8 *Supreme Court Review* 305 (1983).

35. E.g., Ronald J. Tabak, 'The Death of Fairness: The Arbitrary and Capricious Imposition of the Death Penalty in the 1980s,' 13 *N. Y. U. Rev. of L. & Social Change* 797 (1986), and the sources cited above in Endnote 25.

36. *New York Times,* 14 Sept. 1994, A12.

37. For discussion of the Racial Justice Act (also called the Fairness in Sentencing Act of 1991), see House Hearings Before the Subcommittee on Civil and Constitutional Rights, Committee of the Judiciary, 'Death Sentencing Issues,' 102nd Congress, 1st Session, July 1991; David C. Baldus, George Woodworth, and Charles A. Pulaski, Jr., 'Reflections on the "Inevitability" of Racial Discrimination in Capital Sentencing and the "Impossibility" of Its Prevention, Detection, and Correction,' 51 *Wash. and Lee L. Rev.* (Spring 1994) 359-430; and Don Edwards and John Conyers, Jr., 'The Racial Justice Act-A Simple Matter of Justice,' 20 U. *Dayton L. Rev.* (1995) 699-713.

38. For a general survey of the evidence, see Michael L. Radelet and Margaret Vandiver, 'Race and Capital Punishment: An Overview of the Issues,' *Crime and Social Justice,* No. 25 (1986), 94-113; see also Randall L. Kennedy, 'McCleskey v. Kemp: Race, Capital Punishment, and the Supreme Court,' 101 *Harvard L. Rev.* 1388 (1988), and the sources cited in note 35; and U. S. General Accounting Office, 'Death Penalty Sentencing: Research Indicates Pattern of Racial Disparities' (February 1990).

39. The death penalty for terrorists was criticized by Thomas Perry Thornton, 'Terrorism and the Death Penalty,' reprinted in H. A. Bedau,

ed., *The Death Penalty in America,* 3rd ed., New York, Oxford University Press, 1982, pp. 181-85. For a different view, see Arlen Spector, 'The Time Has Come for a Terrorist Death Penalty Law,' 95 *Dickinson L. Rev.* 739 (1991).

40. *New York Times,* 8 June 1995, A1. See also *The New York Times* editorial opposing this legislation, 9 June 1995, A28.

41. On federal habeas corpus generally, see Randall Coyne and Lyn Entzeroth, *Capital Punishment and the Judicial Process,* Durham, N.C., Carolina Academic Press, 1994, 495-647.

42. Amnesty International-USA, 'Death Penalty Newsletter,' July-Sept. 1995,.4.

43. Michael L. Radelet, Hugo Adam Bedau, and Constance E. Putnam, *In Spite of Innocence: Erroneous Convictions in Capital Cases,* Boston, Northeastern University Press, 1992; H. A. Bedau and Michael L. Radelet, 'Miscarriages of Justice in Potentially Capital Cases,' 40 *Stanford L. Rev.* 21 (1987); Senate Hearing Before the Committee on the Judiciary, 'Innocence and the Death Penalty,' 103rd Congress, 1st session, April 1994; and Staff Report by the Subcommittee on Civil and Constitutional Rights, Committee on the Judiciary, 'Innocence and the Death Penalty: Assessing the Danger of Mistaken Executions' (October 1993).

44. *N. Y. Times,* 22 Sept. 1989, B20.

45. See NCADP, '1994 Survey of State Legislation'.

46. *N. Y. Times,* 8 March 1995, A1.

47. *National Coalition to Abolish the Death Penalty Newsletter,* 'Lifelines,' April-June 1995, 10.

48. See *National Interreligious Task Force on Criminal Justice, Capital Punishment: What the Religious Community Says,* New York, 1978, and *The Death Penalty: The Religious Community Calls for Abolition,* New York, 1988.

49. On Mormonism, see Martin R. Gardner, 'Mormonism and Capital Punishment: A Doctrinal Perspective, Past and Present,' 12 *Dialogue: A Journal of Mormon Thought,* Spring 1979, 9-26. For an unusually thorough defence of the death penalty from a Christian fundamentalist viewpoint, see H. Wayne House, 'In Favor of the Death Penalty,' in H. Wayne House and John Howard Yoder, *The Death Penalty Debate,* Dallas, Texas, Word Publishing, 1991, 3104.

50. See Michael L. Radelet and Margaret Vandiver, *Capital Punishment in America: An Annotated Bibliography,* New York, Garland, 1988.

51. The following paragraphs are based on H. A. Bedau, 'American Populism and the Death Penalty: Witnesses at an Execution,' 33 *Howard J.* 289 (1994), and the sources cited there.

52. For a general discussion of the issue as seen by those who oppose the death penalty, see the debate between Robert R. Bryan and Henry Schwarzschild, 'Lifelines,' July-Sept. 1991, pp. 2, 7; also Wendy Lesser, *Pictures at an Execution: An Inquiry into the Subject of Murder,* Cambridge, Mass., Harvard University Press, 1993, 24-46.

53. See Sam Reese Sheppard, 'In the Belly of the Death Penalty Beast,' in *The Machinery of Death: A Shocking Indictment of Capital Punishment in the United States,* New York, Amnesty International U. S. A., 1995, 59-63; and Bill Pelke, 'The Seeds of Compassion,' in *The Machinery of Death,* 64-68.

54. Louis Joughin and Edmund M. Morgan, *The Legacy of Sacco and Vanzetti,* New York, Harcourt, 1948.

55. Walter and Miriam Schneir, *Invitation to an Inquest,* New York, Doubleday, 1965, 193.

56. Milton Machlin and William Read Woodfield, *Ninth Life,* New York, Putnam's, 1961, 248-49.

57. See *United States of America: The Death Penalty,* London, Amnesty International, 1987; Ian Gray and Moira Stanley, eds., *A Punishment in Search of a Crime: Americans Speak Out Against the Death Penalty,* New York, Avon Books , 1989; *The Machinery of Death.* In 1980, Amnesty urged a special investigation of the death penalty by the U. S. government; see 'Proposal for a Presidential Commission on the Death Penalty in the United States of America,' reprinted in *The Death Penalty in America,* 3rd ed. (1982), 375-82. This was followed an 'Open Letter to the President on the Death Penalty,' London, Amnesty International, 1994.

58. The following paragraphs are based on William A. Schabas, *The Abolition of the Death Penalty in International Law,* Cambridge, Grotius Publications, 1993.

59. See Ramsey Clark, *Crime in America: Observations on Its Nature, Causes, Prevention and Control,* New York, Simon and Shuster, 1970, 330-37.

60. Schabas, 92.

61. The following paragraph relies on *Capital Punishment and the Judicial Process*, 693-701.

62. See, in addition to works already cited, H. A. Bedau, *The Death Penalty in America*, New York, Anchor Books , 1964; Thorsten Sellin, *The Penalty of Death*, Beverly Hills, Calif., Sage, 1980; William J. Bowers, *Legal Homicide: Death as a Punishment in America*, 1864-1982, Boston, Northeastern University Press, 1984; Franklin E. Zimring and Gordon Hawkins, *Capital Punishment and the American Agenda*, New York, Cambridge University Press, 1986; Raymond Paternoster, *Capital Punishment in America*, New York, Lexington Books, 1991; Welsh S. White, *The Death Penalty in the Nineties: An Examination of the Modern System of Capital Punishment*, Ann Arbor, Mich., University of Michigan Press, 1991.

## Cases cited

*Barefoot v. Estelle*, 463 U.S. 880 (1983)

*Blystone v. Pennsylvania*, 494 U.S. 299 (1990)

*Booth v. Maryland*, 482 U.S. 496 (1987)

*Boyde v. California*, 494 U.S. 370 (1990)

*Callins v. Collins*, 114 S.Ct. 1127 (1994)

*Clemons v. Mississippi*, 494 U.S. 738 (1990)

*Coker v. Georgia*, 433 U.S. 584 (1977)

*Coleman v. Thompson*, 111 S.Ct. 2546 (1991)

*Eberhart v. Georgia*, 433 U.S. 917 (1977)

*Enmund v. Eilorida*, 458 U.S. 782 (1982)

*Ford v. Wainwright*, 477 U.S. 399 (1986)

*Furman v. Georgia*, 408 U.S. 238 (1972)

*Godfrey v. Georgia*, 446 U.S. 420 (1980)

*Graham v. Collins*, 113 S.Ct. 892 (1993)

*Gregg v. Georgia*, 428 U.S. 153 (1976)

*Herrera v. Collins*, 113 S.Ct. 853 (1993)

*Johnson v. Texas*, 113 S.Ct. 2658 (1993)

*Jurek v. Texas*, 428 U.S. 262 (1976)

*Lockett v. Ohio,* 438 U.S. 586 (1978)

*McCleskey v. Kemp,* 481 U.S. 279 (1987)

*McCleskey v.Zant,* 111 S.Ct. 1454 (1991)

# CHAPTER 4

# Russia and Other CIS States

## Ger Pieter van den Berg*

This introductory section provides a historical overview of capital punishment in Russia and the rest of the former USSR.[1] In old Russian written law the death penalty did not officially exist until 1397. Thereafter, the number of capital crimes gradually increased, except that the penalty was not executed during the reign of Czarina Elizaveta Petrovna in the middle of the eigthteenth century. During the nineteenth century - between 1826 and 1906 - only 170 persons were executed, but after the 'revolution' of 1905 the annual volume increased to more than 500 in 1906 and more than 1,000 between 1907 and 1909, mostly applied by special military courts.[2]

After 1917, and during the period of socialism, the official doctrine on the death penalty was always ambiguous. This was also the tenor of writings of Karl Marx. When already in power, Lenin had stated: 'No revolutionary government can do without the death penalty and the essence of the question is against whom the weapon of the death penalty is directed'; in other circumstances, however, he deemed it a question of expediency and indicated that the death penalty will 'no longer be maintained as will be required'.[3] To Lenin, this apparently meant that the need for the death penalty would lapse under genuine communism. In fact, under Lenin and, in particular, when Stalin was the Secretary General of the Communist Party and political leader of the country, the practical question was not really whether the death penalty existed under the Criminal Code; people were for the most part executed extra-judicially, and these extra-judicial methods were abolished only in 1953 (officially in 1959).

The official ambiguity towards the institution of the death penalty led to several attempts to abolish it (1917, 1920 and 1947) on grounds of principle; and its reintroduction soon thereafter (1918, 1920 and 1950) for pragmatic reasons. In 1947 the death penalty was abolished during the negotiations on the Universal Declaration of Human Rights in order to demonstrate to the world, and especially to the USA, that a socialist state could do without such a sanction. However, in 1950 the death penalty was restored in the Soviet Union, because of the necessity to justify the execution[4] of several political opponents to whom the death penalty was applied retroactively. Until 1954 the death penalty usually was available under the Criminal Code for political crimes and up to 1947 for serious crimes against state ('socialist') property or the economic system. Thus, its main purpose was to protect state interests. Under Stalin, some years witnessed the execution of more than 300,000 people, either on the sentence of a court of law or in the majority of cases, through extra-judicial channels.[5]

When Stalin died and extra-judicial executions came to an end, the death penalty was only imposed for certain crimes against the state, such as treason, espionage and banditry. In 1954 - for the first time since 1917 - serious crimes against the person became capital crimes as a reaction to the surge in violent crime accompanying the early release of many inmates from the Gulag labour camps.[6] When the criminal law was recodified in the USSR Principles of Criminal Legislation of 1958 and the Criminal Codes of the union republics, the death penalty was called 'an extraordinary measure of punishment, until its complete abolition' (article 23 RSFSR Criminal Code of 1960). This thoroughly hypocritical statement was borrowed from the 1926 Criminal Code and has since been repeated. It did not hamper the tendency towards expanding the number of capital crimes between 1960 and 1973, especially for a number of crimes against the socialist economy in line with the tradition of the 1920s to assign priority to the protection of state interests.[7] In line with the tradition and precedents under Lenin and Stalin the death penalty was likewise applied retroactively in the case of Rokotov and Faibyshenko in 1961.[8]

Under Khrushchev two thousand people were sentenced to death annually, but reliable figures have not yet been published. On average, in the USSR 1,130 people were sentenced to death between 1962 and 1972 and 850 between 1973 and 1984.[9] In 1965 the question of the death penalty was discussed in high political circles, but without results. Only in 1980 did the number of capital crimes register a drop for the first time since 1954 when criminal provisions on rape were changed.[10]

After 1959, the alternative to the death penalty, following commutation, was deprivation of freedom for a maximum of 15 years (before 1937 this was 10 years, between 1937 and 1959 it was 25 years); this was perceived to be much too low and not an acceptable alternative to the death penalty as such.

Under the existing Criminal Code, the statute of limitations (the maximum is 10 years following the commission of a crime) does not apply to capital crimes, but, if the court does not apply the statute of limitations, the death penalty may not be imposed (article 48 Criminal Code), except where war crimes committed during World War II are concerned. Under the terms of a still valid edict of the USSR Presidium of the Supreme Soviet of 4 March 1965 (converted into a law of 2 October 1965) 'nazi-criminals, guilty of the worst misdeeds against peace and humanity and military crimes, are subject to be tried and punished independently of the time period, elapsed since the commission of the crimes.' This law is also valid for Soviet, as well as Russian, citizens.[11] A similar law to punish those responsible for the terror under Stalin has not been enacted, although several interrogators are still alive.

# PERESTROIKA, THE 1993 CONSTITUTION AND THE NEW CRIMINAL CODE

After Gorbachev came to power in 1985, the alternative to the death penalty following its commutation by way of a pardon was raised to 20 years, and this displayed a genuine desire to decrease the actual number of executions, although at the time many persons were still awaiting execution.[12] The USSR Fundamentals of Criminal Legislation of 1991 restricted the death penalty to cases of treason, first degree murder, rape and kidnapping of children with grave consequences (article 40), and this provision came into force upon publication of the Fundamentals. The death penalty could not be imposed on persons who were under 18 years of age when they had committed the crime or on women (previously this had only applied to pregnant women).[13] On 5 December 1991, the Russian Federation abolished the death penalty for most economic crimes, but the provisions in the Code on other capital crimes were not amended. Moreover, the alternative penalty after commutation of the sentence by an act of pardon of the President was raised to 25 years deprivation of freedom and, on 17 December 1992, to lifelong imprisonment.[14]

The Declarations on Human Rights issued in the autumn of 1991 in the USSR as well as in Russia, and especially the amended Russian Constitution of April 1992, restricted capital crimes to 'particularly grave crimes against the person' (article 38). After the amendments of 27 April 1993, article 23 of the Criminal Code reads: 'As an extra-ordinary measure of punishment the death penalty - execution - is permitted for particularly grave crimes in the instances provided in this Code.' The remaining portions of the Code were not brought into line with the amended Constitution, which has caused some confusion, which lasted also after the adoption of a new Constitution in December 1993. Furthermore, it was provided that the penalty may not be imposed on men over 65 years of age.[15]

Between November 1990 and April 1993 several draft versions of a new Constitution were published. Under the draft Constitution by the jurists Sobchak and Alekseev, published in March 1992, the death penalty would have been abolished (article 4), but most other versions followed the old formulation that the state pursues its abolition, and its application is meanwhile restricted to particularly grave crimes.[16] On 30 April 1993 President El'tsin (Yeltsin) published a draft which limited the application of the death penalty to intentional homicide and the killing of people in the course of committing a grave crime (article 26). All drafts provided that the death penalty could be applied only on the basis of a sentence, pronounced 'with the participation of sworn assessors' (interpreted as meaning trial by a jury). The final text of the Constitution, adopted by the referendum of 12 December 1993, provides:

*1. Everyone has the right to life.*

*2. Until its abolition, the death penalty can be established by a federal law as an extraordinary penalty for particularly grave crimes against life, the accused possessing the right to have his case considered by a court with the participation of sworn assessors.* [17]

It is not really certain whether the 1993 Constitution is directly applied. In his comments on the constitutional provision Petrukhin does not say that the death penalty may be imposed only in these cases, but that the Constitution provides a legal ground for abolishing the death penalty. [18] However articles 15 and 18 of the Constitution rule that the Constitution operates directly and the provisions on human rights by themselves. A problem in this connection is that the Constitutional Court has ruled that the ordinary courts are bound to apply any federal law, until it has been declared unconstitutional by this court (in the case of *Avetian*, decided on 3 May 1995).

Reports are published on the prosecution of treason, for which under the Criminal Code the death penalty still is possible. [19] Iashchenko who surrendered to Chechen forces in January 1995 could be sentenced to death if he were found guilty of voluntary surrender. When Iashchenko was released by the Chechens he was locked up in a military jail for several weeks pending trial, which has apparently never been held. [20] A group of experts from the Council of Europe was informed in 1994 that a court had reversed a death sentence for the offence of counterfeiting as unconstitutional, because this was not an offence against life. [21]

Reports that death sentences, pronounced prior to the new constitutional provisions of 1992 and 1993 but not carried out at the time that these provisions came into force, have been reconsidered by the courts on the basis of protests by way of judicial supervision, are lacking, although such a policy would square with the ordinary interpretation of the retroactive operation of laws mitigating punishment in Russia (article 6 Criminal Code). Such laws also have to be applied to final sentences, assuming the individual involved had not completed his sentence. [22]

A 1992 draft Criminal Code (articles 41, 55) and the new Constitution still contain the clause 'until its abolition', but this hypocrisy is no longer encountered in the 1994 draft Criminal Code. The draft discussed in the State Duma (the lower house of parliament, hereinafter referred to as 1995 draft [23]) also omits such language (article 58). If the clause 'until its abolition' were to have any meaning other than that of simple logic or magic formula, it should at least connote that a general policy must be formulated to abolish this penalty. However, no public policy is prompting discussion in this field.

The 1992 draft Criminal Code designated several war crimes (article 96); assault on a representative of a foreign state in order to provoke war (article 100); first degree murder (article 102); assault on the President (article 252); and terrorist actions (article 253) as capital crimes. The 1994 draft Criminal Code only mentions 'particularly grave crimes against life'. The 1995 draft defines the scope of capital crimes as extending to 'particularly grave crimes, infringing on life' (article 58), which is somewhat broader than the Constitution allows. This version lists as capital crimes: intentional homicide marked by various aggravating circumstances itemized in the Code (first degree murder) or when committed by 'a criminal community' (article 103); terrorism committed by a criminal community (article 196), and genocide (article 335).[24]

First degree murder is in general quite clearly defined, because the aggravating circumstances are enumerated in the Criminal Code and the successive draft editions thereof. Less clear is homicide 'out of hooliganistic motives'; 'out of social, ethnic, racial or religious hatred or enmity'; or homicide committed 'with special cruelty' or 'out of sadist motives'.[25] Homicide committed without any apparent reason may be qualified as committed out of hooliganistic motives, and murdering a rich man may be classified as homicide out of social hatred. In addition if homicide is committed 'by a group of persons on the basis of a prior agreement or by an organized group' or 'an organized community' the death penalty is possible. Terrorism committed by a criminal society and genocide are defined in such a way that they need not be directed against specific persons or result in death; whereas under the 1994 draft capital punishment for terrorism was possible only if the act was coupled with intentional homicide.

A criminal community is defined as a group of 'persons united in a stable and cohesive organization founded for committing grave or particularly grave crimes'. In that case the organizer or leader of the community is also liable for the crimes where they are encompassed by his intent. Other participants of the community are only liable for the crimes in the preparation or commission of which they have engaged (article 36). The 1995 draft further allows resort to the death penalty for intentional actions by illegal armed groups which result in the killing of a single person, but when the State Duma adopted a law to that purpose the Council of the Federation (the upper house of parliament) rejected the idea: only if such actions resulted in more human deaths could the death penalty be invoked. This prompted the Duma to formulate a new provision under which such actions would qualify as capital crimes if they were coupled with mass violence, human deaths or the infliction of other grave harm', but the law has not yet been promulgated.[26] In January 1995 the State Duma discussed amendments to the Criminal Code under which a mercenary could incur punishment by deprivation of freedom or the death sentence, and this is included in the 1995 draft Criminal Code.[27]

Compared with the Russian Constitution, the draft Criminal Code gives greater scope for applying the death penalty. It is no longer necessary for the crime to be directed at taking the life of another person. As far as several forms of terrorism and genocide are concerned, the 1995 draft is not in tune with the Constitution.

**Table 1: Intentional Homicide and Attempts in the Russian Federation**

| | Reported killings | | final sentences for murder/intentional homicide | | | |
|---|---|---|---|---|---|---|
| | total | of which attempts | total | attempts as % | under aggravating circumstances | death sentences |
| 1986 | 9437 | 2112 | 9358 | 32.4 | 2477 | 212 |
| 1987 | 9199 | 1621 | 7619 | 17.9 | 1711 | 111 |
| 1988 | 10572 | 1361 | 6854 | 13.9 | 1386 | 107 |
| 1989 | 13543 | 1537 | 8203 | 10.3 | 1553 | 97 |
| 1990 | 15566 | 1900 | 10290 | 9.3 | 2099 | 206 |
| 1991 | 16122 | 11100 | | 8.8 | 2424 | 144 |
| 1992 | 23006 | 12400 | | | | |
| 1993 | 29213 | 18800 | | | | |

Sources: N. Wijngaard-van Es, *Chuliganstvo in de Sovjetunie*, thesis Leiden 1993, 223; *Naselenie SSSR 1988*, 498; *Prestupnost' i pravonarusheniia v. SSSR 1990*, 36-41; *Prestupnost' i pravonarusheniia v. 1991*, 132; *Statisticheskie dannye*, 7-10; *Argumenty i fakty* 1994 No.15

The question of the preciseness of the definition of the crime is not so important in soviet or in Russian criminal law because, aside from attempts, the preparation of a crime (draft Criminal Codes: grave crime) also incurs the same punishment as the crime itself. In 1985, attempts accounted for more than 20% of all homicides, but in 1990 this figure fell to only 12%. Among all sentences in the Russian Federation, attempts accounted for 32% in 1986 and 9% in 1991 (see *Table 1*). The same phenomenon exists with regard to rape.[28] The data show that the subjective opinions of the police and the courts play a large role in the classification of a crime. It may be assumed that the anti-alcohol campaign waged between 1985 and 1989 affected the then prevalent classification of the crime. Hence, an actual homicide would not seem to be necessary for resort to the death penalty, notwithstanding dicta in the Constitution.

## PARDON AND COMMUTATION

If the death penalty is imposed, the case is reviewed by the courts at the regional level (the court of a republic, province or similar area), with the possibility of further appeal to the federal Supreme Court. This court may also act as the court of first instance. Since the constitutional amendments of April 1992, the accused person has a constitutional right to have his case heard in two instances (see current article 50). The Supreme Court has proposed that the law be amended in such a way that if the case is considered in the first instance by the criminal or military chamber of the federal Supreme Court, the accused has a right of appeal to an internal college within the Supreme Court, but this is not yet done in practice.

So far, the Russian appeal procedure does not give the accused the right to have his case heard in two instances because the appeal court may confine itself to delivering a judgement on the basis of the files of the case without inviting the accused or his defence counsel to attend. Against a final sentence 'protests by way of judicial supervision' are available without any time limit, but they may be filed only by the chairman of the Supreme Court or the procurator general (his deputy), while the convict can only petition them to file a protest. This procedure, however, does not give him a right of appeal.

Precise data on the fate of the sentences in the courts of first instance are not published. During 1993 the Criminal Chamber of the Supreme Court considered on appeal 194 cases in which 207 persons had been sentenced to death and during that year 157 final death sentences were pronounced.[29] According to the data available during 1993 and the first half of 1994 courts of first instance sentenced 350 people to death, but over the same period the sentences with regard to 61 people were changed or quashed and only 239 sentences became final. Final sentences with regard to 10 persons were changed or quashed after a protest, but this number is not included in the usual data published on death sentences, apparently because such protests frequently deal with rather old sentences. All in all, review of cases by the Supreme Court is successful in about 20% of cases.

Under a decree of 1934, most death sentences were carried out immediately after their pronouncement and a right of appeal did not exist,[30] but this is no longer possible since the recodification of criminal law under Khrushchev. By virtue of edicts of 1961, all death sentences and all petitions for pardon were subject to verification by the USSR Supreme Court and the Presidium of the USSR Supreme Soviet (the collective head of state at the time) had the power to grant a pardon after hearing the report of a special commission set up for these purposes; since 1990 the President has had this power. In 1990 a special USSR commission was created to consider all requests for pardon. A similar commission exists in the Russian Federation. Until 1990 the commission consisted of the ministers of internal affairs and justice, the chairman of the Supreme Court and the Procurator General, but in 1990 they were replaced by members of parliament. In 1994 the President staffed it with well known public personages, such as the writer Anatolii Pristavkin (chairman), the poet Bulat Okudzhava, the writers Lev Razgon, Arkadii Vainer, the lawyer Igor Bezrukov, a priest and others, who seem quite immune to outside pressure. The department for pardon within the Administration of the President employs 60 jurists who assist the commission in its work. Pristavkin has stated that the commission has to read 200 case files each week, of which 10 involve death sentences.[31] Apparently only those people are pardoned who confess to their crimes, which does not guarantee, however, that the accused is telling the truth: in a situation where the number of death sentences is much higher than the number of actual executions, people may feel impelled to confess to crimes they did not commit.

Counsellor of Justice Vladimir Indiriakov insists that the pardon must not be used as a way of abolishing the death penalty: the Criminal Code still contains this penalty and the will of the popularly elected lawmaker is required to repeal it. Pristavkin has argued that people are sentenced to death to convey the impression that the war against crime is being waged ruthlessly, but he forgets that the court only applies the measures sanctioned by law to the body of evidence presented by the prosecution.[32] The head of the sector for criminal law within the apparatus of the government, V. Vlasov, has proposed making pardons conditional: if a new crime is committed, the first sentence will be implemented.[33] Indiriakov recommends the following: 'A democratic society must first learn to protect the life of its law abiding citizens and only after the rule of law is established when terrorist acts and gangsterism have become a rare phenomenon in our life can we switch to discussing the abolition of the death penalty.'[34]

Persons sentenced to death are kept in remand prisons, apart from fellow inmates, but otherwise their legal position has not been defined differently from that of other persons held in custody, which means that visits to them are governed by especially strict regulations.[35] Moreover, the conditions under which people are held have been described as brutal and prisoners are not allowed to leave their windowless cells for weeks at a time.[36]

Executions, which are carried out in these remand houses, are by a bullet to the head once the last request for pardon has been turned down. The body is not returned to the family for aesthetic reasons. On occasion, prisoners have to 'wait' 4-5 years before they meet their fate.[37] Doctors are only involved in the procedure after the execution, to certify that the executed person is indeed dead.[38] Individuals whose sentence is commuted to lifelong imprisonment serve time in special prisons.[39]

## STATISTICS ON THE DEATH PENALTY

Between 1934 and 1990 statistics on the application of the death penalty were not published, and only some indirect data were known to the outside world. In 1990 the head of the department for citizenship and granting pardons of the USSR Supreme Soviet's Secretariat, G. G. Cheremnykh, provided for the first time some information on the application of the death penalty.[40] Later on, additional, but never full and clear, details were released. They show that the number of final death sentences decreased after 1986: from 790 in 1985 to

284 in 1990, parallel with the decrease in the number of trials of capital crimes which fell rapidly due to the anti-alcohol campaign of 1986-88 (figures for the USSR). In 1989-90 the number of capital crimes (especially homicides) increased again and so did the number of death sentences, but the total number of death sentences did not return to its previous level. In Russia from 1991-94, between 150 and 160 death sentences were passed. In 1985 the death sentence was imposed in 6% of all capital cases, between 1986 and 1990 in 5%, but thereafter this percentage decreased to 2.5 to 3%.[41]

---

**Table 2: Average Annual Number of Death Sentences in the Russian Federation, 1961-1994**

| | |
|---|---|
| 1961-1970 | 854 |
| 1971-1980 | 327 |
| 1981-1985 | 443 |
| 1986-1990 | 157 |
| 1991-1994 | 154 |

Source: M. Detkov, V. Kondroev, 'Smertnaia kazn i pozhiznennoe lishenie svobody', *Prestuplenie i nakazanie* 1995 No. 4, 52

---

After 1954 most death sentences were handed down for first degree murder, which was not a capital crime before 1954: between 1954 and 1973 every fifth person tried for murder with aggravating circumstances was sentenced to death; between 1973 and 1985 every seventh; and thereafter every tenth or less. In 1991 the rate was less than 6%. The number of people sentenced for economic crimes was high under Khrushchev and probably also during the short anti-corruption campaign of 1982-1984 initiated by Andropov. During the 1980s, 201 persons were sentenced to death for crimes against the state: 59 for treason (including espionage)[42] and 142 for banditry and disruption of the regime in penal camps. In 1985 four persons were sentenced to death for theft of especially large amounts and in 1989 one, between 1985 and 1987 four persons for receiving bribes, but in 1988 and 1989 none (figures for the USSR). The death penalty was frequently imposed on war criminals, but figures are not known. In 1992 Russian Federation courts pronounced 94 death sentences for murder and one for assault on a police officer, apparently resulting in his death.[43] In 1993 and the first half of 1994, 8,399 capital charges were heard by the courts and the death penalty was imposed by courts of first instance in 350 cases (4.2% of all capital crimes).

# Table 3: Death Sentences and Capital Crimes in the USSR and the RSFSR/RF, 1985-1994

| year* | sentences for capital crimes | | death sentences | | p a r d o n s | | executions | |
|---|---|---|---|---|---|---|---|---|
| | USSR | Russia | USSR | Russia | USSR | Russia | USSR | Russia |
| 1985 | 13,081 | | 790 | | 20 | | 654 | |
| 1986 | 11,744 | | 552 | 225 | 41 | | 666 | |
| 1987 | 7,592 | | 359 | 120 | 47 | | 440 | |
| 1988 | 5,826 | | 284 | 115 | 72 | | 210 | |
| 1989 | 5,387 | 2,814 | 284 | 100 | 23 | 4 | 186 | 93 |
| 1990 | | 4,035 | 459 | 223 | 208 | 2 | 195 | 76 |
| 1991 | | 4,977 | | 147 | 195 | 37 | | 59 |
| 1992 | | | | 159 | | 54 | | 18 |
| 1993 | | 5,250 | | 157 | | | | 3 |
| 1994 | | 4,271 | | 153 | | | | 7 |

*For the years 1985-1991 the data have to be read as follows: of those sentenced for capital crimes in 1985 (13081) 790 people were sentenced to death, but some of these were changed after a protest procedure. In 1985 654 persons were executed. The data for 1994 are provisional.

Sources: Z. Iakovleva, 'O smertnoi kazni v SSSR', *Sotsialisticheskaia zakonnost'* 1991 No.4, 45; V. Gordeev, 'O prestupnosti i sudimosti v SSSR', *Vestnik Verkhovnogo suda SSSR* 1991 No.3, 31; No.7, 38; *Summary of World Broadcasts SU/0973 i*, 18 January 1991; *Izvestiia* 1 October 1990; V. Rudnev, *Izvestiia* 6 April 1991 (1990: 445); Oschlies, *op.cit.*, 27; *Argumenty i fakty* 1991 No.28; L. Kolodkin, *Trud* 11 January 1992; A. Illesh, V. Rudnev, 'Kak i za chto sudiat v Rossii', *Izvestiia* 10 april 1992; *Sovetskaia militsiia* October 1992 (1990 196); *Current Digest of the (Post) Soviet Press* 1991 No.14, 29; 1992 No.15, 24; No.32, 24; V. Rudnev, 'Komu u nas zakon ne pisan', *Izvestiia* 2 October 1992; A. Naumov, V. Rudnev, 'Smertnaia kazn': za chto', *Izvestiia* 9 June 1993; *Argumenty i fakty* 1993 No.19; M. Khazin, *Izvestiia* 7 December 1993 (18 in 1992); *Prison Reform in the Former Totalitarian Countries*, II, 8; *Izvestiia* 27 April 1994; *Prestupnost' i pravonarusheniia 1991,* Moscow 1992, 128; *Mezhdunarodnye normy i pravoprimenitel'naia praktika v oblasti prav i svobod cheloveka*, Moscow 1993, 85; Kushen, 'The Death Penalty', (1993), 565; Iu.Kalinin, A. Mikhlin, 'Kaznit' nel'zia pomilovat'', *Rossiiskaia gazeta* 1 September 1994; interview with Kalinin, 'Slushat' takoe obidno', *Rossiiskaia gazeta* 1 November 1994; *Summary of World Broadcasts SU/2150 B/4-5*, 11 November 1994; *Iuridicheskii vestnik* 1994 No.15-16, 25; V. Rudnev, *Izvestiia* 14 April 1995 (*Current Digest of the (Post) Soviet Press* 1995 No.15, 13); *Rossiiskaia iustitsiia* 1995 No.6, 51; *The Moscow Times* 30 July 1995, 17; A. Mikhlin, 'Smertnaia kazn': pravo na pomilovanie i 'pravo na smert''', *Rossiiskaia iustitsiia* 1995 No.10, 44

While the number of death sentences in Russia is still rather high, it seems likely that this number will decrease only if courts are allowed to sentence people to penalties of more than 15 years or to lifelong imprisonment,[44] as is contemplated in the 1995 draft of the Criminal Code: the alternative to the death sentence will become a custodial punishment for a fixed term, i.e. between 6 months and 20 years or lifelong imprisonment. In cases of terrorism or genocide, the penalty will entail either lifelong imprisonment or the death penalty.

Before 1917, only about one third of the sentences were in fact carried out and the same may have been true in the 1950s and 1960s. When the number of capital sentences started to decline during Brezhnev's reign, this portion may have increased and the annual number of executions probably remained at a level of 600-800 in all those years up to 1985, when 654 individuals were executed. Thereafter the number of actual executions (including persons sentenced in earlier years) decreased annually from more than 650 in 1985-86 to less than 200 in 1989-90 (figures for the USSR). This was partly the result of the decrease in the occurrence of capital crime due to the anti-alcohol campaign during those years, which had the effect of halving the number of death sentences; but also the result of the introduction of a more humane and realistic alternative: in 1986 the head of state was vested with the power to convert a death sentence after pardon into deprivation of freedom for 20 years, instead of the traditional 15 years. In 1992 the alternative was raised in Russia to 25 years and, later, also to lifelong imprisonment. This was followed by a sharp decrease in the number of actual executions: from 59 executions in 1991, to 18 in 1992, and 3 in 1993. In 1993 and the first half of 1994 the President pardoned 266 persons and 6 persons were executed, apparently only serial or professional killers or killers of children and soldiers who had killed during initiation ceremonies. In 1994 137 persons wrote to the presidential commission requesting pardon, and only 13 petitions were rejected.[45] During 1994 the President rejected 14 appeals for pardon. It seems likely therefore, that the number of executions will rise, but even then this number will be remarkably less than under Gorbachev.[46]

A consequence of the low number of executions is that the number of inmates on death row increases: it has been reported that as of 9 March 1992, 332 persons were awaiting execution; on 31 August 1993, 505; in the autumn of 1994 this number was put even higher at 640; and in July 1995 at 500.[47] These figures do not seem to tally with other data, circulating within the RF. Between 1 January 1993 and 1 July 1994, 350 persons had been sentenced to death by courts of first instance, but through appeals and judicial supervision protests 71 sentences were quashed or changed;[48] in the same period 266 persons were pardoned; six persons were actually executed. Thus the number of persons on death row cannot have increased during that time by more than 18 persons. According to Iurii Kalinin, the head of the department for the execution of punishments, the Committee for pardons did not consider a single case over a period of seven months.[49] These data cannot be reconciled with other data published relating to these years. A major problem with all such data is that the authorities fail to give clear current data on the application of the death penalty, even in periods where the numbers are very low. The politicians in charge who usually stress the need for a strong state do not seem to want to convey an impression to the public that they are 'weak' and that their actual policy is quite humane. Only a few cases where the death sentence is possible or invoked are reported in the central press and this has been the norm during all of the past 40 years in the USSR and Russia.[50]

## DISCUSSING THE DEATH PENALTY

Open discussion of the death penalty did not occur during the soviet era.[51] In 1965 the death penalty was discussed in high political circles, but this happened largely behind closed doors. During the *perestroika* period several jurists and representatives of the intelligentsia started a debate on this question. It is usually said that public opinion, the police, and the procuracy (public prosecution service) support the death penalty, while attorneys (advocates) and the intelligentsia are against it.[52] As long as it existed, the USSR parliament did not want to abolish it: appointments to high positions in law-keeping bodies (minister of justice, procurator general) were still dependent on the candidate's positive support for the death penalty and specific questions to elicit views on the subject were posed.[53]

In an opinion poll conducted in 1990 in 28 regions, 28% of the respondents wanted to apply the death penalty more frequently; 34% favoured maintaining the current level; 19% preferred a gradual decrease and only 5% opted for immediate abolition (13% expressed no opinion). A July 1994 poll showed that two-thirds of the population support the death penalty.[54] Although a poll conducted among 1,325 Russians in 1989 and 2,957 in 1994 shows no appreciable changes with respect to abolishing the death penalty, demands to expand its application are weakening at a time when the number of capital crimes in the Criminal Code has decreased considerably, even as the actual number of capital crimes rose substantially (*Table 4*).

| Table 4: Attitudes Towards the Death Penalty in Russia | | |
|---|---|---|
| | 1989 | 1995 |
| Abolish immediately | 3 | 5 |
| Gradual abolition | 15 | 15 |
| Retain | 33 | 37 |
| Extend | 35 | 25 |
| Undecided | 14 | 18 |

Source: Iu. Levada, *Segodnia* 24 January 1995; *Current Digest of the (Post) Soviet Press* 1995 No. 6, 10

Under Khrushchev the argument commonly advanced for maintaining the death penalty was that criminal law must become more humane, but not only for the criminals: combatting crime itself was also considered to be an aspect of humanization of criminal law. Such theories can still be heard and the jurist Iurii Demidov insisted in 1994 that 'humanism cannot be one-sided'.[55] These views are based on the idea that ultimately the state may decide everybody's fate, that the state thus stands above man, and on populist conceptions of people's power and a collectivist doctrine of human rights. Another quite common argument for preserving the death penalty is that the legal consciousness of the population is still very low,[56] but this sounds rather unconvincing: it only points to the need to develop that consciousness. Moreover, the trend in the number of executions closely depends on the outlook of the lawmaker: each increase, between 1986 and 1993, in the maximum term of imprisonment after pardon caused a dramatic drop in the number of actual executions to the accompaniment of only a few protests from law enforcement officers. Some argue that the legal possibility of the death penalty in a given case works to deter people from committing the crime, and there are, as the jurist A. Mal'ko wrote in 1993, also 'persons (or better non-persons) for whom limits do not exist'.[57] This would in any event call for the death penalty to be only rarely applied.[58] Moreover, if the death penalty were only applied in such cases, the question of miscarriage of justice would be irrelevant.

Several serial killers have been tried in recent years. In 1994 Golovkin was sentenced to death for having killed 11 young boys over a period of 8 years and Gordovenko for the rape and killing of five women.[59] In the spring of 1995 Riakhovskii stood trial for 19 homicides and 6 attempts on women.[60] One of the prisoners who ate his cell-mate and had been sentenced for murder three times already, was sentenced to death on July 28.[61] In July 1995 two soldiers, who killed six of their comrades at a Far Eastern base in March 1994, were sentenced to death by a military court.[62]

If the actual number of executions is as low as is the case in Russia, the question arises as to why the death penalty is maintained. Part of the argument is that the number of death sentences is still high and the lawmakers may believe that this serves as a deterrent[63] but, if the actual number of executions is low, this effect will become marginal. Partly, the policy is a vestige of the programme of social defence which influenced soviet criminal policy in the 1920s: only those persons who pose a big risk to society are actually executed.

The main problem is that the low number of actual executions apparently reflects the policy endorsed by President El'tsin [Yeltsin], but he has never defended it in public, not even when assured of the support of a majority of the population. A special Society for the Right to Life and Civil Dignity, headed by Viktor Kogan-Iasnii, was founded in 1990, and there is also a Society Against Capital Punishment.

# THE RISE OF CRIME IN RUSSIA

The frequency of murder in Russia is appalling, and in the years 1993-95 annually about 20 homicides occurred per 100,000 inhabitants, and in 1994 nearly 48,000 people were murdered. In 1993, 18.8 per thousand and in 1994, 21.3 per thousand persons were sentenced for homicide (including preparation and attempts).[64] Contributing factors include the relatively low price of vodka, the drinking habits of a part of the population and the resulting fights and domestic violence. The high number of offences is not the result of a decline in the application of the death penalty over the past years, because the number of homicides in Russia has always been rather high in years when vodka was available in large amounts and at affordable prices. However, the number of homicides and especially the killing of policemen play an important role in discussions of the death penalty: when it was claimed that 69 law-enforcement officers had been killed by criminals and 236 seriously wounded in the first six months of 1994, the 'crisis' was attributed to the fact that in 1993 only 4 of the 72 bandits who had killed police officers were sentenced to death and three of them were granted clemency.[65] Another question is the growing number of professional murders: for 1992, 102 high-profile contract killings were reported, but for 1994 586, of which only 132 were solved.[66] When television personality Vladimir List'ev was killed in the spring of 1995, President El'tsin commented: 'In Uzbekistan six groups of bandits were simply executed by firing squad in one go, they were executed by the internal affairs' bodies! And the situation has immediately started to improve.'[67] The first deputy minister of the interior, Vladimir Kolesnikov, stated when he was appointed to this post that all persons having committed a murder under aggravating circumstances 'should face the supreme penalty. That and nothing else. I am sure that there will be positive [results] . . . Do you understand that we love mother Russia, and we love its people. I want you to believe that we are not afraid of anybody. I am not afraid of anybody. The law should be above everything . . .'.[68]

In Leninist or Stalinist times, such a remark would have been sufficient ground to unleash a campaign by overzealous people at the grass roots level, but there is no sign of such a reaction at the moment. Such remarks today attest to the rather helpless attitude of the authorities in trying to deal with the rising tide of crime.

# AVOIDING MISCARRIAGES OF JUSTICE

Some widely publicized miscarriages of justice in the first half of the 1980s have played a role in discussions about the death penalty. They occurred in several cases of serial murders: in Belarus in the Vitebsk case in the first half of the 1980s, at least one innocent person was executed; the same happened in the case of the serial killer, Andrei Chikatilo, when Aleksandr Kravchenko was executed.[69] These incidents may have strengthened the hand of those who argue for introducing jury trials in capital cases.

Jurors were introduced in Russia in October 1993 in some provinces on an experimental basis. Under the original text of the draft Constitution, the death sentence was only possible after a court trial with the participation of a jury, but at the last moment this was changed: the accused is free to choose between trial by jury or without a jury. This is a constitutionally guaranteed right and, if the wish of the accused is ignored, a gross violation of the law is committed which requires the higher court to quash the verdict and order a jury trial to be held. However, this right operates only experimentally in a small portion of the territory of Russia, which does not seem to sit easily with the equality principle, although it could be argued that the interim provisions of the Constitution allow for this.

In the case of *Efimov*, decided by the Criminal Chamber of the Supreme Court on 25 October 1994, the court ruled that article 20(2) of the Constitution provides the accused with the right to have his case tried by a jury. In this case, the accused had read all the materials of the case before the law on trial by jury went into force (1 November 1993); as for Efimov, he was sentenced only on 23 June 1994.[70]

In the cases of *Panchishkin* and *Filippov* tried in Rostov-na-Donu the jury found both defendants guilty and one of them was sentenced to death.[71]

## OTHER MEMBERS OF THE CIS

The Constitutions of the other republics belonging to the Commonwealth of Independent States (CIS) are usually more vague as to the death penalty than is the case in Russia. In Belorussia the death penalty is possible for particularly grave crimes and only pursuant to a court sentence (article 24 Constitution of 1994). The Armenian Constitution of 1995 provides nearly the same. In Georgia alone, the Constitution forbids the death penalty, but that Constitution was the social democratic Constitution of 1921, revived in 1992. In 1994 draft amendments were published in two versions, one allowing the death penalty for grave crimes against life and health, the other forbidding it. The 1992 Constitution of Turkmenistan and 1993 Constitutions of Kazakhstan and Kyrgyzstan decree that the death penalty may be applied 'only in extraordinary cases'. The Uzbek Constitution proclaims the right to life as 'the inalienable right of every human being', and 'an encroachment on it is the gravest crime' (article 24), but this only means that nobody may be deprived of this right extra-judicially (article 19).[72] The Constitution of Moldova of 1994 contains the same formula, but embellishes it with the magic passwords 'until its complete abolition' (article 21).[73] The Ukrainian Criminal Code was amended in 1992 and specifies that the death penalty is still possible in cases of particularly grave crimes. In many republics the right of the accused to have his case considered in two instances is not guaranteed and is often violated.[74]

A draft of a model Criminal Code discussed by the Inter-Parliamentary Assembly of the Commonwealth of Independent States provides: 'The death penalty - execution - may be imposed as an exceptional punishment only for especially grave crimes, accompanied by the intentional deprivation of human life under aggravating circumstances. The death penalty may not be applied to women; to persons who committed the crime before they reached eighteen; and men over the age of sixty five. The death penalty may by way of pardon be commuted to lifelong imprisonment or deprivation of freedom for a term of twenty five years' (article 60).[75] Pardon may be conditional and in that case a person committing a new crime within the probationary period may be sentenced to death even if the second crime was not a capital crime (articles 71 and 87). The court may not apply the death penalty in a jury trial, if the jury recommends clemency.

The 1992 Constitution of Lithuania restricts itself to declare that 'the right of a human being to life is protected by law' (article 19), but abolition of the death penalty may feature in a draft of a new Criminal Code. The 1992 Constitution of Estonia contains similar language but adds that 'nobody may be deprived of life arbitrarily' (article 16); on the other hand Estonia has signed the Sixth Protocol to the European Convention on Human Rights concerning the abolition of the death penalty.

A draft of the Latvian Criminal Code of 1993 provides either for the complete abolition of the death penalty or a reduction of the number of capital crimes to the single count of aggravated murder, but in September 1995 parliament decided to maintain the death penalty.[76] Its current Criminal Code was amended in 1992, but it still allows for the death penalty in cases such as counterfeiting, in which nobody has been killed.

The practice in several CIS republics was less liberal than in Russia; for example, in Ukraine 79 persons were sentenced to death during 1992; 117 during 1993; and 200 during the first nine months of 1994. In those years 103, 78 and 60 persons, respectively, were executed on the basis of sentences pronounced that year or earlier. For 1992 and 1993 taken together, the death sentence was quashed or changed with regard to 25 persons, and 7 persons were pardoned. Seventy-four people were sentenced to death in the first half of 1995, but only one person was executed.[77]

As part of an effort to fight a rising tide of crime in Kazakhstan, the authorities decided to allow live televising of executions. The first such broadcast took place in July 1995 and the second in September 1995. Kazakhstan executed 134 people in 1994 and 45 in the first half of 1995.[78] In April 1995 the Kyrgyz commission for pardons turned down thirty appeals from criminals to have their death sentences commuted to terms of imprisonment.[79] In Georgia a moratorium on actual execution expired on 5 May 1994. At that time twenty persons had been sentenced to death and the sentence of only four of them was commuted. President Shevardnadze has declared that he was against the death penalty, but confirmed that it would be applied as long as the law provided for it.[80] The Tajik Supreme Court returned death sentences on three men involved in the assassination of businessman,

Vladimir Nirman, who headed a Tajik-American joint venture. A man who is said to have played an active role in atrocities committed against civilians during the civil war in Tajikistan in 1992 was sentenced to death in 1995.[81] In Moldova two persons were sentenced to death in 1993, but it is not known whether they have been executed.[82] After the country's admittance to the Council of Europe, Moldovan President Mircea Snegur sent to the parliament a legislative proposal calling for the abolition of the death penalty. In November 1995 Moldova became the first former USSR state to abolish the death penalty for all offences. Armenia and Azerbaijan do not seem to actually execute people, although the death penalty is still included in the Armenian Constitution or in the Criminal Codes of other states, and sometimes people are sentenced to death.[83] In Armenia 12 persons have been awaiting execution for four years. The last person to be executed was in 1992, but this had to be carried out in Saratov because of a lack of local experience.[84]

In July 1995 Lithuania carried out its first execution since 1990. Mafia boss Boris Dekanidze was executed for the premeditated murder of a journalist, who had reported on Dekanidze's gang. Government spokesman Vilius Kavaliauskas has insisted that while capital punishment was not a symbol of good democracy, its abolition was not on the agenda because it was considered an effective weapon against organized crime.[85]

## CONCLUSIONS AND PROSPECTS

In the field of Russian law many things have changed, but it is not always easy to trace the real effects of the efforts to change the totalitarian system to one where the human being occupies pride of place not in some abstract ideological sense, but in conformity with democratic principles and respect for human dignity. The Russian Constitution adopted in 1993 proclaims in article 2 that '[t]he individual and his rights and freedoms are the highest value. Recognition, observance and protection of the rights and freedoms of man and citizen is the obligation of the state'. It is one of the great virtues of President Boris El'tsin (Yeltsin) that his actions attest to his belief in these principles on a matter where his personal decisions and his moral judgement play a crucial role. It is his decision to establish a commission composed of outstanding personages who advise him on the question of clemency for people who frequently do not deserve such mercy and to follow most of its recommendations. The fact that executions still occur in Russia should not belittle the progress made by Elt'sin which is striking when compared to the lack of progress elsewhere in the former USSR.

However in the mid-1990s, it has been reported that El'tsin has turned tougher on crime and is less and less inclined to commute death sentences to life in prison; if so, one can expect a rise in the number of actual executions. The most acute problem here is that no open policy with regard to the death penalty has yet emerged which makes for real discussion of this topic quite difficult. El'tsin has never defended his policy on this question in public, and his silence frustrates public debate. When specifically asked in 1994 about its readiness to consider ratification of Protocol No. 6 to the European Convention on Human Rights (which deals with the abolition of the death penalty), no answer was forthcoming.[86] But the draft of the new Criminal Code and the 1993 Constitution already contain the necessary information: complete abolition of the death penalty in the near future is not likely, although, as already pointed out in this chapter, one may argue that such a low number of executions as now occur in Russia would make it rather easy to abolish it. Another problem is that in reality individuals are not executed because of their crime, but because of individual factors. While exempting women and elderly men from the death penalty seems a humane measure, it also strikes as discriminatory and not consistent with the equality principle. An exemption for minors (and in the past for pregnant women) is defensible, and also fits the tenor of the international covenants on human rights.

Prospects for other members of the CIS tend to resemble those of Russia, but in several states such as Kazakhstan and Ukraine, the number of death sentences and executions is still very high and the politicians in these countries apparently believe that this has a deterrent effect. This is most clearly in Kazakhstan which is one of the few countries in the world to execute people in public.


## ENDNOTES

* When writing this paper, the research done by Floor Lauwaars, a student at the University of Amsterdam, was most helpful.

1. For a recent account see, R.A. Kushen, 'The Death Penalty and the Crisis of Criminal Justice in Russia', *Brooklyn Journal of International Law* 1993 No. 2, 523-581. See for the soviet past G. P. van den Berg, 'The Soviet Union and the Death Penalty', *Soviet Studies* 1983 No.2.

2. 'Repressii', *Ezhegodnik gazety Rech' na 1912 god*, St.Petersburg 1912, 517; S. S. Ostroumov, *Prestupnost' i ee prichiny v dorevoliutsionnoi Rossii*, Moscow 1980, 99-100; M. G. Minenok, *Nakazanie v Russkom ugolovnom prave*, Kaliningrad 1985; O. F. Shishov, in *Smertnaia kazn': za i protiv*, Moscow 1989.

3. V. I. Lenin, *Polnoe sobranie sochinenii* Vol. XXXIX, 184-185; Vol. XL, 114. In 1994 the rehabilitation of the first victim of a death sentence after the October revolution (admiral Shastnyi) was urged, *Izvestiia* 2 July 1994. Shastnyi was sentenced by an ad hoc tribunal, founded on the day of his arrest on the basis of a decree of the justice ministry. This decree provided that tribunals are not bound by any limitations in the choice of the means to combat counter-revolution, sabotage etc. It seems to have been a act of

revenge by Trotskii, *Izvestiia* 25 October 1990; 'Pervyi smertnyi prigovor', *Chelovek i zakon* 1991 No.3-4, 112 ff.

4. The word execution (*rasstrel'*) is used to denote carrying out the death penalty by a bullet to the head, which is still the practice in Russia and the other countries of the former USSR except in cases of war criminals, when the sentence is execution by hanging.

5. Between 1930 and 1950 a number of extra-judicial agencies could also apply the death penalty and in this period 786,098 persons were sentenced to death, charged with crimes against the state, *Izvestiia* 13 February 1990. In 1937 and 1938 alone 681,692 persons were executed, V. Zemskov, *Argumenty i fakty* 1990 No. 5,8; *Summary of World Broadcasts SU / 0731 B/ 4*, 5 April 1990; *Voprosy istorii KPSS* 1991 No. 8, 85; V. P. Popov, 'Gosudarstvennyi terror v sovetskoi Rossii. 1923-1953 gg. (istochniki i ikh interpretatsiia)', *Otechestvennye arkhivy* 1992 No. 2, 23, transl. as 'State Terror in Soviet Russia, 1923-1953 (Sources and Interpretation)', *Russian Law & Politics* 1994 No. 3; V. V. Luneev, 'Politicheskaia repressiia', *Gosudarstvo i pravo* 1994 No. 7, 115 (for crimes against the state).

6. *Vedomosti Verkhovnogo Soveta SSSR* (the official gazette of the USSR, hereinafter *Ved. SSSR*) 1954 No. 11; V. Rostovtsev, *Iuridicheskii vestnik* 1992 No. 14 (16), 12.

7. *Ved.SSSR* 1961 No. 19 item 207; No. 27 item 291; 1962 No. 8 item 83-85; 1973 No.1 item 3.

8. *Ved. SSSR* 1961 No. 27 item 291; *Pravda* 21 July 1961; H. J. Berman, *Justice in the U.S.S.R.*, New York 1963, 86, 403; *Chelovek i zakon* 1988 No.12. See also the comments in *Nauchno-prakticheskii kommentarii UK RSFSR*, Moscow 1964, 13, *Sovetskoe ugolovnoe pravo. Chast' obshchaia*, Moscow 1962, 55; *Kurs sovetskogo ugolovnogo prava* Volume I, Leningrad 1968, 119-121.

9. Z. Iakovleva, 'O smertnoi kazni v SSSR', *Sotsialisticheskaia zakonnost'* 1991 No. 4, 44-46; between 1962 and 1984 22,235 (until 1989 24,422) people were executed, between 1973 and 1989 12,000, *Trud* 11 January 1992; *Komsomol'skaia pravda* 26 February 1992; *Tiuremnaia reforma v stranakh byvshego sotsializma*, Moscow 1993, 19.

10. *Ved. SSSR* 1980 No. 19 item 347; 1986 No. 22 item 364; 1990 No. 45 item 946; see also *Ved. SSSR* 1987 No. 28 item 437.

11. *Ved. SSSR* 1965 No. 10 item 123; No. 37 item 532; No. 39 item 569.

12. *Ved. SSSR* 1986 No. 22 item 364.

13. *Ved. SSSR* 1991 No.30 item 862.

14. *Ved. Rossiiskoi Federatsii* 1993 No. 1 item 9. The President interprets this as imprisonment for a period up to 15 years or for life, decree of 16 March 1994, *Sobranie aktov Prezidenta i Pravitel'stva Rossiiskoi Federatsii* 1994 No. 12 item 879. Such sentences to lifelong imprisonment create problems, because such people have hardly anything to lose, Iu. Kalinin, A. Mikhlin, 'Kaznit' nel'zia pomilovat'', *Rossiiskaia gazeta* 1 September 1994. Mikhlin argues that this is not a penalty, because it is not provided by the Criminal Code and not assigned by a court, but by the President, A. Mikhlin, 'Zakliuchen pozhiznenno', *Rossiiskaia iustitsiia* 1995 No.7, 24.

15. *Ved. Rossiiskoi Federatsii* 1993 No. 22 item 789.

16. Shakhrai's draft, article 5 ; the Communist draft (Slobodkin): article 38; and the draft of the Fond Reform (article 11). The draft of the Christian Democratic Party and the Party of the Constitutional Democrats recognizes the right to life (article 1) and does not contain a provision which allows restriction of this right in order to combat criminality. The 1992 Constitution of Tatarstan provides that 'the life of man [. . .] is protected by the state' (article 25).

17. An earlier text of this draft stated 'and only pronounced in a sentence of a court with the participation of sworn [jurors]', but this was changed at the last moment.

18. *Konstitutsiia Rossiiskoi Federatsii. Kommentarii*, Moscow 1994, 136.

19. A spokesman for the Russian chief military prosecutor's office said in September 1995 that Western intelligence services are expanding their operations in Russia, acting both openly and covertly, in covert operations by using Russian citizens whom they are recruiting for the purpose. The spokesman recalled that in old Soviet judicial practice, Russian citizens exposed as working for foreign intelligence services usually received the death penalty. But since 1992, nobody sentenced to death in Russia for high treason was actually executed, thus suggesting that such people are still sentenced to death, *Jamestown* 26 September 1995. In September 1995 Russia dropped the death penalty for illegal trading in hard currency (article 88 Criminal Code), Peter Rutland, *OMRI Daily Digest* (electronic version, hereinafter *OMRI*) 22 September 1995.

20. *Izvestiia* 6 June 1995; *Jamestown Monitor* (electronic version, hereinafter *Jamestown*) 7 June 1995. It is said that the death penalty has not been abolished in war-time conditions, *Moskovskie novosti* 12-19 February 1994, 4.

21. *Report on the Conformity of the Legal Order of the Russian Federation with Council of Europe Standards*, prepared by R. Bernhardt, S. Trechsel, A. Weitze, F. Ermacora, Strasbourg AS/Bur/Russia (1994) 7, at p. 34.

22. *Vestnik Verkhovnogo suda SSSR* 1991 No. 7, 8. See for the theory V.N. Kudriavtsev, *Teoreticheskie osnovy kvalifikatsii prestuplenii*, Moscow 1963, 226; V. M. Galkin, 'Konkretizatsiia norm ugolovnogo zakona', *Problemy sovershenstvovaniia sovetskogo zakonodatel'stva* Vol. XXXXVII, Moscow 1990, 100-111. A remarkable case was the case of Kamskii, who had been sentenced to death for receiving bribes under aggravating circumstances in 1986. An edict of the head of state had pardoned him and the penalty was commuted to deprivation of freedom for 20 years. By a Law of 5 December 1991 the death penalty for Kamskii's crime was abolished and the maximum penalty was set at 15 years. Thereupon he asked the Chairman of the Supreme Court and the procuracy to file a protest to have his sentence adapted to the new law. However they deemed the Supreme Court not entitled to review an edict of the head of state. Jurists commented that the law decreased the penalty and that Kamskii's situation was discriminatory, because for other persons in his position who were not yet granted a pardon, the sentence was changed automatically to 15 years. Several jurists sent a letter to the Chairman of the Supreme Court, and thereupon this chairman filed a protest and the Presidium of the court changed the sentence to 15 years imprisonment, *Rossiiskaia iustitsiia* 1994 No. 4, 6.

23. The draft was adopted by the Duma on 17 July 1995, but has not been signed by the President within the prescribed time. The Council of the Federation considered the Code on 4 October 1995, but has rejected the draft, *Izvestiia* 6 October 1995 (Iu. Feofanov).

24. See also an interview with Viktor Pokhmelkin. *Segodnia* 2 August 1995 (condensed text in *The Current Digest of the Post-Soviet Press* 1995 No. 31, 2.

25. Under Article 28 of the Constitution everybody may have 'religious and other convictions and act in accordance with them'. This right cannot be restricted (article 56.3), but apparently the term 'convictions' is explained quite narrowly.

26. *Rossiiskaia Federatsiia* 1995 No. 7, 16.

27. *Kommersant'-Daily* 21 January 1995; *Current Digest of the (Post) Soviet Press* 1995 No. 3, 23.

28. *Prestupnost' i pravonarusheniia 1991*, 132-133.

29. *Biulleten' Verkhovnogo suda Rossiiskoi Federatsii* 1994 No. 10, 8.

30. *Sobranie Zakonov . . . SSSR* 1934 No. 64 item 459.

31. N. Vedernikov, 'Kaznit' ili milovat' ?', *Pravo i zhizn'* Vol. I (Moscow 1992) 131; *Sobranie zakonodatel'stva* 1994 No. 16 item 1903; interview with Pristavkin, *Rossiiskaia Federatsiia* 1995 No. 5, 50-51. It is not clear whether this commission reviews all death sentences, or only if pardon has been asked for. Mikhlin argues that persons have the right to life under the Constitution, but they must have the right to die too, A. Mikhlin, 'Zakliuchen pozhiznenno', *Rossiiskaia iustitsiia* 1995 No. 7, 24.

32. V. Indiriakov, 'Snachala zashchitite grazhdanina, a uzh potom miluite ubiitsu', *Rossiiskaia gazeta* 12 July 1995. He reacts to an interview with Pristavkin in *Argumenty i fakty* 1995 No. 12.

33. V. Vlasov, 'Na pervom plane - zaschita lichnosti', *Rossiiskaia iustitsiia* 1995 No. 3. See also A. Mikhlin, 'Smertnaia kazn': pravo na pomilovanie i 'pravo na smert'", *Rossiiskaia iustitsiia* 1995 No. 10, 44.

34. V. Indiriakov, 'Psikh v inter'ere 'zony'', *Rossiiskaia gazeta* 6 June 1995.

35. Article 33 Law of 15 July 1995 'On Keeping in Custody Persons Suspected or Accused of the Commission of a Crime', *SObranie zakonodatel'stva RF* 1995 No. 29 item 2759.

36. M Taibbi, *The Moscow Times* 30 July 1995, 17.

37. *Izvestiia* 29 October 1991; A. Natashev, 'Mnogo shuma i . . nichego', *Iuridicheskii vestnik* 1992 No. 11 (13), 13; 'Chas 'Iks'", *Argumenty i fakty* 1993 No. 23, 4; *Rossiiskaia Gazeta* 22 April 1994 (Tula); interview with Iu. Kalinin, 'Slushat' takoe obidno', *Rossiiskaia gazeta* 1 November 1994; A. Pashkov, 'I ne kazn', i ne milost'", *Izvestiia* 22 November 1994.

38. *Izvestiia* 12 April 1994 contains a report on doctors' protests against their involvement with the death penalty in the USA.

39. *Izvestiia* 25 May 1995 (A. Ekhalov). See for the conditions in the special prisons built for them V. Filippov, 'Osuzhdennye na vechnuiu muku', *Izvestiia* 18 May 1994; A. Pashkov, 'I ne kazn', i ne milost'", *Izvestiia* 22 November 1994, Their legal position has not yet been regulated.

40. Interview with G.G. Cheremnykh, 'Posleslovie k vysshei mere', *Izvestiia* 1 October 1990. See for the present day commission *Izvestiia* 23 October 1993.

41. In fact the decrease is larger because in 1985 capital crimes encompassed economic crimes as well and also other crimes not directed against the person. For such crimes the death penalty was only rarely applied.

42. A number of them fell victim to the treason of the American Aldrich H. Ames, *Izvestiia* 15 June 1995.

43. *Izvestiia* 4 June 1987; *Literaturnaia gazeta* 10 June 1987, 11; V. Gordeev, 'O prestupnosti i sudimosti v SSSR', *Vestnik verkhovnogo suda SSSR* 1991 No. 3, 21-22; Z. Iakovleva, 'O smertnoi kazni v SSSR', *Sotsialisticheskaia zakonnost'* 1991 No.4, 44-46; W. Oschlies, *Alle anderthalb Stunden ein Mord . . .*, *Berichte des BOIS* 1991 No. 21; *Summary of World Broadcasts SU/0232 B/6*, 17 August 1988; /0746 C1/3, 24 April 1990; *Moscow News* 1988 No. 40, 7; V. Rudnev, 'Komu u nas zakon ne pisan', *Izvestiia* 2 October 1992.

44. See also M. Seleznev, 'Usilit' garantii zakonnosti pri vynesenii smertnogo prigovora', *Rossiiskaia iustitsiia* 1995 No. 6, 48.

45. Pristavkin in *The Moscow Times* 11 December 1994; *Izvestiia* 27 January 1995. See however also *Summary of World Broadcasts SU/2150 B/4*: up to 1 November 154 criminals have been sentenced to death and for 152 of them the sentence was commuted.

46. See on this point Pristavkin in *The Moscow Times* 11 December 1994 and an interview with Pristavkin in *Argumenty i fakty* 1995 No. 12, 1, 6. Most cases considered by the commission deal with hopeless alcoholics without the financial means to hire a good lawyer.

47. S. Chugaev, *Izvestiia* 10 March 1992; *Report on the Conformity of the Legal Order of the Russian Federation with Council of Europe Standards*, AS/Bur/Russia (1994) 7, 34; *Ekspress Khronika* 1995 No.9 ,5; interview with Iu. Kalinin, 'Slushat' takoe obidno', *Rossiiskaia gazeta* 1 November 1994; Pristavkin states 'more than 500', *The Moscow Times* 11 December 1994; M. Taibbi, *The Moscow Times* 30 July 1995.

48. During 1994 154 persons were sentenced to death, *Summary of World Broadcasts SU/2150 B/4-5*, 11 November 1994, and for 152 persons the sentence was commuted to long-term imprisonment.

49. Interview with Iu. Kalinin, 'Slushat' takoe obidno', *Rossiiskaia gazeta* 1 November 1994. According to Pristavkin the commission had considered 137 addresses during 1994 and rejected the appeals for mercy of 13 persons, *Izvestiia* 27 January 1995.

50. See e.g. in *Izvestiia* the case of the brothers Novinov in Donetsk, Ukraine (7 July 1995), of Maduev, in St. Petersburg (12 July 1995).

51. See however P. P. Osipov, *Teoreticheskie osnovy postroeniia i primeneniia ugolovno-pravovykh sanktsii (aksiologicheskie aspekty)*, Leningrad 1976, 81.

52. G.M. Reznik, 'Prestizh professii advokata', *Sovetskoe gosudarstvo i pravo* 1987 No. 3, 69; V. Kogan, 'Nakazanie: problemy gumanizatsii', *Sovetskaia iustitsiia* 1987 No. 19, 25-26; V. Kardin, S. Kelina, *Moscow News* 1987 No. 16, 13; A. Iakovlev, *Ogonek* 1987 No. 33; S. Alekseev, S. Kelina, G. Pavda, 'Prava cheloveka i sila zakona', *Izvestiia* 29 December 1988; A. Adamov, A. Iakovlev, ' Vysokaia tsena sudebnoi oshibki', *Literaturnaia gazeta* 1 February 1989; A. M. Iakovlev, *Pravda* 25 February 1988; *Summary of World Broadcasts SU/0088 B/4*, 1 March 1988; N. Zagorodnikov, A. Naumov, A. Sakharov, 'Ischerpan li potentsial gumanizma?', *Izvestiia* 24 January 1989; *Izvestiia* 20 September 1990; interview with L. Kolodkin, *Trud* 11 January 1992; L. Kolodkin, Iu. Karpukhin, 'Po kom zvonit kolokol. Smertnaia kazn': za i protiv', *Militsiia* October 1992, 5 ff.; A. V. Mal' ko, 'Smertnaia kazn' kak pravovoe ogranichenie', *Gosudarstvo i pravo* 1993 No.1, 73 ff.; Iu. Goriacheva, *Nezavisimaia gazeta* 13 August 1992; *Current Digest of the (Post) Soviet Press* 1992 No.32, 24; E. Maksimova, 'Smertnaia kazn'. Chto - za? Chto - protiv?', *Izvestiia* 23, 24 December 1993. See also A. Motivans, E. Teague, 'Capital Punishment in the Former USSR', *RFE/RL* 1992 No. 26, 71-72.

53. See for Smolentsev (Chairman Supreme Court) *Pervaia sessiia Verkhovnogo Soveta SSSR* (1989), 157; for Trubin (Procurator General) *Izvestiia* 12 December 1990; for Lushchikov (Minister of Justice) *Summary of World Broadcasts SU/0973 i*, 18 January 1991. See for the point of view of RSFSR deputies in 1990 *Argumenty i fakty* 1990 No. 46, and also Pristavkin, *The Moscow Times* 11 December 1994.

54. *The Moscow Times* 11 December 1994, 31.

55. See G. P. van den Berg, 'The Soviet Union and the Death Penalty', *Soviet Studies* 1983 No. 3; G. Shakhnazarov, *Izvestiia* 14 May 1961; V. Terent'ev, *Izvestiia* 10 January 1989; I. V. Bestuzhev-Lada, 'Gumanizm i psevdogumanizm', *Smertnaia kazn': za i protiv,* Moscow 1989; V. Mukhin, *Ekonomika i zhizn'* 1990 No.24, 15; A. E. Iakubov, 'Gumanizm i smertnaia kazn'', *Vestnik Moskovskogo un-ta. Seriia 11, pravo* 1990 No. 4, 41 ff.; Z. M. Chernilovskii, 'Smertnaia kazn': istoriko-filosofskii aspekt', *Sovetskoe gosudarstvo i pravo* 1991 No. 8 128 ff.; I.I. Karpets, 'Vysshaia mera: za i protiv', *Sovetskoe gosudarstvo i pravo* 1991 No.7, 49 ff.; A. V. Naumov, 'Obnovlenie metodologii nauki ugolovnogo prava', *Sovetskoe gosudarstvo i pravo* 1991 No. 12, 26; Iu. Demidov in *Rossiiskaia iustitsiia* 1994 No. 7, 51.

56. For this argument see A. S. Nikiforov, 'Kontrol' nad prestupnodt'iu v. Rossii', *Gosudarstvo i pravo* 1994 No. 5, 74. Nikiforov lists the arguments against the death penalty: it does not deter people, and certainly not fanatics, terrorists, sexual maniacs, persons who commit murders under the influence of alcohol, and also professional murderers, for whom it is only a professional risk. Its special preventive effect is of course high, but this poses the question of miscarriages of justice. According to Pristavkin such people usually do not seek pardon, *Izvestiia* 27 January 1995.

57. A. V. Mal'ko, 'Smertnaia kazn' kak pravovoe ogranichenie', *Gosudarstvo i pravo* 1993 No. 1, 74-75; see also V. Baranov, 'Protiv otmeny smertnoi kazni', *Ekspress Khronika* 1995 No. 9, 5.

58. See also the interview with Pristavkin in *Argumenty i fakty* 1995 No. 12, 1, 6. Most cases considered by the commission are degraded alcoholics, who cannot hire a good lawyer. Only maniacs and persons who commit violence against children are in fact executed.

59. *Izvestiia* 27 September, 21 October 1994; *The Moscow Times* 23 October 1994.

60. *Moskovskie Novosti* 1995 No. 31.

61. *OMRI* 10, 27 July 1995; *The Moscow Times* 16 July 1995, 19.

62. *OMRI* 24 July 1995.

63. For the same reason it seems to occur that persons are housed in death row cells before they are finally sentenced, Taibbi, *op.cit.*

64. *Rossiiskaia iustitsiia* 1995 No. 6, 51.

65. *Summary of World Broadcasts SU / 2048 B/2*, 15 July 1994.

66. *Summary of World Broadcasts SU / 2242 B/6*, 3 March 1995; *Rossiiskaia Federatsiia* 1995 No. 7, 16. However according to other data the detection rate would be 75%, but only 39% in Moscow, where 96 murders of this type were reported for 1994, A. L'vov, *Rossiiskaia gazeta* 13 April 1995. However, Pristavkin declared in 1994 that his commission did not consider any case with regard to people from the 'mafia', speech at the Sakharov lectures of 21 May 1994, *Prava liudyny v Ukraine*, IX (Kiev-Khar'kov 1994), 35.

67. *Summary of World Broadcasts SU / 2242 B/3*, 3 March 1995. The Uzbek authorities denied that such an incident has occurred. As far as it is known it happened in Turkmenistan.

68. *Summary of World Broadcasts SU/* 29 August 1995.

69. *Literaturnaia gazeta* 2 March 1988 (case of Mikhasevich); V. Ogurtsov, 'Rasstrelian po oshibke?', *Rossiiskaia gazeta* 23 April 1992 (case of Kravchenko); A. Pristavkin in *Izvestiia* 23 October 1993.

70. *Biulleten' Verkhovnogo suda Rossiiskoi Federatsii* 1995 No. 1, 14-15.

71. *Izvestiia* 23 April 1994 (condensed text in *The Current Digest of the (Post)Soviet Press* 1994 No.16, 18).

72. In Uzbekistan the death penalty may be commuted - by pardon - into imprisonment for 25 years by a law of 7 May 1993.

73. A 15-year-old boy was killed and a woman badly beaten after stealing potatoes in a village in the Dnestr. The teenager was thrown into a canal by furious villagers who tied a bag of potatoes around his neck. The beaten woman was paraded through the village and tied to a pole. The incidents occurred amid serious food shortages in the region, Dan Ionescu, *OMRI* 4 August 1995.

74. See for Azerbaijan, Georgia, Kazakhstan, Tajikistan, Uzbekistan, *Ekspress Khronika* 1995 No.9, 5.

75. *Informatsionny biulleten'* 1995 No. 8, 144, appendix to a decree of the Assembly of 13 May 1995.

76. *Summary of World Broadcasts,* SU/2416 E/1, 23 Sept. 1995.

77. *Prava Liudyny v. Ukraine,* IX (Kiev-Khar' kov 1994), 3. Legal experts advising the Council of Europe have said that Ukraine has made 'spectacular progress' in political reform and that it now complies with the organization's principles on democracy and human rights. Ukraine is obliged to ratify a series of international conventions within one year, including the European Convention on Human Rights and a convention on protection of minorities. It must also abolish the death penalty within three years and introduce an immediate moratorium on executions, Chrystyna Lapchak, *OMRI,* 27 Sept. 1995.

78. *Jamestown* 14 July 1995. See for Kazakhstan I. Novikov, 'The Death Penalty in Kazakhstan', *Review of Central and East European Law* 1994 No. 6.

79. *Vechernii Bishkek* 26 April 1995; *Summary of World Broadcasts* SU/2294, G/1, 4 May 1995.

80. *Ekspress Khronika* 1995 No. 9, 5. In March 1995 two persons were sentenced to death because they had committed a number of crimes, including participation in an attempt to kill Ioseliani. *Ekspress Khronika* 1995 No.5; No.10. In August 1995 several prisoners awaiting capital punishment went on hunger strike because of the conditions in their cells, *Summary of World Broadcasts* SU/2379 F/3, 11 August 1995.

81. *Ekspress Khronika* 1995 No. 9, 5; *Summary of World Broadcasts* SU/2395 G/2, 30 August 1995.

82. *Ekspress Khronika* 1995 No. 9,5; Michael Shafir, *OMRI* 3 Nov 1995.

83. Former Defence Minister Ragim Gazyev has been sentenced to death *in absentia* by a Baku court on charges of embezzling and surrendering two towns to Armenia in 1992, and for his role in Azerbaijan losses to Armenia in 1993. Gazyev was arrested in November 1993 but escaped from prison, Liz Fuller, *OMRI, Jamestown* 16 May 1995; *Ekspress Khronika* 1995 No.12, 2. A Russian was sentenced to death for planning to plant a bomb in Baku in 1994, *Summary of World Broadcasts* SU/2406 F/1, 12 September 1995.

84. *Izvestiia* 9 September 1995.

85. *OMRI* 18 July 1995. In September 1995 in Lithuania the fifth death sentence was carried out since 1990 , *Summary of World Broadcasts* SU/2121 E/5, 8 October 1995.

86. Explanatory notes to the Council of Europe on the state of the legal system and plans of its improvement in the Russian Federation as of 18 January 1995.

# CHAPTER 5

# The People's Republic of China

## Michael Palmer

In post-Mao China, the leadership has accorded the criminal process a central place in its efforts to institutionalise a socialist legal system.[1] The Criminal Law and Criminal Procedure Law were key features of the substantively and symbolically important step taken in 1979 to commit China to a rule of law. The two codes were essential elements in a package of seven major laws[2] designed to move China away from the radical and almost anarchic policies pursued during the Cultural Revolution in the direction of a society that is both stable and prosperous.[3] The Criminal Law has since become one of the most amended areas of the laws of the People's Republic of China (hereinafter, 'the PRC'), an indication of its continued central position in the legal and, indeed, the economic, reforms.

Although a key tool in the PRC's modernisation programme, the criminal justice system bears the imprint of many traditional Chinese legal norms and values. In traditional Chinese society, law was often equated with criminal law, criminal law with punishment, and punishment regarded as an instrument for the maintenance of state control. This view continues to be important today. The death penalty was a crucial feature of the imperial Chinese legal system, and it has remained central in the criminal justice process of the People's Republic of China.[4] A substantial number of offences now carry the death penalty, and one fifth of the world's population has found that the post-Mao liberalisation of the economy has not necessarily been accompanied by greater freedoms in other areas of social life. Indeed, in many important respects the Chinese people have been subjected to an increasingly draconian criminal justice system, as the Communist leadership has tried to maintain control, preserve social order and ensure political stability during a period of very rapid economic growth. That is, the criminal law has become a key mechanism for ensuring that China's population continues to uphold the Four Basic Principles as outlined in the preamble to the 1982 Constitution: Marxist-Leninist-Mao Zedong thought, the leadership of the Chinese Communist Party, the people's democratic dictatorship, and the paramount role of socialism.

As popular commitment to socialist ideals has drained away, so the Chinese Communist Party (hereinafter 'the CCP' or 'the Party') and the state have sought to maintain the people's democratic dictatorship through a mixture of enhanced material rewards and a more rigorously coercive system of criminal justice. Ideological mobilization has been replaced by the rewards of capitalism and the pressures of coercion. As a result, it is not the politically symbolic crime of counterrevolution that now most often gives rise to a death sentence or actual execution[5] but, rather, cases of homicide and to a lesser extent, corruption and economic crime.

In a number of crucial respects the revival of a formal legal system[6] in the post-Mao era was meant to prevent a return to the arbitrary and wilful exercise of official power that occurred during the Cultural Revolution. However, in the area of the criminal law - including the provision for and exercise of the death penalty - political campaigns and policy considerations remain centrally important mechanisms that often severely limit the autonomy of the people's criminal courts. Law, including in particular the criminal law and its provisions on the death penalty, are seen as 'weapons' (*wuqi*) by means of which the Chinese Communist administration continues its dominance of the Chinese people. Although market forces and the rule of law are now both promoted, in a very real political sense *both* the economy and the legal system are still 'owned' by the Party and this does, in my view, make the Party reluctant to grant autonomy to the courts in particular and the legal system in general.

This essay outlines the system of capital punishment in the People's Republic of China, attempts to explain the role that it plays in China's criminal justice system and offers some concluding observations on the PRC's continued heavy reliance on the death penalty.


## IDEOLOGICAL AND CULTURAL UNDERPINNINGS

The Criminal Law of the PRC (1979) is written in language that is in places redolent with socialist ideology, but the code also bears strongly the imprint of traditional Chinese legal values - for example, it does not provide clear definitions of criminal offences but, rather, in keeping with traditional Chinese norms it primarily sets out the punishment to be applied when a serious infraction of norm has occurred.[7]

The code is divided into two main sections, the first providing general principles and the second dealing with particular crimes. Article 1 stresses that the Criminal Law takes 'Marxist-Leninist-Mao Zedong thought as its guide' and that the code has been formulated in accordance with the policy of 'combining punishment with leniency'; article 2 makes one of the most important - perhaps even the most important - task of the Law the 'use of criminal punishments to struggle against all counterrevolutionary and other criminal acts in order to defend the system of the dictatorship of the proletariat ...'.

The Criminal Procedure Law in its General Principles section contains similar sentiments but adds that it is based *inter alia*, on the 'actual need to attack the enemy [*diren*] and protect the people [*renmin*]' (article 1). The Organic Law of the People's Procuracy (1979, amended 1983), requires China's prosecuting authorities to 'correctly differentiate and handle contradictions between the enemy and the people, and those among the people themselves' (article 7). This distinction between the 'enemy' and the 'people' is an important basis for the application of severe punishment in serious cases, and is an ideological reinforcement of the traditional view of law (especially criminal law) as punishment. It is a manifestation in statutory form of Mao Zedong's highly significant development in the Chinese context of the distinction which Lenin drew between non-antagonistic and antagonistic contradictions.[8] Mao's thoughts on the nature of contradictions in society continue to have a crucial influence on both the formal and informal (non-adjudicatory) justice systems in the People's Republic. I have considered this feature of Mao's continuing influence elsewhere.[9] Suffice it to say here that non-antagonistic contradictions arise between persons who share an identity of interests because they are 'of the people'. Such differences are seen as politically unproblematic and therefore to be treated by the 'gentle' and 'democratic' methods of education, persuasion and criticism, especially as these are conducted through the processes of people's mediation.[10] In contrast, antagonistic contradictions are those differences that have developed between parties with essentially conflicting stakes in the system, namely the enemy and the ordinary people. This second type of contradiction is viewed as threatening, potentially at least, the political future of the regime, and must therefore be dealt with by the full force of dictatorial methods including, of course, the death penalty. The distinction between the two forms of contradiction has also reinforced the traditional Chinese tendency to deal with a wide range of deviant acts by administrative methods, and to refrain from labeling such conduct as criminal, while reserving the law for the harsh punitive treatment of those who have committed serious offences, especially those deviants whose conduct has given rise to, or is likely to create, antagonistic contradictions.

Until quite recently, the identification of the law with heavy punishment was explicitly linked to a class theory of Chinese society in which private property in the means of production was identified as the most important cause of criminal conduct, because such property underpinned the power of the enemies of the people.[11] This view has become increasingly untenable with an economy that is becoming ever more private, and the concern has now switched to a need to maintain public order and ensure loyalty to the system in a period of dramatic economic reform. The ideology of contradictions has remained in place, however, albeit to a certain extent depoliticised in that it is asserted that increasingly the enemies are those whose serious *criminal* conduct - rather than their political disloyalty *per se* - gives rise to antagonistic contradictions. The Criminal law is an important mechanism for preserving political order and maintaining social stability, and since the early 1980s there has been a series of anti-crime campaigns in which the death penalty has played a central role.

From the earliest times imperial China maintained a system of 'Five Punishments' (*Wu Xing*) and this always contained a death penalty. But the system of punishments that lay at the heart of law in early China was so antithetical to the Chinese Confucian tradition that its origins were ascribed to barbarian peoples.[12] The Confucian view was that social order was best maintained by the consensual means of exemplary conduct on the part of the ruler and a willingness to compromise on the part of the ordinary people, and that when punishment was regrettably necessary it had to be accompanied by education in order that the offender might be reformed.

The excessive use of authoritarian measures by China's unifying dynasty, the Qin (221 B.C. - 206 B.C.), had a profound effect on popular Chinese attitudes to law. The Qin had been inspired by the Legalist school of thought,[13] and the Legalists influence encouraged the Qin rulers to administer the country through bureaucratic methods and legal codes containing heavy punishment, which were equally applicable to all persons. There was no separation of powers, with executive, legislative and judicial functions all being carried out by the imperial bureaucracy. The excessively despotic nature of Qin rule encouraged the succeeding dynasty - the Han - to make Confucianism the official ideology of the state. It remained so until the ending of the imperial system in 1911, but the exigencies of ruling the world's largest society encouraged the Han and succeeding dynasties to rely also on many Legalist methods to ensure order and continuity in social life.

Thus, criminal law, including the Five Punishments, was reinstated by the Han although in places modified by Confucian benevolence (*ren*) and humanity (*hu*). In particular, a number of changes were made to the system by which deviant conduct was corrected through punishment, and Emperor Wen introduced beatings in 167 BC to replace the physically mutilating punishments involving various forms of amputation, justifying the change with the argument that a limb which had been amputated could not grow again. By the sixth century the basic forms of punishment had become more or less fixed and those found in the Sui Code of 581 A.D. persisted until the early years of this century: beating with the light bamboo, beating with the heavy bamboo, penal servitude, exile, and death. There were also various supplementary punishments and within the five main categories a number of divisions were made. These additional penalties and variations within the five main categories were intended to provide precision in sentencing, for the belief was that a punishment should correspond as nearly as possible to the seriousness of the offence. Such precision was necessary in order to restore the universal harmony that had been threatened by the offending conduct itself.[14] If the precise punishment to be applied in a particular case was not provided for in the Code, a magistrate was able to impose the punishment applicable in a similar set of circumstances by a process of analogical reasoning. A magistrate who applied an incorrect punishment was liable to punishment himself, and a system of obligatory review of all cases by higher levels of the bureaucracy was put into place in order to ensure the application of the correct punishment. Moreover, in the interests of preserving universal harmony offenders were encouraged to surrender themselves voluntarily and to make a full confession before the discovery of their offence. In this way, the state learned of offences that had escaped its attention, and was therefore in a position to take the necessary corrective action. Those who voluntarily surrendered were given reduced sentences or even exempted from punishment.

The emphasis throughout was on physical punishment. There were, it is true, various provisions for the redemption of physical punishment by means of payment in cash or kind, but these were relatively unimportant in the overall scheme of things. The most serious punishment was the death penalty, and during much of the later period of imperial rule three forms of death penalty existed, namely, strangulation, decapitation, and slicing of the body. Of the three strangulation was considered the lightest penalty as it left the convicted prisoner's body intact; decapitation and slow slicing symbolically broke the line of patrilineal descent running through the offender's body and in a society which defined social identity in terms of descent through the male line and ancestor worship, these were seen as being graver forms of punishment.[15]

In the *lingchi* or 'death by slow slicing' the purpose was to render the criminal's body useless for any future life, as Alabaster emphasised nearly one hundred years ago in a memorable passage:

The most ignominious of all penalties is *slicing to pieces* [*lingchi*] *and extinction of the family*. Here the offender is tied to a cross, and, by a series of painful but not in themselves mortal cuts, his head is sliced beyond recognition. The head of the offender is subsequently exposed in a cage for a period.
This punishment, known to foreigners as "lingering death", is not inflicted so much as a torture, but to destroy the future as well as the present life of the offender - he is unworthy to exist longer either as a man or a recognisable spirit, and, as spirits to appear must assume their

previous corporeal forms, he can only appear as a collection of little bits. It is not a lingering death, for it is all over in a few seconds, and the *coup de grâce* is generally given [by] the third cut; but it is very horrid and the belief that the spirit will be in need of sewing up in the land where needles are not, must make the unfortunate victim's last moments most unhappy.[16]

This particularly inhuman form of death penalty is - like the Five Punishments themselves - thought to have originated not from within Chinese society but, rather, from barbarian people - in this case the tribal communities of the Tungus who governed parts of northern China from the tenth to the twelfth centuries.[17]

The gravity of the punishment of death by slicing is further reflected in the fact that this mode of execution was always characterised as 'immediate' (*lijue*) whereas the other two forms - strangulation and decapitation - were divided into either 'immediate' or 'after the assizes' (*jianhou*). In the former category of punishment there could be no review, and the convicted prisoner was put to death as soon as possible after the emperor had upheld the death sentence.[18] In the latter, however, the death sentence was subject to re-examination by senior officials at a special meeting held in the season of death namely, the autumn. This re-examination offered various possibilities of a reprieve.

The system of capital punishment was neither applied uniformly nor was it without certain safeguards. Confucian values discouraged the punishment of disadvantaged classes of person and the penal codes, reflecting these values, generally refrained from imposing the death penalty for the elderly, the infirm, minors and other special categories.[19] As noted earlier, a system of obligatory review for all cases meant that higher level tribunals examined the merits of decisions made by the local courts and there was, as a result, a 'careful scrutiny of every capital case at the highest level, including imperial ratification, before life may be taken.'[20] As we have also noted, a decision to characterise a capital punishment as *jianhou* or 'after the assizes' diverted a case into a range of possibilities of delay and commutation including, in particular, the system of imperial amnesties. The latter often enabled convicted capital offenders to escape death through the granting of a reprieve and a reduction in punishment. A variety of considerations underlay this system, including not only a desire on the part of the Emperor to display his benevolence but also a belief that miscarriages of justice were threatening the universal harmonious order and that this harmony or balance needed to be restored by the corrective action of an amnesty.[21]

In their struggle for power in the two decades before their 'liberation' of the Chinese mainland in 1949 the Chinese communists relied on the death penalty as an important instrument for dispensing revolutionary justice.[22] In order to eliminate counterrevolutionaries and to impose political control, executions were carried out fairly extensively, and this policy continued after the establishment of a people's republic in 1949. Tensions between the left

110

and right wings of the Party were reflected acutely in the legal system as legal development oscillated between an approach based on the Soviet (and, indeed, more generally the continental or civilian) model which stressed the need for formal law and orthodox legal institutions such as the court and the people's procuratorate, and a more radical - almost millenarian approach - which, in criminal matters, meant large public trials, summary justice and frequent executions:

> During the Common Program era[23] 'people's tribunals' were often organised outside the regular court system to carry out nation-wide movements for social reform and to inflict severe punishment upon the enemy . . . the 'people's tribunals' were *ad hoc* in nature and only lasted through the duration of a given movement. As one of the major instrumentalities for wielding the power of the state, these tribunals were used extensively in the Agrarian Reform,[24] Three-Anti, and Five-Anti Campaigns.[25] So ruthlessly did they wage war against the 'hostile classes,' particularly during the Land Reform that a reign of terror was created.[26]

Leng provides an illustration of the sort of climate that prevailed:

> the Peking Municipal People's government held a huge public meeting for the accusation of counterrevolutionaries on May 20, 1951. Speaking before the aroused crowd Lo Jui-ching, Minister of Public Security, 'suggested' that some 220 criminals be sentenced to death. He was followed by Mayor P'eng Chen who wound up the drama by saying: "What shall we do with such a group of beast as these vicious despots, bandits, traitors and special agents?" "Shoot them!" the audience shouted. "Right, they should be shot," the Mayor replied. "Following this meeting we shall hand over the cases to the Military court of the Municipal Military Control Commission for conviction. Tomorrow, conviction, the next day, execution." The crowd responded with wild applause and loud cheers.[27]

Throughout much of the 1950s and, indeed at various times in the 1960s and 1970s, policy and practice fluctuated between this flexible populist approach, which often encouraged indiscriminate and unsanctioned executions, and the more formal, bureaucratic and Soviet inspired approach which laid stress on the need for a regular system of criminal justice. The latter encouraged the development of a conventional criminal code and one such code was on several occasions very nearly introduced, first in 1957 and then again in 1963. But the general dominance of the populist approach for the first three decades of socialist rule meant that such a code could not be introduced until 1979. The legislative framework for the sanctioning of criminally deviant behaviour - when it was applied - consisted instead of a variety of specific laws and administrative directives. The most important of these for the purpose of sanctioning sentences of death included the 1950 General Rules for the Organisation of People's Tribunals, the 1951 Law for the Punishment of Counterrevolutionaries, the 1951 Provisional Law on Guarding State Secrets, the 1951 Provisional Law on Penalties for Undermining the State Monetary System, the 1952 Law on Penalties for Corruption, and the 1952 Instructions Relating to the Suppression of Counterrevolutionary Activity.

Some of this legislation included the principle of crime by analogy. Thus, Article 16 of the 1951 Law for the Punishment of Counterrevolutionaries provided that 'persons who have committed other crimes with counterrevolutionary intent that are not specified in the law shall be punished according to analogous specified crimes in these Regulations.'[28] In this and a number of other ways traditional influences were fused with socialist attitudes to produce an authoritarian system of rule in which capital punishment was used fairly extensively - and without any meaningful procedural safeguards - as a weapon of class justice and retribution. It is not possible to determine with any accuracy the number of executions that took place in the first thirty years of socialist rule, but Mao Zedong himself acknowledged that by the mid-1950s more than 800,000 persons had been sentenced to death by the people's tribunals, and so the number certainly was not small.[29]

## CAPITAL PUNISHMENT IN THE ERA OF REFORM

The absence of criminal and criminal procedure laws was remedied in 1979 with the introduction of the Criminal Law and the Criminal Procedure Law. This legislation now provides the basic framework for capital punishment, although both laws are something of a synthesis of earlier provisions and have been modified in ways significant for the death penalty since they came into force on 1 January 1980.

The only method of execution permitted is that specified in article 45 of the Criminal Law: 'the death penalty is to be executed by means of shooting' - that is, by shooting the prisoner in the back of the head while he or she is kneeling. There are some fifty[30] - perhaps more[31] - capital crimes on the PRC statute books, and more than one half of these have been added since 1979 even though article 43 of the Criminal Law stipulates that 'the death penalty is only to be applied to criminal elements who commit the most heinous [*zuida eji*] crimes'.

Not surprisingly, in a people's democratic dictatorship, the largest category of capital offfence is *fangeming zui* or the crimes of counterrevolution,[32] although the evidence suggests that relatively few executions are now carried out for such offences.[33] Article 103 of the Criminal Law - echoing the emphasis in article 43 - lays down that the death penalty may be applied in such cases 'when the harm to the state and the people is especially serious and the circumstances especially odious.'[34]

The specific counterrevolutionary offences identified in the chapter of the Criminal Law dealing with 'Crimes of Counterrevolution' include 'colluding with foreign states in plotting to harm . . . the motherland' (article 91), conspiring (*yinmou*) to 'subvert the government or dismember the state' (article 92), encouraging a member of the armed forces, or the police, or the people's militia 'to defect to the enemy and turn traitor or to rise in rebellion' (article 93), defecting to the enemy and turning traitor 'when the circumstances are serious or it is a case of leading a group to defect to the enemy and turn traitor' or taking the principal role in leading 'members of the armed forces, people's police or people's militia to defect to the enemy and turn traitor' (article 94), leading or playing a significant role in an 'armed mass rebellion' (article 95), leading a raid on a prison or organizing a jailbreak (article 96), participating in espionage and related activities (article 97), carrying out acts of sabotage to promote counterrevolution such as causing explosions, theft of state records, hijacking aircraft, manufacturing arms (article 100), and mass poisoning or spreading infectious diseases for the purpose of promoting counterrevolution (article 101).

A second category of offences in the 1979 Criminal Law carrying the death penalty is *weihai gonggong anquan zui* or crimes of endangering public security. Here two forms of criminal conduct give rise to the possibility of capital punishment. Thus, article 106 makes it a capital offence to commit arson or similarly dangerous acts that 'lead to people's serious injuries or death or cause public or private property to suffer major losses'. Sabotage of public transport or the supply of utilities such as gas and electricity 'causing serious consequences' may also be a capital offence according to article 110.

A third area in which the 1979 Criminal Law contains important death penalty provisions is offences against the person.[35] Article 132 provides for the death penalty for intentional killing (*guyi sharen*). Rape, including statutory rape 'with a girl under the age of fourteen', in circumstances that are 'especially serious or a person's injury or death is caused' - including when two or more persons have jointly committed the offence - are punishable by death (article 49). The Criminal Law 1979 also made provision for the application of the death penalty in certain types of property offence (*qinfan caichan zui*) including cases of robbery with violence (article 150), and in cases of corruption by state officials in circumstances that are particularly serious.

The number of capital crimes has expanded very significantly in two main directions since 1980. On the one hand, there has been a growing preoccupation with crimes of violence, exploitation of women, and other conduct reflecting an essentially professional criminal life style. On the other hand, there has been a spiraling concern with the problems of corruption and 'economic crime' (*jingji fanzui*).[36] In addition, the scope of the death penalty has been expanded to protect the interests of the state in several ways. Both service personnel and ordinary citizens may be subject to the death penalty in a wide range of situations according to the 1981 Interim Regulations on the Punishment of Servicemen Who Commit Crimes Contrary to their Duties.

113

These Regulations provide for the imposition of the death penalty on 'any person who steals, collects or furnishes military secrets for the enemy or foreigners' (article 4), any person hindering by force or by threats service personnel from carrying out their duty in 'circumstances that are especially serious' or if 'a person's serious bodily injury or death is caused' (article 10), any person who destroys important weapons, equipment or military installations in very serious circumstances (article 12), any person colluding with the enemy to 'spread rumours so as to mislead others and undermine army morale' and the 'circumstances are especially serious' (article 14), persons whose desertion causes 'serious losses to a battle or campaign' (article 16), service personnel who disobey orders with the result that 'serious losses are caused to a battle or campaign' (article 17), any service personnel who intentionally make a false report jeopardizing military operations such that serious losses are caused to a battle or a campaign (article 19), and any service personnel who work for the enemy after surrendering (article 19), any service personnel who 'plunder or mistreats innocent residents in areas of military operations . . . and the circumstances are serious' (article 20). Moreover, divulging state secrets was made a capital offence in the 1988 Supplementary Provisions of the Standing Committee of the National People's Congress Concerning the Punishment of Crimes of Divulging State Secrets: 'persons who steal, spy on, buy or illegally provide state secrets for institutions, organizations and people outside the country . . . if the circumstances are especially serious . . . shall be sentenced to ... the death penalty.'

A more important area in which the death penalty has been extended is, however, serious 'professional' and 'organised' crime. Within a few years of the introduction of the Criminal Law in 1980, the Standing Committee of the National People's Congress supplemented that Law with a Decision Regarding the Severe Punishment of Criminal Elements who Seriously Endanger Public Security. This extended the death penalty, *inter alia*, to 'ringleaders of criminal hooligan groups or those who carry lethal weapons while engaging in criminal hooligan activities', to persons who injure state personnel or citizens reporting criminal conduct, or who abduct and sell people, or who manufacture arms, or who organise religious sects and secret societies,[37] or who lure women into prostitution and act as their pimps, or who teach others their criminal methods.

The concern with trafficking in human beings noted above has continued to grow and in September 1991 further rules were introduced regarding both involvement in prostitution and trading in women and children. Thus, the Decision of the Standing Committee of the National People's Congress on Strictly Forbidding Prostitution and Whoring extended or confirmed the possible application of the death penalty to a range of offences relating to prostitution. These include - when the 'circumstances are serious' - organising prostitution activities, forcing or inducing a female under the age of fourteen into prostitution, forcing more than one person into prostitution, repeatedly forcing a woman into prostitution, forcing a woman into prostitution after rape, causing serious injury or death 'or other serious consequences' to anyone forced into prostitution, and patronising a prostitute who is under the age of fourteen. This Standing Committee Decision also confirmed the provisions extending the death penalty to criminals who force or lure women into prostitution contained in the 1983 Decision on the Severe Punishment of Criminal Elements who Seriously Endanger Public Security.[38]

The Standing Committee also introduced in September 1991 a Decision on the Strict Punishment of Criminals who Abduct, Sell and Kidnap Women and Children. This provides more detailed provisions on the circumstances in which abducting and dealing in women and children may lead to the imposition of a sentence of death. These now include: leading a group that abducts and trades women and children, abducting and selling three or more women and children, raping an abducted woman, inducing or forcing women into prostitution, selling abducted women to others for prostitution, selling women and children outside the territory, and using force, threats or narcotics on women or children in order to sell them to others. This Decision also confirms the provisions contained in the 1983 Decision on, *inter alia*, the application of the death penalty on those who intentionally cause serious injury to or the death of another, or who injure state personnel or ordinary persons who supply information to the authorities on criminal conduct (for example, dealing in women and children).

The second area in which there has been a major expansion of offences carrying the death penalty since the early 1980s is corruption and economic crime. The shift in economic organization away from a state planned economy to one in which market forces and private ownership of the means of production have a significantly greater role to play has, since the early 1980s, created a vast array of new opportunities for corruption and commercial crime.

This transformation was not anticipated in the 1979 Criminal Law. In that code only one such offence was characterised as a capital offence. Thus, article 155 provided that the death penalty would be applied in especially serious cases in which 'state personnel take advantage of their office to engage in corruption involving articles of public property'. However, the rapid proliferation of corruption and economic crimes in the early 1980s[39] quickly encouraged the Standing Committee of the National People's Congress to introduce a further set of measures designed to strengthen the Criminal Law: the Decision of the Standing Committee of the National People's Congress Regarding the Severe Punishment of Criminals who Seriously Undermine the Economy (in force, 1 April 1982). This made soliciting or acceptance of bribes an offence of corruption under article 155 of the Criminal Law, and therefore punishable by death in serious circumstances. The Decision also made possible the imposition of the death penalty, as well as confiscation of property, in the more critical cases of smuggling, currency offences, speculation, large-scale theft, sale of dangerous drugs, and theft[40] and export of cultural relics. Moreover, according to the Decision state personnel who take advantage of their official position to commit such crimes are to be given particularly heavy punishment (including the death penalty). The traditional concern with voluntary surrender is given express emphasis, with the old law applying to those surrendering prior to 1 May 1982, or if already arrested 'truthfully confessing and acknowledging the entirety of [their] crimes, and in addition truthfully bringing accusations regarding the facts of crimes of other criminals.' Offenders refusing to surrender or to confess, and unwilling to collaborate, were subject to the new law.[41] More recently, article 2(1) of the Supplementary Regulations Concerning the Severe Punishment of Corruption and Bribery Offences, enacted in January 1988, provides that, 'where an individual receives through corruption (appropriation of public property) an amount in excess of 50,000 RBM' and 'the circumstances are especially serious, the death penalty will be imposed'. In June 1995. the Standing Committee of the National People's Congress adopted new rules on dealing with various financial irregularities - the Decision on the Punishment of Criminals Who Disrupt Financial Order. This Decision makes capital punishment a possible outcome in serious cases of counterfeiting, bogus insurance claims, bank fraud and so on.

The concern with economic offences has continued to grow, and in 1988 further steps were taken to strengthen the law in this area. A particularly important development was the introduction in 1988 of new rules governing smuggling. Article 4(1) of the Supplementary Regulations Concerning the Severe Punishment of Smuggling Offences, also enacted in January, 1988, stipulates that, 'where the value of the smuggled goods or articles exceeds 500,000 RMB', and 'the circumstances are especially serious, the death penalty will be imposed.'

Since the mid-1980s, there has also been a growing concern on the part of the authorities with narcotics. This problem has assumed particular importance in the south and west of the country, where drugs are illicitly imported from Burma and Thailand and either consumed locally or transported to Hong Kong and thence to Japan, the Philippines and the United States. The PRC's law enforcement agencies have attempted to deal with the problem by extensive propaganda campaigns aimed particularly at the young. But along with preventative measures, the criminal law has been further amended to allow for the application of heavy punishments. In particular, the Standing Committee of the National People's Congress introduced at the very end of 1990 an important Decision on the Prohibition of Dangerous Drugs. This provides, *inter alia,* that in a wide variety of circumstances 'smugglers, sellers, transporters and producers of narcotics' may be sentenced to death for their criminal conduct (article 2) and further stipulates 'severe punishment' (most probably, that is, the death penalty) in cases where adult offenders have involved minors in such activities as dealing and production. Moreover, heavier punishment is to be applied to state personnel who commit narcotics offences (article 11), increasing the possibility of a death sentence in cases involving such persons.

# PROCEDURAL DIMENSIONS

From the earliest days of socialist rule in China, the political campaign (*yundong*) has been used to play an important role in correcting deviant conduct. In a number of respects, these campaigns have served as an alternative to the application of law,[42] but since the early 1980s the two forms of social control have been used to supplement each other. There have been vigorous campaigns to deal with serious crime, juvenile crime, economic offences, narcotics, prostitution, political dissent and so on. Such campaigns have typically involved mass arrests, extensive propaganda work including large-scale sentencing rallies, and widespread use of the death penalty (sometimes with the courts being given specific death penalty quotas that must be met).

A very important dimension of these campaigns against crime has been the mass sentencing rally, often heavily publicised in the press as well as on radio and television. There is some reluctance to rely on the mass trial as a form of proceeding, presumably because of possible international criticisms. Nevertheless, the requirement in article 8 of the Criminal Procedure Law 1979 that all trials be held in public should not be seen as encouraging due process. The purpose is, rather, to educate the public. As a result, entry to many trials requires a ticket, and factories, schools and other units are encouraged to apply for tickets in order that their members might learn about criminal justice. The lessons to be learned are substantive, not procedural, and in cases involving the death penalty the outcome of the trial is determined beforehand in accordance with article 107 of the Criminal Procedure Law 1979:

> All major and difficult cases, where the president of the court considers it necessary to submit the matter to the adjudication committee [*shenpan weiyuanhui*] for discussion, are to be submitted by the president of the court to the adjudication committee for discussion and decision. The collegial panel [that is, the trial court] shall carry out the decision of the adjudication committee.

Moreover, the Supreme People's Court long ago stipulated that this direct involvement of the adjudication committee in a particular case may not be made known to the public. The adjudication committee is a very important feature of the PRC's criminal justice system. It is the mechanism by means of which the interests of the Chinese Communist Party and the state and other policy considerations can be brought to bear in a particular case.[43]

Thus, in a serious criminal case the verdict and the punishment are determined, on the basis of the dossier, in a meeting of various judges held before the trial itself. The trial court is bound by the decision of the Committee and the trial therefore becomes little more than a sentencing ritual – a system popularly referred to as *xian pan hou shen* or 'first the verdict, then the trial'. Defence lawyers are usually appointed no more than one week before the trial: 'after a people's court has decided to open a court session, it shall proceed with the following work . . . (2) deliver to the defendant a copy of the bill of prosecution of the people's procuracy no later than seven days before the opening of the court session and inform the defendant that he may appoint a defender or, when necessary, designate a defender for him' (article 110, Criminal Procedure Law 1979). The role of the defence lawyer therefore often consists of little more than putting forward pleas of mitigation. The trial is not conducted on the basis of any presumption of innocence - the courts are merely required to 'base themselves on the facts and take the law [that is, rather than political or class status] as the criterion' (article 4, Criminal Procedure Law, 1979). As noted above, there is in the Criminal Procedure Law of the PRC a requirement that trials be conducted in public (article 8) but this is to help ensure that the trial performs an educative function rather than to guarantee due process. Many news reports indicate that this process of education continues with a mass rally for sentencing in a capital case.[44]

The campaign element in the treatment of serious crime has also been manifested in a concern with rapid procedures. In particular, in 1981 the Standing Committee of the National People's Congress introduced a Decision that enabled Supreme People's Court approval of death sentences to be dispensed with if the defendant does not appeal and the capital offence is neither a crime of counterrevolution nor of corruption.[45] The Decision was originally introduced for two years as part of the anti-crime campaign but has been extended for cases of 'serious endangerment to public safety and public security in which death sentences are imposed' by article 13 of the revised Organic Law of the People's Courts (1983). The drive to speed up the handling of capital and other serious offences was taken one step further in September 1983 when the Standing Committee of the National People's Congress introduced its Decision Regarding the Procedure for Rapid Adjudication of Cases Involving Criminal Elements who Seriously Endanger Public Security. The Decision applies to cases in which the offence has been committed by 'criminal elements on whom death sentences should be imposed for killing another, rape robbery, causing explosions and other serious endangerment to public security, where the main criminal facts are clear, the evidence irrefutable and the people's indignation is very great'. In such circumstances 'the case should be rapidly and promptly adjudicated.' In particular, the Decision empowers the court to waive the requirement in the 1979 Criminal Procedure Law that it must inform the defendant no less than seven days before commencement of trial of the bill of prosecution and of her or his right to a defence lawyer (article 110(2)). The Decision also enables the court to disregard the requirements of notice laid down in article 110(4) of the 1979 Criminal Procedure Law namely, that it summon parties, notify defendants, witnesses, expert witnesses and interpreters, and deliver the subpoenas and notices, no later than three days before the opening of the court session. The trial of cases likely to lead to the death sentence is hastened still further by the Decision's reduction of the period within which an appeal may be brought from the ten days given in article 131 of the 1979 Criminal Procedure Law to a mere three days.

On the other hand, it should be borne in mind that speed is not always the essence in serious cases, especially if the authorities find it difficult to obtain sufficient evidence to secure a conviction. In such cases the prosecuting authorities may apply article 92 of the Criminal Procedure Law. This allows the Supreme People's Procuracy to petition the Standing Committee of the National People's Congress to approve postponement of a case. The Standing Committee's 1981 Decision Regarding the Question of Time Limits for Handling Criminal Cases relaxed the custody restrictions still further. The Decision provides that, *inter alia,* in a small number of criminal cases in which 'the circumstances are complex' the time limits regarding investigation, prosecution, trial of first instance, and appeals may be extended' with the approval not of the National People's Congress but, rather, of the relevant *local* people's congress. In addition, the PRC practices a system known as *shourong shencha* or 'custody and investigation' in which the Public Security Bureau (the principal police force in China) is able to detain suspicious persons for up to three months - the police are not subject to any external scrutiny of their operation of the system, and there are many reports of the three month limit being exceeded and the system being used to detain those suspected of criminal offences. Details of the system are unclear, in large part because the rules governing its operation are still not available to the public.

As we have indicated, much deviant behaviour in the PRC is dealt with extra-judicially. The application of the Criminal Law tends to be reserved for the more serious acts of deviance; very minor acts are likely to be dealt with informally by local mediation committees and similar bodies, while a great deal of fairly serious offending conduct is treated by means of the middle-range sanctions of administrative penalties (*xingzheng chufen*) and discipline (*ji*). There are several forms of discipline, of which the most important are work-place discipline and party discipline. The latter consist of warnings, demerits, serious demerits, demotion in grade, removal from office, probationary expulsion, and expulsion from the Communist Party. The Criminal Procedure Law 1979, at article 4, insists that 'no special privilege whatever is permissible before the law' and that the law applies equally to all citizens (see also article 5 of the Organic Law of the People's Courts). In reality, the existence of disciplinary sanctions - in particular, party discipline - creates something of a two track system. In many cases this means that cadres, reluctant to see fellow cadres severely punished, ensure that a problem is dealt with by the more lenient methods of party discipline only; in a small number of cases it means that a party member's guilt will be in effect determined by the Communist Party's Discipline Inspection Commission and her or his case then transferred to a court for trial and the application of the death penalty in the relevant circumstances. This direct involvement of the Party in the criminal process is justified on the ground that the problems of corruption and other forms of economic crime are so serious that Party must take the lead in dealing with such matters. In theory, of course, Party discipline and state law are meant to be kept apart, but the practice is often rather different.

The people's courts in the PRC are organised into a hierarchy consisting of four principal levels: Basic, Intermediate, Higher (that is, provincial level) and, at the apex, the Supreme People's Court in Beijing. The courts at all levels have a criminal division, and jurisdiction to try capital cases in the first instance lies with the Intermediate People's Courts: 'the Intermediate People's Courts have jurisdiction as courts of first instance over the following criminal cases - (1) counterrevolutionary cases; (2) ordinary criminal cases in which there may be a sentence of life imprisonment or death; and (3) criminal cases in which foreigners [are alleged to] have committed crimes or in which PRC citizens [are alleged to] have violated the lawful rights of foreigners' (Article 15, 1979 Criminal Procedure Law). The Criminal Procedure Law further stipulates that the trial court is to consist of one judge and two people's assessors[46] (article 105), although from my observations of criminal proceedings in China the *heyi ting* or collegial panel (as the trial court is officially called) is now more typically composed of three judges, especially in serious cases. If there is an appeal (*shangsu*) by the defendant, or a protest (*kangsu*) from the procuracy, the court consists of three or five judges. A majority decision by the judges suffices to secure conviction (article 106). According to the Criminal Procedure Law (article 125) judgement must be made within one month to six weeks of the court accepting the case. However, as we have noted, in major or complex cases - including those to which the death penalty may be applied - the time limit may be extended almost indefinitely.

As observed earlier, in traditional China a sharp distinction was drawn between death sentences that had to be carried out immediately, and those which were to take place 'after the assizes', the latter being a form of suspended death sentence which offered possibilities of reprieve and commutation to a lesser type of punishment. In the People's Republic something of this tradition has been maintained, with the development of the penalty of the 'death sentence with a two-year reprieve' (*sixing huanqi zhixing,* or *'sihuan'* as it is popularly referred to in China). Apparently first used in the early 1950s in legislation on corruption, waste and bureaucracy, it has developed in the 1980s into one of the most important kind of penalties handed down by the Chinese people's courts. Indeed, there are now calls in academic law circles to make *sihuan* into a penalty quite distinctive and separate from the death penalty itself,[47] as well as claims that it is a uniquely Chinese contribution to the global panoply of penalties. The suspended death sentence is seen as reflecting a 'spirit of revolutionary humanitarianism' (*geming rendao zhuyi jingshen*) which infuses the PRC's criminal process,[48] and is provided for in article 43 of the 1979 Criminal Procedure Law: 'in the case of a criminal element who should be sentenced to death, if immediate execution [*liji sixing*] is not essential, a two-year suspension of execution may be announced at the same time that the sentence of death is imposed, and reform through labor carried out and the results observed . . . Sentences of death with suspension of execution may be decided or approved by a Higher People's Court.' The norms used for determining whether the convicted offender has repented sufficiently and conducted herself or himself well enough in other respects to warrant the subrogation of the death penalty by life imprisonment at the end of the two years are not publicly available.

This concern with inducing a change of heart on the part of the offender and encouraging confession (the only mode of proof in traditional Chinese criminal courts) is reflected in other areas of the criminal law. In particular, we should note the system of *zishou* or voluntary surrender. As indicated above, this traditional Chinese institution is relied on to encourage confession, and the 1979 Criminal Law at article 63 provides: 'those who voluntarily surrender after committing a crime may be given a lesser punishment . . . if their crimes are relatively serious, they may also be given a mitigated punishment or be exempted from punishment if they demonstrate meritorious service [*ligong*].' Subsequent legislation, especially in the area of corruption and economic crime, has continued this emphasis as we have already observed in our discussion of the Decision of the Standing Committee of the National People's Congress Regarding the Severe Punishment of Criminals who Seriously Undermine the Economy (1982). In addition, the 1988 Supplementary Provisions of the Standing Committee of the National People's Congress Concerning the Punishment of the Crimes of Embezzlement and Bribery, stipulate at article 2(1) that, 'where the value of the smuggled goods or articles exceeds 500,000 *yuan*', and 'the circumstances are especially serious, the death penalty will be imposed.' However, for lesser offences hope was held out in paragraph 3(3) for persons willing to surrender themselves: 'if an individual who embezzles not less than 2,000 *yuan*, but less than 5,000 *yuan*, after committing the crime, voluntarily surrenders himself' renders meritorious service or shows signs of repentance and gives up the embezzled money of his own accord, he may be given mitigated punishment or exempted from criminal punishment and subjected to administrative sanctions by his unit or by the higher competent authorities.'[49] Further, paragraph 8 provides that those persons offering bribes 'may be given a mitigated punishment or exempted from criminal punishment' if they voluntarily surrender and confess before a prosecution has been initiated. It may be assumed from these provisions that in considering the application of the death penalty in the more serious corruption offences, a decision not to confess at an early stage of the investigation will render a suspect more liable to the application of the death penalty under article 2(1).

We should note that there are two categories of person against whom the death penalty may not be applied, regardless of the circumstances of the case: pregnant women and children under the age of eighteen. Both restrictions are long-standing and were repeated in the 1979 Criminal Law at article 44: the death penalty is not to be applied to persons 'who have not reached the age of eighteen at the time the crime is committed or to women who are pregnant at the time of adjudication.' In fact, the effective age limit for minors is sixteen because article 44 continues: 'persons who have reached the age of sixteen but

121

not the age of eighteen may be sentenced to death with a two-year suspension of execution if the crime committed is particularly grave.' It should be noted that the prohibition on capital punishment for women apparently applies also to women who have recently undergone an abortion.[50]

The PRC relies on a two trial system, with the defendants being permitted one appeal. This must be made to the court at the immediately superior-level. In order to ensure that defendants are not deterred from exercising their right of appeal should they so wish, the 1979 Criminal Procedure Law stipulates that the appellate court may not increase the punishment should the appeal fail. A first-instance decision may, however, also be protested against by the Procuracy under article 130 of the Criminal Procedure Law, and article 137 also provides that if there is both appeal and protest the court may increase the penalty. A second instance trial is a trial *de novo,* and the appellant is able to challenge findings of both fact and law, as well as the sentence. The court is required by article 134 to carry out a complete review of the facts and the law, and is not bound by the scope of the appeal or protest.

Not all trials, however, are completed with the conclusion of the appeal or the protest. It is also possible to re-open a legally effective judgement made by the court of second instance through the process of *shenpan jiandu* or 'trial supervision'. There are no time limits on this re-opening of the case. The extent to which this supervision system assists a defendant on whom the death penalty has been passed is, however, not clear. The case may be reopened on the application of not only the defendant but also a wide range of persons including 'the parties, victims, and their family members and citizens' (article 148) as well as a court president (article 149). Moreover, the execution of the original judgment is not suspended pending the outcome of the adjudication supervision. Somewhat worryingly, one academic commentator has concluded that 'adjudication supervision, by allowing broad discretion in the reopening judgments, renders case results vulnerable to temporal changes of state and Party policy.'[51]

Moreover, as we noted earlier, rights to appeal in serious criminal cases have been limited by the legislation accompanying the anti-crime campaigns of the early 1980s. Article 131 of the 1979 Criminal Procedure Law provides that an appeal may be lodged against a judgement within ten days, but should the defendant decide initially not to appeal, it appears that under the provisions of the Decision of the Standing Committee of the National People's Congress Regarding the Procedure for Rapid Adjudication of Cases Involving Criminal Elements Who Seriously Endanger Public Security (1981), the approval of the sentence by the relevant Higher People's Court may result in an execution being carried out within a few days.

## THE JURISPRUDENTIAL DEBATE

It will come as no surprise to the reader to learn that there is little or no genuine public debate in the PRC on the death penalty. In contrast to the experience of a number of other socialist regimes in the 1980s and early 1990s, China has both retained a people's democratic dictatorship and increased its reliance on the death penalty. The restrictions on the ability of the public in China to comment on the actions of the state are considerable, and they are particularly important in politically sensitive areas such as the death penalty. It is not possible to assess accurately the state of public opinion in China on the use of capital punishment and the possible abolition of this type of penalty. However, traditionally the popular Chinese view was that the death penalty is essential. Thus, *sharenzhe si* (those who kill [should] be killed) and *sharen peiming* (a life for a life) were important social values, and there is little sign that such thinking has changed in recent times. Nevertheless, it is possible to identify a number of arguments within legal circles which amount to fairly strong criticism of current policies and practice.

We noted above the continuing influence of Mao's theory of contradictions on China's system of justice, and justifications for the retention of a vigorous application of the death penalty are still redolent of the language and thought of Mao and his approach to social conflict. We may take as a recent example an essay published in mid-1991 in the law journal of one of China's most important law schools. In a study[52] of the thoughts of Mao Zedong on the death penalty, Kang Runsen argues that a correct understanding of the theory and practice of Mao's approach to the death penalty is highly relevant for 'the current fight against crime, protection of China's social stability, and beating back the adverse international anti-Communist current.' Drawing also on Marx and Engels he argues that after seizing power the proletariat must rely on the methods of dictatorship, including the weapon of the death penalty, to deal with bourgeois reactionaries: 'only in this way is [the proletariat] able to maintain its authority in the transition to socialism.' Lenin, too, had insisted that the death penalty must be boldly put to use in order to suppress counterrevolutionaries. Kang also emphasises that Mao recognised the need to maintain the people's democratic dictatorship with the aid of the death penalty, especially in the Movement to Suppress Counterrevolutionaries (1950-1951), when the enemies of the people and imperialists refused to accept their defeat with equanimity and engaged themselves in all kinds of disturbance and trouble. As a result, a number of counterrevolutionaries - those who had committed extremely heinous crimes - were executed. Without executions there could not be a satisfactory pacification of the wrath of the people (*minfen*). One of Mao's contributions, according to Kang, was his emphasis on the need for continued reliance on the death penalty even after the revolution had been consolidated in order to deal with reactionary elements who continue to plot and scheme for a restoration of the old order. However, continues Kang, it is important not to overlook the fact that Mao also insisted that there should be neither widespread arrests nor indiscriminate executions. Moreover, it is important not to drag in elements who are innocent. Overkill would have the adverse effect of transforming a non-antagonistic contradiction into an antagonistic contradiction, that is, alienating the people from socialist rule.

As a result, the Party's attempts to eliminate the reactionary classes and the system of exploitation did not resort to a policy of eliminating the reactionary elements themselves. The Party permitted neither individual nor class retribution but, instead, sought to deal with reactionary elements by subjecting them to reform through labour and reeducation in political ideology so that they might become new people (*xinren*). This policy of limited killing (*shaosha zhengce*) encourages a democratic spirit among the people, and fosters support for the Party. Too many killings will turn the masses away from the Party and leave it isolated. The Party has also stressed the importance of striking against the enemy in terms of certain standards, that is, not to kill erroneously (*buyao shacuo*). In doubtful cases, an arrest should not be made, and if guilt is not certain then an execution should not be carried out.

Nevertheless, in this description of the policy of limited killing, Kang reminds us that the policy does mean that capital punishment has an important role to play in the recreation of Chinese society. Where there are 'debts of blood' (*xue zhai*) or other serious offences have been committed, capital punishment has to be imposed, and carried out immediately, in order to quell public anger and to protect national interests. Kang places great stress on the continuing need to deal with the problem of public wrath because, he argues, it is an expression of the will of the people. A party committed to following the mass line must pay attention to the democratic expressions of the masses. Moreover, Kang stresses, full consideration must be given to the deterrent and educational effects of capital punishment - *sha yi jing bai* or 'to kill one will frighten one hundred'. According to Kang, China now pursues a policy of only *limited* executions, and this is manifested in a number of ways including, in particular, the system of the death sentence with a two year reprieve. Moreover, asserts Kang, in the Movement to Suppress Counterrevolutionaries, some ninety-nine per cent of those criminal elements sentenced to death with a two year reprieve behaved themselves and became transformed into new persons. The policy of limited killing and committing few mistakes eliminates counterrevolutionaries while preserving substantial amounts of labour power, thereby benefiting economic development.

In this analysis one may see within the rhetoric the outlines of some very familiar justifications for use of the death penalty: punishment (especially, we might add, through immediate executions), retribution or atonement (despite Mao's strictures against revenge), deterrence, prevention, and reform (through, in particular, the system of the death penalty with a two-year reprieve). Justifications of continued reliance on capital punishment, infused with this sort of rhetoric and these vindications, appear in many of the commentaries on the death penalty published in China, and as noted above in a people's democratic dictatorship there is little opportunity for meaningful public debate about the status and role of capital punishment. Nevertheless, the emphasis on punishment and deterrence contained in Kang's writing is not in fact as strong as it might be in the context of contemporary China, and the chief architect of China's post-Mao reform programme, Deng Xiaoping, has a very hard line approach to this issue. He identifies criminal law with punishment: 'in cracking down on crime and correcting unhealthy tendencies, we should use the legal system in criminal cases and education in non-criminal ones.'[53] The reference to 'the legal system' means, in particular, application of the death penalty.

China's policies on the continued use of the death penalty during the post-Mao reforms are not simply a reaction to a worsening crime situation. Even at the very beginning of the 1980s - that is, before the concern with the deteriorating crime situation had become acute - some commentators stressed the need to retain the death penalty in order to deal with serious crime as well as class struggle. Although acknowledging that China had succeeded in abolishing class divisions the argument is, in effect, that class struggle continues in modified form because it is necessary to deal with the conduct of counterrevolutionaries and those who carry out 'the most serious crimes' (*zuida ezui*). This argument also asserts that while the PRC does pursue a policy of carrying out as few executions as possible - 'the fewer executed the better [*sharen yueshao yuehao*]' - and while recognising that the death penalty's historical role has been to enable feudal and capitalist forces to oppress the proletariat, it would be wrong to abolish capital punishment in China's particular circumstances lest the minority of dangerous elements (*shehuishang shaoshu weixian fenzi*) who are incapable of reform get out of control. According to this view, western creeds promoting abolition, such as 'humanitarianism' (*rendao zhuyi*) and 'human rights' (*renquan*) are infused with class characteristics and are therefore unsuitable for the socialist context of the PRC. Protecting the small minority of counterrevolutionaries and other criminal elements, at the expense of the vast majority of the people, lacks humanity and seriously infringes human rights.[54] Since the early 1980s, the arguments in favour of continued use of the death penalty have been extended to include the need to correct the problem of economic crime. To these justifications may be added the claim that quite simply, the death penalty clearly works as a deterrent.[55]

There are, however, indications that some commentators see continued reliance on the extensive use of the death penalty as inappropriate for modern China. Calls for a more restrained approach have been made. It is argued that China and its Communist Party need to adhere to the PRC's self-proclaimed policy of 'restricting the use of the death penalty' (*xianzhi sixing shiyong*). According to this view,[56] the various decisions of the Standing Committee of the National People's Congress introduced in the 1980s,[57] have expanded excessively the range of crimes for which the death penalty may be applied. The authorities in the PRC should take heed of the arguments made in favour of abolition developed in capitalist societies in the seventeenth and eighteenth centuries. These arguments included a number of strands: capital punishment is outdated and irrational, punishment should be focused on reforming people rather than revenge (*fuchou*) or retribution (*baoying*), erroneous cases can not be corrected ('the head that has dropped to the ground can not be put back'[58]), the death penalty runs counter to humanitarian principles, the death penalty is an act of retribution that makes it impossible for the offender to repay her or his debt to the victim or the victim's family, capital punishment does not work as a deterrent, and so on. This 'restrictionist' analysis of capital punishment in the PRC asserts that the current international situation encourages abolition, and that many jurisdictions have either abolished the death penalty in law or in practice without undermining their social stability. Many of the countries that have retained the death penalty execute less people each year than does the PRC.

A third component of this argument is that China's current circumstances also require a more tempered approach to the death penalty. In this context it is important to note that, somewhat retrospectively, the PRC has justified its post-Mao shift to more capitalist economic policies by, *inter alia,* characterising its current state of development as manifesting only a 'primary stage' of socialism. During this stage expansion of the forces of production should be emphasised, and China's system of punishments accordingly must also protect and promote this expansion. It is therefore inappropriate to view the death penalty in terms of punishment or retribution, especially as most of those guilty of capital offences are able to reform themselves provided they are reeducated correctly. More specifically, the death penalty is not suitable in the two major areas in which the death penalty has been expanded in recent years. Thus, China has too many capital offences relating to economic and financially deviant conduct. The 1988 regulations on corruption and embezzlement[59] allow for an excessive application of the death penalty, and China's enhanced reliance on capital punishment for dealing with this sort of problem is exceptional when looked at comparatively. This observation comes close to a plea for attention to be given to the notion of proportionality - that the PRC's punishments for economic crimes simply do not fit those crimes. Secondly, there is a need to reduce the number of executions of young people. The official view that an increase in crime levels must be met by increased use of capital punishment is considered to be erroneous. The death penalty is the effortless solution for 'to execute people is easy, to reform people is difficult' (*sha ren rongyi; gaizao ren nan*). At present in China the majority of offenders are young people, and many of those on whom the death penalty is carried out are a mere nineteen or twenty years of age. The state has a duty to save (*wanjiu*) such people. Indeed, while China has well-developed organs for 'striking against criminal elements', it lacks mechanisms for preventing juvenile crime, and prevention work must therefore be strengthened.[60]

## THE DEATH PENALTY IN PRACTICE

The authorities in the PRC do not publish accurate and detailed statistics relating to either the number of death sentences that are passed, or the number of executions that take place, each year in China. But even though there is a dearth of official statistical evidence, we may speculate on the possible patterns of death penalty practice in the People's Republic. Various sources published in China do confirm, however, that the number of death sentences is steadily increasing and that the volume of executions actually carried out is also on the rise.[61] Assessments based on surveys of published Chinese sources made by Amnesty International indicate that since the early 1990s, between 1,800 and 2,400 death sentences have been passed each year with between 1,100 and 1,700 actual executions annually.[62] That China has the world's largest population, with between one quarter and one fifth of the total, must be borne in mind in this context, but it is clear nevertheless that the latter figures, if correct, gives the PRC one of the highest execution rates in the world.[63] In fact, the figures given above may well understate the true position. In the post-Tiananmen crackdown of political dissidents that took place in 1989 and 1990, it is likely that a substantial number of unpublicised executions took place,[64] primarily of those who had been involved in the pro-democracy movement of April and May 1989. Moreover, in the *Report of the Visit to China by the Delegation led by Lord Howe of Aberavon*, a 'reliable source' is quoted as indicating the number executed 'in the 18 months following August 1990 (and the commencement of a new Law and Order Campaign) may have been as many as 20,000.' Regardless of whether we accept this last figure, it does seem highly likely that the calculations based on information gleaned from various published reports in the PRC do not reflect the true extent of capital punishment in China.

The most important official source of annual statistics on criminal trials in the PRC is contained in the work reports presented each year by the President of the Supreme People's Court to the National People's Congress. These reports, however, only furnish figures for very broad categories of case, and refrain from providing any analysis of the statistics that would help us to assess more accurately the position on capital punishment. The language of the latest report,[65] which covers the year 1994, indicates nevertheless that the number of death sentences and executions very probably continued to increase in the year 1994. According to President Ren Jianxin 'courts across the country stepped up the struggle against and severely cracked down on serious criminal activity.' Nearly two-fifths (that is, 208,267 persons) of those found guilty of criminal offences (547,435) 'were sentenced to fixed term imprisonment of five or more years, to life imprisonment, or to death (including the death sentence with a two year reprieve).' Some 276,800 persons were convicted of offences relating to endangering public security, and some 168,000 of these convicted offenders were given sentences of five years' fixed term imprisonment or more for committing offences that endangered public security - that is, for offences against which the authorities urge the relevant bodies such as the courts to *daji* or 'strike', language again suggestive of the use of the death penalty. With official statistics of this scale, it does indeed seem safe to conclude that the 1,800 death sentences and 1,100 executions annually are conservative estimates.

The system of capital punishment in the PRC is, it would seem, directed primarily against young persons who are members of a gang[66] and who have been convicted of a crime of violence: their crimes are seen by the authorities as particularly onerous or, if the suspended death penalty is applied to them, their conduct during the two year period of the sentence is viewed by the authorities as insufficiently repentant to justify commutation to life or fixed term imprisonment. According to the analysis of one academic commentator, whose findings have been published in a leading PRC law journal,[67] more than fifty per cent of those persons executed in recent years have been between eighteen and twenty-five years of age. Another source states that the majority of those offenders who are executed are eighteen or nineteen years of age.[68] These are persons who, in the opinion of that commentator, often have little experience of the world, whose knowledge is limited, whose personalities are 'wild', and who could be reformed despite the fact that they have committed extremely serious crimes. Supreme People's Court statistics furnish some other clues to the likely social backgrounds of those given criminal convictions. In 1993, 451,920 persons were convicted of criminal offences, and nearly sixty-five per cent of these offenders are reported to have been 'peasants' (*nongmin*), some twelve per cent were 'workers' (*gongren*), eleven per cent were 'social idlers' (*shehui xiansan*), and just over two per cent were civil servants or 'state working personnel' (*guojia gongzuo renyuan*).[69] The high figure for those of 'peasant' status does reflect to some extent a lack of effective state control and a deteriorating crime situation in many parts of the countryside, a problem that the authorities have apparently been attempting to remedy since mid-1993. The President of the Supreme People's Court provided the National People's Congress with an example of the sort of trouble that has to be dealt with in the countryside when he reported that in recent times the courts have:

> actively taken part in a concerted drive to rectify and improve public order in rural areas throughout the country, forcefully striking at flagrant hooliganism and other evil criminal activities in the countryside, and severely punishing according to law a group of criminal offenders who had seriously disrupted public order in rural areas. Take, for example, the serious case of the Wang Hanying group of hooligans [*liumang zatuan*] in . . . Hainan Province. The Wang father and son, called the 'southern despots of modern times' by the local masses, bullied and oppressed the people and committed all kinds of evil. The Hainan Provincial Higher People's Court sentenced five principal members of the gang of hooligans to death and other members to severe punishment according to the law,[70] winning applause from the people.[71]

It also very likely, however, that the high number of convictions for the peasants includes a substantial portion who are the so-called *mangliu* namely, the newly emerging transient or floating population - persons of rural domicile who are 'temporarily' working in the cities. Estimated to number some 100 million (approximately 8 per cent of the total population)[72] these persons provide the mobile labour and many of the entrepreneurs that have been crucially important in China's economic reforms. For a variety of reasons, the Chinese authorities have been unwilling to offer such persons equal 'rights, welfare, or security' so that they 'occupy the secondary track in a dual labour market as do migrants the world round.'[73] Statistical research indicates that the floaters are mainly young men. Moreover, like migrant workers in many other societies, China's floating population is seen in stereotyped fashion as prone to criminal conduct and therefore liable to attract the suspicion of the police, and to be treated in an arbitrary fashion. According to one observer:

> supposedly these people were responsible for 30 percent of the crimes in Wuhan in 1986, and committed 32.2 percent of the robberies, 33.7 percent of the swindling, and 22 percent of the looting, rapes, and murders in Shanghai in 1987. Floaters are also held for scalping transportation tickets and selling pornography; but larceny is the most frequent charge. As of 1988, the Beijing public security arrested as many as forty to fifty of them daily.[74]

In these circumstances, it seems safe to conclude that the floating population supplies a disproportionately large number of the convicted offenders of 'rural status' who are in fact executed.

Serious crimes in the area of economic activity, and corrupt conduct by government officials, are viewed in a particularly grave light by the PRC authorities because of the adverse effects that they have on China's development as a modern socialist society. As we have seen, these are areas in which the use of the death penalty has been significantly expanded on several occasions since the Criminal Law came into force at the beginning of 1980 - first, in the Standing Committee 1982 decision on severe punishment for those who commit economic offences, and secondly in the 1988 decisions on embezzlement and bribery and on smuggling offences. Many cases reported in official and semi-official sources emphasise the willingness of the authorities to take the 'correct' line of action with even quite senior officials and to punish them severely. Emphasis is laid in the 1979 Criminal Procedure Law on equality before the law (article 4) but sentences for officials in many kinds of offences are to be more severe. Nevertheless, as we have also noted, this is an area in which administrative sanctions and discipline have been used to treat leniently senior and other important party members. The statistics of the Supreme People's Court on criminal convictions suggest that economic offences and corruption are areas that now occupy second place in the official concerns with deviant conduct.[75] In 1994, some 20,000 persons were convicted of offences such as embezzlement, bribery and diverting public funds, and of those convicted some 6,400 were given sentences of 'fixed term imprisonment' of five years or more, life sentences, or the death sentence (including the death sentence with a two year suspension). In addition, some 13,600 persons were convicted of offences related to undermining the economic order, with no details being provided of the incidence of heavy punishments. Clearly, then, convictions for corruption and related offences and for economic crimes are currently running at a rate of less than one eighth of the rate for offences against public order. In these circumstances, one would expect the incidence of capital punishment also to be substantially lower for this sort of offence. Nevertheless, the use of capital punishment in this area is given great public emphasis, with deterrence apparently its most important function. Thus, the 1995 work report of the Supreme People's Court not only notes that in 1994 one of those convicted of corruption offences included a deputy minister but in addition highlights an embezzlement case:

> not long ago the Guizhou Provincial High Court sentenced to death Yan Jianhong, formerly Deputy Director of the Guizhou Provincial Planning Commission and formerly Chairman of the Board of Directors of the Guizhou International Trust and Investment Company for . . . embezzling 2.2 million *yuan*, pocketing 2.4 million *yuan* in oublic funds, obtaining 400,000 *yuan* though speculation, and receiving a bribe of 20,000 *yuan*. In addition, the former director of the Public Security Department for Guizhou, Guo Zhengmin, was given the death penalty with a two year suspension for receiving a bribe of 170,000 *yuan*. In order to . . . strengthen the struggle against corruption, the people's courts enhanced their propaganda work by holding open trials and by pronouncing judgments publicly. Since the beginning of [1994] the Supreme People's Court . . . made public through news conferences and . . . reporting . . . the results of the trials of forty-nine major cases that had worried the masses and that had a very significant social impact. [76]

Many news reports published recently indicate a broadly similar policy in cases of economic crimes other than corruption related activities.

## CONCLUSIONS

The data and the interpretations presented in this paper are necessarily tentative, for the death penalty - like the criminal law in general - is a politically sensitive issue in the PRC, and it is difficult to construct an accurate picture on the basis of information that often has been filtered by and infused with ideological values. There is a great deal of material available from Chinese sources, but much of it is repetitive and it lacks the kind of detail that is needed for accurate and full analysis. However, it has been possible to assert certain facts with confidence and to draw some broad conclusions.

It is clear that the death penalty remains central to the Chinese leadership's policies and practices of social control. Heavy punishment, especially capital punishment, is one of the two faces of Chinese justice, and as an expression of the people's democratic dictatorship its use is designed to ensure that those seriously intent on criminal or rebellious conduct are too frightened to transform their felonious or seditious thoughts into action. At the same time, much routine social conflict is handled through the ostensibly consensual and democratic methods of people's mediation, [77] and from the Chinese leadership's point of view there was little or no inconsistency in their

130

decision in June 1989 not only to crackdown severely on democratic protesters but also, just a few days later to introduce new rules governing the organization and work of people's mediation committees.[78]

The Chinese leadership as presently constituted is unlikely to relax current policies emphasising capital punishment, even though it is aware of international criticism of China's policies in this area and despite jurisprudential discussions within legal circles which point to some serious problems in these policies, especially in relation to the expansion of the scope of capital punishment through the various decisions of the Standing Committee of the National People's Congress and other developments subsequent to the introduction of the Criminal Law in 1979. China views herself as a society which is moving away from the anarchy and chaos of the Cultural Revolution to a position of wealth and power on the international scene. Law is viewed as a crucial element in this process because, *inter alia*, it provides the social stability and political certainty that the Chinese leadership regards as essential for economic development. However, this law is understood in a melange of traditional and ideological terms, so that it remains closely associated with heavy punishment. China is unlikely to cast off easily its traditions of, and ideological commitment to, capital punishment, and given that its leaders are extremely sensitive to international criticism, there very probably will be no shift in policy on the death penalty until major political changes have occurred. The lack of judicial independence (as that value is understood in common law jurisdictions), and the domination of the legislative process by the Party,[79] do not encourage optimism. The prospects for such political change in the short term or in the medium term are not at all good, if only because the current leadership played a central role in the post Tiananmen crackdown. However, a system that is now based politically on a mix of material benefits and coercion, with little real support being generated by the radical socialist ideology that the regime once espoused and used so effectively to mobilise people, is probably a great deal less secure in its rule than the current leadership apparently believes.

# ENDNOTES

1. A number of very useful discussions of various aspects of post-Mao China's efforts at legal reform may be found in Stanley B. Lubman (ed.), *China's Legal Reforms*, in *The China Quarterly*, (Special Issue), No. 141, March 1995.

2. For an interesting description of these legislative developments see Peng Zhen, 'Explanation of the Seven Draft Laws,' in Legislative Affairs Commission of the Standing Committee of the National People's

Congress, *The Laws of the People's Republic of China, 1979-1982,* (Beijing, Foreign Languages Press, 1987), pp. 420-431.

3. A succinct account of the significance of the new direction in legal development followed in the People's Republic of China since 1979 is provided in Stanley B. Lubman, 'Introduction: the future of Chinese Law,' in Stanley B. Lubman (ed.), *China's Legal Reforms,* in *The China Quarterly,* (Special Issue), No. 141, March 1995, pp. 1-21.

4. For earlier accounts of the death penalty in modern China see, in particular, the excellent essays by Davis and Scobell: Stephen B. Davis 'The Death Penalty and Legal Reform in the PRC,' *Journal of Chinese Law,* Vol. 1, No. 2 (1987), pp. 303-334; Andrew Scobell, 'The Death Penalty in Post-Mao China,' *The China Quarterly,* No. 123, September 1990, pp. 503-520, and 'Strung up or shot down?: the death penalty in Hong Kong and China and implications for post-1997,' *Case Western Reserve Journal of International Law,* Vol. 20, No. 1 (1988), pp. 147-167.

5. In addition, now that the threat from counterrevolution is seen as having been contained the belief that political deviance should be corrected through reforming the deviant's consciousness means that long-term imprisonment is the preferred way for dealing with political dissent.

6. This formal legal system is the product of three legal traditions: Chinese, socialist and civilian - the last means, *inter alia,* that statutory law takes the form of codes, interpretation of law is primarily legislative rather than judicial, and the system of criminal prosecution is essential inquisitorial in nature.

7. Article 1 of the *Da Qing Lü Li* or *Qing Penal Code* laid out not general principles of the law but, rather, provided a table of punishments.

8. See Mao Tse-tung, *Selected Works of Mao Tse-tung* (Vol.5) (Beijing: Foreign Languages Press, 1977), pp. 384-421.

9. See, in particular, Michael Palmer, 'The Revival of Mediation in the People's Republic of China: Extra-Judicial Mediation,' in W. E. Butler (ed.) *Yearbook on Socialist Legal Systems 1987,* (New York, Dobbs Ferry: Transnational Books, 1988), pp. 219-277, at pp. 228-230; 'What makes socialist law socialist? - the Chinese case' in F. J. M. Feldbrugge (ed.) *The Emancipation of Soviet Law,* Dordrecht: Kluwer Academic Publishers, 1992), pp. 51-72, at pp. 68-70.

10. See Michael Palmer, 'The Revival of Mediation in the People's Republic of China: Extra-Judicial Mediation,' in W. E. Butler (ed.) *Yearbook on Socialist Legal Systems 1987*, (New York, Dobbs Ferry: Transnational Books, 1988), pp. 219-277

11. On changing views of property relations in post-Mao China see Michael Palmer, 'China's New Inheritance Law: Some Preliminary Observations,' in T. H. Pairrault, S. D. R. Feuchtwang, and A. Hussain (eds.) *Transforming China's Economy in the Eighties: (1) the Rural Sector, Welfare and Employment*, Boulder, Colorado: Westview Press, 1988), pp. 169-197.

12. Derk Bodde and Clarence Morris, *Law in Imperial China*, (Cambridge, Massachusetts: Harvard University Press, 1967), at pp. 13-14.

13. On the contrasts between Confucian and Legalist approaches to law and social control, see Benjamin Schwartz, 'On Attitudes toward Law in China,' in Milton Katz, *Government Under Law and the Individual*, (Washington D.C.: American Council of Learned Societies, 1957), pp. 27-39.

14. See, for example, A. F. P. Hulsewé, 'Ch'in and Han Law,' in *The Cambridge History of China, Vol. 1, the Ch'in and Han Empires 221 B.C.- A.D. 200*, (Cambridge, England: Cambridge University Press, 1980), pp. 520-544, at p. 522, Derk Bodde and Clarence Morris, *Law in Imperial China*, (Cambridge, Massachusetts: Harvard University Press, 1967), pp. 43-48, and Jonathan K. Ocko, 'I'll Take it All the Way to Beijing: Capital Appeals in the Qing,' *Journal of Asian Studies*, Vol. 47, No. 2, pp. 291-315, at p. 292.

15. Derk Bodde and Clarence Morris, *Law in Imperial China*, (Cambridge, Massachusetts: Harvard University Press, 1967), p. 92.

16. Ernest Alabaster, *Notes and Commentaries on Chinese Criminal Law and Cognate Subjects*, (London: Luzac & Co., 1899), pp. 58-59.

17. Derk Bodde and Clarence Morris, *Law in Imperial China*, (Cambridge, Massachusetts: Harvard University Press, 1967), pp. 94-95.

18. In particular, the application of the death penalty for one of the so-called Ten Abominations (Shi E) could not wait until after the assizes. These offences included treason, parricide, mutliation for witchcraft

purposes of a person still alive and so on, and they were punished 'immediately' by means of death by slow slicing.

19. For a detailed account of the special legal provisions protecting weaker members of society see Derk Bodde, 'Age, Youth, and Infirmity in the law of Ch'ing China,' in *Essays on China's Legal Tradition*, (eds.) Jerome Alan Cohen, R. Randle Edwards, and Fu-mei Chang Chen, (Princeton, New Jersey: Princeton University Press, 1980).

20. Derk Bodde and Clarence Morris, *Law in Imperial China*, (Cambridge, Massachusetts: Harvard University Press, 1967), p. 131.

21. B. E. McKnight, *The Quality of Mercy: Amnesty and Traditional Chinese Justice*, (Honolulu: University of Hawaii Press, 1991).

22. See, for example, Hiroshi Oda, 'Chinese Law and Procedure in the Chinese Soviet Republic,' in W. E. Butler (ed.), *The Legal System of the Chinese Soviet Republic 1931-1934*, (New York, Dobbs Ferry: Transnational Books, 1983), pp. 53-70, at p. 54.

23. That is, during 1949 and the early 1950s when the Common Programme of the Chinese People's Political Conference served as the constitution of the new People's Republic. Article 7 of the Common Programme called for the severe punishment (that is, in most cases, the death penalty) for those who continued to carry out counterrevolution.

24. That is, the land reform campaigns of 1949-1953. These not only redistributed much land to the peasants but also involved trials by people's tribunals and subsequent executions of landlords and other class enemies.

25. The 'Three-Anti' movement was designed to combat corrupt, wasteful and excessively 'bureaucratic' conduct among Party and government members. The 'Five-Anti' movement was aimed at the problems of bribery, tax evasion, fraud. theft of state economic secrets, and theft of other state property. These movements, which were closely co-ordinated, commenced late in 1951 and came to an end in the middle of 1952.

26. Leng Shao-chuan, *Justice in Communist China: A Survey of the Judicial System of the Chinese People's Republic*, (Oceana Publications: Dobbs Ferry, New York, 1967), p. 35.

27. Leng Shao-chuan, *Justice in Communist China: A Survey of the Judicial System of the Chinese People's Republic,* (Oceana Publications: Dobbs Ferry, New York, 1967), p. 35.

28. The principle of determining guilt by analogical reasoning is still present in the criminal law (at article 79 of the 1979 Law), but all the indications are that it has not been used very much - perhaps because in the Criminal Law crimes are defined so broadly and the distinction between minor and serious circumstances affords the courts a great deal of discretion (see, also, n. 34, below).

29. See, Mao Tse-tung, 'On the Correct Handling of Contradictions among the People (Speaking Notes),' in Roderick MacFarquhar, Timothy Cheek, and Eugene Wu (eds.), *The Secret Speeches of Chairman Mao: From the Hundred Flowers to the Great Leap Forward,* (Cambridge Mass.: Harvard University Press, 1989), pp. 131-189, at p. 142.

30. Wang Minghu reports that by 1994 the number of offences which carried the death penalty had risen to fifty - see Wang Minghu, 'Jianchi yi Mao Zedong renmin minzhu zhuanzheng sixing guan zhidao sixing lifa yu sifa,' (Persist in using the death penalty [as found] in Mao Zedong's people's democratic dictatorship to guide our legislation on, and judicial administration of, the death penalty), *Faxue Pinglun,* No. 1 for 1994, pp. 9-15, and p. 32, at p. 12).

31. For a variety of reasons, it is not possible to be precise about the number of crimes for which the death penalty actually applies - for example, secret legislation may exist that extends the range of capital crimes, provincial legislation sometimes contains punishments more severe than national law and this discrepancy is not always corrected, and so on.

32. Defined in article 90 as any act 'endangering the People's Republic of China committed with the goal of overthrowing the political power of the dictatorship of the proletariat and the socialist system.'

33. Certainly, the number of convictions for counterrevolutionary offences is now very small - according to official statistics there were only 187 concluded cases for counterrevolutionary crimes in 1993 - see Zhongguo Falü Nianjian Bianji Bu, *Zhongguo Falü Nianjian 1994,* (Law Yearbook of China, 1994), (Beijing, Zhongguo Falü Nianjian Chubanshe, 1994), at p. 1027. It should be noted, however, that it seems that political dissidents

are increasingly charged with ordinary criminal offences rather than the 'controversial' crime of counterrevolution and this may have a significant impact on the figures.

34. The distinction between 'minor' and 'serious' circumstances runs right through the criminal law. If the circumstances are minor the court may deem that no offence at all has occurred (article 10, 1979 Criminal Law). If the circumstances are considered to be serious then a convicted offender is likely to face a substantial sentence. Clearly, this distinction gives the courts a great deal of discretion when sentencing. The seriousness of the circumstances is assessed in accordance with a number of factors. These include the motive for and method used in the crime, the underlying cause of the offence, whether there were previous offences, whether the individual was the instigator or the principal member of a gang, whether the crime was 'plotted', whether the effects were especially harmful (including the degree of economic harm to the state or society) and whether the individual has cooperated with the authorities during the investigation and so on. See, for example, Ge Ping and Wang Honggu, 'Lun sixing,' (On the death penalty), *Faxue Yanjiu*, No. 1 for 1980, pp. 29-32, and p. 44, at p. 30.

35. These are contained in Chapter 4 of the second section of the Law: 'Crimes of Infringing the Rights of the Person and the Democratic Rights of Citizens' (*qinfan gongmin renshen quanli, minzhu quanli zui*).

36. The concept of 'economic crime' corresponds very broadly with what is known in the West as 'commercial crime', although it does include certain forms of conduct - such as speculation - that would not be considered as crimes in non-socialist jurisdictions. For a general discussion of the problems of economic crime on the PRC see: Deborah E. Townsend, 'The Concept of Law in Post-Mao China: A Case Study of Enonomic Crime,' *Stanford Journal of International Law*, Vol. 24, No. 1, pp. 227-258.

37. That is, a traditional form of organised crime in China that has resurfaced in the 1980s in response to the more liberal economic climate.

38. Although, as noted below, it would seem that as a result of an unannounced change in policy the death penalty is not in practice to be applied to persons convicted of these particular offences.

39. As the early 1950s legislation and the 'Three Antis' and 'Five Antis' indicate, this sort of deviant conduct has always been viewed with a great deal of concern by China's socialist authorities.

40. The amounts involved in theft cases being revised upwards from time to time in order to take into account inflation.

41. See S. C. Leng and H. D. Chiu, *Criminal Justice in Post-Mao China: Analysis and Documents*, C. Albany: State University of New York Press, 1985), at pp. 139-140.

42. As Leng and Chiu clearly indicate in the following passage: 'during political campaigns or mass movements, legal procedures were often totally disregarded and ad hoc organs were set up to arrest, investigate, and detain alleged offenders for almost unlimited periods. Mass trials and public judgment meetings were held to dispense people's justice, which performed not only a deterrent function but a propaganda education function of raising the people's political awareness' (S. C. Leng and H. D. Chiu, *Criminal Justice in Post-Mao China: Analysis and Documents*, Albany: State University of New York Press, 1985), at p. 25.

43. The President of the Court usually chairs this committee, even though he has often been appointed because he is a trustworthy member of the Communist Party rather than someone solidly trained in the law. The overwhelming majority of judges in China are members of the Party.

44. See for example, in the section below entitled 'The Death Penalty in Practice' and the observations contained therein on sentencing rallies.

45. See paragraph 2 of the Decision of the Standing Committee of the National People's Congress Regarding the Procedure for the Rapid Adjudication of Cases Involving Criminal Elements Who Seriously Endanger Public Security, (1983).

46. People's assessors are intended to provide a lay element, as well as in many cases specialised knowledge, in the adjudication process.

47. See, in particular, the arguments of Cheng Liangwen, 'Sihuan gai ying wei duli xing zhong,' (The death sentence with a two year reprieve should be made an independent type of penalty), *Xiandai Faxue*, No. 2 for 1990, pp. 6-9.

48. Ge Ping and Wang Honggu, 'Lun sixing,' (On the death penalty), *Faxue Yanjiu*, No. 1 for 1980, pp. 29-32, and p. 44.

49. Moreover, by article 5 of the Supreme People's Procuracy Regulations on the Exemption from Prosecution in Corruption and Bribery Cases (1991) those who have committed this particular offence but voluntarily surrendered themselves may be exempted from prosecution.

50. Xiao Shengxi, 'Sixing fuhezhong ying zhuyi de jige wenti,' (Several issues that should be given attention in the review of cases in which the death sentence has been passed), *Zhengzhi yu Falü*, No. 6 for 1985, pp. 46-47, at p. 47.

51. Margaret Y. K. Woo, ' Adjudication Supervision and Judicial Independence in the P. R. C.,' *The American Journal of Comparative Law*, Vol. 39, pp. 95-119 at p. 119.

52. Kang Yunshen, 'Lun Mao Zedong dui Ma-Liezhuyi sixing lilun chuangzaoxing de fazhan,' (On Mao Zedong's creative development of the Marxist-Leninist theory of the death penalty). *Zhengfa Luntan*, No. 6 for 1991, pp. 29-32.

53. Deng Xiaoping, 'Political Structure and Sense of Legality,' in *Fundamental Issues in Present Day China*, (Beijing: Foreign Languages Press, 1987), pp. 145-148, at p. 146.

54. Ge Ping and Wang Honggu, 'Lun sixing,' (On the death penalty), *Faxue Yanjiu*, No. 1 for 1980, pp. 29-32, and p. 44, at p. 29.

55. One Chinese source baldly makes the claim that 'China has a large population, but a relatively low crime rate, and social stability has been maintained, so the death penalty is working. It protects the life and property of the vast majority of our citizens' - Zhao Bingzhi, 'Guanyu sixing cun fei ji qi fazhan qushi de sikao,' (Reflections on the retention, abolition, and the trend of development of the death penalty), *Faxue* (Beijing), No. 5 for 1991, pp. 106-110, at p. 110.

56. See, in particular, Li Yunlong, 'Chuji jieduan sixing wenti yanjiu,' (Research into several questions concerning the primary stage of the death penalty), *Faxue*, [Beijing] No. 9 for 1989, pp. 111-114.

57. In particular, the 1981 Decision on escaped prisoners, the 1982 Decision on economic crimes, and the 1983 Decision on criminals who endanger public order.

58. That is, in Chinese *'rentou luodi buneng zai zhuangshang'* - Li Yunlong, 'Chuji jieduan sixing wenti yanjiu,' (Research into several questions concerning the primary stage of the death penalty), *Faxue*, [Beijing] No. 9 for 1989, pp. 111-114, at p. 111.

59. That is, the 1988 Supplementary Provisions of the Standing Committee of the National People's Congress Concerning the Punishment of the Crimes of Embezzlement and Bribery.

60. This prevention has mainly consisted to date of the introduction at both the national and the provincial levels of special codes for the protection of the rights and interests of minors. See Michael Palmer, 'Minors to the Fore: juvenile protection legislation in the PRC,' in M. Freeman (ed.) *Annual Survey of Family Law: 1991*, vol. 15, London: The International Society on Family Law, 1992, pp. 299-308.

61. See, for example, Wang Minghu, 'Jianchi yi Mao Zedong renmin minzhu zhuanzheng sixing guan zhidao sixing lifa yu sifa,' (Persist in using the death penalty [as found] in Mao Zedong's people's democratic dictatorship to guide our legislation on, and judicial administration of, the death penalty), *Faxue Pinglun*, No. 1 for 1994, pp. 9-15, and p. 32, at p. 13.

62. See *Report of the Visit to China by the Delegation led by Lord Howe of Aberavon*, (London: HMSO, 1993) at p. 39. Amnesty's figures for 1994, the latest year for which annual statistics have been compiled, are 2,496 death sentences passed and 1,791 executions carried out. However, Amnesty International takes the view that its 'figures are far below the actual number of death sentences passed and executions carried out during the year' (Amnesty International, China: Death Penalty Figures Recorded for 1994. March 1995, AI Index, ASA 17/17/95).

63. For 1991 there were nearly 2,100 executions documented by Amnesty International for the entire world, and the executions that took place in China therefore very probably totalled more than one half of the global figure. See *Report of the Visit to China by the Delegation led by Lord Howe of Aberavon*, (London: HMSO, 1993) at p. 39.

64. In addition, that is, to the '400 to 800' who were extra-judicially executed in the official assault on the Square itself during the night of 3-4 June 1989. See International League for Human Rights and The Ad hoc Study Group on Human Rights on China, *Massacre in Beijing: the events of 3-4 June 1989 and their aftermath*, (New York, 1989), at p. 18.

65. 'Zuigao Renmin Fayuan Gongzuo Baogao,' (Supreme People's Court Work Report 1995), *Xinhua Yuebao*, No. 4 for 1995, pp. 37-42.

66. Especially if this gang takes the form of a 'secret society' or *heishehui* -- an institution which has traditionally been China's principal form of organised crime and which, as noted above, has been reviving in importance in recent times.

67. See, for example, Wang Minghu, 'Jianchi yi Mao Zedong renmin minzhu zhuanzheng sixing guan zhidao sixing lifa yu sifa,' (Persist in using the death penalty [as found] in Mao Zedong's people's democratic dictatorship to guide our legislation on, and judicial administration of, the death penalty), *Faxue Pinglun*, No. 1 for 1994, pp. 9-15,and p. 32, at p. 13.

68. Li Yunlong, 'Chuji jieduan sixing wenti yanjiu,' (Research into several questions concerning the primary stage of the death penalty), *Faxue*, [Beijing] No. 9 for 1989, pp. 111-114, at p.114.

69. Dong Wenpu, 'Xingshi shenpan' ('Criminal Adjudication') in Zhongguo falü bianjibu, *Zhongguo Falü Nianjian 1994 (Law Yearbook of China 1994)*, (Beijing: Falü Chubanshe, 1994), pp. 95-96.

70. It should be noted here that the phrase 'according to law', or *yifa* in the original Chinese text, refers not to due process but, rather, to the heavy punishment that is involved in the application of the criminal law, as opposed to administrative penalties and discipline.

71. 'Zuigao Renmin Fayuan Gongzuo Baogao,' (Supreme People's Court Work Report 1995), *Xinhua Yuebao*, No. 4 for 1995, pp. 37-42, at p. 37-38.

72. Estimates of their number vary. Thus , one observer writing in the early 1990s suggests 80 million - see Dorothy J. Solinger, *China's Transients and the State: a Form of Civil Society*, (Hong Kong: Hong Kong Institute of Asian-Pacific Studies, 1991), at p. 10. Others, writing more recently, suggest that the figure may now be as high as 150 million - see W. Wo-lap Lam and F. Fook-lun Leung, *China After Deng: a report submitted to the Sub-*

140

*Committee on Asia and the Pacific, Committee on International Relations, U.S. Congress,* (July 20, 1995) at p. 12.

73. Dorothy J. Solinger, *China's Transients and the State: a Form of Civil Society,* (Hong Kong: Hong Kong Institute of Asian-Pacific Studies, 1991), at p. 11.

74. Dorothy J. Solinger, *China's Transients and the State: a Form of Civil Society,* (Hong Kong: Hong Kong Institute of Asian-Pacific Studies, 1991), at p. 20.

75. See those presented in 'Zuigao Renmin Fayuan Gongzuo Baogao,' (Supreme People's Court Work Report 1995), *Xinhua Yuebao,* No. 4 for 1995, pp. 37-42.

76. 'Zuigao Renmin Fayuan Gongzuo Baogao,' (Supreme People's Court Work Report 1995), *Xinhua Yuebao,* No. 4 for 1995, pp. 37-42, at p. 38.

77. For a fuller account of this system of people's mediation see Michael Palmer, 'The Revival of Mediation in the People's Republic of China: Extra-Judicial Mediation,' in W.E. Butler (ed.) *Yearbook on Socialist Legal Systems 1987,* New York, Dobbs Ferry: Transnational Books, pp. 219-277.

78. Michael Palmer, 'What makes socialist law socialist? - the Chinese case' in F. J. M. Feldbrugge (ed.) *The Emancipation of Soviet Law,* (Dordrecht: Kluwer Academic Publishers, 1992) at p. 69.

79. See Scott Tanner, 'How a Bill Becomes a Law in China: Stages and Processes in Lawmaking,' in Stanley B. Lubman (ed.), *China's Legal Reforms,* in *The China Quarterly,* (Special Issue), No. 141, March 1995, pp. 38-64 at p. 57 and p. 64.

141

# CHAPTER 6

# Commonwealth Caribbean

## Edward Fitzgerald*

This chapter is concerned with the death penalty in the Commonwealth Caribbean - that is to say, in the Caribbean states that were former English colonies but have gained independence in the last few decades.

It is possible to generalise about capital punishment in the Commonwealth Caribbean because there are certain common features about the death penalty system that these countries inherited upon independence, and significant similarities in the way in which that system has continued and developed since independence. To summarise, the Commonwealth Caribbean states all inherited, at the time of independence, both the death penalty as the mandatory penalty for murder, and many features of the death penalty system that had existed in England during the early part of the twentieth century - before its use was restricted in 1957, and abolished in 1965 in the 'mother country'. The independence constitutions of the Commonwealth Caribbean universally recognised the death penalty as a lawful form of punishment, and the criminal codes of each of them to this day retain the death penalty as the mandatory penalty for murder, or at least certain forms of aggravated murder. More importantly, despite periods of controversy and de facto moratoria on executions during the past two decades, and despite increasing legal challenges to the actual executions of individuals sentenced to death, the governments of the vast majority of the Commonwealth Caribbean states[1] continue to assert the will to enforce the death penalty, and continue to justify the use of the death penalty by reference to the incidence of violent crime, and popular demand.

Against that background, this chapter is intended to provide a critical analysis of the death penalty system in the Caribbean both in its origins upon independence, its recent development, and its present form. It will do so with particular reference to Jamaica. This is firstly because the Jamaican death penalty system upon independence was typical of the great majority of Commonwealth Caribbean states, and exemplified the common inheritance of these states from the colonial past. Secondly, it is because Jamaica has over the last two decades experienced a particularly intense controversy over the retention of the death penalty, because it has been the subject of some of the most significant constitutional challenges in the death penalty field, and because it was the first to introduce a system of classification of murder into capital and non-capital murder (which may prove to be a first step towards total abolition).

143

# COMMON FEATURES OF THE COLONIAL INHERITANCE

There are a number of crucial aspects of the death penalty system which were inherited from the colonial past by Jamaica, and by almost all the other states of the Commonwealth Caribbean, which have conditioned the use and development of the death penalty thereafter. These include the mode of execution (death by hanging); the mandatory nature of the death penalty as the penalty for all crimes of murder; the wide common-law definition of murder; the important role played in the system by a secretive process of executive clemency; the two-tier appellate system; and the constitutional protection of the death penalty as a lawful form of punishment.

## Execution by hanging

Death by hanging was the penalty for murder at common law, and death by hanging remains the mode of execution in all those Caribbean states that have retained the death penalty. As a form of execution it is immunised from constitutional challenge by the independent constitution of Jamaica and almost all the other Commonwealth constitution states despite the growing evidence that death is not instantaneous in many cases, and despite the gruesome and degrading nature of the actual ritual of hanging.

## The death sentence as the mandatory penalty for murder

The second aspect of the colonial system that was retained upon independence was the mandatory nature of the death sentence as the penalty for all crimes of murder. In depriving the trial court of all discretion to mitigate the penalty in the light of the individual circumstances of the offender, and the particular facts of his or her case, such a system is manifestly unjust. It contrasts with the system in the United States where the common law approach has been rejected by the Supreme Court in such cases as *Woodson v North Carolina*[2] as rigid and inhumane. This is because the common law approach fails to provide for the judge or jury to determine whether, upon conviction of murder (even first-degree murder), the sentence of death is really merited in the light of the particular circumstances of the offence and the offender.

## The wide definition of murder

The injustice of the common law approach inherited from the colonial system was compounded by the wide definition of the offence of murder which attracted the inflexible and mandatory penalty of death. Jamaica, along with most Caribbean states, retained the common law definition of murder which does not require an intent to kill for a conviction, but, where death results, allows for a conviction on the basis of an intent to inflict grievous bodily harm, or recklessness as to the infliction of grievous bodily harm or death. (Belize is a notable exception and its criminal code does require an 'intent to kill'). Furthermore, Jamaica and most Caribbean states allow for conviction of murder even in respect of those aiders and abettors who did not physically strike the fatal blow, or fire the fatal shot, on the basis of the doctrine of 'joint enterprise'. Finally the colonial legal system inherited upon independence allowed for a limited range of defences - such as provocation and diminished responsibility - but does not even permit a defence of duress. It seems wholly unacceptable to allow for a conviction for murder, and the imposition of the death penalty, where the offender acted under duress.

## A two-tier system of appeal

A fourth feature of the Commonwealth Caribbean death penalty system inherited from colonial times, and typified by Jamaica, is the appellate system. Thus the court system inherited by Jamaica from its colonial past, and protected by the constitution, consists of a trial court, then a domestic appeal court, and finally a further Court of Appeal in the Judicial Committee of the Privy Council (hereafter JCPC) sitting in London. In recent years the Judicial Committee as the final Court of Appeal, has played an increasingly active role in reviewing individual death penalty convictions, and imposing basic human rights standards on the death penalty system in Jamaica and other Caribbean countries. The most important decision was that in the case *of Pratt v Attorney General of Jamaica*[3] which outlawed execution after a delay of more than five years. Yet both the Jamaica Court of Appeal and the JCPC, operate within the limits imposed by the Judicature (Appellate Jurisdiction) Law 1962 which severely restricts the circumstances in which the appellate courts can interfere with convictions and does not permit a reconsideration of the merits of the conviction by the appeal court. The existence of a final court of appeal in England undoubtedly provides a vital additional safeguard against unjust convictions and an important final arbiter of constitutional and human rights issues. But the constitution of almost all the Caribbean states protects the death penalty itself from direct constitutional challenge in the courts - so that the scope for review is heavily circumscribed.

## Executive clemency

A fifth common feature of the Caribbean system is the crucial role played in it by executive clemency. After the death penalty has been imposed, and any appeals exhausted, the question of whether the death penalty should actually be carried out or commuted to life imprisonment is typically taken by the governor-general or some other executive figure acting on the advice of an advisory committee or mercy committee. In Jamaica, the governor general acts on the advice of the Privy Council of Jamaica, and similar systems operate in Belize, Trinidad and the Bahamas. But the proceedings of the advisory committees are conducted in secret, and the prisoner is not shown the reports placed before it, or afforded a hearing. Moreover, most Caribbean constitutions protect both the proceedings of the mercy committees and the decision of the executive on respite of sentence, from challenge or review in the courts. These mercy decisions are crucial to the operation of a system that has deprived the trial judge of any discretion as to the imposition of the death penalty. In such a system, it is only at this later executive stage that the real question of whether the death penalty is merited by the individual

145

circumstances of the case can be considered. But the process is carried out secretly, unfairly, and without regard to any clear or accessible criteria. Given that in over 50% of cases mercy is granted, those who are denied clemency have a genuine grievance that the procedure by which their fate is determined should be conducted openly and they should be afforded an oral hearing - as happens in many states in the United States of America.

### Constitutional protection of the death penalty

The final common feature in the Commonwealth Caribbean is the constitutional protection afforded to the death penalty as a lawful form of punishment. The exact extent of the protection is not absolutely clear. The majority of Commonwealth Caribbean constitutions recognise the legality of execution where it is prescribed by law, and prohibit a frontal attack on execution by hanging as a 'cruel' or 'inhuman' or 'degrading' form of punishment. In the cases of *Riley*[4] and *Pratt,*[5] the JCPC certainly interpreted the constitutional protection to extend to the imposition of the death penalty for murder on the basis that the constitution protected all forms of punishment that were lawful before independence. But it is at least arguable that the protection goes no further than to prevent an attack on the death penalty as an inhuman punishment in itself. That would still leave open the argument that to impose the death penalty as the mandatory sentence for all forms of murder, or even as the mandatory penalty for all aggravated forms of murder, would be unconstitutional because it fails to allow the court to take account of the individual circumstances of the offence or offender. The appeal would be on the basis that, if the death penalty is to be preserved, a civilised system of law must leave the court with the discretion as to whether it is proportionate and merited in any particular case - so as to take account of the kind of mitigating circumstances that courts are required to consider before imposing any other, lesser penalty.


# DEVELOPMENT OF THE SYSTEM IN JAMAICA

In the last two decades, the death penalty system Jamaica inherited from colonial times has been challenged, questioned and modified. There have been substantial periods during which no executions have taken place. Many death sentences have been commuted on grounds of delay, and the introduction of the system of classification of murder into capital and non-capital has led to a further restriction in the circumstances in which the death penalty can be imposed. However there seems a real likelihood that executions will now be resumed in respect of those offences still classified as capital. The history has many parallels in other Caribbean jurisdictions and is worth recounting.

### Post-independence practice

After independence, the death penalty continued to be imposed in Jamaica and there were, on average, some five executions a year, but opposition to the death penalty was growing and a period of intense public debate and re-examination of the case for retention of the death penalty led to a moratorium on executions in the latter part of the 1970s.

## The period of debate and suspension

This crucial period of debate on the merits of the death penalty, and suspension of its use, can be dated from the report of the Barnett Commission[6] in June 1975. The Commission was appointed to inquire into disturbances in the security wing of St Catherine's prison where death row inmates were held. As part of its report the Commission questioned the deterrent effect of the death penalty and stated that 'most men who commit the crime of murder can be adequately rehabilitated to lead normal productive lives'. It recommended the abolition of the death penalty.

Following the publication of the Barnett Report, a Select Committee of the House of Representatives[7] was formed to consider the question of whether to retain or abolish the death penalty. In the end the Committee did vote for retention, but only by a small majority. There followed an intense debate in the House of Representatives on a motion to retain the death penalty which was only narrowly carried by 24 votes to 19. At the same time, the House of Representatives voted unanimously that the governor general should review the cases of all 79 prisoners on death row.

However, the matter did not rest there as shortly afterwards the Senate passed a resolution by a majority of 10 to 5 recommending that 'capital punishment be suspended for a period of 18 months pending a detailed study and assessment of the sociological and psychological effect of capital punishment in Jamaican society'. Furthermore, that vote led to the setting up of the Fraser Committee (chaired by Sir Aubrey Fraser, an Appeal Court judge)[8] whose brief was 'to consider and report within a period of 18 months whether liability under the criminal law in Jamaica to suffer death as a penalty for murder should be abolished, limited or modified'.

## The Fraser Report

The Fraser Committee, which commissioned its own research, drew attention to certain significant facts about the crime of murder and the death penalty in Jamaica.

First, the committee drew a broad distinction between, on the one hand, the kind of spontaneous killings committed for personal and emotional reasons by individual criminals - which still represented the majority of murders - and, on the other hand, the growing incidence of gun murders by 'social criminals' operating in groups or gangs whose crimes were often committed in the course of robbery. Second, the committee noted that the death penalty continued to be imposed disproportionately on those of low socio-economic status who had been poorly represented on legal aid. Third, it revealed that, of those convicted of murder, some 70% were reprieved.

In its conclusions, the Fraser Committee recorded its own view that the death penalty should be abolished, and, in doing so, stressed the unequal application of the death penalty: 'In every country of the world history shows that the death penalty has been unjustly imposed. It bears unequally and irrevocably on the poor, on minorities, and on opposition groups within the population.'[9]

Nonetheless, the Fraser Committee acknowledged that such a move would not be acceptable to public opinion and reached a compromise (which was later to result in the Offences Against the Person (Amendment) Act 1992) by recommending the introduction of two categories of murder - capital and non-capital. It further recommended that the death sentence should be reserved only for those convicted of murders committed with firearms, and, even then, only for the principal in the first degree, or actual perpetrator (the precursor of the modern-day 'triggerman' test). This distinction was justified by reference to the particular public concern with the gun murders that had so greatly increased during the 1970s.

## Period of resumption

The Fraser Report put a powerful case for the abolition of the death penalty and a strong pragmatic case for the restriction of its use to the worst cases of murder. But its recommendations were not implemented at once and, by the time it was published in 1981, executions had resumed as a result of a change of government and increasing public concern at violent crime. In 1982, the JCPC - by a narrow majority - declined to intervene in the case of *Riley*,[10] on behalf of four defendants who had received death sentences in 1975 and 1978 but not issued with warrants of execution until 1979. Their claim, that to execute them after such delay was inhuman and degrading treatment, was rejected by the majority of the Privy Council. That decision was characterised by a narrow and legalistic approach to constitutional review and a spirit of judicial non-interference with the rights and wrongs of capital punishment in far-away Jamaica. So although the number of executions remained low, the numbers of prisoners held on death row awaiting execution over many years greatly increased throughout the 1980s.

## Period of judicial activism

The last execution in Jamaica was in 1988, though on occasions death warrants have been read and executions have been narrowly prevented by last minute legal activity involving domestic courts, the JCPC, the Inter-American Commission for Human Rights and the UN Commission of Human Rights. In this sense the battleground on the death penalty has shifted from the legislature to the courts, and has been internationalised as outside bodies (such as the Inter-American Commission and the UN Commission of Human Rights) have intervened to protect the rights of those under sentence of death.

At the same time a new judicial activism has been displayed by the JCPC in a series of decisions on capital cases where convictions were based on flawed identification such as *R v Reid and Others*,[11] and also in the landmark decision of *Pratt v Attorney-General for Jamaica*[12] which reversed the earlier decision in *Riley*[13] and held that substantial delays in carrying out executions

148

did constitute inhuman and degrading treatment or punishment contrary to section 17(1) of the Constitution.

The Privy Council's decision in *Pratt* has to be seen in the wider context of a process of internationalisation. In *Pratt*, adverse decisions against the Jamaican government had already been made, firstly by the Inter-American Commission on Human Rights, and then by the UN Human Rights Committee because of the delay of four years by the Jamaican Court of Appeal in giving its reasons for a decision to reject the appellant's appeal. Moreover, the European Court of Human Rights had ruled - in the context of an extradition to America - that it would be inhuman and degrading treatment contrary to article 3 of the European Convention to return a person to the U.S.A. to face a trial for capital murder because of the protracted stay (on average 8 years) on death row awaiting execution (the death row phenomenon).[14] (See Chapter 2 for a fuller account of the *Soering* judgement)

The JCPC's decision in *Pratt* was part of a general international move towards the imposition of more exacting standards on states that wish to retain the death penalty. The nature and effect of the *Pratt* decision can be summarised as follows: the Privy Council held that delays in carrying out executions of over five years were presumptively unconstitutional, even when the defendant had himself contributed to these delays by the exhaustion of domestic or international avenues of appeal. (The ruling left it open that delays of less than five years might still be unacceptable where they were wholly the fault of the state). As a result of this ruling a large number of those on death row in Jamaica (some of whom had been there for over ten years) had their death sentence commuted to life imprisonment. However, it must be emphasised that the JCPC did not suggest in any way that the death penalty per se was unconstitutional - and indeed reaffirmed that the Constitution implicitly protected the right to impose the penalty of death by hanging on people convicted of murder.

**Restriction of the death penalty to capital murder**
So much for the impact of international legal developments on the imposition of the death penalty in Jamaica. It is necessary now to turn to a further and yet more significant development introduced by the Jamaican legislature itself, namely, the introduction of the distinction between capital and non-capital murder, and the restriction of the death penalty to those aggravated forms of murder identified as capital in the new classification system.

This new system was introduced by the Offences Against the Person (Amendment) Act 1992. It followed a renewed debate about the retention of the death penalty, and a vote by the Jamaica Bar Association which, at one and the same time, described abolition of the death penalty as a desirable goal, but, in rejecting the case for immediate abolition, recommended the introduction of a classification system in order to restrict the death penalty to the worst kinds of aggravated murder. The 1992 Act which gives effect to the recommendations of the Fraser Committee (albeit expanding the types of murder which will still attract the death penalty), adopts the practice of

149

classifying murder offences into capital and non-capital that was briefly employed in England between the years 1957 and 1965 - before the complete abolition of the death penalty in 1965.[15]

The essential features of the Jamaican legislation is that it reserves the death penalty for the actual perpetrators of particular types of aggravated murder. The categories of murder classed as capital include the murder of certain officials (such as police officers, prison officers, and members of the judiciary) and murders committed in aggravating circumstances such as murder in the course of robbery, theft, burglary or sexual offences. But the Act further restricts the death penalty to those who actually cause the death of the deceased (such as the 'triggerman' in a shooting) or who inflict some personal violence on the victim. This is intended to save from the death penalty those convicted of murder on the basis of the doctrine of joint enterprise who play no direct or physical part in the causation of death.

## Operation of new system

The restriction of the death penalty to those convicted of the new offence of capital murder is a welcome modification of the harshness of the mandatory death penalty previously imposed on all those convicted of murder. However, most of those convicted of the types of murder now categorised as non-capital were probably reprieved under the old system. The introduction of the new aggravated offence of 'capital murder' was expressly intended to identify what might be regarded as the worst type of murder cases so as to more easily justify their execution.

Since 1988, up to February 1996, no-one has been executed despite the introduction of the new offence of capital murder. This is because there have been a number of individual appeals in the Jamaica Court of Appeal and JCPC, and because of the continuing uncertainties surrounding the precise meaning of the statutory provisions defining the new types of 'capital murder', which have yet to be resolved in a number of forthcoming appeals in the JCPC. But there is a real danger that the time is fast approaching when executions will begin again. Thus, despite periods of uncertainty and intense debate, despite numerous legal challenges and the increasing use of international avenues of appeal, the death penalty continues to be imposed by the courts, and the political will to carry it out appears to be as strong as ever.

# OVERVIEW AND FUTURE PROSPECTS

The detailed analysis of developments in Jamaica may, it is hoped, serve as a starting-point for some wider generalisation about trends in the Caribbean as a whole. For, as in Jamaica, so elsewhere in the Caribbean, the history of the last twenty years has witnessed certain common developments. There have been periods of intense debate, of de facto moratoria, and in many jurisdictions there have been significant delays in execution - produced partly by political uncertainty, and partly by the existence of a two-tier appellate system, and of further avenues of appeal to international bodies. However, as in Jamaica, there is evidence that the public in the Caribbean still supports the use of the death penalty, at least for specified forms of murder - and that the political will to continue executions still exists.

However, there are certain developments which might be anticipated. First the notion that only the worst forms of aggravated murder should attract the death penalty seems to be gaining ground throughout the Caribbean. The Colonial legacy of a mandatory death penalty for all murder offences has been rejected. Both Jamaica and Belize have introduced the capital/non-capital distinction, though not in an identical manner. It seems likely that other jurisdictions will follow suit. One has to welcome any restriction on the unjust and arbitrary system of condemning to death all those convicted of the widely defined common law offence of murder (even if this move does not in fact prove a first step to total abolition in the near future). Second, the extent to which the death penalty for murder or for certain classes of aggravated murder is protected constitutionally requires careful scrutiny. It is arguable that all that the Jamaican-style constitutions do is to recognise that hanging may be a legitimate form of execution, and is not in itself to be considered an inhuman and degrading form of punishment. That leaves it open to argue that the penalty of death by hanging for all crimes of murder, or even for all crimes of capital murder, is nonetheless disproportionate and therefore inhuman in any case where, despite the murder conviction, there are any mitigating factors in the circumstances of the offence or the offender's background. It is a continuing feature of the colonial legacy that the mandatory death penalty system allows no *discretion* to *judge* or *jury* to consider the individual circumstances of offenders and to spare those offenders from the death penalty once they have been convicted of murder.

A third area that requires further scrutiny is the unsatisfactory and secretive system whereby the executive considers the question of reprieve - on the advice of various advisory committees or mercy committees. This 'clemency' stage is crucial to a system which retains a mandatory death penalty upon conviction for murder or upon conviction of certain categories of murder. In many Caribbean constitutions, the proceedings of the mercy or advisory committees that decide whether to remit the death sentence are immunised from judicial review. The JCPC has upheld this immunity in the Bahamian case of *Reckley v Minister of Public Safety*.[16] Fairness requires that, if a person's life is to be decided by such mercy committees, then he should see the reports submitted to them and have an opportunity to comment. But, only Belize in the case of *Lauriano v Attorney-General of Belize*[17] has recognised such a right. In the light of the JCPC's negative ruling on the *Reckley* case, consideration will have to be given throughout the Caribbean to further appeals to the Inter-American Commission and/or the UN Human Rights Committee if the irrevocability of the mercy decisions is to be further challenged.

Finally, although many Caribbean constitutions do expressly protect the death penalty by hanging from constitutional attack, not all do. The time may yet come when the JCPC will have to consider the merits of the retention of the sentence to death by hanging. In view of the recent powerful judgement of the Constitutional Court of South Africa abolishing the death penalty for murder,[18] and the strong humanitarian arguments against the barbarity of the ritual of death by hanging, there is at least some prospect of a favourable ruling.

But clearly in the majority of states the issue will ultimately be decided by local legislators and therefore by public opinion. In that context, there is at least some comfort to be drawn from the concurring conclusions of the Barnett and Fraser Reports that the death penalty should be abolished, the Jamaican Bar Council's conclusion that this is a desirable objective in the long-term, and from the fact that some Caribbean jurisdictions and most Central American jurisdictions have already abolished the death penalty. Although the United States of America is clearly set on a course of regular executions there is no unanimity on the issue in the Americas as a whole. There is some hope that the Inter-American Commission may itself operate as an influence in favour of abolition, or at least further restriction of the death penalty in the Caribbean.

# ENDNOTES

*I am very grateful to Emma Scott-Williams, law graduate from Univeristy of Westminster and Bar Vocational student for her help in editing and referencing this chapter.

1. Antigua, Bahamas, Barbados, Belize, Jamaica, Dominica, Grenada, St. Lucia, St. Vincent, St. Kitts and Trinidad and Tobago are British Independent Territories that retain the death penalty and for who the Judicial Committee of the Privy Council remains the last court of appeal. The other British Independent Territory Guyana has the death penalty but relinquished the link with the JCPC. Of the British Dependent Territories, the British Virgin Islands, Cayman Islands, Turks and Caicos, Monserrat and Anguila have abolished the death penalty. Only Bermuda retains the death penalty but here the convention is for the Governor-General to commute all death sentences to life imprisonment. The last executions in retentionist countries were: Antigua (1991), Bahamas (1986), Barbados (1984), Belize (1985), Bermuda (1977), Jamaica (1988), Dominica (1986), Grenada (1978), St. Lucia (1995), St. Vincent (1995), St. Kitts (1987), Trinidad and Tobago (1994).

2. *Woodson v North Carolina* 428 U.S. 28096 S.Ct. 2978, 49 L.Ed.2d 944 1976.

3. *Pratt v Attorney General for Jamaica* [1993] 3 W.L.R 995, [1993] 4 All ER 769.

4. *Riley v Attorney General for Jamaica* [1983] 1 A.C. 719, [1982] 3 W.L.R. 557.

5. op. cit., n. 3.

6. The Barnett Commission of Inquiry was established under the chair of Lloyd Barrett Q.C., Kingston, Jamaica, June 1975.

7. Select Committee of the House of Representatives of Jamaica.

8. *Report by the Committee to consider death as the penalty for murder in Jamaica* (chair Sir Aubrey Frazer, 1981).

9. See Endnote 8.

10. See Endnote 4.

11. *Junior Reid and Others v. The Queen* 1990, 1 *Appeal Cases* 363, PC.

12. *Pratt.* See Endnote 3.

13. *Riley.* See Endnote 4.

14. *Soering v United Kingdom* 1989 11 E.H.R.R. 439.

15. Homicide Act 1957 ( England and Wales).

16. *Reckley v Minister of Public Safety, The Times* Law Report 6 February 1996.

17. *Lauriano v Attorney-General of Belize* (unreported 20 September 1995).

18. *The State v Makwanyane and Mchunu Case No. CCT/3/94* Judgement of 6 June 1995.

# CHAPTER 7

# Commonwealth Africa

## John Hatchard and Simon Coldham

This chapter constitutes something of a landmark in that it is the first analysis of the current status and operation of the death penalty in Commonwealth African countries (hereafter 'CAC') a description which includes Nigeria, Ghana, Sierra Leone, The Gambia, Uganda, Kenya, Tanzania, Zambia, Malawi, Zimbabwe, Botswana, Lesotho, Swaziland, Namibia, South Africa, Mauritius and Seychelles. The last four countries, of course, have rather distinctive histories and some of the generalisations made in the text (e.g. those based on the conventional distinction between the pre-colonial, the British colonial and the post-independence periods) may not apply to all of them. Some people might query whether it is possible to make any useful generalisations about seventeen countries differing widely in the nature of their political systems and in their levels of economic development. However, the view is taken here that traditional approaches to crime and punishment enjoyed certain features in common throughout most of sub-Saharan Africa and that most of the countries under consideration shared a similar colonial experience and were subject to similar penal policies. Moreover, since independence the governments of these countries have adopted a broadly comparable stance on questions of penal policy, regardless of their particular political ideology. The intention is not to undertake a country by country analysis of the death penalty but rather to introduce the reader to some of the principal themes and trends that bear on the debate in Commonwealth Africa. A practical problem relating to the exercise is the lack of reliable information on the death penalty in the CAC. The literature is extremely sparse[1], and with the exception of South Africa, very little research has been done on the death penalty. Indeed, the absence in many countries of accurate and meaningful criminal statistics makes any such research difficult. This explains why the discussion that follows is, in parts, impressionistic and the conclusions that it draws tentative.

After a brief historical overview, the chapter examines the current status of the death penalty, trial and post-trial procedures, the death penalty and the constitution, and death row conditions. The final section considers prospects for change in the near future.

## HISTORICAL OVERVIEW

Reliable information on the pre-colonial period is, for obvious reasons, fairly limited and much of our understanding of notions of crime and punishment in traditional African societies derives from the research carried out by anthropologists and others in the course of the colonial period. Central to their preoccupations were the ways in which wrongs were classified and wrongdoers dealt with in different societies and the extent to which a distinction was recognised between criminal/public wrongs on the one hand and civil/private wrongs on the other.

The answers to these questions vary inevitably from society to society, given the wide diversity of political and social systems that existed. At one end of the spectrum were the strongly centralised chiefly societies with specialised institutions for the making and enforcement of laws and for the settlement of disputes. At the other end of the spectrum were the acephalous communities of agriculturists living in scattered settlements and of nomadic pastoralists, where authority was exercised by clan elders. However, while there certainly were differences in the ways that wrongs were categorised and dealt with, it is generally accepted that all societies distinguished between offences that must be publicly punished by society at large and those that should be left to private redress.[2] Broadly the emphasis was on compensation, on restoring social equilibrium and on reintegrating the offender within the community, and even offences like theft and homicide were normally settled by making the offender compensate the victim or the victim's family for their loss. However, there were always offences which were seen as threatening the security or well-being of the community as a whole and which could not be redressed simply by the payment of compensation to the party injured. Such offences were few and were generally punishable by death or, its equivalent, expulsion.[3] One such offence was witchcraft, since a witch was seen not merely as a disturbing influence in the community but also as a threat to its supernatural governance. In this sense it was akin to treason, which itself was a capital offence in the more centralised chiefly societies. Finally, while a person who committed homicide would usually be able to settle the matter by the payment of 'blood money' to the victim's family, recidivists or those guilty of wilful killing would be regarded as a danger to the whole community and punished by death.[4]

The introduction of British rule had a profound effect on this area of law. The power of traditional authorities to exact punishment was severely curtailed and customary law was recognised only in so far as it was neither repugnant to natural justice, equity and good conscience, nor inconsistent with imperial or local legislation. Moreover, by 1935 codes of criminal law and procedure of very similar (if not identical) origin had been introduced throughout most of British colonial Africa.[5] These codes, which remain largely unreformed even today, were closely based on nineteenth-century English law and make few concessions to their African context.[6] Under the dual system of courts introduced by the British, the Native or African Courts would have a very limited criminal jurisdiction and most Penal Code offences would be triable only in the Magistrates' Courts or the High Court. The Criminal Procedure Codes provided modes of trial closely based on those followed in England, one important and interesting difference being the use of

156

assessors (of the same race/tribe as the accused) rather than juries in High Court trials.[7] The superimposition of this formal system of criminal justice was accompanied by the introduction of a range of punishments that were largely unknown to customary law and by the adoption of sentencing policies based on principles of retribution and general deterrence.

In most territories the death penalty was mandatory for murder[8], treason and certain forms of piracy and in a few, e.g. Kenya (1927-1955), it was available for the rape of a European woman by an African man.[9] Moreover, in times of emergency, e.g. during the Mau-Mau crisis in Kenya or under the Law and Order (Maintenance) Act of Rhodesia, the death sentence was extended to a variety of 'security' offences. The usual method of execution was hanging, although shooting was common in the first years of colonial rule and death by beheading continued in Northern Nigeria until 1936. At first capital sentences were often carried out in public, sometimes at the scene of the crime, but by the 1930s most executions took place in central government prisons. There was also an expectation that executions would not be long delayed after sentence. It was the responsibility of the Governor of the territory either to confirm a capital sentence or to grant a reprieve, and it appears that clemency was fairly frequently exercised.[10]

## STATUS OF THE DEATH PENALTY TODAY

Political independence did not result in any significant changes in penal policy. In most countries customary criminal law was abolished[11] and steps were taken to integrate the courts structure. In spite of the stress that many governments place on African values, African socialism, African traditions and the like, there has been no attempt to incorporate such values into the penal system. Furthermore, there has been no real attempt to amend the Penal Codes in line with criminal law reforms in England nor to take into account developments in penological ideas that have occurred over the past few decades. Penal policy shows a marked continuity with the colonial period and remains committed to the goals of retribution and general deterrence. Maximum sentences have been increased and both minimum and mandatory sentences have become more common. The retention, and in many countries the extension of the death penalty is symptomatic of this approach.[12] Given that the majority of the CAC are parties to the International Covenant on Civil and Political Rights (ICCPR), it is regrettable that it remains a punishment for rape in some countries and has frequently been extended to non-fatal offences contrary to article 6(2) of the Covenant.[13]

The abolitionist movement has had relatively little effect. Only in Seychelles, Mauritius and Namibia has the death penalty been expressly abolished by law.[14] In The Gambia, capital punishment was abolished but following a military coup in the country, was reinstated in August 1995 by the ruling Armed Forces Provisional Resistance Council. As is discussed below, the Constitutional Court in South Africa has declared the sentence

157

unconstitutional as regards murder. In view of this situation, it is not surprising therefore that Seychelles and Namibia are the only two CACs that are party to the Second Optional Protocol to the International Covenant on Civil and Political Rights aiming at the abolition of the death penalty.

The retention of the mandatory death sentence for murder seems particularly harsh today, given that the definition of the offence contained in the Penal Codes is usually considerably broader than its definition in contemporary English law. Two examples may be given. Firstly, the definition of malice aforethought in the Penal Codes includes 'constructive malice', which was abolished in England by section 1 Homicide Act 1957. While the exact formulation does vary between the Penal Codes, the Tanganyikan provision, under which malice aforethought includes 'an intent to commit a felony' and 'an intention by the act or omission to facilitate the flight or escape from custody of any person who has committed or attempted to commit a felony', is typical.[15] Secondly, the definition of malice aforethought in the Penal Codes includes recklessness, whereas the House of Lords in *Moloney* confirmed that nothing less than an *intention* to kill or cause grievous bodily harm would suffice.[16] Again the Tanganyikan provision is typical, whereby malice aforethought includes 'knowledge that the act or omission causing death will probably cause the death of or grievous harm to some person, whether such person is killed or not, although such knowledge is accompanied by indifference whether death or grievous bodily harm is caused or not, or by a wish that it may not be caused'.[17] Thus even though the 1984 ECOSOC safeguards state that the scope of crimes punishable by death 'should not go beyond intentional crimes', it is clear that an unintentional homicide may amount to murder under the Penal Codes and attract a mandatory death sentence.

The steadily increasing incidence of crimes against property, frequently involving the use of arms, has prompted a draconian response from many governments including the introduction of a mandatory death sentence for certain offences. In Zambia, for example, the death penalty was extended in 1974 to aggravated robbery where a fire-arm or other offensive weapon is used or grievous harm is done.[18] The Minister of Home Affairs forecast optimistically that '. . . it will not be long before we completely eliminate robbers, even if we might be forced to use crude and extremely ruthless methods in the interests of law-abiding citizens'.[19] In Nigeria, in an attempt to combat the sharp increase in armed robbery following the end of the civil war, the Federal Military Government promulgated the Robbery and Firearms (Special Provisions) Decree 1970 which introduced the death penalty for robbery where the accused is armed with a firearm or other offensive weapon or where he wounds any person.[20] Similar legislation was introduced in Uganda in 1968 to deal with the problem of Kondos (groups of rural bandits). The Penal Code (Amendment) Act 1968 introduced a mandatory death sentence for robbery where the accused uses or threatens to use a deadly weapon or where he causes death or grievous harm to a person.[21]

Not only has the death penalty been extended in several jurisdictions to various forms of aggravated robbery,[22] but it has also on occasion been extended to certain economic crimes. The deterioration in the economies of many Commonwealth African countries over the last thirty years has often been accompanied by an increase in corruption, sabotage, smuggling, black-marketeering and the like, and this has frequently led governments to create new offences, to impose harsh penalties, to introduce new trial procedures and to move away from the general requirement of *mens rea*. The use of the criminal law to sustain or revive the economy has been most striking in Nigeria, where successive military regimes have not hesitated to introduce the death penalty in an attempt to deter acts of economic sabotage. Thus the Petroleum, Product and Distribution (Anti-Sabotage) Decree 1975 created an offence for which the sentence was death or 21 years imprisonment. The Counterfeit Currency (Special Provisions) Decree 1984 prescribed the death penalty for various counterfeiting offences, while the Special Tribunal (Miscellaneous Offences) Decree of the same year introduced the death penalty for arson, for tampering with electricity, telephone cables etc., and for dealing in cocaine.[23] Other examples come from Uganda where section 301 of the Penal Code was amended in 1987 to make armed smuggling a capital offence and from Ghana where a variety of economic and political offences were made capital under the Public Tribunals Law.[24]

Finally, in countries suffering from a degree of civil unrest it is common for the death penalty to be introduced for a variety of 'political' offences. Thus a number of serious public order offences were made capital during the Nigerian State of Emergency 1966-1970, for example, under the Suppression of Disorder Decree 1966. Again, a variety of capital offences were created by the Rhodesian Law and Order (Maintenance) Act to deal with the African nationalist movement; while the statute remains in force today, it is largely in disuse[25] and the death sentence for these offences was abolished in 1992. Similarly, in South Africa in the 1960s, sabotage together with child-stealing and kidnapping were made capital offences after a number of politically-motivated incidents of these kinds had occurred.[26]

## USE OF THE DEATH PENALTY

In spite of the trend towards extending death penalty offences, such information as is available indicates that in most countries the death sentence is seldom carried out. For example, in The Gambia between independence in 1965 and 1993 when the sentence was abolished, only one of the eighty-seven persons sentenced to death was actually executed. In Zambia between 1966 and 1978, 406 persons were sentenced to death but there were only 34 executions. In very many cases the President has exercised his prerogative of mercy.[27] In Zimbabwe since independence in 1980 there have been 49 executions, in Lesotho there has been on average about one execution every ten years[28], in Mauritius there have been no executions since 1987 whilst in

159

Botswana and Malawi the death penalty is reportedly rarely used.[29] Two exceptions are Nigeria where, between 1976 and 1985 there were 1,110 executions,[30] and South Africa where between 1980 and 1989 1,123 people were hanged. Hanging is the usual method of execution in the CAC, although in Nigeria, Ghana and Sierra Leone death by firing squad has been introduced.[31]

## THE DEATH PENALTY DEBATE

It is against a background of rapidly increasing crime and calls for deterrent sentences in most of the CACs, that the death penalty debate must be seen. Given the prevalence of government-controlled media and rubber-stamp legislatures, the debate has been extremely limited in scope and the following discussion therefore focuses on those jurisdictions where at least some debate has occurred.

In Zambia, hopes that the death sentence would be abolished with the coming of the Third Republic in 1991 were not realised. However, in 1994, the Government decided in principle to become a party to the Second Optional Protocol but before doing so, held a series of nation-wide consultations including meetings with representatives from the trade union movement, non-governmental organizations, the police and judiciary. The overwhelming response was in favour of retaining the death penalty as a deterrent because of the escalating crime rate in the country and its destabilising effect on both the economy and democracy. Accordingly the government did not proceed with its proposal. The issue was also debated by the Constitutional Review Commission which reported in June 1995. The majority of Commissioners did not support the abolition of the death penalty and this is reflected in the new draft constitution.

In Tanzania the Report of the Nyalali Commission, whose membership represented a broad cross-section of society, unanimously reached the conclusion that the death sentence is to be regarded as a barbaric form of punishment in democratic societies and morally insupportable.[32] However, public opinion seemingly remains firmly in favour of retaining the penalty although it has been argued that this is based on 'the erroneous belief that capital punishment is the most effective deterrent' and that 'the government has a duty to put the true facts before the public instead of holding out to them that the death penalty is an instant solution to violent crime'.[33]

When Zimbabwe became independent in 1980, government policy was not to carry out executions. The courts continued to sentence to death those found guilty of murder because they were required to do so in the absence of extenuating circumstances, although it was known that sentences of death were not being carried out. Even so, the wide range of capital offences was retained despite a recommendation in 1982 by the Advisory Committee on Law Reform for a re-consideration of the situation.[34] That this did not take place was probably influenced by the emergence of serious civil unrest in

Matabeleland[35] and instead the execution of 'dissidents' commenced. There is no evidence that this policy had any effect on a problem which was a wholly political one and which ended in 1987 as soon as a political settlement was reached.[36] Thereafter several influential figures, including the then Chief Justice, Enoch Dumbutshena, publicly called for the abolition of the death penalty and, as discussed below, several constitutional challenges were mounted. This certainly had some impact because no executions took place after 1988 and in 1990 the government announced a moratorium on executions. Non-governmental organizations such as the Legal Resources Foundation remain actively involved in the debate.[37] The Catholic Commission for Justice and Peace has also consistently campaigned for the abolition of the death sentence which included organising a nation-wide petition which was later presented to the President. Despite this, the moratorium was lifted in 1992, and executions have since resumed.[38] The issue of the retention of the death penalty continues to receive attention and the government of Zimbabwe has pledged to keep the matter under review. It may well be that the ruling of the Constitutional Court in South Africa, discussed below, will have an important bearing on its future policy.

In Namibia the matter was debated by the Constituent Assembly which drew up the 1990 independence constitution. The arbitrary use of the death sentence during the colonial period and a resultant determination that it should have no place in the new nation resulted in the Constitution providing for the abolition of the sentence.[39]

In South Africa the death sentence was an integral part of the apartheid regime and bitterly opposed by the African National Congress (ANC) and leading NGOs such as Lawyers for Human Rights and Black Sash. No executions took place after November 1989 and with political developments moving apace towards the creation of the New South Africa, the future of the death penalty came into question. In 1991 the South African Law Commission in its Interim Report on Group and Human Rights described the imposition of the death penalty as 'highly controversial' and, as a result of comments received, adopted a 'Solomonic solution' under which the matter was left to the Constitutional Court to decide (discussed below). The debate thus moved on to the familiar issue of whether, in the face of a sharp increase in violent crime, capital punishment was a necessary deterrent. Opinion polls of all races invariably showed considerable support for its retention and a pro-hanging Capital Punishment Campaign (CPC) was launched. However the South African Government remained abolitionist as did most NGOs.

The decision of the Constitutional Court of South Africa in *S v Makwanyane and Mchunu*[40] in June 1995 that capital punishment for murder was unconstitutional thus provoked a mixed reaction. Government, leading Church leaders, including Archbishop Desmond Tutu, head of the Anglican Church, together with organisations such as the Legal Resources Centre (which was actively involved in the constitutional case itself), Black Sash, Human Rights Committee and Lawyers for Human Rights all warmly welcomed the decision, the latter declaring 'South Africa was once known as the capital punishment capital of the world but now takes up its position as a pioneer of human rights in the international community'.[41] However the CPC maintained that the decision went against majority opinion and it was also criticised by the National Party (NP), the former ruling party, as well as several other right wing parties. The NP called for a referendum on the issue and proposed that the Constitution be amended to allow capital punishment in serious cases of murder and rape. Its motion, which was debated in Parliament in June 1995 and backed by the Inkatha Freedom Party and Freedom Front, was rejected by the National Assembly which has an ANC majority. Clearly however, despite the decision of the Constitutional Court, the debate is set to continue.

The issue of the deterrent effect of the death sentence has received scant attention in the CAC. In Zambia the introduction of the death penalty for aggravated robbery in 1974 coincided with a sharp fall in the numbers of reported robberies but this was sustained for only a brief period before they rose again to record levels. There is nothing to suggest the fall was connected with the passing of the Act whilst the rise thereafter is mainly attributable to the fact that the 'clear-up' rate remained very low and the 'failure to apprehend offenders means that the most effective deterrent to crime is largely absent, and thus the fear of punishment is much reduced because the chances of detection are so low'.[42] In 1995, Chaskalson P in the Constitutional Court of South Africa also found that there was no proof that the death sentence was a greater deterrent than imprisonment[43] and emphasised that the greatest deterrent to crime is the likelihood that offenders will be apprehended, convicted and punished - something that was presently lacking in the criminal justice system. He quoted police statistics that in the previous five years on average 20,000 murders were committed and 9,000 murder cases brought to trial although only 243 death sentences were imposed with 143 of these being confirmed on appeal. He posed the telling question: Would the carrying out of the death sentence on these 143 persons have deterred the other murderers or saved any lives?[44] Similarly in Nigeria studies on murder and armed robbery have demonstrated that the death penalty does not act as a deterrent.[45] Certainly the only conclusion that can be drawn is that the deterrent effect of the death sentence remains questionable.

Issues which are increasingly coming to the fore in the debate concern traditional values and religious influences. As noted earlier, the death penalty had no basis in African traditional societies and there have been calls for a revival of traditional approaches to crime and punishment. For example, Adeyemi argues for a strategy of educating the public about the lack of any deterrent value of the death penalty and suggests that this would encourage an abolitionist movement because:

the non-invocation of the death penalty had been the most conspicuous policy of our pre-colonial and pre-Islamic criminal justice system.[46]

162

This approach was emphasised by Mokgoro J in *S v Makwanyane and Mchunu* (above). She noted that one shared traditional value and ideal in South Africa that ran 'like a golden thread' across cultural lines is *ubuntu* which generally translates as 'humaneness' and which embodies both the right to life and dignity. In her view the spirit of *ubuntu* was embodied in the new Constitution and thus impacted on the death penalty. In contrast, the influence of Islam in some CACs such as Nigeria and Tanzania undoubtedly affects the debate and, indeed Adeyemi suggests that Islam has now become an obstacle to the total abolition of the death penalty in Africa. Given the uncompromising retentionist position of Islamic countries worldwide this assessment is probably correct.

Overall, and in spite of its limited use and questionable effectiveness, most of the CACs remain in favour of retaining the death penalty. This is well illustrated by the deliberations of the 57th meeting of the Third Committee of the United Nations held in December 1994. Here a draft resolution[47] entitled 'Capital Punishment' called, *inter alia*, for all States which had not done so to consider becoming parties to the Second Optional Protocol and encouraged all retentionist states:

> to consider the opportunity of instituting a moratorium on pending executions with a view to ensuring that the principle that no State should dispose of the life of any human being be affirmed in every part of the world by the year 2000.[48]

Lesotho, Malawi, Nigeria, Sierra Leone, Swaziland, United Republic of Tanzania, Zambia, and Zimbabwe joined Singapore in calling for no action to be taken on the motion, Botswana and The Gambia abstained, and only Namibia and South Africa voted for the motion.

## CAPITAL TRIALS

It is essential that defendants on trial for their lives should be given scrupulously fair trials for otherwise the death penalty is open to political abuse and the danger of innocent persons being executed is increased. Article 14 of the International Covenant on Civil and Political Rights sets out certain standards for a fair trial and it is particularly important that these standards are respected in capital trials.[49] Nevertheless, it is clear that a number of Commonwealth African countries fall significantly short of these standards and it is the aim of this section to highlight some of the more glaring deficiencies. In the first part we shall look at court procedures and the question of representation, and in the second part we shall examine certain special factors that may have a bearing on the outcome of a case.

163

**Court procedures**

In most of the jurisdictions under consideration there are constitutional provisions guaranteeing an accused person 'a fair hearing within a reasonable time by an independent and impartial court established by law', and capital offences are, as a general rule, triable in the High Court, before a single judge. Juries have largely been abolished,[50] but the use of assessors has been retained in some countries.[51] It is common for a preliminary investigation to be conducted by a magistrates' court before a person is committed for trial by the High Court. Procedure at the trial is governed by the Criminal Procedure Code, which is derived from the English law. English is generally the language of the High Court and where the accused does not understand the language of the court, he is entitled to the assistance of an interpreter without payment.

Not only does an accused have a constitutional right to defend himself in person or by an advocate of his own choice,[52] but he (or she) may be entitled to legal aid at the trial stage.[53] Given that the vast majority of persons charged with capital offences will not be able to afford the services of an advocate, the interests of justice demand that such a person should be entitled to be represented by an advocate at public expense.[54] Although a person may be entitled to legal aid at the appellate stages as well, he is not entitled to it at the committal stage.[55] Whether a person accused of a capital offence can rely on receiving satisfactory representation on legal aid is questionable. Such evidence as exists suggests that, in general, advocates taking on 'pauper briefs' are noted neither for their calibre nor for their commitment. In Tanzania, in a case where the constitutionality of the death penalty was raised, the trial judge pointed out that the risk of executing the innocent is increased by the fact that 'most poor persons do not obtain good legal representation, as they are defended by lawyers on dock briefs who are paid only T Shillings 500 (the equivalent of US $1)'.[56] In Kenya the poor remuneration means that such briefs are turned down by older, more experienced advocates and left to be taken up by their younger colleagues.[57] In Nigeria there has been a number of appeals against convictions for murder on the ground that the accused's counsel had failed to discharge his professional duty in a proper manner.[58] Finally, the *pro deo* system of representation in capital trials in South Africa has come in for strong criticism.[59] Without effective representation an accused can hardly be said to have had a fair trial.

Although it is the general rule that capital offences are only triable in the High Court, it is not invariably the case. For example, in Kenya, capital robbery is triable in the magistrates' courts and this works to the disadvantage of the accused in at least two ways: it deprives him of a trial with assessors and it means that he is not entitled to legal aid. His situation is still weaker in those countries where the official courts are denied jurisdiction over capital offences. Thus the Nigerian Robbery and Firearms (Special Provisions) Decree 1984 (as amended), which is largely based on the 1970 Decree of the same name, provides for the constitution of a special tribunal or tribunals for the trial of the offences of robbery, attempted robbery and the illegal possession of firearms. Such a tribunal consists of a High Court Judge (chairman), a high-ranking military officer and a high-ranking police officer. The tribunal can impose the death sentence for armed robbery and, while the sentence has to be confirmed by the Military Governor, there is no provision for appeal to the courts. The Decree also provides for a stream-lined procedure for the investigation, trial and disposal of cases.[60] A further example of the use of special military tribunals is provided by the Treason and Other Offences (Special Military Tribunal) Decree 1986 (as amended), which largely re-enacts the 1976 Decree of the same name. This Decree provides for the constitution of a Military Tribunal to try offences (including murder and treason, both capital offences) committed in connection with any act of rebellion against the Federal Military Government. Again there is no provision for appeal to the courts, nor are the tribunals bound by the normal rules of evidence and procedure.[61] It is questionable whether a person is sure of receiving a fair trial before such tribunals.[62]

No less controversial was the Malawian Traditional Courts Act 1969, which created the Regional Traditional Courts (with unlimited original criminal jurisdiction) and the National Traditional Appeal Court. These courts consisted of a panel of five persons, including three chiefs, a trained chairman and a qualified lawyer. They were not governed by either the Criminal Procedure Act or the Evidence Act, nor were lawyers permitted to appear before them. Although the English-type courts (the magistrates' courts, the High Court and the Supreme Court) continued to exist in parallel with the Traditional Courts, murder and treason, both capital offences, were invariably tried before the Traditional Courts. One analysis of homicide cases revealed that none of the defendants called witnesses of their own and many failed to offer any defence other than a simple denial. Defendants had little idea how to conduct their cases, and the courts, far from attempting to assist them, created an intimidating environment.[63] In treason cases they operated in a harsh and politically controversial manner,[64] so that it was not surprising that their criminal jurisdiction was removed under the new constitution.[65]

## Special factors

In this part consideration is given to a variety of factors which may have an effect on the question whether the death sentence is imposed or not. The four factors considered here (youth, mental incapacity, provocation and extenuating circumstances) are not the only ones, but they are ones that have generated attention in the literature.

### Youth

Virtually all the countries under consideration have laws specifically providing that the death sentence shall not be imposed for crimes committed by persons below eighteen years of age and shall not be carried out on pregnant women.[66] In Nigeria the age is seventeen and in a few states the relevant date is the date of conviction. In countries which lack a reliable system for the registration of births it may be difficult for a court to establish the age of the accused with any certainty and consequently it is possible that juveniles are occasionally executed.[67]

## Mental incapacity

Although it is generally agreed that persons who are not of sound mind should not be held criminally responsible for their actions, it would appear that a narrow and out-dated legal definition of insanity combined with a shortage of expertise in the field of mental illness may have resulted in mentally incapacitated persons being sentenced to death and executed in Commonwealth African countries. Insanity is a defence to a criminal charge in all the jurisdictions under consideration. If an accused is found to have committed the offence and to have been insane at the time of committing it, a verdict of guilty but insane (in some jurisdictions) or of not guilty by reason of insanity (in others) is entered and he is liable to be detained in custody. The definition of insanity in the Penal Codes is broadly based on the M'Naghten Rules, but whereas these much-criticised rules have lost most of their importance in England since the introduction of the defence of diminished responsibility for murder by the Homicide Act 1957, this is not generally the case in Commonwealth Africa.[68]

The burden of proof is on the accused and this may be difficult for him to discharge, not only because of the outdated and narrowly-formulated definition of insanity,[69] but because of the practical problem of getting hold of expert evidence. Outside South Africa there is an acute shortage of psychiatrists in sub-Saharan Africa and many penal institutions do not have full-time medical officers, let alone specialised psychiatric services. Such a situation must have serious implications for the legal adjudication of responsibility. While the courts have generally accepted that the defence can be properly established without expert evidence, such evidence is clearly of vital importance where the accused's sanity is in issue. In practice, the accused, typically illiterate and unsophisticated, will be fortunate if he can even rely on the support of a government-appointed medical officer.[70] It is therefore possible that among those convicted and sentenced to death there are some who should not have been regarded as responsible for their actions.[71]

## Provocation

Following the English common law, the Penal Codes provide that provocation may be a defence to a charge of murder entitling the accused to be convicted of manslaughter. There are variations in the formulation of the defence, but in essence it incorporates a mixed subjective/objective test. Not only must the accused have been provoked to lose his self-control, but it must be shown that an ordinary/reasonable person would have been provoked to lose his self-control.[72] In applying the law of provocation it seems that the courts are less willing to make concessions to human frailty than to stress the sanctity of human life and the importance of maintaining public order. Thus, even where the codes do not expressly refer to the need for the retaliation to be reasonable, the courts have interpreted them to require proportionality. One commentator argues that the proportionality criterion is applied too strictly in Nigeria and that too much weight is given to the objective test. He points out that in most cases the defence is unsuccessful and he concludes that the number of murder convictions would be 'greatly reduced' if the legal definition of provocation was 'less stiff'.[73]

Any general conclusions to be drawn from this discussion are necessarily tentative, but it does seem that serious obstacles confront persons accused of murder who wish to rely on the defences of insanity or provocation, and that this can result in wrongful convictions.[74] Where an accused is uneducated and inadequately represented, there is a danger that a defence to which he may be entitled may not be raised at all, and even where it is raised, it may not find favour with a court less concerned with the individualisation of sentences than with general deterrence. While much of the material comes from Nigeria, commentators on Ghana conclude in similar vein: 'In general questions of *mens rea* and specific problems of intent, mistake, mental abnormality, provocation and absolute liability, [the Ghanaian courts] have given the Code a common law interpretation which has forced it in the direction of objective *mens rea* and general deterrence.'[75]

*Extenuating circumstances*
In southern Africa (Botswana, Lesotho, South Africa (until 1990), Swaziland, Zambia (since 1990)[76] and Zimbabwe) the death penalty is mandatory for murder unless there are extenuating circumstances. If extenuating circumstances exist, the death penalty is discretionary, as it is indeed for a number of other offences. The burden of proof lies on the accused and the range of factors that may be taken into account is narrower than those that would bear on the exercise of a sentencing discretion. A widely accepted definition of extenuating circumstances is 'any facts, bearing on the commission of the crime, which reduce the moral blameworthiness of the accused, as distinct from his legal culpability'.[77] Extenuating circumstances should be weighed against any aggravating circumstances in determining whether they have any appreciable bearing on the moral blameworthiness of the accused. Such an assessment is inevitably highly subjective and it is inevitable that inconsistencies occur.[78] Nevertheless the trial court must give reasons for its finding on extenuating circumstances and among the factors that have been held to extenuate are mental abnormality (falling short of insanity), provocation, intoxication, absence of an intent to kill, youth, a good motive, and a belief in witchcraft.[79] Judges (at least in Zimbabwe) tend to lean in favour of finding extenuating circumstances and it would be rare for a judge to exercise his discretion in favour of the death penalty where such circumstances were found to exist.[80] However, much depends on evidence being led in extenuation, and where the accused is inadequately represented or where the accused has pleaded not guilty, this may not be done; unless the judge calls for evidence himself, the death sentence will be passed.

A preferable approach was adopted in South Africa in the Criminal Law Amendment Act 107 of 1990.[81] This provides that a sentence of death shall be imposed only after the presiding judge conjointly with any assessors has made a finding on the presence or absence of any mitigatory or aggravating factors and if the presiding judge is satisfied that a sentence of death is the only proper sentence. This means that the death sentence can be imposed only in exceptionally serious cases, i.e. where 'it is imperatively called for' and the court must take into account all relevant factors, including those unrelated to the crime. Accordingly, the behaviour of the offender after the commission of the crime or the fact that he/she was poorly educated; susceptible to rehabilitation; or immature are all possible mitigatory circumstances.[82] An inordinate delay in the hearing of an appeal would certainly be another relevant consideration. In addition, an appeal court can set aside a death sentence if it considers that it would not itself have imposed such a sentence and impose the sentence which it considers appropriate.

*Conclusions*

The foregoing discussion indicates that, whatever constitutional guarantees may exist, in many countries a person accused of a capital offence cannot rely on receiving a fair trial. All too often proceedings are subject to error and prejudice and in the absence of an effective system of legal representation the odds are heavily weighted against the accused in a variety of ways. These deficiencies would be lamentable in any event, but where the life of the accused is at stake they become indefensible.

# POST TRIAL PROCEDURES

There are generally three avenues for a condemned person to pursue following conviction: (a) appealing to a higher court; (b) seeking the exercise of the prerogative of mercy; and (c) mounting a constitutional challenge.[83]

**Appeals**

The United Nations Safeguards guaranteeing protection of the rights of those facing the death penalty require that anyone sentenced to death shall have the right to appeal to a court of higher jurisdiction, and steps should be taken to ensure that such appeals become mandatory.[84] In contrast, as noted above, in Nigeria there is no provision in some cases for a formal appeal with sentences being merely confirmed or otherwise by the Military Governor. Elsewhere, the approach of the UN Safeguards is adhered to although many countries still do not provide an automatic right of appeal. In addition, the standard of legal representation for indigents remains a cause for concern in many countries and even an automatic appeal system does not necessarily correct any deficiency in representation especially when, as is often the case, the same lawyer represents the condemned person at the appeal.[85]

168

## Clemency and pardon

The United Nations Safeguards guaranteeing protection of the rights of those facing the death penalty also require that anyone sentenced to death shall have the right to seek pardon, or commutation of sentence. In the retentionist states, whilst the prerogative of mercy is invariably vested in the Head of State, there are considerable procedural differences. In Zambia the President effectively controls the whole process in that he appoints members of the Advisory Committee on the Prerogative of Mercy, is entitled to preside at its meetings and determines procedure.[86] A very similar procedure operates in Tanzania and Kenya. In Sierra Leone the President must act in accordance with a committee appointed by the Cabinet over which the Vice-President presides[87] whilst in Zimbabwe the President must act on the advice of the Cabinet,[88] although the comment by the Minister of Justice that the President 'has absolute power to pardon whoever he wishes' perhaps gives an insight into the decision-making process within the administration.[89]

In view of the need for an informed, independent and objective assessment of each case, the approach adopted in the Constitution of Uganda merits attention. Here the President may act on the advice of the advisory committee on the Prerogative of Mercy which consists of the attorney-general and six prominent citizens of Uganda, appointed by the President. A person is not qualified for appointment to the committee if a member of parliament or a district council or the Uganda Law Society.[90] This is similar to the position in Ghana, where the President acts in consultation with the Council of State (a body including representatives from the regions, the judiciary, traditional leaders, armed forces and police), and in Lesotho.[91]

The seeming lack of transparency and potential lack of objectivity in the procedure in many countries are a cause of concern[92] but the approach in Ghana, Sierra Leone and Uganda, where the respective Advisory Committees are given considerable discretion as to the information which they might consider, offers a potentially excellent model for others to follow. Here a written report of the case from the trial judge(s) together with 'such other information derived from the record of the case or elsewhere as may be necessary must be submitted to the committee'.[93] Arguably the function of the committee is quasi-judicial and thus the condemned prisoner has a right to see the materials placed before the committee and to have a hearing at which he or she is legally represented.[94]

In practice the operation of advisory committees is shrouded in secrecy and there is little information as to the extent to which the prerogative is exercised. In Zimbabwe and Zambia confidential reports are prepared by the Social Welfare Department based on interviews with the condemned prisoners and their relatives. Reports are also obtained from the trial judges and a memorandum from the Minister whilst the judgements of the High Court and Supreme Court are supplied. A similar procedure is probably followed elsewhere.[95]

169

## Constitutional challenges

Constitutional challenges are separate from the appeal process,[96] whilst the exercise of the prerogative of mercy in no way limits the jurisdiction of a court to hear and determine an alleged contravention of fundamental rights provisions.[97] Two questions have preoccupied the courts: (i) the constitutionality of the death sentence itself and (ii) the effect of delay in carrying out the death sentence.

### (i) Constitutionality of the death sentence

As *Table 2* indicates, the death penalty is specifically provided for in many of the national constitutions of the CAC. However, the past few years have seen several attempts to test the constitutionality of the sentence.

In Zimbabwe, section 15(1) of the Constitution provides that 'No person shall be subjected to torture or to inhuman or degrading punishment or other such treatment'. In 1990 in *Chileya v S*[98] the Supreme Court asked for full argument on the issue of whether the use of hanging contravened section 15(1). Before the hearing could take place the Government rushed through a constitutional amendment Act which included a provision specifically upholding the constitutionality of executions by hanging.[99] The Minister of Justice, Legal and Parliamentary Affairs informed Parliament that any holding to the contrary 'would be untenable to government which holds the correct and firm view . . . that Parliament makes the laws and the courts interpret them'.[100] He added that the abolition of the death sentence was a matter for the executive and legislature and that 'government will not and cannot countenance a situation where the death penalty is *de facto* abolished through the back door . . .' Given the supremacy of the constitution and the role of the Supreme Court to 'hear and determine constitutional issues', this response was particularly surprising and disappointing.[101]

In 1994 the issue was raised again in Tanzania in *Republic v Mbushuu.*[102] In the High Court, Mwalusanya J held that the death penalty was a cruel, inhuman and degrading punishment both inherently and in the manner of its execution (by hanging) and further that delays in carrying out executions and the dreadful conditions on death row were relevant in determining the issue.[103] Further, the imposition of the death sentence was not saved by article 30(2) of the Constitution i.e. it was not a provision which was 'lawful and in the public interest'. This finding was based on factors such as (i) the possibility of erroneous convictions, including the fact that most poor defendants did not receive adequate legal representation; (ii) the fact that sentences of life imprisonment provided protection against violent crime no less effective than the death sentence; and (iii) the mode of execution, the inhumane conditions on death row and delays. On appeal, the Court of Appeal agreed that the death sentence itself and the mode of execution offended the constitution but held that the sentence was saved by article 30(2). It was not an arbitrary sentence because decisions as to guilt or innocence were taken by the judges, there was no proof one way or another as to whether or not the death sentence was a more effective punishment than a period of imprisonment; and in any event it was for society and not for the courts to decide whether the death sentence was a necessary punishment. Having satisfied itself that society did favour the sentence, it held that in the circumstances 'the reasonable and necessary' standard had been met and the death sentence was a valid punishment.

In 1995 the Constitutional Court of South Africa also considered the matter in *S v Makwanyane and Mchunu* (above). Chaskalson P, giving the judgement of the court,[104] noted that section 11(2) of the Constitution of South Africa prohibited 'cruel, inhuman or degrading treatment or punishment' and emphasised that the section should not be interpreted in isolation but in its context, which included the history and background to the adoption of the Constitution, other provisions of the Constitution and, in particular, the fundamental rights provisions. He added that rights which were associated with section 11(2) and which were of particular importance to the case included section 9 (Every person shall have the right to life); section 10 (Every person shall have the right to respect for and protection of his or her dignity); and section 8(1) (Every person shall have the right to equality before the law and to equal protection of the law). Thus a punishment must meet the requirements of sections 8, 9 and 10, whether these sections were treated as giving meaning to section 11(2) or as prescribing separate and independent standards with which all punishments must comply.

The two issues which were addressed in particular were: the present state of public opinion; and the issue of proportionality. As regards the first, the court was prepared to assume that the overwhelming majority of the public was in favour of retaining the death penalty but Chaskalson P pointed out that public opinion was no substitute for the duty vested in the courts to uphold constitutional provisions without fear or favour. He added that if the decision of the Tanzanian Court of Appeal in *Mbushuu v Republic* was inconsistent with that conclusion, then he must express disagreement with it. Be that as it may, whilst public opinion is not decisive, as Kentridge J rightly pointed out, if public opinion on the question was clear it cannot be entirely ignored because 'the accepted mores of one's own society must have some relevance to the assessment'. However, he said the court had no evidence that this was the case. As noted earlier, the death sentence debate in South Africa certainly suggests that there was such evidence, a point that was forcefully put by the State in the case.

As for proportionality, this was said to be an 'ingredient' to be taken into account when deciding whether a penalty is cruel, inhuman and degrading. Factors included: the disparity between the crime and the penalty; the irredeemable character of the death sentence in circumstances where neither error nor arbitrariness can be excluded;[105] and disparities based on the race, poverty and other subjective factors relating to the accused. These were to be evaluated with other relevant factors, including the right to dignity and the right to life. Chaskalson P then concluded that the death penalty was indeed a cruel, inhuman and degrading punishment and proceeded to consider the limitation clause in section 33(1) of the Constitution. Concentrating on the issue of whether capital punishment for murder was reasonable and justifiable, he rejected the argument that the death sentence was a deterrent to violent crime. Further, the execution of persons each year would not provide any solution to the high crime rate.[106] On the issue of retribution, the court held that whilst a punishment must be commensurate with the offence, it need not be equivalent or identical. Further, retribution ought not to be given undue weight in the balancing process in the New South Africa in which a need for understanding and reparation had replaced vengeance and retaliation.[107]

Having balanced these issues against the alternative punishments available and the factors which, taken together, made capital punishment cruel, inhuman and degrading: the destruction of life, the annihilation of dignity, inequality and the possibility of error in the enforcement of the penalty and the existence of a severe alternative punishment, Chaskalson P held that it had not been shown that the death penalty would be more effective to deter or prevent murder than the alternative sentence of life imprisonment. Accordingly section 277(1)(a) of the Criminal Procedure Code (which provided for the death sentence for murder) was inconsistent with section 11(2) of the Constitution.[108]

The decision of the Constitutional Court has been hailed by Amnesty International as 'a huge step forward of international significance' and emphasises the important contribution that courts in the CAC are making in defending constitutional rights in death penalty cases.[109] Its impact remains to be seen but it has clearly focused attention on the issue in a manner which retentionist countries (and their courts) cannot ignore.

### (ii) Delay and the death penalty

Prolonged delays in carrying out the death penalty are not uncommon in many CACs with periods of over ten years being reported in Tanzania[110] and six years in Zimbabwe.[111] In 1993 the constitutional position regarding delay was considered by the Zimbabwe Supreme Court in *Catholic Commission for Justice and Peace in Zimbabwe v Attorney-General*[112] (the *CCJP* case). In March 1993 it was reported in a national newspaper that four condemned murderers were to be executed shortly.[113] Sentenced between 1987 and 1988, in all but one case their appeals were not heard and dismissed by the Supreme Court until 1991.[114] The court considered whether by March 1993 the dehumanizing factor of prolonged delay, viewed in conjunction with the harsh and degrading conditions in the condemned section of the holding prison, meant that the executions themselves would have constituted inhuman and degrading treatment contrary to section 15(1) of the Constitution of Zimbabwe (set out above). The case aroused considerable public debate with all views on the abolition debate being aired although, as the Supreme Court emphasised, the case concerned neither the constitutionality of the death sentence itself nor the manner of execution. In approaching its task, the court adopted a progressive and enlightened approach towards the plight of the condemned men noting that: 'prison walls do not keep out fundamental rights and protection' and no matter the magnitude of the crime, prisoners 'are not

172

reduced to non-persons [but] retain all basic rights, save those inevitably removed from them by law, expressly or by implication'.[115]

The first substantive question was whether reliance could be placed on the factor of delay at all. The Supreme Court adopted the view of Lords Scarman and Brightman in *Riley v Attorney-General of Jamaica*[116] who, in a 'haunting dissent' noted that the jurisprudence of the civilised world 'has recognised and acknowledged that prolonged delay in executing a sentence of death can make the punishment when it comes inhuman and degrading', adding that a sentence of death is one thing but 'sentence of death followed by lengthy imprisonment prior to execution is another'. This approach was surely correct since due process does not end with the pronouncement of sentence but goes on to offer constitutional protection for condemned persons against any abuse of executive power. It is thus 'an inhuman act to keep a man facing the agony of execution over a long extended period of time' and the cause is irrelevant.

Turning to the question of whether the delays constituted a breach of section 15(1), the court recognised that the section is a 'provision that embodies broad and idealistic notions of dignity, humanity and decency' and that its application is dependent upon the exercise of a value judgement that takes into account not only the emerging consensus of values in the civilised international community but of contemporary norms and sensitivities of individual societies. In making such a judgement, the court considered, amongst other things, the average period from the date of sentence to the carrying out of executions in previous years (much shorter than in the current case) and the fact that, in any event, the delays were almost entirely outside of the control of the condemned men. Accordingly, the delays were inordinate. As regards the appropriate remedy, it was held that whilst the power to 'commute' a sentence of death was constitutionally vested in the executive, the court had a separate role, mandated by the Constitution, to protect and enforce fundamental rights. In doing so, it was essential that, in the exercise of its wide discretion, the court should award a meaningful and effective remedy for the breach of section 15(1) and this was best achieved by ordering that the sentences of death be vacated and substituting a sentence of imprisonment for life.

The immediate impact of the *CCJP* decision was that death sentences on some twenty condemned prisoners who had endured lengthy periods on death row were commuted to life imprisonment. Regrettably the decision resulted in a highly critical response from government which asserted, untenably, that the court was usurping the functions of the executive. Indeed within weeks the Constitution of Zimbabwe Amendment (No 13) Act 1993 was passed which sought to overturn the decision by retrospectively exempting the death penalty from the scope of section 15(1).[117]

Overall, in view of the many prisoners on death row in the CAC, the CCJP decision could have a profound effect if other jurisdictions are prepared to follow suit, especially since it has received support from the Court of Appeal in Tanzania and the Constitutional Court in South Africa.[118] The decision is obviously inconvenient for retentionist governments but nevertheless, the retention of the death sentence carries with it the responsibility for ensuring that the whole procedure is carried out with all possible expedition. [119]

## DEATH ROW CONDITIONS

By its very nature, death row is a terrifying place and, by statute, condemned persons in the CAC generally enjoy very limited rights, such as access to a minister of religion and a legal representative, and limited privileges such as visits by family members and friends. The available information indicates that in practice conditions in African prisons make the plight of condemned prisoners particularly desperate. In Nigeria, living conditions of some 12 juveniles sentenced to death for armed robbery by the Lagos State Armed Robbery and Firearms Tribunal in June 1988 were reportedly 'unfit for any human, much less young adolescents. They are mixed into cells with other condemned convicts, six to a cell, approximately eight by ten feet [2.4 to 3 metres].' [120] In the *CCJP* case, the Zimbabwe Supreme Court painted a grim picture of condemned prisoners being subjected to mental and physical torture from warders, confined to tiny cells alone for a minimum of almost twenty two hours per day, deprived of all clothing for much of that time, even during the cold winter months and with little or no exercise facilities and no reading material save that of a religious nature. Similar conditions reportedly also exist in Zambia and Tanzania [121] and were a hallmark of the death penalty regime in South Africa. [122]

Governments appear reluctant and/or unable to alleviate the plight of condemned prisoners and it has been left to the courts to act, with the Supreme Court of Zimbabwe again taking the lead. In *Conjwayo v Minister of Justice* [123] a condemned prisoner claimed that the treatment being received on death row constituted degrading and inhuman treatment contrary to section 15(1) of the Constitution of Zimbabwe. Gubbay CJ recognised that, in many jurisdictions, courts had adopted a broad 'hands off' attitude towards matters of prison administration but that:

a policy of judicial restraint cannot encompass any failure to take cognisance of a valid claim that a prison regulation or practice offends a fundamental constitutional protection. [124]

He added that section 15 guaranteed that punishment or institutionalised treatment of offenders be exercised within the ambit of civilised standards. Turning to the facts of the case, he held that to confine a human being in a tiny cell for lengthy periods with little or no exercise facilities was:

174

plainly offensive to one's notion of humanity and decency. It transgresses the boundaries of civilised standards and involves the infliction of unnecessary suffering. [125]

As a result, the court directed that the applicant enjoy specified improvements in his living conditions.

Overall, given death row conditions in at least some of the CACs, a policy of judicial intervention is both timely and essential and courts in other jurisdictions should follow the lead of Zimbabwe. Prison walls are not an impenetrable barrier to the exercise of their constitutional rights by condemned prisoners and courts have a duty to uphold them.

Of course the practical impact of prison conditions litigation depends on two main factors. Firstly, the commitment on the part of governments and prison authorities to take active steps to re-assess penal policy and improve conditions. [126] Here the economic card is sometimes played i.e. unsatisfactory conditions on death row are inevitable, given the poor state of the economy of developing countries. This does not explain much of the suffering experienced by condemned prisoners and, in any event, the argument was firmly rejected by Mwalusanya J in *Republic v Mbushuu* with the words 'It is my view that the defence of poverty can be offered elsewhere, but not when the basic human rights of an individual are at stake'. [127] Secondly, it pre-supposes that prisoners know of their rights and have access to outside assistance. In *Conjwayo* the applicant was able to afford legal representation, but this is a luxury few can afford. In view of this, if the constitutional rights of condemned prisoners are to have any lasting and far-reaching effect, then the work of the courts must be reinforced by other institutions and mechanisms such as the right of prisoners to complain to an Ombudsman and the practice of regular prison visits by judicial officers.

## CONCLUSIONS AND PROSPECTS

This chapter has shown that, with some notable exceptions, in the CAC there remains a continuity in penal policy with the colonial period with an emphasis on retribution and general deterrence. This in turn has led to the retention of the death penalty for a wide range of offences and in some countries the introduction of new capital offences in apparent disregard of the ICCPR provision limiting its use to the most serious offences. A contributory factor is the almost universal rise in levels of serious crime, especially in urban areas, which has helped maintain public support for retention despite the fact that there is little evidence that the death sentence has had any effect on crime levels. Indeed the available evidence points to socio-economic factors and a failure of effective policing as the major contributory reasons for the crime problem and for which the death penalty is not a solution. [128]

The chapter has also highlighted procedural deficiencies in many countries and the critical need for transparency and accountability in the whole process. Particular concern centres on the lack of and the quality of legal representation and the plight of mentally disordered persons. This emphasises the need for states to re-assess their current laws and procedures, many of which also date back to the colonial period, and to bring them in line with their international commitments. In this connection, it is essential that persons charged with capital offences should receive free and meaningful legal representation throughout the entire criminal justice process. Admittedly these resources are often scarce and expensive. Whilst the state bears the prime responsibility for their provision, it is suggested that the appropriate local professional bodies actively assist in ensuring that such assistance is given to those involved in capital trials.

A more positive trend has been a willingness on the part of the courts in a few countries to deal with death penalty issues, particularly in the constitutional context. Together with enhanced access to comparative and international materials and an increasing awareness of international human rights norms, this should encourage not only courts elsewhere in the CAC to recognize and uphold the constitutional rights of condemned persons but also human rights bodies and activists to be prepared to bring appropriate cases to court.

Prospects for change remain uncertain. Despite the abolition of the death sentence in several CAC countries, the perceived belief that capital punishment is necessary to combat the continuing rise in crime and the limited scope of the debate on the issue makes it unlikely that more of the CAC will become abolitionist, at least in the near future. What is clear is that the capital punishment debate in the CAC cannot take place in isolation but must form part of a reconsideration of penal policy as a whole. The task of encouraging and assisting governments to undertake this task falls especially on institutions of civil society. This must be backed up by the necessary research. As this chapter has revealed, information on CAC is scattered and patchy and no in-depth studies yet exist. A major reason for this is the veil of secrecy under which death penalty matters are handled. This is almost inexplicable for if the aim of capital punishment is general deterrence or pure retribution, then it is surprising that governments do not seek to carry out executions in the full blaze of publicity. It is hoped that this chapter will act as a catalyst for that further research.

ENDNOTES See page 179

## Table 1: Offences Attracting the Death Penalty in the CAC

| | |
|---|---|
| **The Gambia** | Murder (re-introduced in 1995) |
| **Ghana** | Attempted murder, economic offences, murder, political offences, treason |
| **Kenya** | Armed robbery, murder, treason |
| **Lesotho** | Murder, rape |
| **Malawi** | Armed robbery, murder, rape, treason |
| **Mauritius** | Drug trafficking, murder (both abolished in 1995) |
| **Namibia** | None |
| **Nigeria** | Armed robbery, arson, drug offences, economic sabotage, murder, treason |
| **Seychelles** | None |
| **Sierra Leone** | Murder, robbery with violence, mutiny, treason |
| **South Africa** | Treason |
| **Swaziland** | Murder |
| **Tanzania** | Murder, treason |
| **Uganda** | Armed robbery, armed smuggling, kidnap with intent to murder, murder, mutiny, treason |
| **Zambia** | Aggravated robbery, murder, treason |
| **Zimbabwe** | Murder, treason |

## Table 2: Constitutional Provisions Regarding the Death Penalty

**The Gambia**  No person shall be deprived of his life intentionally except in execution of the sentence of a court ... s.14(1).

**Ghana**  As The Gambia, s.13(1).

**Kenya**  As The Gambia, s.71(1).

**Lesotho**  Every human being has an inherent right to life. No one shall be arbitrarily deprived of his life: but not so deprived if done in execution of the sentence of death imposed by a court in respect of a criminal offence under the law of Lesotho of which he has been convicted. s.5.

**Malawi**  As Lesotho, s.16.

**Mauritius**  As The Gambia, s.23.

**Namibia**  The right to life shall be respected and protected. No law may prescribe death as a competent sentence. No Court or Tribunal shall have the power to impose a sentence of death upon any person. No executions shall take place in Namibia. art. 6.

**Seychelles**  Everyone has a right to life and no one shall be deprived of life intentionally. A law shall not provide for a sentence of death to be imposed by any court. art.15.

**Nigeria**  As The Gambia, s.32(1).

**Sierra Leone**  As The Gambia, s.16

**South Africa**  Every person shall have the right to life. s.9.

**Swaziland**  No constitutional document in force.

**Tanzania**  Everyone has a right to life and to receive from the society protection of his life, in accordance with the law. art.14.

**Uganda**  No person shall be deprived of life intentionally except in execution of a sentence of a court of law in a fair trial in respect of a criminal offence under the law of Uganda of which he has been convicted. No law shall be made by Parliament depriving any person of his right to life except in very grave circumstances acceptable in a democratic society. s.52 (draft Constitution).

**Zambia**  As The Gambia, art.12(1).

**Zimbabwe**  As The Gambia s.12(1). Note s.15(4): The execution of a person who has been sentenced to death by a competent court in respect of a criminal offence of which he has been convicted shall not be held to be in contravention of subsection (1) solely on the ground that the execution is [by hanging].

178

# ENDNOTES

1. For example, UNSDRI, *The Death Penalty: a Bibliographical Research*, Publication No. 32, 1988 contains only a handful of references on Commonwealth Africa. There is more material on extra-judicial executions but this topic is outside the scope of the chapter.

2. For a full examination of the distinction between civil and criminal law in African societies see T. O. Elias, *The Nature of African Customary Law* (Manchester, 1956), ch.VII.

3. For Nigeria see Alan Milner, 'The sanctions of customary criminal law: a study in social control', [1965] *Nigerian Law Journal* 173, at 186 ff. and A. G. Karibi-Whyte, *History and Sources of Nigerian Criminal Law* (Spectrum, 1993), Chapter 4. For East Africa see James S. Read, 'Crime and Punishment in East Africa: the Twilight of Customary Law', (1964) 10 *Howard Law Journal* 164.

4. The mode of execution varied. Where guilt was uncertain, trial by ordeal might take place.

5. In Sierra Leone the criminal law is based on the uncodified common law supplemented by local legislation together with a number of applied English statutes. In southern Africa, English criminal law was introduced subject to being interpreted according to the principles of Roman-Dutch law.

6. See H. F. Morris, 'A history of the adoption of criminal law and procedure in British Colonial Africa', *Journal of African Law*, 1974, 18, 1, 6; J. S. Read, 'Criminal law in the Africa of today and tomorrow', *Journal of African Law*, 1963, 7, 5; S. F. R. Coldham, 'Crime and Punishment in British Colonial Africa', *Recueils de la societe Jean Bodin pour l'histoire comparative des institutions*, 1991, LVIII, 4, 57; John Hatchard and Muna Ndulo, *Readings in Criminal Law and Criminology* (Lusaka, 1994), especially Chapter 1.

7. Trial by jury was confined to West African colonies (not protectorates) and to Kenya and Southern Rhodesia (where it was further confined to Europeans).

8. In Southern Africa, although originally mandatory for murder, it was subsequently made discretionary where there were extenuating circumstances. It was, moreover, discretionary for a number of other offences.

9. Offences of this kind, so called 'Black Peril' offences, were capital in parts of Southern Africa too.

10. For example, in Ghana between 1952 and 1960, clemency was exercised in about 50% of cases. See R. B. Seidman and J. D. Abaka Eyison in Alan Milner (ed.), *African Penal Systems* (Routledge, 1969), at 75.

11. Thus, for example, section 33(12) of the Independence Constitution of Nigeria provided: No person shall be convicted of a criminal offence unless that offence is defined and the penalty therefor is prescribed in a written law.

12. See *Table 1* at the end of the chapter for a country-by-country list of capital offences.

13. This provides that a sentence of death may be imposed only for the most serious crimes.

14. While the constitutions of most of the countries under consideration protect the right to life, exceptions are made in respect of death sentences imposed by the courts (see *Table 2*). The constitutionality of the death sentence is discussed below.

15. The Penal Code (Chap. 16 of the Revised Laws of Tanzanie 1966), s. 200(c) and (d). The Penal Code Amendment Act of Uganda, no. 29 of 1970, abolished implied malice and constructive malice, but retained express malice and recklessness in its definition of malice aforethought.

16. [1985] AC 905.

17. Penal Code, s.200(b).

18. Penal Code Amendment Act (No. 2) 1974, s. 12.

19. Quoted in Kalombo T. Mwansa 'Aggravated Robbery and the Death Penalty in Zambia: an Examination of the 1974 Penal Code Amendment Act (No. 2)', *Zambia Law Journal*, 1984, 16, 69 at 71.

20. The Decree (as amended) was re-enacted under the same name in 1984. Death may be by hanging or by firing squad. See, generally, M. A. Owoade, 'Death Penalty - The Nigerian Experience', *Indian Socio-Legal Journal*, 1985, XI, 16.

21. Act no. 12 of 1968, replacing the 1966 Act of the same name which the courts had interpreted in a restrictive way in order to avoid passing a death sentence. See F. M. Ssekandi, 'Uganda and Kondos: Capital Punishment revisited', *Eastern Africa Law Review*, 1970, 3, 83.

22. In Cameroon it has even been extended to various forms of theft by a draconian 1972 amendment to the Penal Code. See W. P. Capstick, 'Capital theft and the Cameroon Penal Code Amendment Ordinance', *British Journal of Criminology*, 1973, 13, 284.

23. This decree had retroactive effect and it appears that at least one person was executed in respect of a drugs offence committed before the decree was introduced: see Amnesty International, *When the State kills. The death penalty v. human rights* (London, 1989), at 38. All these decrees were subsequently amended, in response to public pressure, so as to remove the death sentence. See, generally, M. A. Owoade, 'The Military and the Criminal Law in Nigeria', *Journal of African Law*, 1989, 33, 2, 135, and A. A. Adeyemi,' Death Penalty: Criminological Perspectives: the Nigerian Situation', *Revue internationale de droit penal*, 1987, 58, 485.

24. PNDC Law No. 78 of 1984 s.9. Section 16(1) of the same law empowered a Public Tribunal to impose the death penalty 'for such offences as may be specified in writing by the [Provisional National Defence Council] and in respect of cases where the tribunal is satisfied that very grave circumstances meriting such a penalty have been revealed'. The law was repealed by the Courts Act No. 459 of 1993, s. 120(1).

25. Ch. 65, enacted in 1960.

26. See David Welsh, 'Capital Punishment in South Africa', in Alan Milner (ed.), op. cit., at 405.

27. Figures given by Mwansa, op. cit. at 73. The exercise of the prerogative of mercy is normally announced on or about October 24 during the Independence Day celebrations or during the Labour Day celebrations: information furnished by the Ministry of Legal Affairs.

28. Information received from the Ministry of Law and Constitutional Affairs.

29. However, five persons were reportedly executed in Botswana in August 1995.

30. Figures given by Adeyemi, op.cit. Even so, this was a relatively small percentage of the 33,599 convictions for capital offences during that period.

31. For example, between July and September 1995 78 persons were executed in public by firing squad in Nigeria.

32. *Report of the Nyalali Commission*, vol III, at 25

33. Mwalusanya, J in *Republic v Mbushuu* [1994] 2 LRC 335 at 351.

34. Report entitled *Aspects of Capital Punishment* Harare, 1982

35. Dumbutshena, infra. Note n. 80, 531.

36. John Hatchard, *Individual Freedoms and State Security: The Case of Zimbabwe*, London/Harare/Ohio, 1993, 20.

37. For example, in its quarterly publication, *Legal Forum*, the Legal Resources Foundation has carried several articles and comments presenting all aspects of the death sentence debate.

38. In fact many of the prisoners on death row had their sentences commuted as a result of the Supreme Court decisions in *CCJP* and *Nkomo* (see below).

39. Following a return to multi-party politics, the Seychelles also saw a break with the past with the abolition of the death sentence in the new 1993 Constitution.

40. 1995 (3) SA 391.

41. Reported in *South African Times* 7 June 1995.

42. John Hatchard, 'Crime and Penal Policy in Zambia', (1985) 23 *Journal of Modern African Studies* 483, 487-88.

43. As did Mwalusanya J. in *Republic v Mbushuu* (above) at 352-3.

44. In *S v Makwanyane and Mchunu*, at paragraph 126, Mahomed J. also emphasised that successful deterrence of serious crime involved the need for substantial redress in socio-economic conditions in South Africa: see paragraphs 286-295.

45. See Adeyemi, op.cit., 489.

46. Op.cit., 501

47. Draft resolution A/C.3/49/L.32.

48. Paragraph 4.

49. The Gambia, Kenya, Lesotho, Mauritius, Malawi, Namibia, Nigeria, Seychelles, Tanzania, Zambia and Zimbabwe are all parties to the ICCPR. South Africa is a signatory. The African Charter on Human and Peoples' Rights, art. 7, sets out standards for a fair trial.

50. Kenya abolished them in 1963.

51. E.g. in Kenya and Zimbabwe. It has been abandoned in Nigeria.

52. This is a feature of all Commonwealth African constitutions. See, for example, the Kenya Constitution s.77(2)(d).

53. An accused also has the right to an interpreter as part of fair trial provisions. In the Mauritian case of *Kunnath v State* [1993] 2 LRC 326, where the accused had been sentenced to death for drug trafficking, the Privy Council held that the failure of the trial court to ensure adequate interpretation for the accused meant that the trial, for all practical purposes, had been conducted without his presence and he had accordingly been deprived of a fair trial and a substantial miscarriage of justice had occurred. The appeal was allowed and the conviction quashed.

54. Most countries run either legal aid schemes, albeit of rather limited scope or a *pro deo* scheme. In Ghana, Lesotho, Malawi and Zambia legal representation is available as of right to those facing a capital charge.

55. Bwonwong'a points out the danger that an unrepresented accused runs the risk of incriminating himself at this stage and recommends that legal aid should be extended to such proceedings. Momwanyi Bwonwong'a, *Procedures in Criminal Law in Kenya* (East African Educational Publishers, 1994), at 176.

56. *Mbushuu v Republic,* above at 353, *per* Mwalusanya, J.

57. *Bwonwong'a* at 177.

58. See *Udifua v. The State,* (1988) 7 SCNJ 118 (retrial ordered) and *Okosi and Another v. The State,* [1989] 1 NWLR (Pt 100) 642 (appeal dismissed

in spite of finding that the defence had been handled in a casual manner).

59. David Welsh, 'Capital punishment in South Africa', in Alan Milner (ed.), *op.cit.*, at 418 and Christine Murray and others, 'The Death Penalty in the Cape Provincial Division: 1986-1988', *South African Journal on Human Rights*, 1989, 5, 154 at 165 and 169. Also see J. Mihalik, 'Articled clerks, legal aid and capital offenders', *South African Law Journal*, 1991, 108, 4, 718 on the unsatisfactory operation of the *pro deo* system in Bophuthatswana and in Zimbabwe see G. Feltoe, 'Reliability of decisions about when to execute in Zimbabwe', (1991-92) 9-10 *Zimbabwe Law Review* 162.

60. In one instance the accused were sentenced to death one day, the sentences confirmed the following day and carried out on the day after confirmation. Amnesty International, *op.cit.*, at 45.

61. A large number of alleged coup plotters have been executed under this decree. There are a number of other decrees providing for the constitution of military tribunals to deal with a variety of offences, some of which originally attracted the death penalty. See, generally, M. A. Owoade, *op.cit.* (1989). The Public Tribunals set up by the military regime in Ghana in 1982 also aroused controversy. Composed largely of non-lawyers, they had broad jurisdiction and were not bound by strict rules of evidence and procedure. Although it was possible for an accused to be represented by counsel, the tribunals were largely boycotted by the local legal profession.

62. There were worldwide expressions of concern at the legitimacy of the trial process following the executions in November 1995 of Ken Saro-Wiwa and eight others convicted of murder by a special tribunal.

63. Paul Brietzke, 'Murder and Manslaughter in Malawi's Traditional Courts', *Journal of African Law,* 1974, 18, 1, 37.

64. For an analysis of the Traditional Courts' handling of a well-known treason trial, see M. Nzunda, 'Criminal law in internal conflict of laws in Malawi', *Journal of African Law,* 1985, 29, 2, 129.

65. Constitution of Malawi 1994, art.110(3).

66. This in accordance with article 6 of the ICCPR.

67. In one Nigerian case twelve young persons were sentenced to death for armed robbery even though they all maintained that they were

under the age of seventeen and even though the prosecution conceded that one of them was. The Civil Liberties Organization of Nigeria considered that the prosecution arbitrarily assigned ages to the defendants. See Civil Liberties Organization, *Annual Report on Human Rights in Nigeria, 1993*, 50. After five years of incarceration the defendants were released, in response to local and international pressure.

68. Uganda introduced the defence of diminished responsibility in 1960 (Penal Code s. 188A) and this was followed by Lesotho. Section 28 of the Nigerian Criminal Code is unusual in admitting (see the italicised words) the defence of irresistible impulse. It provides: A person is not responsible for an act or omission if at the time of doing the act or making the omission he is in such a state of mental disease or natural mental infirmity as to deprive him of capacity to understand what he is doing, *or of capacity to control his actions*, or of capacity to know that he ought not to do the act or make the omission.

69. In *R. v. Eriyamremu*, [1959] W.R.N.L.R. 270 the defence of insanity was rejected because any mental infirmity afflicting the accused was induced by her worship of *juju* and witchcraft; it was not 'natural'.

70. See, generally, Alan Milner and T. Asuni, 'Psychiatry and the Criminal Offender', in Alan Milner, *African Penal Systems, op.cit.*, at 317. It is doubtful whether things have improved markedly in the past 25 years. One writer gives examples of psychiatrists testifying without having actually examined the accused, relying simply on the accused's statement or on an account of the accused's history. K. S. Chukkol, *The Law of Crimes in Nigeria* (ABU Press, Zaria, Nigeria, 1988), at 83. In *S v Musimwa* (High Court of Zimbabwe, unreported) Smith J noted 'In December 1992 I visited Harare Remand Prison. One of the inmates who made a complaint was a person I had convicted of murder in 1984 and sentenced to death. His appeal was heard in 1987. The Supreme Court set aside the conviction because it felt that the mental state of the appellant should be investigated. Six years later the unfortunate person is still in prison waiting for the assessment of his mental state when he committed the offence which is now more than 10 years ago'. In June 1993 in Zimbabwe there was just one government psychiatrist in post.

71. It has been noted that an increasing proportion of convicted murderers in Nigeria are mentally abnormal, though not legally insane: M. A. Owoade, op.cit., at 20. A shortage of appropriate facilities means that those who are found to be insane are often simply returned to the prison system.

72. Some Codes define the 'ordinary person' by reference to the 'class to which the accused belongs', but even in those jurisdictions where there is no statutory definition, the courts have tended to interpret the expression in a similar way. See, for example, *R. v. Fabiano Kinene*, 8 E.A.C.A. 96 (Uganda, 1941).

73. M. A. Owoade, *op.cit.* (fn 17), at 19. See also M.A. Owoade, 'Defence of provocation in Nigeria', 2 *Nigerian Behavioural Sciences Journal,* 1979, 2, 87 and K.S.Chukkol, *op.cit.*, at 142.

74. One commentator on the Nigerian penal system wrote that most murders were committed under the influence of mental abnormaility or uncontrolled passion. Alan Milner, *Nigerian Penal System* (London, Sweet and Maxwell, 1972), at 341.

75. R. B. Seidman and J. D. Abaka Edison, 'Ghana' in Alan Milner (ed.), *op.cit.*, at 75. They find the same inclination reflected in the sentencing patterns.

76. The Penal Code (Amendment) Act 1990 provides that a death sentence for murder need not be imposed where there are 'extenuating circumstances'. It was possibly no coincidence that at the time the Act was passed, the son of the then President of Zambia was facing a murder charge: see further, M. Mbao, 'The Criminal Justice System on Trial in Zambia', (1992) 36 *Journal of African Law* 175

77. *S. v. Letsolo*, (1970) (3) SA 476 (A).

78. Research in South Africa has shown that the personal disposition of a judge towards the death penalty is significant in explaining disparities in sentencing patterns. Christina Murray and others, *op.cit.* There has also been evidence of a racialist bias in the conviction and sentencing patterns of South African courts. See B. Van D. Van Niekerk, 'Hanged by the neck until you are dead', *South African Law Journal,* 1969, 86, 457, and *South African Law Journal,* 1970, 87, 60. Also see David Welsh in Alan Milner (ed.), *op.cit.* 414. No extenuating circumstances were found, notoriously, in the case of the Sharpeville Six convicted of murder on the basis of 'common purpose' even though none of their acts had contributed causally to the death of the deceased.

79. See G. Feltoe. 'Extenuating circumstances: a life and death issue', *Zimbabwe Law Review*, 1986, 4, 60; K. Frimpong and A. McCall Smith, *The Criminal Law of Botswana* (Juta, 1992), at 75ff. Feltoe argues that a 'scientific' approach is required in order to reduce these inconsistencies and that the courts should be given more guidance on what constitutes

extenuating circumstances. However, a reduction in judicial discretion works against an individualised death penalty determination.

80. A former Chief Justice of Zimbabwe considers that it has been common practice among judges to lean towards a finding of manslaughter or of extenuating circumstances: E. Dumbutshena, 'The death penalty in Zimbabwe', *Revue internationale de droit penal*, 1987, 58, 521 at 524.

81. Although the death sentence for murder has been declared unconstitutional in South Africa (see below) the 1990 statute is an excellent model for retentionist states.

82. See generally J. van Rooyen, 'South Africa's new death sentence: is the bell tolling for the hangman?', (1991) 4 *South African Journal of Criminal Justice* 79.

83. There have been no references to the United Nations Human Rights Committee from any of the CAC.

84. Safeguard 6.

85. A notorious example comes from Zimbabwe where a lawyer representing a condemned person *pro deo* informed the appeal court that he could offer no extenuating circumstances. The court thought otherwise and requested him to address it on the issue whereupon the lawyer was forced to admit that he was unable to do so as he had not read the brief. See generally G. Feltoe, 'The reliability of decisions about when to execute in Zimbabwe', (1991-92) 9-19 *Zimbabwe Law Review* 162.

86. Article 60 Constitution of Zambia.

87. Article 63, Constitution of Sierra Leone.

88. Section 31H(5) Constitution of Zimbabwe.

89. See (1994) 6(1) *Legal Forum* 4. For a fuller assessment of the power to pardon in southern African countries see John Hatchard 'Undermining the Constitution by Constitutional Means: Some Thoughts on the New Constitutions of Southern Africa' (1995) 28 *Comparative and International Law Journal of Southern Africa*, 21-35.

90. Article 121 Constitution of Uganda.

91. In Lesotho the three members of the Pardons Committee on the Prerogative of mercy are appointed 'by the King acting in accordance with the advice of the Judicial Service Commission from amongst persons who are not public officers or members of the [legislature]': section 102(1). This has the capacity to be relatively objective particularly because the Commission consists of the Chief Justice, Attorney General, Chairman of the Public Service Commission, and others who have held high judicial office.

92. In *Republic v Mbushuu* (above, at 353) Mwalusanya J. states that in Tanzania 'many murderers are set free at the President's whims, under the guise of commuting the sentence or death or pardon'.

93. Article 72(2) Constitution of Ghana, section 63(2) Constitution of Sierra Leone and article 121(5) Constitution of Uganda. The Constitution of Sierra Leone also requires a medical report on the condemned prisoner to be made available.

94. In *R v Secretary of State for the Home Department, ex parte Doody* [1994] 1 A.C. 531 the House of Lords recognised a right to review the exercise of prerogative powers.

95. The use of amnesties is also a feature of countries in the southern African region in particular. In Zimbabwe, for example, periodic amnesties, normally reserved for special occasions, have led to the commuting of death sentences or the pardoning of condemned prisoners. Indeed much of the evidence on death row conditions relied on by the Supreme Court in Zimbabwe in the *CCJP* case (see below) came from a former condemned prisoner who had spent three years on death row for dissident related murders before being given a free pardon to mark Zimbabwe's Tenth Anniversary of Independence in 1990.

96. *Nemi v The State* [1994] LRC 376.

97. For example in *Nkomo and Moyo v Attorney-General* (1994) 20 Commonwealth Law Bulletin 56, the Supreme Court of Zimbabwe held it had the power to hear a constitutional challenge even after executive clemency had been refused.

98. SC 64/90 unreported.

99. This became section 15(4) of the Constitution of Zimbabwe which is set out in *Table 2*.

100. *Parliamentary Debates*, 6 December, 1990.

101. For a full discussion see John Hatchard, 'The Constitution of Zimbabwe: Towards a Model for Africa?' (1991) 35 *Journal of African Law*, 79.

102. [1994] 2 LRC 335 (High Court of Tanzania)

103. These factors are considered separately below.

104. The other ten judges concurred but wrote separate judgements emphasising different reasons for declaring the death penalty unconstitutional. These are noted below where appropriate.

105. Judge Ackermann also emphasised the issue of arbitrariness in the implementation and application of the death penalty which meant it was inconsistent with section 9, the right to life.

106. A point noted above.

107. See paragraph 130

108. Chaskalson P did not consider whether the death penalty would be inconsistent with the constitutional rights to life, to equal protection under the law and to dignity if they had been dealt with separately and not treated together as giving meaning to section 11(2). However Judges Didcott, Ackermann, Kreigler, Langa, Mohamed and O' Regan all found the death sentence violated the right to life.

109. In Mauritius the Court of Appeal has held in *Amasimbi v S* [1993] M.R. 227 that even though the Constitution permits the use of the death penalty, it is always open to the courts, pursuant to other constitutional provisions regarding inhuman punishment, to determine that any form of punishment is unconstitutional in certain cases.

110. Information contained in an article in the *Business Times* (Tanzania) of 2 April 1993 referred to in *Mbushuu* (above).

111. The long delays in Zambia involving condemned prisoners were strongly criticised by the attorney general in 1992 who blamed the courts for delaying dealing with cases resulting in condemned prisoners being kept in suspense for many years. Address to a seminar on homicide organized by the Zambia Law Development Commission, May 1992. In January 1996 it was reported that there were 123 condemned prisoners in Kalowg's Mukobeko prison who had been there up to 30 years (*Times of Zambia*, 31 Jan 1996). In Nigeria the period is generally at least two years or more: see Owoade, op.cit.

112. SC 73/93, unreported.

113. The information was apparently leaked to the press for hitherto the official announcement of executions was made only after they had taken place.

114. In the case of the fourth man, his appeal was dismissed by the Supreme Court in 1988.

115. At 9. See also the case of *Conjwayo v Minister of Justice* 1991 (1) ZLR 105 (SC).

116. [1982] 3 All ER 469.

117. In *Nkomo and Moyo v Attorney-General* (above) the Supreme Court was still able to protect the rights of condemned prisoners who had also endured lengthy delays by holding that their pre-existing rights remained unaffected by the new Act because (i) *litis contestatio* had already occurred and (ii) where fundamental human rights and freedoms were conferred on individuals under a constitution, derogations therefrom, as far as the language permitted, must be narrowly or strictly construed.

118. In *Mbushuu* (above) and *Makwanyane and Mchunu* (above) respectively.

119. On this point the Supreme Court made specific recommendations to expedite the consideration of cases.

120. Referred to in Civil Liberties Organization, *Behind the Wall*, (Lagos, 1991) 9.

121. Mwalusanya J in *Republic v Mbushuu* (above, at 350) states ' As regards the horrible conditions in the death cells, it is common knowledge that the cells are small, dirty, overcrowded, [prisoners endure a] very poor diet, are under watch 24 hours per day, and medical facilities will only be available to these prisoners if the Prison Department is allocated enough funds to pay for their treatment'.

122. See P Naidoo, *Waiting to Die in Pretoria* Harare, 1990.

123. 1991 (1) ZLR 105.

124. At 109.

125. At 113-114.

126. Certainly the Supreme Court of Zimbabwe in the CCJP case found little change in death row conditions even after the *Conjwayo* decision.

127. *Op.cit.* at 350

128. Indeed the prevalence of instant justice i.e. the attacking and beating (and often killing) of alleged wrong-doers by members of the public, emphasises lack of public confidence in the ability of the authorities to combat crime effectively.

CHAPTER 8

# The United Kingdom and the European Union

## Peter Hodgkinson*

The purpose of this chapter is to review the status of the death penalty in the United Kingdom and that country's continued abolitionist stance. It also considers, albeit briefly, the position of other countries within the European Union.

## THE UNITED KINGDOM

The history of the death penalty in England has been explored by V. A. C. Gatrell[1] and Peter Linebaugh,[2] whilst Harry Potter has charted major changes in practice, legislation and religious attitudes that led to eventual abolition.[3]

Gatrell estimates that there were between 6,322 and 7,713 executions in England and Wales for the period 1770-1830 and that for the same period some 36,566 death sentences were passed.[4] From 1832 the death penalty was gradually abolished for certain crimes and by 1861, for all practical purposes, treason and murder remained the only capital offences. Between 1837 and 1868 (the date of the last public execution), according to Gatrell, there were 347 executions. In the final years of the death penalty in Britain, from the Homicide Act 1957 until the eve of abolition in 1964, 48 people were sentenced to death of whom 29 were executed.

### The road to abolition
The Murder (Abolition of the Death Penalty) Act 1965 abolished the death penalty except for treason and piracy, initially for a period of five years, after which it was ratified by a free vote in Parliament, allowing members of both Houses of Parliament to vote according to their conscience and not on party lines. This vote, which was brought forward a year to avoid a clash with the general election, led to a confirmation of abolition by resolution of both Houses of Parliament on 18 December 1969. The death penalty is retained for treason in peacetime and in wartime under the Treason Act 1351 (as amended in 1914) and in England and Wales for piracy with violence under the Piracy Act 1837. It is also retained for a number of offences committed by members of the armed forces (e.g. treason and espionage) under the Army Act 1955; the Air Force Act 1955; and the Naval Discipline Act 1957. Under the Armed

Forces Act 1981 the death penalty was abolished for civilians convicted of spying whilst on a naval vessel or in an overseas naval establishment.

There had been a number of occasions prior to the 1965 legislation when moves towards abolition were debated and defeated. Successful amendments were passed on three occasions in the House of Commons only to meet defeat in the House of Lords. The bishops were instrumental on a number of occasions in carrying this opposition.[5] In the late 1950s after the last such defeat the government convened a Royal Commission on Capital Punishment (the Gowers Commission)[6] which sat between 1949 and 1953. The major recommendations of the Gowers Commission were as follows: to retain hanging as the mode of execution; to reject the establishment of 'degrees' of murder; to raise the minimum age from eighteen to twenty-one years; to argue against the notion of 'diminished responsibility' and the abolition of the death penalty for women. It suggested that the jury should have a say in imposing life or death. The terms of reference of the Royal Commission excluded from consideration the issue of abolition. As Potter remarks 'They had looked for a compromise and found none. In doing so they had rendered the division between retention and outright abolition all the starker. Only with abolition, they seemed to be hinting, would all the anomalies and ambiguities of the present system . . . be put right'.[7]

Few of these modest and sometimes surprising recommendations were implemented, in part because by the time the Commission reported Labour had lost an election and the Conservatives had formed the government. Instead energies were devoted to drafting legislation to distinguish between capital and non-capital homicide, a proposal expressly not recommended by Gowers. The Homicide Act 1957 introduced two bases under which murder might be reduced to manslaughter, namely, provocation and diminished responsibility. Success under either of these defences had the effect of reducing murder to manslaughter. While the legislation departed significantly from the spirit and recommendations of the Gowers Commission it would seem, flawed though it was, that its intention was to further reduce the number of crimes attracting the death penalty and provide gradations of murder.

In this sense, the 1957 Act was in line with the legislation of the late nineteenth century and early twentieth century which reduced the number of offences attracting the death penalty. The Children Act 1908 abolished capital punishment for those under 16 years of age; the Infanticide Act 1922 abolished hanging for mothers who killed new-born children; the Sentence of Death (Expectant Mothers) Act 1931 abolished hanging for pregnant women and the Children and Young Persons Act 1933 abolished hanging for those who were aged under 18 when the offence was committed.

Opportunely for the abolitionist movement, the Homicide Act 1957 was so poorly constructed as to make the distinction between capital and non-capital homicide even more anomalous. The Act attempted to define as capital those crimes which might be deterred by the death penalty. There seemed to be no consideration of the moral dimension and it was suspected that there was a risk of perverse jury decisions. This, reinforced by controversies following the executions of Derek Bentley[8] (1953), Timothy Evans[9] (who although executed in 1950 received little public attention until the miscarriage of justice unfolded a few years later) and Ruth Ellis[10] (1955), the last woman to be hanged, brought about the climate for a successful campaign (see Chapter 11). The last executions in the UK were carried out on 13 August 1964 when Peter Allen and Gwynne Evans were simultaneously hanged at Liverpool and Manchester prisons respectively.

There have been ten occasions since abolition when restoration amendments have been debated and defeated with increasing majorities. There was also a motion in 1974 stating that whilst terrorist murders were to be condemned the re-introduction of capital punishment would neither deter terrorists nor increase the safety of the public and which was approved by 361 votes to 232. A number of strategies have been deployed by those seeking restoration and in the debates of the 1980s the 'terrorist murderer' was one for whom restoration was sought, together with killers of police and prison officers. In the debate of 1983 six restoration amendments were tabled, although each was defeated[11]. Many observers at that time believed that the focus on terrorists was emotional or even irrational when the amendment, which was supported by the home secretary (Leon Brittan), was defended on the grounds of deterrence. In 1981 Bobby Sands (who had been elected to the House of Commons) and nine other Republican prisoners died following hunger strikes in the Maze prison in Northern Ireland, actions which hardly suggest that they and others with such strength of commitment were susceptible to being deterred. Restoration motions up to the 1990 debate continued to include terrorist murderers but the focus since then has been on those who murder police or prison officers. In the last such debate on 21 February 1994, one of the two amendments tabled was for the restoration of capital punishment for all murders with the 'safeguard' that there would be an automatic appeal to the Court of Appeal whose responsibility it would be to determine which homicides remained capital. This was rejected by 403 votes to 159. Apart from any other objections, this has never been the traditional role of the Court of Appeal and in urging rejection of the amendment the home secretary, Michael Howard, declared that it was for Parliament not the Court of Appeal to determine penal policy.[12] The other amendment called for restoration for people who kill police officers. It was rejected by 383 votes to 186.

A debate in the House of Commons on 17 December 1990 attracted amendments for complete abolition as well as for restoration. The sponsors of the abolition clauses sought to remove the last vestiges of peacetime use of the death penalty in the relevant provisions dealing with treason and piracy. The amendment, tabled by Peter Archer QC recommended that the words 'sentenced to imprisonment for life' replace the words 'hanged by the neck until he be severely dead' in section 1 Treason Act 1790; 'hanged by the neck until such person be dead' in section 1 Treason Act 1814; and 'suffer death' in section 2 Piracy Act 1837. In introducing this amendment he noted that 'The last person to be executed for treason was William Joyce, known derisively as

Lord Haw-Haw, immediately after the second world war. Capital punishment for piracy is dealt with under the Piracy Act 1837 and the last person to be executed for piracy was executed in the nineteenth century.' Kenneth Baker, home secretary, although opposed to restoration, urged the House not to support the abolition amendment but promised future Parliamentary time to discuss the issues in more detail. The amendment was narrowly defeated by 289 votes to 257. [13] However lack of Parliamentary time or will have so far failed to provide further opportunity to debate this issue. In addition to the offences already mentioned, it is still possible, technically speaking, to be sentenced to death for imagining the death of the sovereign; violating the sovereign's eldest daughter, provided that she is unmarried; and slaying the Chancellor or the King's Justices, provided that they are 'in their place undertaking their offices'. [14]

## Public opinion

Most research on and surveys of public opinion have been carried out in the USA where, as reviewed in Chapter 3, support for the death penalty remains consistently high, something above 75% in favour of retention or restoration though commentators in that country describe this support as being a mile wide but only an inch deep. Hazel Erskine in 1970 reviewed data from surveys about the death penalty conducted in the USA, Australia, Canada and Western Europe. [15] This and other survey research showed that opinions differ between countries, by gender, by age, by employment, by social class, by religion and by justification for the death penalty - deterrence, retribution (revenge), incapacitation. Most such surveys show that men favour the death penalty more than women; whites more than people of colour (certainly so in the USA); support for the death penalty drops if respondents are offered the choice of life without parole together with some form of restitution to the victim's family. [16]

The most recent scientific samplings of public opinion in the United Kingdom were conducted by NOP [17] in 1983 and in 1990, Gallup [18] in 1992 and MORI [19] in 1990 and 1994, all of which showed ambivalent results. The 1983 NOP poll revealed that 32% were in favour of restoration for all types of murder, 55% for some murders and 13% totally against; the 1990 poll indicated the same level for all murders, a drop to 49% for some murders and a rise to 18% of those opposed to restoration. This same poll revealed that 62% were still in favour of restoration even if there was a risk of executing the innocent. A further 23% were unsure. Lethal injection was the preferred mode of execution and it was felt that the prime minister or home secretary should have the power to approve the sentence of the court. The Gallup poll in 1992 showed for the first time since the 1950s that a majority, albeit narrow, was opposed to the restoration of the death penalty for murder - 42% for and 44% against with 14% undecided. However, 66% of the same sample wanted the death penalty restored for terrorist murders and of those who supported restoration in general 62% would still support the death penalty even if it could be shown that innocent people had been executed. Included in this survey was the question of the alternative of a life sentence meaning life imprisonment. The survey took place at a time when faith in the British legal system had been seriously undermined following a number of high profile miscarriages of justice - the Guildford Four, the Birmingham Six, Judy Ward and others. The murders that these and others were originally and wrongly convicted of committing would certainly have attracted the death penalty and this realisation may have influenced respondents to the general question but obviously did not influence the views of those in support of restoration. The 1994 Gallup poll showed the usual level of support for restoration but when asked whether it would be restored 72% said no.

**The media**

The majority of the British popular press - the tabloids - are active in promoting restoration. The broadsheets are largely opposed to restoration. A *Sunday Telegraph* editorial did not directly advocate the return of the death penalty but argued that there needed to be someone to better marshall the arguments for restoration. It stated: 'For 30 years we have had no political lead from those who support the death penalty, whereas those who oppose it have argued eloquently and mobilised successfully. Should Mr. Howard be giving that lead, and forcing the best minds in the public service to turn to the subject, instead of recoiling in fastidious horror from a question of unique public importance?'[20]

Fascination with the death penalty is shared by all the newspapers as was illustrated by the hefty coverage of the execution of a Briton, Nicholas Ingrams, in Georgia in 1995. The frenzy of eleventh hour appeals, the stays of execution and the war of words between Ingram's lawyers and the attorney general's office were covered in minute detail, as were interviews with the surviving victim and the mother of the condemned man. His British origin was an issue as was the fact that the lawyers representing him were British (two were representatives of the Bar of England and Wales Human Rights Committee and the third, Clive Stafford-Smith, a Briton is qualified as a US attorney). Perhaps it was because of this 'British' ingredient that traditional supporters of the death penalty were ambivalent in their coverage and occasionally highly critical of the process and the mode of execution which in this case was the electric chair. What was different about this episode was the 'responsible' and informed nature of the coverage among the tabloids. One British journalist, Peter Hitchens of the *Daily Express* was a witness to Ingram's execution, yet still remains supportive of capital punishment. The last occasion when a news reporter was present at an execution in Britain was at the hanging of Parker and Probert at Wandsworth Prison in May 1933. This is in sharp contrast with the practice in the USA where executions are attended by media representatives, seventeen at the execution of Robert Alton Harris in California in 1992.

Radio and television in the UK generally provides a more informed and balanced account. The 'Lethal Justice' series produced by Channel 4 and transmitted in 1995 did an excellent job of covering the issue of capital punishment by use of documentary film and studio discussion. The general flavour of such programmes is abolitionist.

## Parliamentary procedures, politics and the death penalty

The convention adhered to in most debates leading up to abolition and since has been to allow Members of Parliament the freedom to exercise their own judgement rather than require them to take the party whip. This freedom is exercised in different ways by MPs, some taking the view that they ought to canvass the opinion of their constituents and be bound by the outcome. The majority seem to take the view that they serve as representatives and not delegates and as such are elected to exercise their own judgement on such occasions, even when this is contrary to the majority view of their constituents. Most declare their views on this and other issues of conscience whilst canvassing at elections and some of those who change their position on restoration will inform their constituents. It is for the constituency party to decide whether their MP's position on the death penalty justifies subsequent deselection.

The 'fear' that such a position will be punished at the polls is unfounded. Members who vote contrary to the majority of their constituents' wishes continue to be re-selected and re-elected. This is a very different practice and experience to that of the USA where politicians are expected to represent the views of the 'vocal' majority on this issue and where there are numerous examples of dissenting politicians being severely punished at the polls. Former Governor Ann Richards of Texas, a southern Democrat, lost the race for re-election in November 1994 to George Bush, Jnr., a Republican. Both had campaigned on law and order; both were strong supporters of the death penalty, but Richards had used her powers to stay executions on two occasions and had vetoed legislation that would have allowed Texans to carry concealed weapons. Most people in Texas supported her other policies but these 'lapses' coupled with the strength of the Christian Coalition in Texas toppled her at the polls. Texas continues to lead the USA in terms of the number of executions it carries out. Governor Clinton of Arkansas, opposed in principle to the death penalty during one of his terms of office, lost the next election, changed his mind on the issue and was re-elected as governor. During the Presidential campaign in 1992 he made it clear that he would have to return to his home state as an execution was taking place. Ricky Ray Rector's journey to the death chamber was paralleled by Governor Clinton's journey to the White House. It would seem that active support for the death penalty is a prerequisite for success at the polls in the USA which is not the case in the UK or elsewhere in the European Union.

From 1979 Britain was governed by a Conservative administration which until 1992 enjoyed significant majorities in the House of Commons. The Conservative Party has a natural majority in the largely hereditary second chamber, the House of Lords, and in the years when Margaret Thatcher was in office it had a prime minister who was an enthusiastic supporter of capital punishment and a majority of over 100; Mrs. Thatcher being the first and only serving prime minister since abolition to support restoration. The other pivotal government minister in the restoration debates is the home secretary and here again there have been only two serving home secretaries (Leon Brittan and David Waddington) who have supported the restoration of the death penalty since abolition. Michael Howard, who became home secretary in 1993, formerly in favour of partial restoration, became totally opposed and voted against restoration in 1994. He told the House of Commons:

> Miscarriages of justice are a blot on a civilised society. For someone to spend years in prison for a crime he or she did not commit is both a terrible thing and one for which release from prison and financial recompense cannot make amends. But even that injustice cannot be compared with the icy comfort of a posthumous pardon. When we consider the plight of those who have been wrongly convicted, we cannot but be relieved that the death penalty was not available. We should not fail to consider that the irreparable damage that would have been inflicted on the criminal justice system had innocent people been executed.

In the mid-1990s, a right-wing government whose penal policy is arguably one of the most punitive in the European Union and whose reliance on imprisonment leaves it at the top of the league of imprisonment of all Council of Europe member states thus persists with what many would see as an inconsistent, anti-restoration, stance on the death penalty.

## Criminal justice practitioners and the machinery of death

A countervailing force to public opinion is that most legal and criminal justice personnel are opposed to restoration. The exceptions are the police and the Prison Service, but even here enthusiasm for restoration appears to be lukewarm and restricted largely to the lower ranks. The Prison Officers Association which represents the rank and file of prison staff last debated this issue in 1978 and their 'position' on the death penalty is to leave it to individual members to decide. No prison officer has been killed in the line of duty in the United Kingdom with the significant exception of prison staff in Northern Ireland. The Police Federation, on the other hand, which represents police officers up to the rank of superintendent does support calls for the restoration of the death penalty. Their statement of January 1994, just before a restoration debate, supported the amendment tabled by Harry Greenway, seeking the death penalty for murders of police officers. The Police Federation sought to extend the remit of this amendment to include members of the public who were murdered whilst going to the aid of the police, or attempting to prevent a crime. Their concern is fuelled by the evidence that in the thirty years since abolition 57 police officers have been murdered whilst on duty, more than twice the number (24) killed in the thirty years before abolition. The Police Federation's fall-back position is that the mandatory life sentence for murder should mean natural life for those convicted of murdering police officers.

Neither the Bar nor the Law Society, which represent barristers and solicitors respectively, have a collective view on capital punishment. Similarly, little is known about the judges' views on the death penalty, although a spate of miscarriages of justice has probably weakened any residual support. Some indication of judicial opinion emerged following the report from the House of Lords Select Committee on Murder and Life Imprisonment which in 1989 recommended the abolition of the mandatory life sentence for murder and argued for its retention as the maximum sentence for murder and a number of other serious offences. [21]

The advice of the medical profession, represented by the British Medical Association[22] and the General Medical Council, is unequivocally opposed to participation in any aspects of the death penalty. Apart from any moral revulsion felt by doctors, psychiatrists would find it difficult if not impossible to deal with such issues as: predicting future dangerousness; determining fitness to stand trial; advising on diminished responsibility and issues of competence that may arise between sentence and execution; treating someone's return to competence and therefore to execution or leaving them with the despair of their illness. Doctors would be reluctant or would refuse to: play a role in developing execution technology; be involved in determining or certifying death at the execution[23] (see generally Chapter 10).

### The Church establishment: 'From the Bloody Code to abolition' [24]
The Church's view on the death penalty is unambiguously abolitionist, but as Potter demonstrates this was not always the case.[25] Twice in 1948 the Commons passed abolition motions only to have them rejected in the Lords with the support of the bishops; similarly in 1956 a Commons abolition amendment was rejected by the Lords. It was not just the votes of the bishops that helped reject calls for abolition but the influence of the Church Establishment on the laity of the Commons and the Lords. The 1930s and the early 1940s benefited from the rise of an inspiring abolitionist, William Temple, first as Archbishop of York and then all too briefly as Archbishop of Canterbury. William Temple's oratory and interpretation of the scriptures slowly brought the church establishment round to accepting abolition but his death in 1944, after only two years as Archbishop of Canterbury, came before his influence was strong enough to be sustained. The progress of the church was not only arrested but regressed under the leadership of the new Archbishop of Canterbury, Geoffrey Fisher. As Potter puts it 'Fisher's succession rather than that of Bell,[26] even more than the premature death of Temple, had been considered to be the worst misfortune to befall the leadership of the Church of England since the Second World War'. [27]

The prison chaplaincy, in its evidence to the Gower Commission, supported the death penalty, arguing that its role be pivotal in advising the home secretary on questions of reprieve. If this evidence was damning to the cause of abolition then that of Fisher which was to follow was more so. However the unequivocal and uncompromising nature of that evidence may, ironically, have benefited the abolitionist cause in the long term as the clergy and laity of the church soon appreciated that Fisher's views were expressed on their behalf without consultation. The executions of Bentley, Evans and Ellis acted as a further catalyst to the abolitionist movement and this amalgam of views and beliefs had a powerful effect on the vote for abolition in the Commons in 1956 which was then roundly rejected by the Lords though on this occasion Archbishops Fisher and Ramsey supported the motion as did eight other bishops. This shift of opinion in the church establishment added fuel to the wider abolition campaign which together with the 'failure' of the Homicide Act 1957 lead eventually to votes for abolition in the Canterbury Convocation and the York Synod in 1962. Fisher's replacement in 1961 by Ramsey as Archbishop of Canterbury was significant in this sea-change. Sydney Silverman's Private Member's abolitionist bill was afforded time and passed to the Lords in July 1965 where, with Archbishop Ramsey's convincing and objective oration, and the support of nine other bishops the bill was agreed by 204 votes to 104.

The last occasion that the Church of England Synod debated capital punishment was in 1983 when the following motion was approved: 'That this Synod would deplore the reintroduction of capital punishment into the United Kingdom sentencing policy.' In July 1983 the Methodist Conference voted overwhelmingly against the reintroduction of the death penalty with only four representatives dissenting. In that same year, the Religious Society of Friends (Quakers) restated their opposition to capital punishment. Similarly, the Baptist Union and the Salvation Army expressed their opposition in the 1990s and the Roman Catholic bishops have spoken out against restoration though a 1995 Encyclical Letter, *Evangelium Vitae,* is the first to refer to the death penalty and Catholic scholars believe that changes will need to be made to the Catechism to reflect these reservations. [28]

### 'Hangers and floggers'

Most commentators accept that there has been a real increase in all crimes in the thirty years since abolition and the official criminal statistics indicate that there has been an overall increase since 1979 of the order of 20%. The significance of 1979 is that it marked the beginning of a government committed to 'law and order'. Violent crimes against the person (excluding homicide) have increased by something of the order of 200% since abolition. During the same period there has been an increase of some 60% in all homicides - a lower figure and at a lower rate of increase than other crimes and nearly 50% of homicide defendants are eventually convicted of lesser offences, in most instances manslaughter. The homicide rate in England and Wales in 1991 was 0.5 per 100,000 of population; in Scotland it was 1.5; the EU member state with the highest rate was Luxembourg with 2.3 per 100,000.[29] Comparable figures for the USA are: an average of 9.18 per 100,000 in those states that have carried out executions since 1977; 5.74 in those states that have the death penalty but have not executed since 1977; and 4.91 in those states where the death penalty has been abolished.[30] Texas, the state that has executed more people than any other since executions resumed in 1977 (over 100), has a homicide rate of 12.7 per 100,000.

These and other data are the weapons employed by those who debate abolition and restoration. Deterrence is part of the debate, with sprinklings of morality, just deserts and revenge. This is consistent with the generality of British penal policy which since the early 1990s has been characterised by a significant shift to retributive punishment and furthermore guided in every respect by penal policy and practice in the USA. The rhetoric is for harsh, demanding measures with a strong reliance on imprisonment.

Although there have been no successful proposals to restore the death penalty, the debates and coverage in the 'popular' press have had an effect on government policy in that those murderers referred to in amendments have been the subject of calls for life sentences to mean longer terms in prison. The average time served in prison on a life sentence is thirteen years, followed by probation service supervision and the risk of recall to prison during the offender's natural life. The call in 1983 for the death penalty for five types of life-taker led to the home secretary announcing his decision, at the next party political conference, to exercise his right to require such murderers to serve a minimum of 20 years before being eligible for consideration for parole.

A 1994 debate sought the restoration of the death penalty for murderers of police officers and whilst an amendment to this effect was heavily defeated there is already evidence that the 'trade off' of life meaning life is taking effect. Michael Howard, the home secretary in December 1994, identified 20 life sentenced prisoners who would never benefit from discretionary powers to grant parole - the UK's first 'life without parole prisoners'. Murder attracts a mandatory life sentence and attempts in domestic courts and in the Court of Human Rights have failed to challenge successfully the way in which executive discretion concerning release is excercised by the home secretary. This is in stark contrast to the reforms that have been made in relation to the discretionary life sentence, where the home secretary's veto of decisions to grant parole has been removed, and prisoners have gained the right to be represented at tribunals when their cases are heard.[31]

There may, however, be some winds of change. In 1995, the House of Commons Home Affairs Select Committee, after lengthy deliberations, issued an interim report on 'Murder: the mandatory life sentence'. This report concluded that a conviction for murder should continue to attract a mandatory sentence of life imprisonment; and that the home secretary should no longer retain the responsibility for setting the tariff and for making decisions about release.[32] It is significant that a Conservative dominated committee, chaired by a strong supporter of the death penalty, should have come to such far-reaching conclusions.

### The victims movement
Victim Support is the main body set up to meet the needs of victims and to co-ordinate related information and research. It receives funding from the government which in 1995 amounted to £11 million. Schemes arranged by

Victim Support work closely with the police to offer advice and counselling to victims and their families. One project developed by Victim Support was the Families of Murder Victims Support Group, whose aims were to offer counselling support to what were in effect a number of self-help groups arranged on a regional basis. In November 1995 the Home Office in conjunction with Victim Support, Support after Murder and Manslaughter (SAMM), and Justice for Victims published an information pack - 'Information for Families of Homicide Victims'.

Victim Support, while providing a forum for victim issues, will not engage in the 'politics' of victims and does not comment on sentencing issues except where these are of direct relevance to victims, e.g. compensation and mediation. That organization does not, therefore, adopt a stance on the death penalty. In recent years a number of ad hoc groups have been formed whose raison d'être has been to meet a variety of perceived needs of victims. Some of these groups have developed in memory of specific named victims e.g. the Suzy Lamplugh Trust, the Zito Trust, Jill Saward's Trust whilst others focus on particular crimes, such as the Campaign against Drinking and Driving (CADD), Road Peace and SAMM. Victim's Voice, formerly United Survivors Forum is a loose coalition of groups.[33] No register exists of such groups, but it is clear that some of them are focusing on campaigning rather than on counselling.

There is some evidence that such groups have influence especially when they receive support from the tabloid press. In the wake of the trial of two ten year old boys for the murder of two year old James Bulger the judge passed the mandatory sentence of detention during Her Majesty's pleasure (in effect, 'juvenile life imprisonment'). Following established procedure, the trial judge recommended that the offenders serve a minimum of eight years; the Lord Chief Justice later raised this to 10 years. These 'lenient' sentences became public knowledge and the victim's family, friends and the tabloid press mounted a concerted campaign to persuade the home secretary to raise the sentence to 25 years. After some delay he announced that they would have to serve 15 years before they could be considered for parole. Leave to challenge this decision in the European Court of Human Rights has been granted. For every ad hoc group that forms to campaign for alleged miscarriages of justice another emerges to lobby for the victim's cause. The needs and feelings of victims have been the focus of research and debate for over a decade and one response has been the government's *Victims' Charter* which spells out some basic standards to be followed by the relevant agencies. The emergence of these ad hoc groupings with their agenda of campaigning and lobbying for harsher punishments and greater procedural rights does not bode well for the interests of victims in general. There is an inherent deception in the received wisdom that delivering harsh punishments (including the death penalty) reduces crime and the fear of crime, thus making victims or their families feel better. However the mainstream victim and penal reform groups have done relatively little to appreciate and meet victims' needs. A cynic might suggest that it is not in the interests of governments to meet fully the needs of victims because exploiting the fact that victims are ignored or marginalised results in considerable support from the general public. Raising the sentence length of children who kill; stating that prisoners will not be considered for release if doing so would be unacceptable to the public; paying lip-service to the idea of procedural rights for victims, including 'victim impact statements'; suggesting that communities should be told where released prisoners are living, are all measures that are popular with the 'public' and with the tabloid press. But if the legitimate pain, anger and frustration of victims or families of victims is not addressed by those concerned with effective penal policy such groups and individuals are ripe for exploitation. Some of them are beginning to lobby actively for the return of the death penalty.


## THE EUROPEAN UNION

Belgium is the only country in the European Union to retain the death penalty for 'ordinary crimes' and while the last execution was in 1950, as recently as December 1993 two defendants were sentenced to death. On 13 September 1991 the Belgian Council of Ministers approved a bill abolishing the death penalty for peacetime offences. It is significant, however, that parliament has refrained from taking any further action. The reason, according to a leading editor, is that whilst the vast majority of lawyers and professionals who are informed about the issues are in favour of abolition the majority of voters are not. Abolition is therefore a vote loser but the mooted alternative sentence of 10-15 years imprisonment without parole is considered to be a greater evil which possibly explains why it is that Belgium occupies this anomalous position, believing it to be less punitive to have the death penalty but never to use it than to abolish it for the trade off of long determinate sentences. As this editor put it: 'The country cannot move backwards since it is irrevocably committed to abolishing the death penalty in the Council of Europe. And for electoral reasons it cannot move forward. The case is one more example of the way Belgium even when confronted by highly contentious issues, manages to govern without changing anything.'[34] Paradoxically, Belgium like the majority of EU countries has signed both the 6th protocol to the European Convention of Human Rights (ECHR) and the 2nd Optional protocol to the International Covenant on Civil and Political Rights (ICCPR).

France abolished the death penalty in 1981 for all crimes and since then there has been no concerted debate on restoration even though there is evidence that crime is perceived as a problem and an opinion poll in 1991 conducted by *Figaro* showed that 59% of those polled favoured restoration. Most support for restoration is from the political right and 30,000 people attended a National Front march in 1988 in support of the death penalty. With 27% of France's prison population being 'foreigners' and with a spate of bombings being associated with Islamic groups, support for Le Pen and the National Front is growing and so therefore is support in that grouping for the death penalty - very much a penalty to use against foreigners. Public executions were abolished in 1939 and the press were excluded from 1951 onwards.

Denmark abolished the death penalty for ordinary crimes in 1930 though legislation was introduced in 1952 which reintroduced capital punishment for treasonable acts that had been committed during war or occupation and 78 prople were sentenced to death under these powers of which 46 were executed - the last one in 1950. This interim legislation was abolished in 1978. The death penalty was abolished for all crimes in 1994. There is no mandatory life imprisonment, with the sentence being in the range five years to life; there are currently ten prisoners serving life sentences. There is no evidence that there is any support for restoration among the churches, the legal and criminal justice agencies or the medical profession. The last opinion poll was conducted by Amnesty International in 1989 when 25% voted for restoration and 69% against.

Finland abolished the death penalty for ordinary crimes in 1949 and for all crimes in 1972. The general maximum sentence of imprisonment is twelve years and murder carries a mandatory life sentence; there are 38 prisoners serving life sentences. It would seem that there is no public discussion about restoration and no support for it among legal, criminal justice, medical and church bodies.

The Federal Republic of Germany abolished the death penalty for all crimes in 1949 which was the date of its last execution; on unification the new Germany became completely abolitionist. At the time of abolition a statute was passed which puts it beyond parliament's power to alter this. Calls for restoration are heard whenever there are brutal murders and some police make similar calls when police officers are killed but there is no support for restoration amongst police managers or the police union. A now extinct right-wing party tabled a restoration amendment in the 1950s but this was never seriously discussed. There is a mandatory life sentence imposed for murder and Germany has a large life sentence population (1177 as of 31 March 1995). The German government's view remains unambiguously abolitionist and the FRG had been active in the UN since the 1970s seeking support for a world-wide ban on capital punishment.

The Republic of Ireland's commitment to abolition was consolidated during the 1990s when it abolished the death penalty for all crimes, ratified the 6th Protocol to the ECHR and signed the 2nd Optional Protocol to the ICCPR. Ireland abolished the death penalty for most ordinary crimes in 1964, the exceptions being treason, capital murder and certain offences under military law and Defence Acts. Capital murder was defined in Ireland's Criminal Justice Act 1964 as the murder of a member of the Garda Siochana or the Prison Service acting in the course of his or her duty. The 'trade-off' during the debate of 1990 was to substitute a mandatory sentence of 40 years for those convicted of the above capital murders and the life sentence remains mandatory for ordinary murder. In 1995, there were 77 men and two women serving life sentences. In the debate on abolition the minister of justice noted that since abolition for ordinary murder in 1964 there had been no discernible effect on the murder rate.[35] The bill and the abolition amendment had all-party support. The editorial position of the leading broadsheet, *The Irish Times,* is abolitionist and actively critical of any call for restoration. In the mid-1990s, the debate in Ireland was not about restoration but concerned abolition.

The Netherlands abolished capital punishment for all crimes in 1982 having abolished it for ordinary crimes in 1870. There is no mandatory alternative of life imprisonment and only four people serving what is called 'real' life imprisonment. Correspondence with the medical inspector of prisons at the ministry of justice indicates that there is no support for restoration in the medical profession nor amongst political parties. The Reformed Churches in the Netherlands have taken no public stand on the matter as the death penalty is not an issue, however in response to a request from Amnesty International they agreed to debate matters. Seemingly, the purpose of this exercise was to enable the church to state explicitly its opposition to the death penalty and so give moral support to its partner churches in the USA and this debate will take place once they have met with their first partner in the USA.

Spain abolished the death penalty in 1978 for ordinary crimes and for all crimes in 1995. There is no alternative mandatory life sentence and no prisoners serving life imprisonment; indications are that public support for the death penalty is running at about 50%. Luxembourg abolished the death penalty for all crimes in 1979. Sweden abolished the death penalty for ordinary crimes in 1921 and for all crimes in 1972. Support for restoration amongst the young runs at 25-30%. There is no mandatory life sentence. Neither is there in Portugal where the death penalty was abolished for ordinary crimes in 1867 and for all crimes in 1976. Greece abolished the death penalty for all crimes in 1993, Italy in 1994 (having previously abolished it for ordinary crimes in 1947). Austria became totally abolitionist in 1968 (having removed the death penalty for ordinary crimes in 1950).[36]

**Optional protocols**

The European Convention on Human Rights (ECHR) does not outlaw the death penalty in express terms, although article 3 states that: 'No one shall be subject to torture or to inhuman or degrading treatment or punishment' and this provision has successfully been applied to prevent or mediate the extradition of citizens accused of capital crimes to countries with the death penalty. In *Soering,* a judgement of the European Court of Human Rights, the court held that extradition of a person from the UK to the USA to stand trial for capital murder constituted inhuman and degrading treatment or punishment in violation of article 3 of the ECHR. The issue was not that the death penalty *per se* was a violation of article 3 but that the time that would inevitably be spent awaiting execution on death row was (the death row phenomenon). In addition, the court identified several mitigating factors in the *Soering* case. The UN Human Rights Committee limited the scope of that judgement in emphasising the mitigating circumstances rather than the death row phenomenon. Abolitionists see this as a landmark decision whilst others see it as turning the EU into a safe haven for murderers. A full discussion of this and related issues can be found in Chapter 2.[37]

While the Convention itself does not refer to abolition the 6th Protocol to the ECHR adopted by the European Parliament in January 1986 does so, and article 1 states that: 'The death penalty shall be abolished. No one shall be condemned to such penalty or executed.' Article 2 allows for states to make provision in time of war to impose the death penalty and articles 3 and 4 forbid any derogation or reservations under articles 15 and 64 respectively of the ECHR.

---

**Table 1:**

**European Union Countries, Year of Last Execution and Status Regarding the 6th Protocol of the ECHR and 2nd Optional Protocol of the ICCPR.**

| Country | Date of last execution | 6th Protocol | 2nd Optional Protocol |
| --- | --- | --- | --- |
| Austria | 1950 | Ratified | Signed |
| Belgium | 1950 | Signed | Signed |
| Denmark | 1950 | Ratified | Ratified |
| Finland | 1944 | Ratified | Ratified |
| France | 1977 | Ratified | |
| Germany | 1949 (FRG) | Ratified | Ratified |
| Greece | 1972 | Signed | |
| Ireland | 1954 | Ratified | Ratified |
| Italy | 1947 | Ratified | Signed |
| Luxembourg | 1949 | Ratified | Ratified |
| Netherlands | 1952 | Ratified | Ratified |
| Portugal | 1849 | Ratified | Ratified |
| Spain | 1975 | Ratified | Ratified |
| Sweden | 1910 | Ratified | Ratified |
| UK | 1964 | | |

---

An advance on this position was reached on 4 October 1994 when the Parliamentary Assembly of the Council of Europe adopted Recommendation No. 1246 (1994) which called for a further protocol to the ECHR on the issue of abolition. This protocol, unlike the 6th protocol would expect states that ratified it to abolish the death penalty in all circumstances and with no exceptions, furthermore it would insert additional control and monitoring mechanisms which would apply not only to member states of the Council of Europe but to those states which enjoy special guest status.[38] The Parliamentary Assembly made a number of very important recommendations concerning the death penalty, namely: that the committee organize a conference on the abolition of the death penalty; to extend the judgement in *Soering* so as to 'not allow the extradition of any person to a country in which he or she risk being sentenced to death and subjected to the extreme conditions on "death row"'; to 'consider the attitude of applicant states towards the death penalty when deciding on their admission as full members to the Council of Europe.'

The Parliamentary Assembly also adopted resolution No. 1044 (1994) which called for the complete abolition of the death penalty in all member states of the Council of Europe including those holding special guest status. The thrust of these recommendations is unequivocally to require member states and states holding special guest status to ratify the 6th protocol, and states applying for membership to abolish the death penalty as a precondition of this. It also 'calls upon all parliamentarians [in countries] which have not yet abolished the death penalty to do so promptly, following the example of the majority of Council of Europe member states' and 'urges all heads of state and all parliaments in whose countries death sentences are passed to grant clemency to the convicted'.[39]

The 2nd Optional Protocol to the International Covenant on Civil and Political Rights (ICCPR) is concerned with the abolition of the death penalty and was adopted by the General Assembly of the UN in 1989 and came into force in 1991. Article 1 states '(1) No one within the jurisdiction of a state party to the present optional protocol shall be executed; (2) Each party shall take all necessary measures to abolish the death penalty within its jurisdiction.' Reservations are permitted but only in so far as article 2 allows for derogation for acts committed in time of war or imminent threat of war for the most serious crimes of a military nature.

Paradoxically, Belgium, the only retentionist country in the EU, has signed both the 6th protocol to the ECHR and the 2nd Optional protocol to the ICCPR. Three member states, France, Greece and the United Kingdom have yet to sign the 2nd optional protocol of the ICCPR.

The United Kingdom is distinguished as being the only member state which has failed to signed either the 6th Protocol of the ECHR or the 2nd Optional Protocol of the ICCPR.


## CONCLUDING COMMENTS

Observers in the United Kingdom see strong support for the death penalty amongst the general public, the tabloid press and some Conservative MPs in the House of Commons. The pragmatic wing of the Conservative parliamentary party accepts that restoration is remote and even some ardent supporters of the death penalty acknowledge this. The only support in the House of Commons comes from sections of the Conservative Party and the Ulster Unionists. The Police Federation is alone in the criminal justice arena in explicitly supporting restoration. There is no evidence that support exists within criminal justice agencies and it is unlikely that without their unequivocal support no government is going to enact legislation restoring the death penalty. The position of the church has moved from active support of the death penalty to outright opposition, as Potter puts it ' . . . now that the churches are largely united in their opposition to capital punishment, it is almost inconceivable that so long as British society remains broadly Christian that the death penalty could be introduced. To participate in so final a punishment from which the religious sanction has been withdrawn would pose insurmountable difficulties for many people'. [40]

On the other hand the strength of feeling and support for restoration is sufficient to have discouraged governments from tidying up the residual legislation permitting it. The UK's reluctance to deal with its domestic legislation means that it lacks moral authority when commenting on human rights issues in other countries where the death penalty is used. This is in sharp contrast with its partners in the EU, the majority of whom have totally abolished the death penalty and ratified or signed the 6th Protocol and the 2nd Optional Protocol. The UK's isolationist stance in this regard is unhelpful within the EU and detracts from any collective position that the EU may wish to take on the death penalty or other human rights issues. Furthermore, the UK's authority within the Commonwealth is also weakened as partner nations move towards abolition. Not only is the government obstructing progress towards abolition but also resisting calls for the reform of the mandatory life sentence.

A further example of the effect of the United Kingdom's obduracy was its absence from the list of co-sponsors to an initiative by Italy that led the the Third Committee (Social, Humanitarian and Cultural) of the United Nations General Assembly to consider a draft resolution requesting the General Assembly to encourage all states that still retain the death penalty 'to consider the opportunity of instituting a moratorium on pending executions with a view to ensuring that the principle that no State should dispose of the life of any human being be affirmed in every part of the world by the year 2000.' [41] This resolution was eventually withdrawn although there are plans to submit a similar one in 1996. The only EU countries absent from the 49 co-sponsors were the United Kingdom and the Netherlands. The UK's absence was inevitable on account of its position *vis a vis* the abolitionist protocols. An explanation offered for the Netherlands' action is the belief that the draft resolution and the general strategy would harden the position of retentionist countries. As already stated, the Netherlands' stance, of course, is uneqivocally abolitionist.

It is clear that the European Parliament and Commission are of one mind in working towards total abolition, as is the Parliamentary Assembly of the Council of Europe. The influence of these bodies on aspiring members is very powerful as evidence is required of progress towards due process and improved civil rights. This moral authority is encouraging efforts within retentionist countries in Eastern Europe and the former USSR to move towards abolition (see Chapters 4 and 9). The irony is that the EU and the

Council of Europe, which are *de facto* abolitionist, have less influence on their current members than upon their prospective members.

## ENDNOTES

\* I would like to thank Clare Dodd, my research student, and Gaynor Dunmall, my research assistant for all their help and patience and Harry Potter for the inspiration of his book and his helpful comments on this chapter.

1. V. A. C. Gatrell, *The Hanging Tree: Execution and the English People, 1770-1868* (Oxford University Press, 1994).

2. Peter Linebaugh, *The London Hanged: crime and civil society in the 18th century* (London, Penguin, 1993).

3. Harry Potter, *Hanging in Judgment: Religion and the death penalty in England - From the Bloody Code to Abolition* (SCM Press, 1993).

4. op. cit., Endnote 1, at 616-619.

5. op. cit., Endnote 3.

6. Royal Commission on Capital Punishment 1949-53, cmnd. 8932 (London, HMSO, 1953), 300-301.

7. op. cit., Endnote 3, at 159.

8. Derek Bentley, who was executed on 27 January 1953, and Christopher Craig were convicted of the murder of a policeman. Craig who fired the fatal shot was, at age 16, to young to be sentenced to death. Bentley's conviction was based on the much disputed evidence that he was heard to instruct Craig to 'Let him have it, Chris' (words which were, in any event, equivocal, given that Craig was holding a gun at the time). Iris Bentley, Derek's sister continues to campaign for a pardon for her brother. The home secretary granted a partial pardon in 1994. His sister continues to campaign.

9. Timothy Evans was executed on 9 March 1950. He was sentenced to death for the murder of his wife and child and protested his innocence to the end laying the blame on his landlord, John Christie, who acted as the prosecution's chief witness. Some four years later Christie was found to be a mass murderer and executed in 1953. An enquiry, instigated by the Home Office, lead by John Scott-Henderson Q.C. concluded that there

were by coincidence two murderers living under the same roof. Informed opinion were not convinced by this explanation and the comment of the then home secretary, David Maxwell Fyfe that there was no possibility of an innocent man being hanged found little support.

10. Ruth Ellis, the last woman to be executed in Britain was hanged at Holloway Prison on 13 July 1955 for the murder of her estranged boyfriend. There was evidence that she had been subjected to frequent physical abuse by him and that he was regularly unfaithful to her. There seems to be little doubt that after the Homicide Act 1957 the conviction would have been one of manslaughter on the ground of diminished responsibility.

11. Hansard 12 July 1983, col. 892-996.

12. Hansard 21 February 1994, col. 43.

13. Hansard 17 December 1990, col. 120.

14. Hansard 17 December 1990, col. 120.

15. Hazel Erskine, 'The Polls: Capital Punishment', *Public Opinion Quarterly,* 34 (1970), 290-307.

16. See especially, Samuel Gross in A. Sarat and S. Sibley (eds.), *Studies in Law, Politics and Society,* (JAI Press Inc., 1993) 71-103.

17. NOP 9492 (1983) and NOP 6564 (1990). The latter survey was commissioned by *The Sun* newspaper.

18. Gallup. Report 381 (1992) and Report 403 (1994).

19. MORI/4798. (1990) and MORI Crime JN/8300 (1994).

20. The *Sunday Telegraph*, 24 October 1993.

21. The Report of the Select Committee on Murder and Life Imprisonment. House of Lords paper 71/1 (HMSO 1989). In England and Wales there are over 3,000 people held in prison on mandatory life sentences. This is more than the total figure for all other member states of the Council of Europe.

22. British Medical Association, *Medicine Betrayed: The participation of doctors in human rights abuses.* (London: Zed Books, 1992).

23. James Welsh, 'Psychiatry and the death penalty: a human rights perspective' Amnesty International. (AI Index:ACT 75/04/91).

24. op. cit., Endnote 3.

25. ibid.

26. The Bishop of Chichester who had retained contact with the German opposition to Hitler and had publicly condemned the British bombing of Dresden.

27. op. cit., Endnote 3, at p. 143.

28. Pope Paul 11's Encyclical Letter, *Evangelium Vitae,* 30 March 1995.

29. *World Health Statistics 1992.*

30. *FBI Uniform Crime Reports 1992.*

31. Those sentenced to a discretionary as opposed to a mandatory sentence of life imprisonment have their parole considered by a specially constituted panel of the Parole Board. This Discretionary Lifer Panel is chaired by a High Court judge who sits with two other people, a representative of the probation service or a medical practitioner with psychological training and a lay person. The prisoner can be legally represented, call witnesses and have access to all the documentation.

32. The Home Affairs Committee First Report on 'Murder: the mandatory life sentence'. House of Commons, 19 December 1995.

33. The author is grateful for this information to Paul Rock, of the London School of Economics, who is conducting research on the social organization of practical and political responses to the aftermath of homicide.

34. Philippe Toussaint, 'The Guillotine of Damocles', *The Bulletin* ( 6 October 1994).

35. Speech by the Minister for Justice and for Communication, Ray Burke, T.D. Criminal Justice No. 2 Bill, 1990 - Second Stage -Dail, Eireann.

36. *The Death Penalty: List of Abolitionist and Retentionist Countries,* Amnesty International. (AI Index, ACT 50/06/95).

37. See also William Schabus, 'Soering's legacy: The Human Rights Committee and the Judicial Committee of the Privy Council take a walk down death row.' *International and Comparative Law Quarterly,* 43 (1994), 913-923.

38. *Abolition of the death penalty world-wide: developments in 1994,* Amnesty International. (AI Index, ACT 50/07/95).

39. *Report on the Abolition of Capital Punishment,* Parliamentary Assembly document 7154 (15 September 1994) and *The Abolition of Capital Punishment: Answers to the questionnaire,* AS/Jur (1994) 48.

40. op. cit., Endnote 3.

41. *Draft Resolution on Capital Punishment Rejected by Third Committee,* UN Department of Public Information (GA/SHC/3287, 9 December 1994).

# CHAPTER 9

# Post-Communist Europe

## Stanislaw Frankowski[*]

For the purpose of this chapter, the term 'Post-Communist Europe' may be used interchangeably with 'Eastern Europe' to refer to post-communist countries of Central and Eastern Europe, except the former Soviet Union and the countries that emerged after the dissolution of former Yugoslavia.

Those engaged in comparative research on the death penalty often complain about the lack of accurate and reliable information and that charge is certainly justified with respect to Eastern Europe. This is especially the case for the period between 1944 and the late 1950s when the death penalty was almost a taboo subject and no statistical data relating to criminality or the activities of the law enforcement agencies or the courts were published.[1] Therefore, all this chapter attempts to accomplish is to present a rather sketchy picture of the death penalty-related developments in several countries of the region. In particular, an attempt will be made to relate the issue of capital punishment within a given historical period to the socio-political life of the countries under study.

For an abolitionist, the recent developments in this part of the world are simply breathtaking. Everywhere in the region, the collapse of communism and the subsequent advent of democracy resulted either in the elimination of or a significant restriction in the application of capital punishment.

## HISTORICAL SURVEY

### Early beginnings

Some Eastern European countries emerged as separate political entities as early as the ninth or tenth century, while others did so only relatively recently (e.g. Albania in 1912). At one point, the territory of today's countries of Eastern Europe was conquered by the new powers (Turkey, Russia, Austria, or Prussia); in some cases (e.g. Bulgaria, Czechoslovakia) the foreign occupation lasted for several centuries. In most instances, the sovereignty was restored in the past 150 years, with some states re-emerging in 1918 after the end of World War One (Hungary, Czechoslovakia, and Poland).[2] The period of independence usually lasted until the outbreak of World War Two in 1939. During the War or immediately thereafter, the entire region came under heavy Soviet dominance. Russian-style communism was forcibly imposed on the subjugated population from the outside (with the exception of Albania where local communists seized power on their own and later broke with their Soviet

215

sponsors). Finally, the current post-communist period (from 1989 onwards) has been marked, in various degrees, by the emergence of democracy.

Capital punishment was present in the region from ancient times; its existence became even more pronounced with the appearance of statehood (e.g., already the first Bulgarian legal statute, the ninth century Judging of People Law, mentions capital punishment). Sentencing to death was usually a prerogative of local rulers. The scope of capital crimes was broad, and the methods of execution elaborate (e.g. hanging, beheading, stoning, burning at the stake). Two forms of the implementation of the death penalty were later distinguished: ordinary (most often beheading and hanging) and one accompanied by torture.[3] The death penalty began to be used more frequently in the period of early feudalism when the central government was able to exercise effective authority over the entire territory.

When the countries under study were conquered by the neighbouring powers, the criminal laws of the occupants, all of them providing for capital punishment, were imposed upon the subjugated population. The death penalty continued to be considered an essential component of the system of punishments. Generally, the scope of capital crimes was extremely broad (e.g. in the beginning of the nineteenth century there were over 180 such crimes known in today's Hungary).[4] However, during the eighteenth and nineteenth centuries, the ideas of Enlightenment reached Eastern Europe, and some attempts were made to restrict the use of capital punishment. Poland abolished it for witchcraft in 1776. The death penalty was abolished in the Austro-Hungarian Empire in 1780 although it was restored in reaction to the 1789 French Revolution. All in all, the scope of capital crimes was generally curtailed in the region.

## The modern era

In Romania, after the 1859 unification of the Romanian Principalities, the indigenous Penal Code was enacted in 1864. It did not provide for the death penalty except for several offences committed during time of war. The 1866 Constitution confirmed the abolition of capital punishment for peacetime crimes.

The Ottoman Empire's rule over Bulgaria came to an end in 1878 when the country was liberated by Russian troops (full independence was achieved thirty years later). A new Bulgarian Penal Code, adopted in 1896, preserved the death penalty. In addition, several statutes created many capital crimes.

Hungary obtained a substantial measure of independence after the 1867 Compromise which created the Austro-Hungarian Empire. The 1878 Hungarian Penal Code was liberal in nature. The death penalty was retained but was provided only for murder and attempts upon the King's life. Prior to the outbreak of World War One in 1914, capital punishment was applied only in cases of murder. Between 1884 and 1914, thirty-eight executions took place. It seemed at that time that the abolition of capital punishment was at hand.[5]

216

During the inter-war period (1918-1939) many countries accomplished a progressive codification of criminal law. The death penalty was retained, but the scope of its application and the frequency of executions were significantly reduced. However, from the late 1920s together with the deteriorating political situation on the Continent, more repressive tendencies took the upper hand.

The abolitionist principle with respect to peace-time crimes was re-affirmed in Romania by the 1923 Constitution (article16). Already at that time, however, the rising crime rate had produced a shift in favour of capital punishment. In 1924 a special statute provided for capital punishment for communist agitators (the Marzescu Act). The new Criminal Code of 1936 incorporated some sections of the Act despite the drafters' opposition to capital punishment. The 1938 Constitution expanded the scope of capital crimes by authorizing the death penalty for offences against the royal family, against high ranking public figures, for politically-motivated murders, and for killings caused during burglaries. The Penal Code was subsequently amended to implement the constitutional mandate. During World War Two (1940-1944) Romania became an ally of Germany. The prime minister, Marshall Ion Antonescu, usurped all the power and strengthened the country's alliance with Germany. Criminal laws became even more repressive. Burglary, theft of weapons, arson, smuggling, and several other crimes were made capital. A large number of political opponents, including communists and anti-German resistance fighters, were executed.

In Hungary, the stormy political events following the collapse of the Austro-Hungarian Empire in 1918, including the creation of the Hungarian Soviet Republic in 1919 and the counter-revolution led by Miklos Horthy, were accompanied by frequent applications of capital punishment to deal with political enemies.[6] In the 1930s, when the radical right grew in power, the Horthy-controlled regime made many military crimes capital. It must be noted, however, that the courts of regular jurisdiction, continuing the pre-war liberal tradition, used to impose capital punishment almost exclusively in the cases of especially heinous murders. No more than two death sentences per year were imposed. Altogether, special courts imposed six death sentences during the 1931-1941 period.[7]

Czechoslovakia regained independence in 1918 after the collapse of the Austro-Hungarian Empire. The 1852 Austrian Code remained in force in Bohemia and Moravia, while the 1878 Hungarian Code was used in Slovakia. During the entire inter-war period capital punishment was retained, although it was not used widely.

Poland re-emerged on a map of Europe in 1918. The 1932 Penal Code provided capital punishment only for four of the most serious political crimes and murder (in no case, however, was it mandatory). Later on, the scope of capital crimes was broadened by special legislation. This trend, which started after the 1926 coup by Marshall Jozef Pilsudski, reflected the worsening political situation of the country which had at that time Nazi Germany and Stalinist Russia as its neighbours. When Germany and Russia invaded Poland in September of 1939, twenty peacetime offences were punishable by death.[8]

# THE COMMUNIST ERA

This period, which lasted from the mid-1940s until the collapse of communism, requires a more comprehensive treatment in view of its relevance to the most recent developments in the death penalty field.

One may distinguish three essential foundations of the communist criminal justice system. First, the law in general (and the criminal law in particular) is perceived and utilised in a purely instrumental way, that is, solely as a tool to achieve current policy goals as defined and formulated by the Communist Party. Second, severe punishments are believed to be highly effective in controlling criminality. Finally, swift criminal proceedings, free of undue technicalities, are believed to have a substantial deterrent effect.[9]

Based on such foundations, the system is extremely harsh, often resorting to the death penalty, primarily to intimidate large segments of the population. Second, it pays little attention to the rights of an individual to strengthen the deterrent effect of punishment. Third, and perhaps most importantly, the manner of application of criminal measures, in particular of capital punishment, is not dictated by penal policy considerations (e.g. fluctuations in crime levels, the need to control *serious* criminality, etc.). Instead, the problem of a death penalty under communism should be viewed in each country's political context. More specifically, capital punishment must be seen as a part of the political structure, as an element of the general policy, including penal policy, promoted and pursued by the communist power centres. In short, under communism, the problem of the death penalty is primarily a 'political' issue rather than a criminal justice issue.

The communist era may be divided into two periods: the Stalinist and the post-Stalinist period, although in some countries the political events took a different course[10]. The Stalinist period started in most countries in 1944-45, and it lasted, roughly speaking, until the second half of the 1950s.[11] For the purpose of this chapter, I will consider 1956 as the first year of the post-Stalinist period. This period, which came to a close with the collapse of communism in 1989-92, was characterized by a relative relaxation of most aspects of socio-political life, although the cardinal foundations of the communist system, including the leading role of the Communist Party, remained intact.

## The Stalinist period.
The Stalinist criminal justice system was marked by the extreme harshness of criminal law measures and the total disregard for procedural rights. These two features found ideological justification in Stalin's theory of the intensification of a 'class struggle' in communism-building countries. Criminality was thus deemed to be a form of a class conflict; every person suspected of committing a crime, especially a major one, was considered an 'enemy of the working

people.' The aim of the criminal law machinery was thus not to distribute justice but to punish and deter 'the enemies.'

Interestingly enough, unlike in Soviet Russia, where the entire pre-revolutionary legislation was fairly quickly abrogated, Eastern Europe retained 'bourgeois' law, including criminal law, sometimes for quite a long time.[12] Understandably, the old codes were soon supplemented by special 'revolutionary' laws that were meant to reflect new socio-political and economic realities. Consequently, the scope of capital crimes was drastically expanded, and the death penalty was used more frequently.

In the last phase of the War and immediately thereafter, capital punishment was used extensively to deal with war criminals. In Poland, at least 1,700 death sentences were passed under the August 1944 Decree that covered the war crimes committed by German officials, and the acts of collaboration engaged in by Polish nationals (the gravest crime was described as 'participating in the commission of killings,' a deliberately broad formula). In several instances the death penalty was mandatory.[13]

In Romania, due largely to Soviet pressure, Marshal Antonescu and many of his anti-communist followers were executed as war criminals (the two statutes dealing with war crimes were passed in 1945). Similar events took place in Bulgaria, another country of the region that initially was an ally of Germany. In September 1944, a special People's Court was created to try former high governmental officials deemed responsible for dragging the country into the War, and for anti-democratic practices before the War. Altogether, the Court rendered 2,680 death penalty sentences.[14] In Hungary, special 'people's courts' were created in 24 cities. At least 414 death penalty sentences were passed on those convicted of war-related and political crimes; at least 180 of these sentences were implemented.[15]

The death penalty was also used to repress broadly defined political opponents of communist regimes. In addition to anti-state crimes, many traditional crimes, including property crimes, became capital. In Poland, the 1945 Decree on Offences Particularly Dangerous in the Period of Rebuilding the State added 13 new capital crimes, including such offences as the manufacturing or storing of weapons or explosives; disclosing a state secret; creating or directing an organization aimed at the commission of a felony; and conspiring to counterfeit money. By the early 1950s, the number of capital crimes reached one hundred.[16] In addition, the death penalty could be imposed for virtually every offence that was tried under the 1945 Decree on Emergency Proceedings, regardless of the penalty provided by the substantive law defining the offence. In the 1945-1947 period, the media reported a large number of death sentences passed each month (in some periods even up to one hundred). These sentences were primarily meant to intimidate the political opposition.[17]

Similar methodology was adopted throughout the region. Several special laws and decrees passed between 1945 and 1950 provided for the death penalty for political, military, and property crimes.[18] The new Bulgarian Penal Code of 1951 characterized capital punishment as 'exceptional and temporary', but provided for it as the sole penalty for twenty-five types of offences, mostly military and anti-state. Several other crimes were punishable by death or long term imprisonment, so the total number was fifty. Such crimes included major property crimes, among them large scale theft and embezzlement, and crimes against the 'socialist' economy such as the crime of non-fulfillment of important economic tasks. Altogether, almost 10% of crimes known under the Code were capital. Many of these crimes were tried summarily by 'people's courts.' The number of death sentences passed and implemented is unknown but was certainly considerable.

In Romania, a new law providing the death penalty for offences against the communist state and the planned economy was passed in 1949. The amended 1936 Code provided for the death penalty for some crimes against the state, peace and humanity, for aggravated murder, and for burglary resulting in death. In 1957, large scale embezzlement causing serious damage to the national economy was made a capital offence. According to one Romanian expert, all of these amendments 'turned the criminal law into a tool used by the communist regime primarily to repress anti-communist "enemies". Its secondary role was to combat criminality.'[19]

In Hungary, between 1952 and 1957, courts of regular jurisdiction rendered 140 death sentences. In the aftermath of the 1956 revolutionary uprising against the Soviets, over 300 persons were sentenced to death and executed.[20]

Similarly, in Czechoslovakia, the death penalty was used rather frequently to deal with the alleged political opposition. The 1948 Law on the Protection of the Republic and the 1950 Penal Code provided for capital punishment as the sole penalty for many political crimes. During the period of 1950-53 at least 178 persons, among them such well-known statesmen as Dr. Vlado Clementis, former Minister for Foreign Affairs, were executed after 'show trials.' The National Tribunal (Statni Soud), established in 1948, passed 56 death penalty sentences in 1952 alone.[21]

In every country of the region, the manner in which the penalty was imposed and implemented did not even satisfy the most elementary procedural requirements. Broadly-defined anti-state crimes, most of which were made capital, were transferred to the jurisdiction of military tribunals that applied simplified procedural rules under which defendants' rights, in particular the right to defence, were often reduced to the bare minimum. In many countries, most serious crimes were tried under special procedural rules. The already mentioned 1945 Polish Decree on Emergency Proceedings was a model of simplicity: the indictment had to be filed within thirty days from the date the suspect was apprehended; the accused had only 72 hours to lodge an appropriate evidentiary motion; and the conviction could be appealed within three days and only by the government.[22]

Most importantly, in addition to regular judicial proceedings, capital punishment was imposed outside the formal criminal law apparatus. In most politically-sensitive cases (and during the Stalinist period almost every case could be considered politically-sensitive), security agents fabricated evidence and, when necessary, tortured suspects to obtain confessions. The accused were then tried by special tribunals created on an ad hoc basis at various levels of the military and regular judiciary. The cases were handled in absolute secrecy, in total disregard of the most basic procedural formalities. In the most serious cases, the highest Communist Party body would first approve the charges and 'recommend' the penalty to be imposed; the judge would then merely announce the pre-determined verdict.[23] The number of capital sentences passed and implemented in this manner was very high. At least 2,500 death sentences were passed in Poland between 1946 and 1953.[24] The number of people executed by state security agencies outside the regular system of law enforcement was certainly much higher.

During the peak of the Stalinist period (1949-1953) even some of the highest-ranking and most trusted Communist Party officials (e.g. Rudolf Slansky in Czechoslovakia, Laszlo Rajk in Hungary, Traicho Kostov in Bulgaria) were convicted of espionage in 'show trials,' sentenced to death, and executed.

All in all, the actual number of death sentences passed and implemented in Eastern Europe during the Stalinist period will never be ascertained with any degree of accuracy. There can be no doubt, however, that thousands of people were executed by agents of broadly defined law enforcement bodies, in most cases charged with crimes they had not committed.

### The Post-Stalinist period

Joseph Stalin died in March of 1953. The ensuing 'thaw' in the Soviet Union resulted in a lessening of the Soviet grip over Eastern Europe. In the second half of the 1950s, in the majority of countries of the region, the days of reign by terror and brutal force were over. Most Eastern European criminal justice systems began functioning in a more civilized manner. Almost everywhere the most repressive features of the Stalinist period were sooner or later rejected (except for Albania and, to a lesser extent Romania, where Stalinist practices were continued until the very end of communist rule).

Generally speaking, although the new penal codes adopted in this period usually characterized the death penalty as 'exceptional and temporary,' the scope of capital crimes was still wide. Hungary and Poland, the two countries considered most liberal within the Soviet bloc, were in this respect not markedly different from other countries of the region. Generally throughout the region, in addition to murder, many loosely defined anti-state crimes remained capital; in many countries large-scale appropriations of 'socialist' property and some economic crimes were still punishable by death.

In Poland, the 1945 Decree on Emergency Proceedings was applied until 1970. The new 1969 Penal Code, still in force today, provides for capital punishment in ten cases, including sabotage, armed robbery, and organizing or directing a major economic swindle.[25] The new 1961 Hungarian Penal Code provided for capital punishment for nine political crimes, murder, thirteen military crimes, two crimes against 'socialist' property, and two other crimes (starting a prison riot and creating a serious hazard to public safety).[26] In 1971, capital punishment was abolished in cases of property crimes. The new 1978 Code of Hungary reduced the scope of capital crimes to twenty-five, including eleven military crimes. Under the 1961 Penal Code of Czechoslovakia, thirty-two types of offences were still capital, including murder, military crimes and several political crimes. In particular, the crime of 'sedition' which included participating in mass demonstrations 'against the Republic, its organs or public organizations of the working people,' could, under certain circumstances, also be punished by death.[27] In 1973, hijacking and kidnapping, resulting in death, became capital crimes. In Ceausescu's Romania, twenty-eight crimes, including economic and property crimes, were still capital under the 1969 Code.[28] This number was substantially reduced in the 1970s; in particular, the penalty was abolished against those convicted of economic crimes[29]. The Bulgarian 1961 Code cut the number of capital crimes from fifty under the 1951 Code to thirty-one.[30] The 1977 Penal Code of Albania, which replaced the 1952 one, provided for over thirty capital offences. All anti-state crimes (except for one) were punishable by death, including 'agitation and propaganda against the state' if it resulted in grave consequences.[31] Albania's criminal justice system was liberalised in 1990 following widespread social unrest. In particular, the number of capital offences was reduced to eleven, and women were exempted from the death penalty.[32] Neverless, according to Amnesty International, at least six death sentences were imposed and four executions carried out in 1991; in 1992, at least 12 men were sentenced to death and six executions took place.[33]

Under penal codes adopted in the post-Stalinist period, no person under 18 at the time of the commission of the crime could be sentenced to death (In some countries, e.g. Hungary and Bulgaria, the minimum age limit was 20, at least with respect to civilians committing crimes during peacetime). In addition, there were special restrictions on the application of the death penalty with respect to women. Everywhere in the region, the death penalty was prohibited with respect to pregnant women. Some codes specified that this prohibition applied to women who were pregnant at the time of the commission of the crime or at the time of passing of the sentence or even at the time of the execution. In Romania the death penalty was prohibited with respect to women with children under three years of age. In some countries there were provisions prohibiting death sentences with respect to insane or mentally disturbed persons.

Despite the fact that the scope of capital crimes remained considerable, almost everywhere in the region one notices in the post-Stalinist period a marked decrease in the number of death sentences passed and implemented. It must be emphasized again that the data are often incomplete, unreliable, and do not take into account convictions rendered by military and other special tribunals. In addition, in most instances it is unclear whether the available data pertain to the total number of death sentences (including those later reversed as a result of appellate proceedings) or only to the number of final death sentences.

With these reservations in mind, one may conclude that the death penalty rate (the number of death penalty sentences passed and implemented, relative to the size of the country's population) was probably the lowest in Czechoslovakia, Hungary, and Poland, the three countries of the region with the strongest democratic traditions. In turn, the highest death penalty rates were probably in Bulgaria and Romania. Little reliable information is available regarding Albania, but it is likely that the use of the death penalty was as frequent as in Bulgaria and Romania.

In Poland, courts of regular jurisdiction rendered altogether 318 final death sentences between 1956 and 1988 (the last full year of communist rule), that is, on average 10 death sentences per year. The country's population during this period grew from approximately thirty to thirty six million. It is difficult to tell how many of those sentences were implemented, but it seems that the number was considerable (e.g. between 1970 and 1979, one hundred and thirty-one death sentences were passed, and one hundred and twenty-one were implemented). These death penalty sentences were passed almost exclusively in cases involving especially heinous murder (in the 1960s, there were few capital sentences passed for economic crimes; ultimately one defendant was executed). Seven death penalty sentences were passed on average each year in the 1960s; this number almost doubled in the 1970s. The decade of the 1980s was marked by the emergence of Solidarity, the first independent civic body ever in existence in a communist country, by the imposition of Martial Law in December of 1981, and by the repressive political climate in the subsequent years. However, one notices a pronounced decrease in the number of death sentences compared to the previous decade. Altogether sixty such sentences were passed between 1980 and 1988, an average of 7.7 per year.[34] Although at least three more death sentences were imposed during this period by military courts, it is obvious that Jaruzelski's military regime used more carrots than sticks when dealing with the political opposition.[35] It was indicative of the trend toward the eventual abolition of capital punishment in the last stage of Polish communism that no final death sentence was passed in 1988. Space constraints preclude a more detailed analysis of the fluctuations in the number of death sentences in post-Stalinist Poland.

The data pertaining to other countries are more incomplete and unreliable. In Czechoslovakia (population of 15 million), ninety-one final death penalty sentences were passed during the 1962-1989 period (an average of slightly over three each year). This seems to be the lowest death penalty rate throughout the region. Slightly over 20 person were executed during the 1970s.[36] In Hungary (population of 10.5 million), during the 1962-1987 period, courts of regular jurisdiction passed 118 death sentences (an average of 4.5 sentences each year). Only in six instances was the death sentence imposed for a crime other than murder.[37] During the 1970s, courts of regular jurisdiction passed only 30 death sentences, half of these between 1970 and 1972.[38] The number of sentences actually implemented is unknown.[39] In Bulgaria, according to some sources within the Bulgarian ministry of justice,

133 death sentences were ordered during the 1984-1989 period (an average of 22 per year). Considering that the country's population was at the time slightly below nine million, these figures are simply staggering. Amnesty International reported at least thirty-two executions during that period.[40] In Romania (population of 23 million), altogether seventy-seven death sentences were passed during the 1980-1989 period; at least fifty of those sentenced to death were executed. Most of the convictions involved murder, but some involved large-scale thefts of state property. For example, in 1983, five death sentences were passed for organized and systematic stealing of large quantities of meat.[41] The last and the most famous execution in Romania was that of Nicolae Ceausescu and his wife Elena.[42]

In the post-Stalinist period, the continued existence of the death penalty in Eastern Europe became politically embarrassing. From the very beginning of the workers movement, communist theorists were always doctrinally-opposed to capital punishment because of its inefficiency and barbarity. They often referred to Karl Marx's statement that a society that wants to be deemed civilized cannot tolerate the death penalty. In some countries a question thus began to be asked, first privately and then publicly, whether Marx's words also applied to 'communism-building' societies. The existence of the death penalty was becoming more and more difficult to explain in view of the repeated claims about the progress in the building of communism, and about the gradual elimination of criminality.

In Poland, the problem of capital punishment was raised for the first time in the mid-1950s, a period characterized by unprecedented political liberalization.[43] The first comprehensive examination of the problem took place a decade later. A leading law journal of the prestigious Polish Academy of Sciences published a well researched and passionately written article by Professor Marian Cieslak in which the author strongly advocated the abolition of capital punishment in peacetime.[44] The journal's Board of Editors organized a special conference on the subject, and the report from the conference was published in the same issue of the journal.[45] The majority of the participants expressed their principled opposition to the death penalty. At the same time, however, they claimed that its immediate and total abolition would not be advisable. The only person openly in favour of capital punishment was a representative of the Office of the Procurator-General who argued that as long the imperialist countries threatened the existence of socialism in Poland, the state power had to resort to the death penalty.[46] The adoption in 1969 of a new penal code, which retained the death penalty while characterizing it as 'exceptional' seemed to have put the question of capital punishment to rest. In 1978, Professor Alicja Grzeskowiak's book brought the problem of the death penalty back to light.[47] The author's fundamental conclusion was unequivocal. She stated that capital punishment had no place in a modern, rational penal system, because the bottom line of retributive justification was vengeance, the claimed deterrent effects of the death punishment were uncertain and not subject to empirical validation, and the offender's incorrigibility was too speculative a factor. All in all, she concluded that no satisfactory justification could be offered for a state-authorized killing.[48] A year later, Jerzy Jasinski, a well-respected criminologist from the Polish Academy of Sciences, facilitated future discussions on the subject by making it clear that conceptually, two separate sets of problems should be distinguished in this context: congruence of the application of capital punishment with an accepted system of values (a purely moral question) and the effectiveness of capital punishment in terms of crime prevention (a purely utilitarian question).[49] In consequence, 'one may accept the death penalty even if it proved impossible to demonstrate its efficacy; one may also be against the death penalty even if it could be proven effective.'[50] All in all, the author concluded cautiously that the arguments favouring capital punishment were based on rather weak foundations.[51]

In the early 1980s, during the stormy Solidarity days, the debate over the death penalty intensified. Numerous articles, usually vigorously opposing capital punishment, appeared in the daily press and legal periodicals.[52] The government-sponsored Codification Commission, working on a new penal code, suggested that the following two alternative solutions be examined: Should the penalty be abolished in peacetime? Should it be retained but limited to treason and murder? The Solidarity-sponsored Commission suggested that the penalty be abolished except for most serious wartime crimes.[53] A new round of debates started following the recession of Martial Law in 1983 and intensified in the late 1980s when the communist regime was visibly weakened.[54] It was at that time that a middle-ground solution in the form of a fixed time moratorium began gaining scholarly support.[55]

In Czechoslovakia, the abuses of the Stalinist past were first noted in 1956 and then fully exposed during the 1968-1969 'Prague Spring' period. One scholar claimed at that time that 'it is difficult to find a more convincing argument against capital punishment than the 'staged' trials of the 1950s.'[56] In Bulgaria, Romania and Hungary, scholarly opposition to capital punishment was weaker, but some scholars had enough courage to voice their criticism in public.[57]


## THE TRIUMPH OF DEMOCRACY

As mentioned at the very beginning, the collapse of Soviet-style communism in Europe resulted either in the abolition or restriction of capital punishment. Unlike in most other regions of the world, this change was accomplished with surprising swiftness, usually without any protracted preparatory process. One may briefly ponder on the reasons for this unprecedented phenomenon. It seems that they were complex and varied from country to country. Consequently, they may not be conveniently captured in one paragraph. One must keep in mind that the transformation from communism to democracy did not follow any single pattern. In particular, in most instances a negotiated settlement took place which resulted in a strange symbiosis between communist leaders and the representatives of the emerging new political forces. For example, General Wojciech Jaruzelski, who tried to crush Solidarity by force in 1981, was nine years later, elected President of the Republic of Poland by the Solidarity-dominated Parliament. In addition, almost without exception, communist parties were renamed after the collapse of communism and continued playing an active political role. It is thus quite likely that, at least in some countries, one of the underlying motives behind the abolition of capital punishment was a desire to spare some highly-placed communist officials from facing a possibility of being charged with and convicted of capital crimes. In other countries, however, the abolition of capital punishment was probably accomplished in reaction to the politically motivated abuses during the not so recent Stalinist period. Finally, it is probable that an officially-proclaimed goal of joining the Western community of nations had played a vital role. The new democratic governments realized that full compliance with internationally-accepted human rights standards was a *conditio sine qua non* of their eventual integration with the West.

The current status of the death penalty in the countries under study may be briefly described as follows. Romania, the Czech Republic, and Slovakia have abolished capital punishment by legislation; in Hungary, the death penalty has been declared unconstitutional by the country's Constitutional Court. These four countries have signed the Sixth Protocol to the European Convention, and two of them (Hungary and Romania) have also signed the Second Optional Protocol to the International Covenant on Civil and Political Rights. The death penalty is formally still in existence in Poland and Bulgaria, but a moratorium on its implementation has been declared. As a result, any death sentences which are imposed are not carried out. Albania is the only retentionist country where capital punishment is actually being used, although recent events suggest that this will not be the case for much longer.

Romania was the first post-communist country to abolish capital punishment. This was accomplished immediately after the violent 'Christmas Revolution' of December 1989 during which the Ceasescu regime was overthrown and power was assumed by the National Salvation Front. On 7 January 1990, the Front's Council promulgated a Decree No. 6/1990 which replaced the death penalty by life imprisonment. The death penalty sentences of the twenty-seven convicts awaiting execution on death-row were commuted to life imprisonment. The reaction of the Romanian public was largely negative. On the one hand, the excessive use of the death penalty during the Ceausescu regime was abhorred. On the other hand, however, many believed that the National Salvation Front, headed by Ion Iliescu, a former Central Committee Secretary of the Communist Party who had fallen into disfavour with the former dictator, was guided by purely political considerations, that is, the desire to protect former communist officials (after all, over 1,000 persons were killed in December of the preceding year by security agents trying to protect the falling regime). This belief is widely shared even today. [58] In general, the public sentiment, fueled in large measure by a perceived rise in serious crime, seems to be decisively in favour of capital punishment. [59]

On 27 February 1991, Romania ratified the Second Optional Protocol to the International Covenant (Law No. 7/1991). The new Constitution, adopted in November of the same year, explicitly prohibits the death penalty, precluding in this way its reinstatement even in the most egregious circumstances. A constitutional amendment would be needed to accomplish this goal. However, the Constitution provides that no amendment is allowed if it were to result in the suppression of fundamental rights and freedoms. This has been interpreted to mean that as long as the present Constitution is in force, the death penalty may not be reinstated.[60] Finally, in May of 1994, the Chamber of Deputies adopted a law ratifying the European Convention and the Sixth Protocol.

In Czechoslovakia, following the November 1989 'Velvet Revolution', the campaign against the death penalty became especially vigorous after President Vaclav Havel's characterization of capital punishment as barbarous. In the opinions of some commentators, many former retentionists joined the abolitionist camp for the sake of political conformity. An informal moratorium was then put into effect (the last reported execution in Czechoslovakia took place in 1988). On 3 May 1990, the parliament of the then Czech and Slovak Republic amended the Penal Code, abolishing the death penalty for all offences; the penalty was replaced by long term imprisonment, including life sentences. As explained a few days later by a government representative to the UN Economic and Social Council in New York, by abolishing the death penalty 'Czechoslovakia wants to join those countries that rate the right to life among the most fundamental human rights.'[61] One must note that the Parliament decided to abolish the death penalty despite substantial public opposition.[62] On 18 March 1992, the European Convention and its Sixth Protocol were ratified.

In Hungary, the death penalty was declared unconstitutional by the Constitutional Court on 24 October 1990.[63] The case was brought by the League for the Abolition of the Death Penalty, a leading Hungarian abolitionist group headed by Dr. Tibor Horvath, a long-time crusader against capital punishment.[64] Both the Chairman of the Supreme Court and the Chief Procurator spoke at the Court's Plenary Session in favour of the abolition of capital punishment, although the latter hinted that in his view the Parliament was the 'most appropriate forum' to make the decision. In a written opinion submitted to the Court, the minister of justice expressed the view that capital punishment was unconstitutional. This view was also supported by three well-known scholars who were requested to prepare expert opinions on the subject.

The Court, by a vote of eight to one, eliminated capital punishment from the Penal Code's catalogue of principal punishments and from other provisions of the Code's General Part. The decision also eliminated capital punishment from several provisions of the Code's Special Part, including those penalizing genocide, terrorist activities, and hijacking.[65] The Court held that the death penalty was unconstitutional because it violated the 'innate right to life and dignity of man' as provided by article 54 of the Hungarian Constitution.[66] The Court also noted that article 8 of the Constitution stated

227

that the right to life and human dignity are fundamental rights, the exercise of which may not be suspended or restricted even during the state of emergency. Another clause of the same article declares that 'while regulations concerning basic rights and duties are defined by law, the fundamental content of such rights may not be restricted.' On this basis the Court concluded that the right to life and human dignity is a fundamental, inviolable and inalienable right of every person. It is a right of the highest order because it constitutes the source and foundation for other basic rights; it is so fundamental that it does not even require any specific textual anchoring. The Court stressed further that the right to life and human dignity is an absolute value that sets strict limits on the state's power to punish criminals. In addition, the Court stressed that most criminological studies indicate that neither the level nor the frequency of crime are substantially affected by imposition of the death penalty. Finally, the Court alluded briefly to article 6 of the International Covenant, which was signed by Hungary in 1976, and to the abolitionist initiatives undertaken by the Council of Europe.[67] In November 1992, Hungary ratified the European Convention and its Sixth Protocol. In February of 1994, the country acceded to the Second Optional Protocol of the International Covenant.

In Bulgaria, in July of 1990, the Grand National Assembly passed a Resolution placing a moratorium on executions. The Resolution states simply that carrying out death penalty sentences is suspended until the final decision regarding capital punishment has been reached.[68] Shortly thereafter, the death sentences of 11 of the 12 individuals on death row were commuted by President Zhelev.[69] In July of 1991, the Assembly adopted a new Constitution. Article 28 declares that 'Everyone has the right to life. Any attempt on a person's life will be prosecuted as a grave crime.'[70] However, this statement has not been interpreted to prohibit the application of the death penalty. In fact, the first death sentence since the introduction of the moratorium was imposed in February 1992. In July of the same year, President Zhelyu Zhelev assured Amnesty International that the country was doing its best 'to abolish this anti-human measure.'[71] In September, Bulgaria ratified the European Convention. Nevertheless, several death sentences were imposed in subsequent years (unfortunately, no reliable data is available).[72]

As with all the countries of Eastern Europe, Bulgaria experienced a dramatic surge in traditional crime and the appearance of forms of criminality previously virtually unknown, such as gang and drug related criminality.[73] No wonder that the Bulgarian public has become alarmed and continues to favour capital punishment. In such a climate, President Zhelev hinted at the beginning of 1993 that the temporary reintroduction of the death penalty might help halt a wave of crime. The National Assembly debated the question of lifting the moratorium in February 1994, but no decision was taken. Forty-nine deputies then filed a petition to the Constitutional Court. The Court held that decisions regarding capital punishment are exclusively within the competence of the Assembly.[74]

In March of 1995, the Code of Criminal Procedure was amended. Under the amendment, capital cases will be heard by an enlarged panel consisting of three professional judges and four lay assessors; the decision to impose the death penalty must be unanimous.

In Poland, like in Bulgaria, the decision whether to abolish capital punishment is still being debated, although a bill to abolish the penalty was presented as early as August of 1989 by a group of Solidarity-linked parliamentarians. This was one of the first bills after the June 1989 elections as a result of which Tadeusz Mazowiecki, a close associate of Lech Walesa, became Prime Minister.[75] The bill was laconic. It simply declared that the death penalty should be abolished and replaced by a twenty-five year long imprisonment; the drafters assumed that the burden of proof remained on the shoulders of retentionists. For this reason the only argument raised against capital punishment was a short reference to the highest value assigned to human life. The ensuing debate during the plenary session of Sejm (the Parliament's lower chamber) was generally chaotic and demonstrated a clear polarisation of opinions along party lines (most deputies representing the Communist Party were either openly in favour of capital punishment or supported the idea of a moratorium while the Solidarity deputies argued in favour of abolition). Ultimately, the bill was referred to two parliamentary committees where it was effectively killed.[76]

Parliament was not eager to re-open the debate for at least four reasons. First, other problems (e.g. reforming the country's economic and political structure) were deemed more pressing. Second, the question of capital punishment seemed to have become moot. The last execution in Poland took place in 1988 and since then Polish courts have *de facto* complied with an undeclared moratorium (in the period 1990-1995, the Supreme Court commuted to 25 years of imprisonment several death sentences imposed by first instance courts). Third, public support for the death penalty has for the last thirty years remained vigorous (usually around 55% of those surveyed have declared themselves retentionists) and became even more pronounced after the 1989 collapse of communism.[77] This shift in public opinion may largely be attributed to the rising crime wave (between 1985 and 1992, the number of recorded burglaries rose 250 percent, robberies 100 percent, and murders 50 percent).[78] Not surprisingly, those resisting the abolition of capital punishment claim that in a democratic country such a strong public sentiment should not be ignored. Fourth, the activities of the re-constituted Codification Commission accelerated, and it seemed that the adoption of a new penal code might be accomplished soon. All of the drafts prepared in the 1990s proposed total abolition of capital punishment (at least for peacetime offences).[79] In this situation, those favouring the abolition concluded that it might be expedient to have the death penalty question resolved within the framework of the wholesale reform of Poland's criminal law. Even Poland's ratification of the European Convention in October 1992 failed to trigger a spirited discussion on the subject. Generally, the debates on capital punishment of the 1990s have not been as vigorous as those of the 1980s. One may note, however, the emergence of one new line of analysis: regardless of the position taken, those participating in the debates have addressed the question of whether the

229

retention of capital punishment may be justified in light of the teachings of the Roman-Catholic Church, arriving sometimes at different conclusions.[80]

It became clear around 1994 that the envisaged comprehensive reform of criminal law will not be accomplished in the near future. Therefore, the government decided to pursue a step-by-step strategy. In May of 1994, it proposed a bill containing several amendments to the 1969 Penal Code. In May of 1995, the government offered some amendments to the original draft. One of the amendments recommended adding life imprisonment to the catalogue of punishments. This proposal was based on the reasoning that the gap between the longest prison term under the Penal Code (25 years) and the death penalty was too wide; life imprisonment was thus seen by the drafters as a penal sanction more appropriately reflecting the gravity of the crime in instances in which capital punishment was not imposed. In other words, the government's clear intent was to increase the harshness of the system. The revised version of the bill was then sent again to the parliamentary committees. After heated discussions, the committee agreed to add life imprisonment as a new penalty and, surprisingly, to impose a five year moratorium on the implementation of capital punishment, although no mention of this item was made in the governmental drafts. In July of 1995, after an additional flurry of legislative activities, the Sejm overruled the Senate's amendment deleting the proposed moratorium (160 deputies voted in favour of the moratorium, 99 against, and 33 abstained). The relevant article of the July 1995 Law states simply that 'capital punishment shall not be implemented during the five-year period after the entry of the Law in force.' (article 5). The next article provides that the Law enters into force 3 months after the date of its publication. The law was published on 19 August 1995 and the moratorium started on November 21.[81] The public reaction to the moratorium was mixed. Some commentators have noted an evident awkwardness of the situation of a person sentenced to death: a final verdict has been imposed, but the convict then remains in limbo being uncertain of his fate. This argument carries obviously a lot of weight, despite the fact that it is widely expected that the passage of a new penal code abolishing capital punishment will take place before the expiration of the moratorium. It is also believed that any final death sentence, if such a sentence is every passed is the future, will be commuted by the President of the Republic.

Albania was the last among Eastern European countries to reject Soviet-style communism. Ramiz Alia, who in 1985 succeeded a hard-line communist dictator Enver Hoxha, liberalized some aspects of the system, including criminal justice arrangements[82], in the wake of the December 1990 student demonstrations. Alia allowed functioning of the spontaneously-created Albanian Political Party (APD), the country's first opposition party since World War II, which in the spring 1991 election won almost one-third of the seats in the People's Assembly. One year later, the Communist Party was defeated in the general election. In April of 1992, Sali Berisha, an ADP leader, was elected President, and the first non-communist government was formed.[83] The problem of capital punishment was not at the centre of the new government's attention. However, in June of 1993, President Sali Berisha hinted in Parliament that life imprisonment was preferable to capital punishment. Nevertheless, he concluded that although he was personally in favour of abolishing the death penalty, further discourse on this problem was in order. Death penalty sentences have continued to be imposed and implemented. In 1994, as reported by Amnesty International, seven men were sentenced to death, of whom two were executed. [84]

The situation began to change in 1995 in connection with Albania's efforts to be admitted to the Council of Europe. In April, a Council committee explicitly tied the question of Albania's membership to its progress on human rights issues. In particular, the committee recommended that Albania abolish the death penalty. [85] On 1 June 1995, the first post-communist Penal Code went into force; it slightly reduced the number of capital crimes. [86] On June 29, the Council's Assembly approved Albania's application to join the organization after the President of the Albanian Parliament signed a declaration stating that Albania will 'sign, ratify, and apply Protocol No. 6 of the European Convention on Human Rights on the abolition of the death penalty in time of peace within three years of accession [to the European Convention] and to put into place a moratorium on executions until the total abolition of capital punishment.' [87] It seems that the road to the eventual abolition of capital punishment in Albania has thus been paved.

## CONCLUDING REMARKS

In the post-World War II period many countries have achieved significant progress in humanizing the process of handling convicted criminals. There can be no doubt that the abolition of the death penalty, the most drastic measure at the disposal of state power, is an essential component of this process.

All the post-communist societies under study have either already abolished capital punishment or are resolutely moving in that direction. This has been achieved in a politically challenging period requiring immediate attention to numerous problems connected with a systemic transformation from Soviet-style communism to Western liberal democracy. One must also note that the death penalty reform has been accomplished in the face of substantial public opposition strengthened in large measure by a rising crime wave, in particular, violent crime. However, the realization that abolition of capital punishment has become an explicit condition of membership of the European Union was certainly a factor influencing the decision. Consequently, the new democratically-elected governments have rejected one of the most abhorrent trimmings of the communist past. This seems to prove the point briefly raised at the very beginning of this chapter, namely, that capital punishment is primarily a political, not a crime control issue. Very few politicians really believe that the application of the death penalty has a significant deterrent effect or that one has to resort to such drastic methods to reaffirm the most fundamental social values such as the sanctity of human life. In many instances, ruling élites consider capital punishment as one more measure at their disposal to be used in order to ease social tension, especially when the level of frustration is high and the public is eagerly looking for scapegoats. One must generally agree with a Croatian scholar, Zvonimir P. Separovic, that the 'more unstable the regime . . . the greater the probability of the introduction or retention of the death penalty and its application.'[88] Needless to say, other factors (e.g., religion, national tradition) may also be relevant when it comes to deciding whether to abolish capital punishment or at least curtail its application. But, let us stress again, these factors usually will not be directly related to the alleged crime-control function of the death penalty.

The remaining question worthy of examination is whether the abolition process accomplished in most countries of the region is irreversible. The answer will obviously be of a speculative nature. One may venture to say that the future course of events in the death penalty area will be primarily a function of political developments in Eastern Europe. If the current trends continue, it is almost certain that capital punishment will soon become a relic of the past.

Historically, Eastern Europe has been at a crossroads between the Russian empire and the Western powers. In the past few years, the pendulum has decisively swung toward the West. However, it is still an open question whether Russia's hegemonic ambitions will remain dormant long enough to allow the fledgling democracies to mature and to be fully integrated with Western Europe. The growing political importance of 'reformed' communists in many countries of the region (e.g. Slovakia, Hungary, and most recently in Poland where a high-ranking ex-communist defeated Lech Walesa in the 1995 presidential election) should not be ignored in this context. In conclusion, if Russia's current attempts at democratization fail, if the empire-building tendencies take an upper hand, the future of Eastern Europe is uncertain, unless the integration with the West has been accomplished in the meantime. However, *if* autocratic regimes were to return to power early enough, the question of the death penalty would be re-examined, sooner rather than later.

# ENDNOTES

* The amount of information gathered for the purpose of this study differs widely from country to country. Bulgaria, Poland, Hungary, and Romania clearly come to the forefront. I wish to extend my thanks to Dr. Boris Velchev from Bulgaria, Dr. Tiberiu Dianu from Romania, and Dr. Robert Fico from Slovakia, for preparing short background reports on their countries. Unless otherwise noted, all information pertaining to the above-mentioned countries derives from the country reports. I also want to express my thanks to my teaching fellows who helped me a lot in the preparation of this chapter: Bart Baumstark, Carl Geraci, and Jennifer Roy.

1. It is not even certain whether reliable official statistics of this kind were ever collected. With the passage of time, official documents were lost or misplaced. Some of them were most probably intentionally destroyed in the last stage of communist reign. As a result, in most instances it is difficult, if not impossible, to reconstruct the past.

2. For example, Bulgaria was part of the Ottoman Empire between the end of the fourteenth century and 1878 when it achieved limited autonomy. The today's Czech Republic and Slovakia, as well as Hungary, were under the Hapsburg rule between 16th century and 1867 and then became parts of the Austro-Hungarian Empire until 1918. Poland was partitioned between Russia, Prussia, and Austria in the late 18th century and regained independence in 1918.

3. As noted by a Polish expert on the death penalty, 'until about the eighteenth century, death was not the harshest punishment . . . That punishment was torture. People found guilty . . . were not executed but tortured to death, and the torture was so cruel that death came as a relief.' Krzysztof Poklewski-Koziell, 'The Abolition of the Capital Punishment, The Polish Point of View', Zbigniew Lasocik, Monika Platek, Irena Rzeplinska (eds.) in Abolitionism In History. On Another Way Of Thinking, (1991) 178-179.

4. Tibor Horvath, 'Kara smierci na Wegrzech' [Death Penalty in Hungary], Panstwo I Prawo, (April 1990) 70.

5. It is noteworthy that between 1895-1900 no single death penalty sentence was imposed despite the fact that the level of serious criminality remained unchanged. ibid. at 70-71.

6. Revolutionary tribunals ordered about 590 executions between March and August of 1919; some people were executed for 'crimes against the revolution'. In the period immediately following the coming to power of Horthy's authoritarian government in August 1919, approximately 5,000 executions took place, often without any appearance of legality. Hungary. A Country Study, (1990) 35-37.

7. Tibor Horvath, supra note 4, at 71.

8. Alicja Grzeskowiak, Kara smierci, w polskim prawie karnym [Death Penalty In Polish Penal Law], (1978) 53-58.

9. Stanislaw Frankowski, 'The Polish Criminal Justice System After World War Two-Selected Problems', 44 U.Pitt.L.Rev. (1982) 139, 145.

10. The essentially Stalinist-style regime remained in power in Albania until 1992. Romania, influenced mostly by nationalistic factors, deviated from the Soviet pattern and proceeded along relatively separate and independent lines.

11. In some countries, numerous appearances of the old order were kept in place until the late 1940s (e.g., opposition parties were allowed to function and were represented in parliaments; Romania was a monarchy until the end of 1947; the Hungarian People's Republic was formally established only in 1949).

12. In most instances, new penal codes were promulgated in the 1950s (e.g., in Czechoslovakia in 1950, Albania in 1952, Bulgaria in 1951) or even in the 1960s (e.g. in Hungary in 1961, Romania in 1968, and Poland in 1969). See generally, Igor Andrejew, *Zarys prawa karnego panstw socjalistycznych* [An Outline of Criminal Law of Socialist Countries] (1975) 40-44.

13. Lech Gardocki, *Zarys prawa karnego miedzynarodowego* [An Outline of International Criminal Law] (1985) 90.

14. Jacek Kubiak, 'Kara smierci w europejskich panstwach socjalistycznych' [The Death Penalty in European Socialist Countries], 30 *Palestra* (Sept.-Oct. 1988) 67, 79. Among those sentenced to death were two of the regents, 28 former ministers and 47 generals.

15. Horvath, *supra* note 4, at 71; Kubiak, *supra* note 14, at 73.

16. Aleksander Lesko, *System Srodkow Karnych* [A System of Penal Measures] (1974) 45. The 1953 Decree on Strengthening Protection of Social Property provided the death penalty for the large-scale 'appropriation' of state property.

17. Between 1946 and 1953 Polish military tribunals convicted 64,887 defendants for anti-state crimes. Adam Strzembosz, 'Bezsilne prawo' [Powerless Law], *Nowy Dziennik*, (18 April 1995), at 3.

18. Kubiak, *supra* note 14, at 79.

19. Tiberiu Dianu, 'The Romanian Criminal Justice System', in Stanislaw Frankowski and Paul B. Stephan (eds.), *Legal Reform In Post-Communist Europe. The View From Within* (1995) 258.

20. Horvath, *supra* note 4, at 71; Kubiak, *supra* note 14, at 73-75. In 1957, regular courts passed 60 death sentences. In 1958, Imre Nagy, former

Prime Minister, and his two closest associates, were convicted of conspiracy to overthrow the communist government and executed.

21. Kubiak, *supra* note 14, at 71.

22. Stanislaw Frankowski and Andrzej Wasek, 'Evolution of the Polish Criminal Justice System After World War Two - An Overview', 1 *Europ.J.Crime, Crim.L & Crim.Justice* (1993), 143, 144-45.

23. See generally, Andrzej Rzeplinski, *Sadownictwo w polsce ludowej* [The Judiciary in People's Poland] (1989) 26-50; reviewed by Stanislaw Frankowski, 8 *Arizona J. Int'l.Comp.L*. (1991), 33.

24. The fullest, although far from complete, account of the use of the death penalty during the Stalinist period in Poland is given by Krystyna Kersten, *Te pokolenia zalobumi czarne* [These Generations Marked by Mourning] (1989). Subsequent research demonstrated that the actual number of death sentences passed and implemented during that period was certainly much higher. Military tribunals rendered at least 679 death sentences in the 1944-46 period alone. Adam Strzembosz, *Bezsilne prawo*, *supra* note 17, at p.3. Courts of general jurisdiction passed at least 888 death sentences during the 1949-1953 period (341 death sentences were imposed in 1950). Jacek Kubiak, *Dzialalnosc ONZ na rzecz zniesienia lub ograniczenia stosowania kary smierci i odniesienie do praktyki w Polsce* [The UN Activities Aimed at Abolishing or Restricting the Application of the Death Penalty and Its Relevance for the Polish Practice], 25 *Palestra* 51, Nos.7-9 (1981).

25. Frankowski, *supra* note 9, at 147-148.

26. Kubiak, *supra* note 14, at 74-75; Roger Hood, *The Death Penalty. A World-Wide Perspective* (1989), 12.

27. *Czechoslovakia. A Country Study* (1989) 257-258.

28. 'Penal Code of the Romanian Socialist Republic', in Gerhard O. W. Mueller (ed.), 20 *American Series Of Foreign Penal Codes* (1976).

29. *Romania. A Country Study* (1991) 297-298.

30. Amnesty International. *Europe. Moving toward complete abolition of the death penalty*. February 1992. AI Index: EUR 01/01/92. According to this source, eleven types of criminal homicide and robbery were punishable by an optional death penalty.

31. *When The State Kills. The Death Penalty v. Human Rights* (1989), 98; Kubiak, *supra* note 14 at 81-82. Capital punishment was also provided for several military crimes, including the willful destruction of military property. Other capital crimes included forcible rape resulting in the death or suicide of the victim, assault with intent to rob, and some economic offences (e.g., the large scale appropriation of 'socialist' property and the falsification of currency).

32. *Albania. A Country Study* (1994) 230.

33. *Supra* note 30, and an Amnesty International document *Amnesty International's Concerns* presented at the 49th Session of the United Nations Commission on Human Rights (AI Index: IOR 41/10/92).

34. The data for the 1956-1980 period are derived from an article by Jacek Kubiak (The UN Activities, *supra* note 24). The data for the 1981-1988 period were compiled by the author of this chapter from Polish statistical yearbooks (the Polish Statistical Yearbook is an annual publication of the Polish Statistical Office).

35. On its face, the provisions of the Martial Law Decree were extremely harsh. The most serious offences were tried under emergency proceedings. Altogether eighty-seven types of offences could be tried in this manner. The applicable penalty in such cases was either long-term imprisonment or death; the defendant had no right to appeal the sentence. Stanislaw Frankowski, *supra* note 9, at 157-160 (describing in more detail the changes brought by the December 1981 legislation).

36. Kubiak, *supra* note 14, at 72.

37. Horvath, *supra* note 4, at 71.

38. Kubiak, *supra* note 14, at 75.

39. In July of 1986, Hungary reported to the UN Human Rights Committee that there had been 25 executions in the previous 10 years. *When The State Kills, supra* note 31, at 145.

40. ibid., at 133.

41. ibid., at 195.

42. The couple was captured while attempting to flee the country. A military tribunal was hurriedly convened, and a summary trial was held. Two death sentences were announced and implemented immediately

despite the fact that the Code of Criminal Procedure gave those sentenced to death ten days to decide whether to appeal the sentence.

43. Stanislaw Ehrlich, 'Glos przeciw karze smierci' [A Voice Against the Death Penalty], *Nowa Kultura* No. 28 /1956; Wladyslaw Wolter, 'Zniesc kare smierci' [Abolish the Death Penalty], *Nowa Kultura* (1956) No. 30; Jozef Lipczynski, 'Przeciwko karze smierci' [Against the Death Penalty] in *Zagadnienia prawa karnego i teorii prawa* [The Problems of Penal Law and the Theory of Law] (1959) 91.

44. Marian Cieslak, *Problem kary smierci* [The Problem of the Death Penalty], 21 *Panstwo I Prawo* (1966) 833.

45. Stanislaw Frankowski, 'Sprawozdanie z dyskusji nad artykulem profesora Mariana Cieslaka' [The Report on the Conference on Professor Marian Cieslak's Article] 21 *Panstwo I Prawo* (1966) 846.

46. ibid.

47. Grzeskowiak, *supra* note 8.

48. ibid. at 216-217.

49. Jerzy Jasinski, 'Kara smierci w aspekcie prawnym i moralnym' [The Death Penalty from the Legal and Moral Point of View], *Wiez* (Oct. 1979), at 28.

50. ibid. at 36-37. When it comes to the moral question, the author distinguished its two aspects: the value assigned to human life as an essential component of the value system created within the European civilization, and the problem of capital punishment as a 'just' punishment.

51. ibid. at 45.

52. For example, Alicja Grzeskowiak, 'Zniesc kare smierci' [Abolish the Death Penalty] 26 *Palestra* (Sept.-Oct. 1982); Jerzy Jasinski, 'Glos przeciw karze smierci' [A Voice against the Death Penalty], 36 *Panstwo I Prawo* (Sept.-Dec. 1981), 85; Kazimierz Buchala, 'Niektore problemy nowelizacji przepisow czesci ogolnej kodeksu karnego' [Selected Problems of Reforming the Penal Code's General Part], 37 *Nowe Prawo* (May 1981), 97; Wladyslaw Macior, 'Kara smierci jako *ultima ratio*' [The Death Penalty as *Ultima Ratio*], 36 *Panstwo I Prawo* (Sept.-Dec. 1981), 91 (in favour of capital punishment arguing, inter alia, that it is a necessary evil applied to deter potential criminals).

53. Frankowski, *supra* note 9, at 148-149.

54. Krzysztof Poklewski-Koziell, 'Kara smierci w polskim prawie karnym' [Capital Punishment in Polish Criminal Law], *Tygodnik Powszechny* (1984) No. 3; Jan Switka, 'Refleksje o karze smierci w swietle teorii penalnych' [Reflections upon the Death Penalty in Light of Penal Theories], 32 *Nowe Prawo* (March 1986), 58 (defending the death penalty); Krzysztof Poklewski-Koziell, 'Refleksje o 'Refleksjach o karze smierci' [Reflections on 'Reflections on the Death Penalty in Light of Penal Theories'], 32 *Nowe Prawo* (Oct. 1986), (refuting Switka's arguments); Krzysztof Poklewski-Koziell, 'Wokol postulatu zniesienia kary smierci w Polsce' [On the Argument to Abolish Capital Punishment in Poland], 43 *Panstwo I Prawo* (February 1988) 3 (concluding that the death penalty should be abolished as quickly as possible).

55. An interview with Professor Adam Krukowski, entitled 'I Favour the Moratorium', in a popular weekly *Kultura,* (9 March 1988), at 1, 7.

56. Otto Novotny, 'Za reformu systemu trestu' [On the Reform of the System of Penalties], in *Sbornik praci z trestneho prava,* (1969) 77 (cited by Kubiak, *supra* note 14, at 710.

57. Kubiak, *supra* note 14, at 76, 81.

58. Dianu, *supra* note 19, at 261-262.

59. For example, in February of 1993, taxi drivers brought traffic to a halt in central Bucharest to demand the reinstatement of capital punishment. Occurrences of that kind reflect public anxiety about crime and other negative phenomena, such as a high rate of unemployment, associated with the country's transition from totalitarianism to free-market liberal democracy. Later the same year, *Evenimentul zilei,* the country's most influential newspaper, initiated a campaign in favour of reinstating the death penalty. The organizers expected to collect 250,000 signatures, the number required by the Constitution to start legislative moves. This effort failed when it became clear that the country's integration with Western Europe would be seriously jeopardized by the restoration of capital punishment.

60. Dianu, *supra* note 19, at 261.

61. Amnesty International, *supra* note 30.

62. Public sentiments favouring capital punishment grew even stronger when five especially gruesome murders took place immediately after the abolition vote and before the law took effect on 1 July 1992.

63. The Decision No.23/1990 (X.31) AB, 1 East Europe Case Reporter No. 1 (1994) at 117. (A copy of the entire judgement, in English, is on file with the author of this chapter).

64. The petition challenged the constitutionality of capital punishment on several grounds: the death penalty may not be justified from an ethical point of view; it is incompatible with human rights; it is irreversible and irreparable; it is inefficient in preventing serious crimes; and it does not serve as a deterrent.

65. A relatively short joint decision was signed by all nine justices. One filed a dissent arguing that since the relevant constitutional provisions are in his view inconsistent, it is up to the Parliament to remove this inconsistency by amending the Constitution. Six justices filed rather lengthy concurring opinions. Interestingly enough, some of them referred to the US Supreme Court decision in *Furman v. Georgia* and to the universally accepted international standards pertaining to the death penalty.

66. Article 54 states that 'In the Republic of Hungary, every human being has the innate right to life and the dignity of man, and no one may be arbitrarily deprived of those rights.' 'The 1949 Constitution of the Republic of Hungary (with subsequent amendments)', in Albert P. Blaustein and Gisbert H. Flanz (eds), 8 *Constitutions of The Countries of the World* (1995), 1, 15.

67. Bela Busch, Jozsef Molnar, Eva Margitan, 'Criminal Law, the Law of Criminal Procedure, and the Law of Corrections in Hungary', in Stanislaw Frankowski and Paul B. Stephan (eds.), *Legal Reform in Post-Communist Europe* (1995), 233, at 237.

68. *The National Gazette* No. 60, (27 June, 1991).

69. Amnesty International, *supra* note 30.

70. 'The Constitution of the Republic of Bulgaria of 12 July 1991' in Albert P. Blaustein and Gilbert H. Flanz (eds.) 3 *The Constitutions Of The Countries Of The World* (1992).

71. Amnesty International. *The 1993 Report on Human Rights Around the World* (1993) 77.

72. ibid. According to a ministry of justice source, eight death sentences were passed in 1993 and four in 1994.

73. *Bulgaria. A Country Study,* (1993) 263-265.

239

74. Amnesty International. *The 1995 Report on Human Rights Around the World* (1995) 81.

75. Alicja Grzeskowiak, 'Kara smierci w pracach Sejmu i Senatu Rzeczypospolitej Polskiej w l. 1989-1991' [Capital Punishment in the Activities of Senate and Sejm of the Polish Republic in the Period 1889-1991] in Stanislaw Waltos (ed)., *Problemy kodyfikacji prawa karnego. Ksiega pamiatkowa ku czci Profesora Mariana Cieslaka* [Codification Problems Of Criminal Law. A Book In Honor Of Professor Marian Cieslak] (1993) 171, at 172-173.

76. ibid. at 173-179.

77. Krzysztof Krajewski, 'Opinia publiczna a problem kary smierci' [Public Opinion and the Death Penalty] 45 *Panstwo I Prawo* (May 1994) 60. According to the most recent surveys, approximately 65% of Poles are in favour of retaining the death penalty.

78. Andrzej Wasek and Stanislaw Frankowski, 'Polish Criminal Law and Procedure', in Stanislaw Frankowski and Paul B. Stephan (eds.), *Legal Reform In Post-Communist Europe. The View From Within* (1995) 275, at 299.

79. 'Projekt kodeksu karnego' [A Draft of the Penal Code] 49 *Panstwo I Prawo* (Feb. 1994). Reasons were published in the next issue of the journal. According to the draftsmen, capital punishment should be abolished for the following reasons: the retention of the death penalty cannot be reconciled with the modern understanding of 'human dignity' and with the 'values of society'; most criminological studies have proved that the death penalty is not an effective deterrent; and the protective function of capital punishment may be satisfactorily performed by life imprisonment or even imprisonment for a fixed term of 25 years. These arguments were critically examined by Aleksander Bentkowski, a one time minister of justice. 'Czy nowy kodeks karny bez kary smierci?' [A New Penal Code Without Capital Punishment?] 38 *Palestra* (July-Aug. 1994) 130.

80. Krzysztof Poklewski-Koziell, 'Kosciol katolicki a kara smierci (Nowe elementy)' [The Catholic Church and Capital Punishment (New Elements)] 49 *Panstwo I Prawo* (Apr. 1994) 76 (concluding that in view of the Church's new Catechism all the hopes of abolitionists were extinguished); Jerzy Jasinski, 'Kosciol wobec kary smierci' [The Church's View on Capital Punishment] 50 *Panstwo I Prawo* (July 1995) 50 (concluding on the basis of the Pope's March 1995 encyclical *Evangelium Vitae* - the Gospel of Life - that the Church recognizes the right of state power to introduce and maintain capital punishment, but - at the same time - claims that the death penalty should not be used except in cases of

absolute necessity; the Church's position is thus close to *de facto* abolition); Lech Paprzycki, 'Kara smierci - relikt czy koniecznosc' [Capital Punishment - A Relic or Necessity], *Rzeczpospolita* (3 May 1995) (concluding that especially in view of *Evangelium Vitae* the death penalty cannot be reconciled with the Christian vision of human dignity); Aleksander Bentkowski, *supra* note 79, at 133-134 (concluding that in some extreme instances the death penalty is fully justified in view of the Christian doctrine).

81. The Law of 12 July 1995 on Amending the Penal Code, the Code on the Execution of Penalties, and on Increasing the Minimum and Maximum Fine Limits, published in *Dziennik Ustaw* (1995), No.95, item 475.

82. *supra*, note 32.

83. Albania, ibid., at 171-177.

84. Amnesty International. *The 1995 Report On Human Rights Around The World* (1995) 53. Fourteen former high-ranking communist officials were detained in December 1995. They were charged under the September 1995 Law on Genocide which was passed to deal with the atrocities committed during the past era. It was reported in the media that at least 5,000 people were executed during the communist persecution (Agence France Press, 16 Dec. 1995).

85. Reuters World Service (28 April 1995). Characteristically, the chairman of the Albanian delegation to the Council, emphasised upon returning to Albania from Strasbourg that the abolition of capital punishment was not a precondition for Albania to become a member of the Council of Europe. 'Albania was asked only to sign conventions and agreements just like other CE country members, no more', he said. BBC Summary of World Broadcasts (2 May 1995).

86. Reuters World Service (1 June 1995).

87. Amnesty International. *Death Penalty News* (September 1995), at p. 1 AI Index: ACT 53/03/95.

88. Zvonimir P. Separovic, 'Political Crimes and the Death Penalty', 58 *Revue Internationale de Droit Penal* (1987) 759.

# CHAPTER 10

# Physician Participation

## Michael L. Radelet*

Physicians have a long history of involvement in various facets of capital punishment. Consider four diverse examples. During the reign of Henry VIII in England, a practice began whereby the bodies of executed inmates were given to surgeons for dissection.[1] In 1752, Parliament passed legislation that allocated the bodies of four executed inmates per year to the Company of Surgeons.[2] Second, in 1789, French physician Joseph Guillotin denounced hanging as cruel and unjustifiable and proposed a more swift and certain method; within two years France had a new decapitation machine, bearing Dr. Guillotin's name.[3] Third, one of the first Americans to present a systematic argument for the total abolition of capital punishment was a physician, Dr. Benjamin Rush, a signatory of the Declaration of Independence and today known as the 'Father of Psychiatry.'[4] A fourth example, more modern, involves lethal injection, which today is the most widely used method of execution in the United States. When the Oklahoma Legislature passed the world's first lethal injection statute in 1976, one of their consultants was a physician, Dr. Stanley Deutsch, then chief of Anesthesiology at the University of Oklahoma Health Sciences Center.[5] All of these examples involve individual morals, professional ethics, and, in various ways, classic conflicts between the authority of a state versus the ethical responsibilities of a profession; between duty to a democratic commonwealth and duty to an autonomous individual.

This chapter provides an overview of some aspects of the death penalty, as currently practiced in the United States, that involve, invite, or require participation by the medical profession. I will first address the question of organ transplants by death row inmates, and argue that in the absence of firm and enforced guidelines by professional medical organizations, this question promises to grow in importance. I will then discuss how medical associations in the United States are attempting to draw the lines between acceptable and non-acceptable medical involvements in capital cases. Finally, the involvement of mental health professions in capital cases will be discussed. Here I will argue that in the search for factors that might mitigate a death sentence, more, and not less, participation by mental health professionals is needed. The paper concludes with some thoughts about the necessity for professional medical societies to monitor physician involvement in executions in individual states, to discipline their members who come too close to doing the executioner's work, and to lobby for laws that eliminate the necessity or possibility of most types of medical involvement in executions. Throughout I

243

will speak of physician involvement, but much of what I have to say also has relevance for other health care providers, such as psychologists, nurse practitioners, and physician assistants.

## ORGAN DONATION AND INFORMED CONSENT

Physicians frequently become involved in death penalty cases and debates. The idea is particularly popular in some Asian countries, where the shortage of organs for donation is particularly acute because traditional beliefs hold that bodies should be buried intact.[6] Research conducted on 14 inmates from Taiwan who allowed their kidneys to be transplanted after their executions (by gunshot) shows 'that it is feasible to harvest multiple organs after gunshot injury to the head, and to transplant such organs successfully.'[7] There was no commercial organ selling involved in these 14 cases, and the physicians claimed the executed inmates gave informed consent before their organs were donated. But in mainland China, evidence indicates that the bodies of executed prisoners are being used in a profitable organ trade and without informed consent.[8] The government reportedly gets $30,000 for a kidney.[9] The recipients of the organs are either top Chinese officials or wealthy foreigners from Hong Kong, Japan, Britain, or the United States of America. Estimates of the number of organs transplanted from executed prisoners range from 2,000 to 10,000 per year.[10]

As in Taiwan, Chinese prisoners are executed by a pistol shot to the back of the head, rather than by methods that would render the inmate's organs useless. In some cases, if the corneas are to be used for transplant, the donors are shot in the heart. In testimony before the US Senate Committee on Foreign Relations on 4 May 1995, the Executive Director of Amnesty International USA, William Schulz, estimated that up to 90 percent of the transplant kidneys in China, plus numerous corneas and hearts, come from executed prisoners.[11] To prevent confirmation of organ removal, the body is cremated before it is returned to the family.

Harry Wu, a USA citizen and former political prisoner in China, also testified before the Senate Committee in May 1995. Wu is a human rights activist from the Hoover Institute at Stanford University. He has documented several major human rights abuses in China, including the use of organs of executed inmates for transplant. On 19 June 1995, he was detained by Chinese officials when he attempted to enter the country from Kazakhstan. After two months in confinement and international outrage, he was convicted by the Chinese of spying, sentenced to 15 years, and expelled from the country.[12]

The United States, of course, sees itself as quite different from China in its recognition and protection of human rights. Nonetheless, America has seen analogous types of 'organ theft'.

What if a prisoner wants to donate his body to science or for organ harvesting? Here the issues get a bit more obscure. Consider, for example, the case of Joseph Paul Jernigan, executed in Texas on 5 August 1993. Those who never had the chance to get to know Jernigan still can get to know him, in a sense, because high-quality three-dimensional images of his body are now available on the Internet. Jernigan, now called 'The Visible Man,' has become the world's greatest medical teaching tool. His attorney reports that Jernigan wanted his death to do something good for humanity. Immediately after the execution, Jernigan's body was flown by chartered jet from Huntsville to the University of Colorado and frozen. Later it was cut into 1,870 pieces, filmed, x-rayed, and MRI'd. So much information is now available on Jernigan that it takes two weeks of uninterrupted service on the Internet to download it. The information covers the equivalent of five million typewritten pages - fifty times more abundant than what is found in the entire *Encyclopedia Britannica*. The National Library of Medicine spent more than $1 million on the project. [13]

The project has met no protest. The only exception to this silence is a letter that three Austrian physicians wrote to *The Lancet* demanding withdrawal of the pictures. 'The death penalty itself and all medical participation before, during, and after an execution is unethical under all conditions . . . irrespective of their scientific or teaching merit.' [14] Another writer suggested that it was the death penalty itself that was unethical, but to deny the inmate's last wish was 'unjustifiably paternalistic.' [15]

Some organ donations by death row inmates are virtually immune to criticism. For example, in April 1995, Delaware death row inmate Steven Shelton, whose execution date has not yet been set, donated his kidney to save his mother's life. [16] Still, some would object even to this: Florida death row inmate Joseph Green Brown, later exonerated because of innocence, [17] tried to donate a kidney to his brother while on death row, but prison officials objected for alleged security reasons. The brother died. [18] But allowing donation of body parts to strangers can open up a Pandora's Box of controversies. An example is the case of Daniel Faries, who was sentenced to life imprisonment for a 1986 Miami murder. In 1992, he asked his trial judge to change his sentence to death and to change Florida's method of execution (now electrocution) so that he could donate his organs. [19] A fortnight after this request was denied, Faries, who presumably had been mentally competent to make the decision to request a death sentence and donate his organs, attempted suicide.

The argument that death sentenced prisoners should be permitted to donate their bodies 'to science' met with a more receptive audience in mid-1995. That audience was the US Supreme Court. Two years earlier, Larry Lonchar, a triple-murderer on death row in Georgia, waived all of his appeals and asked to be executed. Just thirty-two minutes before his scheduled execution, he agreed to take up an appeal after a family member threatened suicide, and he won a stay of execution. But when no appeal was filed, a 1995 execution date was scheduled. After learning about the shortage of human organs (primarily through publicity generated by the liver transplant for the former baseball star Mickey Mantle), Lonchar decided to appeal. However, the only claim he would allow in his appeal asserted his right to 'be put to sleep' so he could donate organs, and not to be executed in the electric chair, which would make organ donation impossible.[20] On 29 June 1995, just one minute before Lonchar was scheduled to be electrocuted, the Supreme Court stayed the execution and agreed to hear his claim.[21]

Lonchar enlisted the help of Dr. Jack Kevorkian for advice on alternative methods of execution that would preserve the organs so they could be transplanted. Kevorkian estimated that between three and six lives could be saved by harvesting Lonchar's organs, adding 'What's going to be gained by frying this guy?'[22] Kevorkian claimed that if the execution was done by lethal injection, two kidneys and a liver could be harvested. If Lonchar was anesthetized so he became 'like a brain-dead person' and his organs removed while he was still alive, Kevorkian said that the lungs and heart could also be saved. When asked about the American Medical Association's position that participation by physicians in executions is unethical, Kevorkian stated that he 'knows at least two pre-eminent surgeons in the transplant field who could do the procedure.'[23]

With just over 3,000 death row inmates in America at the end of 1995, an increasing pace of executions, and a constant demand for healthy organs, state legislators are not blind to the potential for death row inmates to will their organs for transplant. In Indiana, for example, State Representative Jon Padfield, who describes himself as a 'staunch' supporter of capital punishment, has initiated a legislative study of the state's new execution method, lethal injection. Padfield is concerned that like electrocution, lethal injection renders many organs unsuitable for transplantation. He therefore wants to search for alternative means of execution so the organs will not be harmed. He has succeeded in scheduling it for study by a committee of state legislators during the summer of 1995. 'If the doctors knew in advance when a donor would die,' said Padfield, 'the process [of organ transplantation] would be much smoother.'[24]

One would think that those who support the death penalty would oppose the use of inmates' bodies for science because they want the inmate to suffer as much as possible, and thus any measure of self-respect that the prisoner might derive - such as by making his death 'meaningful' - should be denied. Abolitionists see it a different way, fearing that another justification for the death penalty will emerge: We need to execute because we need (otherwise) healthy dead people for body parts and medical research. No social advantages should flow from state-ordered homicide: When good things result from bad policies, the bad policy is legitimated.

The question of the propriety of granting a condemned inmate's desire to donate organs was debated by Hugo Adam Bedau and Michael Zeik in the pages of *Hastings Center Report*, America's leading journal of medical ethics, nearly two decades ago.[25] Death row inmate John Evans requested to be executed by lethal injection, rather than by Alabama's practice of electrocution, so that his organs could be preserved and donated. In a move that once again shows the seductiveness of this argument, State Representative Edward Robertson introduced legislation that was designed to grant Evans his wish. Bedau took the position that the legislature ought to focus its attention on giving Evans a meaningful *life* instead of a meaningful death, and that the controversy about methods of execution and organ transplants simply diverted attention from more important questions. Because the proposed measure would give condemned murderers a chance to 'do good,' Bedau felt that it would make executions more palatable to trial juries, judges, and clemency officials than long imprisonment, and eventually more people would be executed. Bedau also worried that the legislation might lead to mandatory organ donation. Zeik, on the other hand, believed that organ donation would make death row inmates look more humane, and therefore might even decrease the appetite for executions. In the end, the proposal did not pass, and Evans was electrocuted. Ironically, the execution was badly botched; Evans literally burned to death in the electric chair.[26]

One might question whether valid informed consent can occur under the stresses of death row confinement and an approaching date with the executioner. And even if the inmate is not acting under intense psychological pressure, his isolation on death row makes it impossible for him to anticipate the costs and benefits of his actions. Inmates choosing to donate organs may do so after making a judgement about how the larger community will view that donation - i.e. the inmate believes the community will give him something (notably acknowledgement of his dignity, of which he has been stripped by his crime, death sentence, and impending execution). But death row inmates have little contact with the community, and are too *isolated* to anticipate or evaluate what symbolic benefits the community might give them, their memory, or their relatives in return for the donation.

Finally, informed consent also necessitates a freedom to choose, and that freedom to chose is simply not present in the death row environment. If an inmate does want to donate organs, he does so in an attempt to atone somehow for his crimes and as a way to achieve at least partial forgiveness. However, by sentencing a person to death, the state has slammed the door to any genuine opportunities for atonement or forgiveness; through a death sentence the state/community has sent a message that it will not forgive. A condemnation to death and life on death row virtually strips inmates of any autonomy,[27] and the principle of autonomy underlies much of the medical and philosophical literature on informed consent.[28] Just as starving a prisoner might lead the prisoner to 'choose' to eat stale bread, giving death row inmates no means to obtain partial forgiveness or to preserve their dignity might lead the inmates to choose to donate organs. However, neither the choice to eat stale bread nor the choice to donate organs can be said to be free. Death row inmates have virtually no other choices available to them that might allow them meaningful repayment to society, and so their ability to choose is so constrained that a free choice to donate organs is impossible. In short, by giving the inmates only one avenue to pursue the rewards that motivate organ donation, the consent is coerced. The right to donate their organs could soon become the duty to do so, as though this was the only way death row inmates can show adequate remorse or concern for their fellow human beings.

## ATTEMPTS BY THE MEDICAL PROFESSION TO DRAW THE LINE

Recently a consortium of four groups was formed to study involvement by the medical profession in capital punishment. These four groups were the National Coalition to Abolish the Death Penalty, the American College of Physicians, Physicians for Human Rights, and Human Rights Watch. In early 1994, they released a report entitled *Breach of Trust: Physician Participation in the Death Penalty in the U.S.* The Report found that of the 36 states that then had the death penalty, 23 require a physician to 'pronounce' or 'determine' death. In 28 states, physicians are required to be present at executions. Hence, no executions can be preformed in these states without the (voluntary) consent and participation of members of the medical profession.

The American Medical Association (AMA) draws a fine line between what a physician may and may not do regarding executions. It last refined that line in 1993.[29] The AMA now considers it a breach of medical ethics for physicians to assist, witness, or attend executions, give technical advice to others about carrying out an execution (an extremely important role in lethal injection states), and from monitoring the vital signs of an inmate during an execution.[30] Under the new policy, physicians may certify death, preferably by not even stepping foot into the prison, but not pronounce it.

While these prohibitions remain controversial,[31] Dr. Robert Truog and Dr. Troyen Brennan argued in the pages of the *New England Journal of Medicine* that 'Medical societies should take the position that involvement in capital punishment is grounds for revoking a physician's license.'[32] But even though the *Breach of Trust* report documented clear violations of these standards and recommended that the medical licences of physicians be revoked for violation of these guidelines, and the AMA report itself clearly implies that physicians in violation should be disciplined, the standards are not being enforced and no state licensing board has ever sanctioned a physician for such violations.[33]

Ronald J. Angelone, the new chief of corrections in Virginia, confirmed that physicians can always be found to participate in executions. He had previously served as the Director of the Bureau of Prisons in Nevada, where five men were lethally injected under his supervision. 'I never had a problem with an execution in Nevada with the medical society of the individual doctors. I've had individuals who say they cannot. I thank them and say I understand that. I've never had an execution held up because I couldn't find a doctor.'[34]

In Florida, both physicians and physician assistants are involved in executions. Despite a 1983 policy of the American Academy of Physician Assistants that prohibits such involvement,[35] the death of inmates executed in

248

Florida is formally announced by a physician's assistant who is present at the side of a physician in the execution chamber.[36]

## PSYCHIATRIC INVOLVEMENT AND THE EXECUTION OF THE MENTALLY ILL

Specifically sidestepped in the latest AMA guidelines were issues related to psychiatric involvement in capital cases, particularly questions relating to the provision of mental health exams or treatment where they are needed for an execution to proceed. The ethically proper role of mental health professionals in death penalty cases is complex, and the lines are difficult to define.

Mental health professionals have had a long history of involvement in death penalty cases, and recent Supreme Court cases have mandated an increased presence.[37] Yet, American history is filled with examples of defendants with severe mental illnesses who have been put to death, and mentally ill people continue to be executed today.[38] Often hearing about an inmate's psychosis causes jurors to fear that mentally ill prisoners cannot be held safely in prisons, so mental illness can become an aggravating, rather than a mitigating factor.[39] Citizens want to feel protected,[40] and if they equate mental illness with unpredictability and dangerousness, they become more likely to vote for death.[41] As a result, a significant but unknown fraction of the 3,000 men and women who today populate America's death rows would fit the clinical criteria for psychosis. As a further result, competence for execution is being raised in cases where the defendant, at least arguably, should have been found not guilty at trial by reason of insanity. In theory the courts have agreed that the mentally ill should not be executed,[42] but in practice it is extremely difficult to amass the psychiatric expertise that is necessary to buttress this claim.

Consider, for example, the 1936 execution in New York of Albert Fish. Although the case is 60 years old, it provides an excellent illustration of two points: mental pathologies can become aggravating (rather than mitigating) factors in sentencing decisions, and second, mental health professionals can always be found who will find normality in even the most severely psychotic prisoners.

Fish was convicted of strangling to death 10-year-old Grace Budd on 3 June 1928.[43] He may have killed as many as 14 additional victims. After his arrest, he gave a detailed and hair-raising confession, admitting that he choked the child to death, cut her body into three sections, and ate part of each. The confession detailed nine days of constant sexual excitement while he cooked Grace's body with carrots, onions, and strips of bacon, and then ate it.

Fish had several relatives who suffered from mental problems: a paternal uncle and a half brother (both of whom died in state hospitals for the insane); a paternal aunt, two brothers, a sister, and his mother. According to Dr. Fredric Wertham - one of the country's foremost forensic psychiatrists in this century - Fish's mother and six other relatives 'suffered from psychosis or were severely psychopathic personalities.'[44] Dr. Wertham, who examined Fish, described Fish's sexual life as one of 'unparalleled perversity . . . There was no known perversion that he did not practice and practice frequently.'[45]

In addition to being a killer, a cannibal, and a sexual pervert, Fish was also a sado-masochist. He enjoyed taking bits of cotton, saturating them with alcohol, inserting them into his rectum, and setting them on fire. He also did that to some of the children he victimized. Dr. Wertham estimated that Fish had assaulted at least 100 children in 23 states (Fish preferred African-American children because the authorities did not pay much attention if they disappeared or were assaulted).

For years Fish enjoyed sticking needles into his body; he preferred the area between his scrotum and rectum (he also did this to some of his victims). Some of the needles were as big as sail needles, and, while Fish usually removed them, some were pushed in too far to be removed. At the time of his arrest, X-rays revealed that 29 needles remained inside his body. Fish was also coprophagic - he ate human feces.

Dr. Wertham testified at Fish's trial on behalf of the defence. In his words, 'In response to a hypothetical question that was fifteen thousand words long, covered forty-five typewritten pages, and took an hour and a half to be read, I declared that in my opinion Fish was legally insane.'[46] Nonetheless, it was not difficult for the state to find physicians who would testify that Fish was completely sane. Four psychiatrists testified for the state, and their statements are revealing:

'Well, a man might for nine days eat that [human] flesh and still not have a psychosis. There is no accounting for taste.'

'Coprophagia is a common sort of thing. We don't call people who do that mentally sick. A man who does that is socially perfectly all right.'

'They [people with coprophagia] are very successful people, successful artists, successful teachers, successful financiers.'

'I know of individuals prominent in society - one individual in particular that we all know. He ate human feces as a side dish with salad . . . I had a patient who was a very prominent public official who did it.'

Post-trial interviews with jurors revealed that most agreed that Fish was insane, but they felt that given his crimes, his mental state was irrelevant. Upon being found guilty, Fish's response was, 'What a thrill that will be, if I have to die in the electric chair. It will be a supreme thrill - the only one I haven't tried.'[47] On 16 January 1936, Fish sat in the electric chair at Sing Sing Prison. More than two dozen needles still remaining in his body caused a minor short circuit in the execution apparatus; a second jolt of electricity was necessary to finish the job.[48]

Sixty years have passed since Fish's execution, but the attitude toward mentally ill killers is still insensitivity. Many examples could be cited to document this point; unfortunately, however, space constraints prohibit the presentation of even a single case fully and fairly. But a brief glimpse of the recent case of Varnall Weeks, executed in Alabama on 12 May 1995, illustrates the point that American courts are failing to exempt the mentally ill from execution. Weeks had a long history of mental illness and use of anti-psychotic medications, and had been committed to a state mental hospital in 1974. None of this was mentioned to his jury prior to his being sentenced to death in a two-day trial in 1982. *Washington Post* columnist Colman McCarthy used these words to describe an April 1995 hearing in which Weeks participated:

> [Weeks] floated in and out of reality. Mostly out. He spoke of cybernetics, of a belief that his execution will transform him into a tortoise, after which he will rule the universe, of a liking for rainy weather, the Koran, Buddhism, Alabama - 'Alabama means albino' - the Garden of Eden and its 'unforbidden fruit,' Aztecs and a king's mace.

The trial judge concluded that Weeks was indeed insane, at least according to 'the dictionary definition of insanity' (whatever that is). Nonetheless, he refused to block the execution. Psychologists testifying for both the state and defence agreed that Weeks was a paranoid schizophrenic. It is clear that Weeks's execution, and those of two or three dozen other psychotic prisoners executed in America in the last two decades, are affronts to both the principle that mentally ill people should not be executed and to those professions which are charged with enforcing it. Forensic psychiatrists have important roles to play in contemporary capital defence,[49] and many inmates facing capital charges are not getting the assistance from mental health professionals that would allow them to avoid execution. In short, there is no equivalency between psychiatric help to avoid execution and psychiatric help to facilitate it.

## THE DANGERS OF NON-INVOLVEMENT

While predictions of dangerousness are unreliable, this does not mean that mental health professionals should totally refrain from predicting an inmate's future behavior during the penalty phase of capital trials. Predictions of *non*dangerousness are much more reliable than are predictions of dangerousness, and can often be very useful to capital defendants.[50] Jurors often believe that if murderers are not executed, they will kill again, and they need to know that the chances for satisfactory adjustment to the prison for certain categories of inmates (e.g. those with no long history of violent criminality, older defendants, or defendants whose previous incarcerations have resulted in a satisfactory adjustment to the prison) might be very high. Since upwards of 90 percent of convicted murderers can and do make appropriate adjustments to prison life, predicting nondangerousness is not especially difficult. On the other hand, mental health professionals who predict dangerousness need to inform jurors that, as the American Psychiatric Association itself says, their predictions are of extremely limited utility. This is because (a) the consequences of a prediction of dangerousness might be death, not simply imprisonment, and (b) predictions of dangerousness are unreliable.

Another area that has attracted much attention in recent years involves psychiatric evaluations of competence to be executed. Although the precise definition of competence to be executed varies by state, Florida's definition is typical: mental health professionals are asked to determine 'whether [the inmate] understands the nature and effect of the death penalty and why it is to be imposed upon him.'[51] The important case here is that of Florida death row inmate Alvin Ford, who in 1983 was examined for competence by a panel of three Florida psychiatrists. After a 25-minute interview, during which Ford could not utter a coherent sentence, two of the psychiatrists concluded that Ford was psychotic, although all three said he was competent to be executed. Ford's attorneys litigated the issue, arguing that the exam was a farce, and that the issue of competence should be decided by the courts, not by the governor. Prior to Ford, the mentally ill were often exempted from execution as a matter of executive grace through clemency authority, not as a matter of constitutional right. In 1986 Ford's attourneys won in the Supreme Court, and hence today the mentally incompetent have not simply a meritorious clemency claim, but also a recognized constitutional right not to be executed.

Some authorities have taken the position that psychiatrists should not be involved in giving opinions on competence for execution.[52] In 1990, for example, a committee of the British Medical Association (BMA) was convened to examine this and other aspects of physician participation in issues related to human rights. In the end, the committee admitted that it was unable to 'satisfactorily resolve' all issues relating to the involvement of psychiatrists in capital cases, but it firmly concluded that 'Providing medical opinion on 'fitness for execution' is not an appropriate role for medical practitioners.'[53]

I am among those who disagree, and urged them to conclude otherwise when I testified in front of the BMA Committee in London in 1990.[54] When a severely psychotic death row inmate faces execution, what would happen if the most ethical and humane psychiatrists declined to help him on the grounds that they did not want to become involved? Only the meanest and most prosecution-prone psychiatrists would do the evaluations. Any boycott would be partial since there would be no way to enforce the ban. Indeed, it could be argued that ethical problems would arise for those physicians who *refuse* to assist defendants who need psychiatric testimony to convince a judge that they are incompetent for execution. At the same time, a physician who evaluates a prisoner and feels that the prisoner probably does meet the criteria for competence may be more ethically justified in telling the courts that he or she cannot render a firm opinion (i.e. one can never be absolutely certain of competence) than in testifying that the proof of competence is conclusive.[55] As with other decisions on the road to execution, the ethical burden is heavier for those whose professional involvement leads to the death of others. As the British Medical Association's committee concluded, 'We . . . note that a doctor testifying on the prisoner's behalf appears to be in quite a different moral position to the doctor testifying for the state.'[56]

252

Another issue that has provoked much discussion in recent years involves what to do after an inmate has been found incompetent for execution. Should physicians provide treatment that might result in competence to be executed? Most commentators have said no, but little thought has been given to what constitutes treatment.[57] A few years ago a colleague and I interviewed a dozen mental health professionals who were faced with such a case.[58] Some were afraid even to say 'Good morning' to the patient/inmate for fear that decent behavior might help restore his competency. Saying 'Hello' or even prescribing drugs with the inmate or his attourney's consent might be justifiable, but there is no clear solution to questions raised by these cases as long as the inmate's stay of execution may be lifted.

The *only* clear solution to this dilemma is to commute death sentences for all prisoners found incompetent for execution.[59] Yet, I am unaware of any medical society in the U.S. that has ever called for such legislation, much less lobbied for it.


## CONCLUSIONS

Three principal conclusions can be derived from the information and judgements above. First, medical involvement in the death penalty internationally is common and in certain areas, such as in securing organ transplants from executed prisoners, a problem of increasing importance.

Second, medical professions have failed to lobby on death penalty issues that affect their members. As described above, courts and legislatures have defined competency for execution in narrow terms that are unconnected with any medical conditions (e.g. psychosis), and they have done so with little or no medical advice and participation in constructing the law. Courts and legislatures have also asked for or demanded medical participation in other aspects of capital punishment. Medical professions are rarely (if ever) consulted on ethical issues before statutes are enacted or judicial opinions rendered that mandate their participation. On the other hand, with the exception of the Missouri law that was changed in 1995,[60] no law concerning the death penalty has ever been changed, and no medical group has ever pushed strongly for a law to be changed, on the grounds that it calls for inappropriate or unethical behaviour by medical professionals. Laws that invite or force medical professionals to act unethically need to be changed, but few (if any) professional associations have given priority to demanding such changes. In issues relating to capital punishment, the medical professions have been tranquil followers, not the leaders.

Third, professional organizations have been slow in disciplining their members who violate ethical codes in capital or potentially capital cases. Professional organizations should demand to know the names of physicians who participate in executions, and these physicians need to be warned in advance of unethical participation and disciplined if these warnings are not heeded.

Two additional thoughts can be offered by way of conclusion. The fact that medical professions are drawing lines about involvement in capital cases is part of a long-term and indisputable trend in western societies to move away from the use of capital punishment. Fifty years ago, it was inconceivable that anyone would seriously challenge a physician's presence at an execution in America.[61] That medical professionals are uncomfortable in execution chambers is one more indicator of society's growing ambivalence about the death penalty.[62] Abolitionists would argue that one means to achieve the disappearance of the executioner is to make everyone involved in carrying out the death penalty increasingly uncomfortable with their involvement.

Once the government determines that some citizens deserve to die, it encounters all sorts of problems in specifying who should be executed, by whom, and how these decisions should be made. Death penalty debates a few decades focused on the question of whether or not we ought to try to get even with people like Lee Harvey Oswald or Charles Manson. Today we are talking about killing teenagers and the retarded, about killing schizophrenics who are no more responsible for their behaviour than they are for the colour of their eyes, and the propriety of placing pictures of their corpses on the Internet. Meanwhile, throughout the world there are untold millions who are suffering and dying because of unmet medical needs. Opposition to the death penalty arises not merely from what it does to offenders, but from what it does to the rest of us.

# ENDNOTES

\* During the Spring semester, 1995, when this paper was drafted, the author was a Visiting Professor at the University of Westminster School of Law, London. I am indebted to Jim Welsh for his advice, to Peter Hodgkinson and his colleagues for their support, and to Hugo Adam Bedau and Henry Schwarzschild for helpful comments on an earlier version of this paper. The first draft of this paper was presented at a public forum at the University of Westminster, 27 March 1995.

1. Scott, George Ryley. *The History of Capital Punishment*. London, Torchstream Books, 1950, p. 50; Cooper, David D. *The Lesson of the Scaffold*. Athens, Ohio: Ohio University Press, 1974, p. 1.

2. 'Advances in one branch of medicine, anatomy, depended as much upon eighteenth-century penal practices as it did upon the idealist transmission of knowledge. ... [p]rogress in anatomy depended upon the ability of the surgeons to snatch the bodies of those hanged at Tyburn.' This practice was met with resistance by the family and friends of the condemned. See Peter Linebaugh, 'The Tyburn Riot Against the

Surgeons,' pp. 65-117 in Douglas Hay, Peter Linebaugh, John G. Rule, E. P. Thompson, and Cal Winslow (eds.), *Albion's Fatal Tree: Crime and Society in Eighteenth-Century England.* New York: Pantheon, 1975, at p. 69.

3. Weiner, Dora B. 'The Real Dr. Guillotin', *Journal of the American Medical Association* 220 (April 3, 1972): 85-89; Donegan, Ciaran F., 'Dr. Guillotin - Reformer and Humanitarian,' *Journal of the Royal Society of Medicine* 83 (Oct., 1990): 637-39.

4. Mackey, Philip English. *Voices Against Death: American Opposition to Capital Punishment, 1787-1975.* New York: Burt Franklin & Co., 1976, pp. 1-13.

5. Colburn, Don. 'Lethal Injection: Why Doctors are Uneasy About the Newest Method of Capital Punishment' *Washington Post* (Health Section), Dec. 11, 1990, p. 15.

6. Nelson, Lane. 'Death Row Donors,' *The Angolite,* Jan.-Feb., 1995, 14-17.

7. Hsieh, H., T. J. Yu, W. C. Yang, S. S. Chu, and M. K. Lai, 'The Gift of Life From Prisoners Sentenced to Death: Preliminary Report.' *Transplantation Proceedings* 24 (Aug., 1992): 1335-36, at 1336.

8. Human Rights Watch, 'Organ Procurement and Judicial Execution in China', *Human Rights Watch/China* 6 (August, 1994): 2-40.

9. Follain, John, 'French First Lady Slams Chinese Human Organ Trade,' *Reuters News Service,* March 20, 1995.

10. Manegold, Catherine S. 'China Is Said to Sell Executed Inmates' Organs', *New York Times,* May 5, p. A10.

11. Copies of Mr. Schulz's testimony can be obtained from Amnesty International, 322 Eighth Avenue, New York, NY 10001-4808.

12. 'China Charges Rights Crusader with Espionage', *Sun,* July 9, 1995, p. 2; 'Chinese Convict Harry Wy as Spy and Order Him Out,' *New York Times,* Aug. 24, 1995, p. A1; 'Wu Greeted by Supporters in California,' *New York Times,* Aug. 25, 1995, p. A4.

13. Laytner, Ron. 'The Visible Man', *Chicago Tribune,* March 15, 1995, p. 1.

14. Roeggla, G., U. Landesmann, and M. Roeggla, 'Ethics of Executed Person on Internet', *The Lancet* 345 (Jan. 28, 1995): 260.

15. Owens, R. Glynn. 'Ethics of Executed Person on Internet', *The Lancet* 345 (March 11, 1995): 653.

16. 'Death Row Inmate Donates Kidney to Save Mother's Life', *Gainesville Sun*, April 28, 1995, p. 5A.

17. Radelet, Michael L., Hugo Adam Bedau, and Constance E. Putnam. *In Spite of Innocence*. Boston: Northeastern University Press, 1992, pp. 290-91.

18. Sherman, Rorie. "Dr. Death' Visits the Condemned,' *National Law Journal*, Nov. 8, 1993, p. 11.

19. 'Convict Seeks Death to Donate His Organs', *U.S.A. Today*, June 5, 1992, p. 2A.

20. 'Court Gives Killer Reprieve Just in Time.' *Washington Times*, July 1, 1995, p. A3; 'Lonchar Gets Another Stay at Last Minute,' *Atlanta Journal and Constitution*, June 30, 1995, p. C6.

21. *Lonchar v. Thomas*, No. 95-5015 (June 29, 1995). In previous cases, inmates under an execution warrant had always been granted stays of execution when their case first entered federal court. In those cases, however, the inmates challenged the constitutionality of their convictions or sentences. It is unclear if the Supreme Court granted certiorari to decide if stays should be automatic when the constitutionality of the conviction or sentence is not being challenged, or if they want to rule on the constitutionality of electrocution when the inmate wants to donate his organs.

22. Cook, Rhonda, 'Condemned Inmate Wants to Donate Organs,' *Atlanta Journal and Constitution*, June 16, 1995, p. D1.

23. *Atlanta Journal and Constitution*, June 16, 1995.

24. Higgins, Will. 'Execution Option Would Create Organ Donors', *Indianapolis News*, July 3, 1995, p. B1.

25. Hugo Adam Bedau and Michael Zeik, 'A Condemned Man's Last Wish: Organ Donation & a "Meaningful' Death"', *Hastings Center Report*, February 1979, pp. 16-17.

26. After the first jolt, physicians examined him and found a heartbeat. A second jolt was applied, and again the physicians found a heartbeat. Amidst smoke, sparks and an 'overpowering stench of burnt flesh and clothing' the third round of electric charges finally ended the prisoner's

life. Russell F. Canan. 'Burning at the Wire: The Execution of John Evans.' pp 60-80 in Michael L. Radelet (ed.), *Facing the Death Penalty: Essays on a Cruel and Unusual Punishment*. Philadelphia: Temple University Press, 1989.

27. Johnson, Robert. *Condemned to Die: Life Under Sentence of Death*. New York: Elsevier, 1981.

28. Faden, Ruth R. And Tom L. Beauchamp. *A History and Theory of Informed Consent*. New York: Oxford University Press, p. 7.

29. Council on Ethical and Judicial Affairs, American Medical Association, 'Physician Participation in Capital Punishment', *Journal of the American Medical Association* 279 (July 21, 1993): 365-68.

30. *The Lancet*, one of the world's top medical journals, has criticized the AMA for not going far enough in denouncing capital punishment. See 'Doctors and Death Row,' *The Lancet* 341 (Jan. 23, 1993), pp. 209-210.

31. Davis, Michael. 'The State's Dr. Death: What's Unethical About Physicians Helping at Executions?' *Social Theory and Practice* 21 (Spring 1995): 31-60.

32. Truog, Robert D., and Troyen A Brennan, 'Participation of Physicians in Capital Punishment.' *New England Journal of Medicine* 329 (Oct. 28, 1993): 1347-1350, at 1349. In a later issue, six letters debated this article, and Truog and Brennan replied. See 'Correspondence,' *New England Journal of Medicine* 330 (March 31, 1994): 935-36.

33. For a description of a physician's participation in a recent North Carolina execution and a call for sanctions on physicians who violate the AMA's ban on participation in executions, see Sonis, Jeffrey, and Katz, Samuel L., 'Is This Medicine? Physician Participation in Capital Punishment in North Carolina,' *North Carolina Medical Journal* 55 (Dec. 1994): 581-86. Following this paper, five physicians debate the authors' points.

34. Arney, June. 'Doctor to be Absent from Execution Amid Debate on Ethics; State Seeks Substitute,' *The Virginian-Pilot* (Norfolk), April 16, 1994, p. D1.

35. Egbert, Lawrence D., 'Should Physicians Oppose P A Participation in Executions?' *Texas Medicine* 90 (January, 1994): 9; Strand, Justine, 'Physician Assistants Don't Participate in Executions,' *Texas Medicine* 90 (March, 1994): 7.

36. Bernard Bolender was executed in Florida on July 18, 1995. 'At 10:09 a.m., the executioner threw the switch. About 10 minutes later, after physicians assistant Bill Mathews and Dr. Jorge Franceschi-Zambrana examined Bolender, he was pronounced dead . . .' Greenberg, David, 'Bolender Executed For Killing 4,' *Gainesville Sun,* July 19, 1995, p. 1B. Our inquiries revealed that Dr. Franceschi-Zambrana is not a member of the Florida Medical Association, so they are unable to conduct an investigation or, if warranted, institute discipline.

37. Kermani, Ebrahim J. and Jay E. Kantor, 'Psychiatry and the Death Penalty: The Landmark Supreme Court Cases and Their Ethical Implications for the Profession', *Bulletin of the American Academy of Psychiatry and the Law* 22 (1994): 95-108.

38. Miller, Kent S., and Michael L. Radelet. *Executing the Mentally Ill.* Newbury Park, Calif.: Sage Publications, 1993, p. 73.

39. Lawrence T White, 'The Mental Illness Defense in the Capital Murder Hearing', *Behavioral Sciences and the Law* 5 (1987): 411-21; Ellen Fels Berkman, 'Mental Illness As An Aggravating Circumstance in Capital Sentencing,' *Columbia Law Review* 89 (1989): 291-309.

40. Three quaters of the American public support the death penalty, but only about half of the adult population supports the death penalty when the alternative punishment is life imprisonment without parole. In a 1991 Gallup poll, 76 percent of Americans supported the death penalty; this dropped to 53 percent 'if life imprisonment with no possibility of parole were a certainty.' Gallup, Alec and Frank Newport, 'Death Penalty Support Remains Strong', *Gallup Poll Monthly* 309 (June 1991): 40-45, at page 40.

41. Lawrence T. White, 'Juror Decision Making in the Capital Penalty Trial: An Analysis of Crimes and Defense Strategies,' *Law and Human Behavior* 11 (1987): 113-30.

42. *Ford v. Wainwright,* 477 U.S. 399 (1986).

43. This account is taken from Heimer, M. *The Cannibal: The Case of Albert Fish.* New York: Pinnacle Books, 1971; Wertham, F., *The Show of Violence.* Garden City, New York: Doubleday, 1949.

44. Wertham, 1949:70.

45. Wertham, 1949:72.

46. Wertham, 1949:84.

47. Heimer, 1949:129.

48. Heimer, 1971:139.

49. McCarthy, Colman, 'Insanity On Death Row', *Washington Post*, May 6, 1995, p. A15.

50. For an overview of these issues, see Redelet, Michael L., and James W. Marquart. 'Assessing Nondangerousness During Penalty Phases of Capital Trials', *Albany Law Review* 54 (1990): 845-61.

51. Miller, Kent S., and Michael L. Radelet *Executing the Mentally Ill*. Newbury Park, Calif.: Sage Publications, 1993, p. 73.

52. 'My best judgement is that the use of psychiatric skills in this context so compromises medicine's therapeutic and compassionate aims that it ought to be regarded as ethically unacceptable.' Bloche, M. Gregg, 'Psychiatry, Capital Punishment, and the Purposes of Medicine,' *International Journal of Law and Psychiatry* 16 (1993): 301-357, at 352. For an overview of contrasting positions, see Heilbrun, Kirk, Michael L. Radelet, and Joel Dvoskin, 'The Debate on Treating Individuals Incompetent for Execution,' *American Journal of Psychiatry* 149 (May 1992): 596-605.

53. British Medical Association, *Medicine Betrayed: The Participation of Doctors in Human Rights Abuses*. London: Zed Books, 1992, p. 108, 201.

54. Professor Richard Bonnie has also indicated that he disagrees with the Committee's conclusions on this point. See Bonnie, Richard J., 'The Death Penalty: When Doctors Must Say No,' *British Medical Journal* 305 (15 August 1992): 381-82.

55. Weinstock, Robert, Gregory B. Leong, and J. Arturo Silva, 'The Death Penalty and nernard Diamond's Approach to Forensic Psychiatry', *Bulletin of the American Academy of Psychiatry and the Law* 20 (1992): 197-210.

56. British Medical Association, *Medicine Betrayed: The Participation of Doctors in Human Rights Abuses*. London: Zed Books, 1992, p. 108.

57. Different activities that may (or may not) be considered 'treatment' are reviewed in Heilbrun, Kirk S., Michael L. Radelet, and Joel Dvoskin. 'The Debate on Treating Individuals Incompetent for Execution', *American Journal of Psychiatry* 149 (1992): 596-605.

58. Radelet, Michael L., and George W Barnard. 'Treating Those Found Incompetent for Execution. Ethical Chaos With Only One Solution', *Bulletin of the American Academy of Psychiatry and the Law* 16 (1988): 297-307.

59. ibid.; Wallace, Donald H., 'The Need to Commute the Death Sentence: Competency for Execution and Ethical Dilemmas for Mental Health Professionals,' *International Journal of Law and Psychiatry* 15 (1992): 317-337.

60. VanDuch, Darryl, 'Is There a Doctor in the Death House?' *National Law Journal*, Sept. 4, 1995, p. A6.

61. For example, one of the country's most outspoken death penalty abolitionists of the early part of this was the physician at New York's Sing Sing Prison, Dr Amos Squire. Yet he regularly participated in executions and in his book, *Sing Sing Doctor*, does not mention any ethical dilemmas or questions that might have arisen because of his participation. He begins his book by stating, 'Standing by the electric chair at Sing Sing, I have given the signal that sent the killing current through the bodies of one hundred and thirty-eight men.' Squires, Amos O, *Sing Sing Doctor*. Garden City, N.Y.: Garden City Publishing Co., 1937.

62. Zimring, Franklin E., and Gordon Hawkins, *Capital Punishment and the American Agenda*. New York: Cambridge University Press, 1986; Zimring, Franklin E. 'Ambivalence in State Capital Punishment Policy: An Empirical Sounding,' *N.Y.U. Review of Law and Social Change* 18 (1990-91): 729-42.

# CHAPTER 11

# Abolitionism: A Tale of Two Struggles

## Andrew Rutherford

The German criminologist, Sebastian Scheerer, one of a handful of scholars who have sought to connect past and present abolitionist concerns, has pointed out that 'most people in the United States associate the term (abolitionism) with the abolition of slavery and/or the death penalty. In Europe, abolitionism stands for "doing away with the prison system wholly", and to some it even means the end of penal law as such.'[1] Furthermore, rather than regarding abolitionism as a theory, Scheerer suggests that 'it seems wiser to speak both more modestly and realistically of it as an incomplete, competing perspective on social control.'[2]

The development of abolitionist perspectives has particularly benefited from the insightful work of Thomas Mathiesen, a sociologist at the University of Oslo. In the first instance, by insisting that 'any reform must be of the abolishing kind' he made the crucial distinction between 'positive' and 'negative' reforms. 'Positive reforms are changes which improve or build-up the system so that it functions more effectively - whereby the system is strengthened and its abolition is made more difficult.' The positive reform bestows 'renewed legitimacy' upon the system, which in turn means that 'the general public interprets the system as more reasonable, better, more correct, more rational, etc.'[3] On the other hand, negative reforms 'are changes which abolish or remove greater or smaller parts on which the system in general is more or less dependent.' To which he added, 'It is correct to work only for negative and *not* for the positive reforms on a short-term basis as well - only if this is done consistently will the otherwise hopeless dilemma between "short-term" and "long-term" objectives be abolished.'[4]

A further strand of Mathiesen's work arises from his exploration of the circumstances under which abolitionist activities appear to have met with some success. He has been particularly interested in the process by which key people with decision-making powers, or who are able to exert considerable influence, become sufficiently sceptical about the issue in question and go on to take a significant initiative. Referring to Norwegian vagrancy legislation, Mathiesen has written that '(a)n abolition of this part of the system required not only scepticism towards the system at the top level, and not only agreement at the grassroots within the system, but, additionally, widespread support of and strong pressure for change from professional groups outside the system. In the climate created through the interaction between these three corners, abolition succeeded. But it should also be noted that the pressure for change came primarily from the professions. The wider lay community was not as intensely involved.'[5]

261

Building upon several case studies of substantial reductions achieved in prison populations, Mathiesen has suggested that 'two levels were involved simultaneously - top level political decision-makers in the sphere of criminal justice on the one hand and the grass roots - the practitioners, of the so-called criminal justice system on the other. Crossing the line between the two levels we find a common culture - a set of norms, values and beliefs - against the prison solution at least for some types of offences . . . Once the battle (over culture) was won by the sceptical side, major and sustained reductions could in fact take place.' [6] Scepticism at the top is not by itself sufficient but it appears to be a crucial component. In tracing the stages of the abolition process, sceptical signals or messages from the top may often be a useful place to begin.

In this concluding chapter, two episodes arising from efforts to remove the death penalty are briefly charted and considered in the light of these strands of Mathiesen's abolitionist thinking. In the early 1960s capital punishment remained in use in both Britain and the United States, but within a decade or so the course of events in these two countries had led to quite different outcomes. In Britain the death penalty for murder was finally abolished in 1969, and subsequent attempts in the House of Commons at restoration have been defeated by widening margins. By contrast, as discussed in Chapter 3 of this work, in the United States there was a rapid head of steam towards abolition in the late 1960s, a victory of sorts in 1972 with the Supreme Court's decision in *Furman v. Georgia*, only to be followed by a new generation of death penalty statutes, a steady stream of executions and a hardening political resolve not only to retain but to extend the scope of capital punishment.[7] Nor were public opinion pollsters reliable indicators as to subsequent events. In the United States, at least for a short period in the mid-1960s, there were more people in favour than were opposed to abolition. In Britain, however, opinion polls reported large majorities in support of capital punishment. Forecasts by closely involved participants were hardly a better guide. It was by no means uncommon for people close to the American struggle against the death penalty in the United States to conclude that with the *Furman* decision there would be no further executions.[8] In Britain there were those who believed, mistakenly as it turned out, that the Homicide Act 1957 had bolstered the death penalty for a generation or more.

Only a brief overview of post-war developments in Britain is required (a fuller treatment is provided in Chapter 8). In 1945, with the election of a Labour government which enjoyed a large majority in the House of Commons, the immediate prospects for abolishing the death penalty had never seemed brighter. The Labour Party Conference in 1934 had unanimously backed abolition, and four years later most Labour Members of Parliament supported a private members motion urging the government to add an abolition clause to the criminal justice bill which was eventually abandoned with the outbreak of war.[9] However, the Labour government's bill, published in November 1947, contained no mention of capital punishment, an omission which represented 'a stunning defeat for the abolitionists'.[10] The Cabinet considered capital punishment on six occasions between June 1947 and July 1948 but did not budge from a collective view that 'this was not an opportune time for abolishing capital punishment'.[11] In due course, it was agreed that there should be a free vote, but that ministers should abstain if they were not able to join the government in supporting the status quo.

At the bill's second reading on 14 April 1948 an abolitionist clause, which sought to suspend the death penalty for an experimental five years, was moved by the Labour backbench member, Sydney Silverman and carried by 245-222.[12] But, as the abolitionists anticipated, this victory was short-lived, and in due course the clause was roundly defeated in the House of Lords. The issue was then put out of touch by the government's announcement of a Royal Commission which began its deliberations in 1949 and reported in 1953, two years after the Conservative Party had been elected to power. The direct question of abolition had been carefully excluded from the Royal Commission's terms of reference, but through a rather tortuous route the Commission indicated 'that the real issue is now whether capital punishment should be retained or abolished.'[13] Although there was an early debate on the report in the House of Lords, it was not until February 1955 that it was considered by the House of Commons. Gwilym Lloyd George, the home secretary who had voted for abolition in 1948, was now a retentionist; whereas James Chuter Ede, the former Labour home secretary, moved in the opposite direction, having apparently been persuaded by the case of Timothy Evans.[14] On this occasion, seven years after the matter had last been put to the vote, Silverman's amendment was defeated by 214-245.

Five months later the hanging of Ruth Ellis, a young divorcee and mother of two children, for the murder of a lover, once again placed the death penalty issue to the fore of national attention. It was this 'national trauma'[15] which led within a month to the formation of the National Campaign for the Abolition of Capital Punishment.[16] The National Campaign, which had thirty thousand members by January 1956, worked closely with parliamentarians. This was reflected in Silverman's abolitionist amendment succeeding by 293-262 the following month. By now the government were on the defensive with forty-eight Conservative members among the abolitionists compared with only fourteen in 1948. But once again defeat in the House of Lords led to the compromise measures framed by the Homicide Bill which sought to create five categories of capital murder. The death penalty would thereby be limited to specific instances of murder, such as in the course or furtherance of theft, where firearms or explosives were used or in the case of a subsequent murder.[17] Having decided that there would not be a free vote, the government carried the third reading of the bill by 217-131.

It was the view of many observers that the Homicide Act 1957 had retarded progress towards abolition. The leading penal reformer, Margery Fry, was by no means alone in believing that the legislation 'indeed went far enough towards abolition: far enough to set back total abolition for another span of years'.[18] But Sir Ernest Gowers was nearer the mark, commenting that the formula adopted by the framers of the Homicide Act represented a 'search for the chimera', and as such had been firmly rejected by the Royal Commission which he had chaired.[19] Furthermore R. A. Butler, the Home Secretary who had steered the legislation through the House of Commons, later remarked that by the end of his time at the Home Office he 'began to see that the system could not go on'.[20]

Further developments, however, had to await the advent of a Labour Government. In July 1963 the new Labour Party leader, Harold Wilson, among the Cabinet members who had abstained on the death penalty vote in 1948, addressing the Society of Labour Lawyers, said that in the event of a Labour victory at the next general election, he was certain the first private member's bill to abolish capital punishment would get through the House and be made law.[21] The sea-change on the death penalty within the leadership of the Labour Party over two decades had been completed. When Labour was returned to office in October 1964 events moved rapidly. Most unusually, it was decided that the programme set forth in the Queen's Speech would make reference to time being made available for a private member's bill on the death penalty. This enabled Silverman to act quickly and, on a free vote, his bill received its second reading by 355-170.[22] The only successful amendment, accepted by the House of Commons in October 1965, was that the Act would expire on 31 July 1970 unless both Houses determined otherwise by affirmative resolutions. The bill was agreed by the House of Lords with a majority of one hundred. In December 1969, with another general election looming, the House of Commons endorsed the legislation by 343-185. After the defeat by 220-174 in the House of Lords of a motion seeking to extend the experimental period by three further years, the affirmative resolution was agreed without a further division. As Lord Windlesham has commented, '(t)he decision was one of the most conspicuous, and courageous, ever taken by parliamentarians, irrespective of party, in the knowledge of the widespread extent of disapproval for their actions.'[23] Royal Assent followed on November 8 and the legislation took effect the following day.

This brief account of developments in Britain has focused mostly upon activities within Parliament, but these were complemented by a growing belief of élite opinion that the death penalty had to go. This powerful 'sphere of influence', to use Mathiesen's term, was closest to Labour, but it had also made significant inroads among Conservatives. In the event, it was the huge shift of opinion among Conservative parliamentarians that was the decisive factor both in the period before and after abolition. From the mid-1950s a solid abolitionist view was shared widely by much of Britain's élite. In short, the public policy position in Britain for abolition enjoyed firm foundations. At that time such a situation did not exist in the United States, and it certainly does not exist thirty years later. In the United States the struggle against the death penalty took a very different shape, but it was not without specific episodes which appeared to hold considerable promise. As Philip Mackey has shown in his historical selection of statements on capital punishment, the period 1955-72 was one of only three eras of reform since the late eighteenth century.[24] As measured by public opinion polls, there was a substantial decline in support for the death penalty from 1953 up to 1966, after which the trend was rapidly reversed.[25] There was also a steady reduction in the number of actual executions which averaged 36 per year for 1960-64 compared with an average of 61 for the preceding five years. Furthermore, there were a few isolated but encouraging events at the state level. The Delaware legislature abolished the death penalty in 1958,[26] and although this decision was reversed four years later, abolitionists could take some comfort from this short-lived victory. A more substantial event occurred in 1964 (but was to be overturned at the polls fourteen years later), when on the heels of a well organized campaign, sixty percent of Oregon voters supported an abolitionist proposition. But as Hugo Bedau has noted, since 1964 public referenda have been used exclusively to restore rather than abolish the death penalty.[27] Two other states, Iowa and West Virginia, abolished the death penalty in 1965, and by the end of the decade three others had severely restricted its availability.[28] Although these developments represented progress, there was little reason to be optimistic about the prospects for state-by-state abolition. By the mid-1960s the belief rapidly gained ground that the most effective way forward lay with the federal courts, and at the end of the decade virtually all abolitionist eggs had been put in the litigation basket, very much to the neglect of a broadly based public policy campaign.

To illustrate aspects of both the promise and the shortcomings of this abolition-by-litigation phase a brief but significant episode is considered here. The legal attack on racial segregation, especially within schools and colleges, had given a tremendous boost to public interest law firms. Litigation was a core component of the civil rights movement, and no organization was more closely aware of the inequities of the criminal justice process, and in death penalty cases in particular, than the nation's largest public interest law firm, the NAACP Legal Defense and Education Fund (hereafter LDF). Between 1950-1954, for example, under the direction of its chief counsel, Thurgood Marshall, the LDF had been involved intensely in a death penalty case in Groveland, Florida, in which it was claimed a white woman had been raped by four black men.

In 1961 Marshall was appointed by President Kennedy to the Second Circuit Court of Appeals, and he was succeeded at the LDF by Jack Greenberg.[29] The origins of the legal assault on the death penalty can be traced to about this time, in connection with a case involving a black man sentenced to death for burglary with intent to commit a rape. The Supreme Court ordered a retrial on the ground that the defendant had been denied counsel at his arraignment. At a subsequent strategy meeting of LDF lawyers (attended, due to unforeseen circumstances, by Anthony Amsterdam, a civil rights advocate and law professor, who was to become the Fund's chief legal strategist between 1965-72)[30], it was agreed that this was an appropriate case in which to raise the issue of racial discrimination in the imposition of the death penalty. Furthermore, the LDF decided to argue that where no life had been taken, capital punishment was a 'cruel and unusual punishment' under the eighth amendment.[31]

In the event, the defendant was sentenced to life imprisonment and matters rested there until the autumn of 1963 when the question of the death penalty resurfaced following an extraordinary initiative taken by Justice Arthur Goldberg, who had the year before been elevated by President Kennedy from Secretary of Labour to the Supreme Court. In Goldberg's view the 'time was ripe for the Court to request argument and explicitly consider this most important issue in an adversary setting'.[32] As one of his clerks for the October Term of 1993, Goldberg had recruited Alan Dershowitz who, in his first clerkship for Judge David Bazelon (United States Court of Appeals for the District of Columbia Circuit), had worked on an opinion to spare a man's life. On the first day of his clerkship Justice Goldberg asked him to prepare a memorandum on the constitutional issues surrounding the imposition of the death penalty. Goldberg put it to his clerk that if torture was cruel and unusual punishment, surely capital punishment also should be prohibited by the eighth amendment. This was regarded by Dershowitz as 'a bold leap of faith', and he 'turned to the books with a sense of mission . . . Here was a real opportunity for the Supreme Court to save countless lives.'[33] Several weeks later Dershowitz gave Goldberg a draft memorandum which concluded that a reasonable constitutional argument could be made against the death penalty. Dershowitz recommended that the Supreme Court should first 'carefully scrutinize the . . . capital cases which came before it, in an effort to define categories of cases where the death penalty is unconstitutional . . . I suggested also that Justice Goldberg should make known his doubts about the constitutionality of the death penalty so that lawyers would begin to raise eighth amendment arguments in death cases. *This would set in motion a process that could gradually chip away at the constitutional legitimacy of the death penalty* and might culminate in a decision declaring capital punishment unconstitutional in all cases'[34]

In the final version of the memorandum, Goldberg stated that the death penalty was 'barbaric and inhuman'. He argued that the eighth amendment, like the others in the Bill of Rights, 'was intended as a counter-majoritarian limitation on government action to be applied to nurture rather than retard our "evolving standards of decency".' He had found disturbing evidence that the application of the death penalty was arbitrary, haphazard, capricious and discriminatory. Goldberg recognized that his brethren might not agree with him that capital punishment, as such, was unconstitutional. He submitted the alternative proposal that the infliction of the death penalty for certain crimes and in the case of certain offenders violated the eighth and fourteenth amendments.[35] According to Dershowitz, when the memorandum was circulated among the justices it had a 'bombshell' effect, but found approval only with Justices Brennan and Douglas. Justice Hugo Black, a liberal member of the Court, disagreed with what he regarded as an attempt to 'rewrite' the Bill of Rights. Furthermore, the Chief Justice, Earl Warren, asked Goldberg not to publish the memorandum, fearing that it would undermine the Court's credibility in other controversial areas such as desegregation.[36]

As Justice Brennan later commented, the memorandum was highly unusual for several reasons. 'First, although not unheard of, it was (and still is) most unusual for an individual justice to take it upon himself or herself to write at length, prior to our conference, about cases which had neither been argued nor even set for argument, and then circulate that memorandum to all of his or her colleagues. Second, the subject matter of the memorandum was the constitutionality of the death penalty, *a subject that had received relatively little attention from the courts and that was not, at the time, an issue upon which either litigants or the press had begun to focus*.' It was particularly unusual, Brennan concluded, because in none of the six cases had any party directly challenged validity of the capital punishment under the eighth amendment.[37]

In due course, the six petitions were denied by the Court, but Goldberg, together with Brennan and Douglas, joined in a dissent on one of the cases in which a black man had been sentenced to death for the rape of a white woman.[38] According to Dershowitz, the purpose of Goldberg's dissent '*was to alert the criminal defence bar to the fact that at least three justices had some doubts about the constitutionality of capital punishment in some contexts . . . (and to send them a message) to raise the issue of cruel and unusual punishment . . . That message was heard clearly and understood fully*.'[39] There can be no doubt as to the effect of the 'Goldberg signal' upon the staff at the LDF who were 'jolted into action'[40] and who took the questions posed in the dissent as an invitation to 'search for the statistics that might isolate the racial factor'.[41]

A subsequent study of decisions between life imprisonment and death taken by juries in rape cases, carried out for LDF by Anthony Amsterdam and Marvin Wolfgang both of the University of Pennsylvania, established that when the defendant was black and the victim was white, the chances of being sentenced to death were high; in all other rape cases such a sentence was remote. These results were used in several cases, but lawyers at the LDF soon became convinced that the broader issues had to be addressed. As two leading participants later explained: 'Once having raised these claims, however, it was not adequate to assert them on behalf of some defendants and ignore other defendants in the hope that they would receive the benefit of a new rule announced at a later date . . . The attack quickly became one against capital punishment as such.'[42] The LDF staff had decided that 'if the death penalty were to wither away it would be necessary to set in motion forces other than those generated by organized abolitionists.'[43]

The litigation line of attack was now formally launched by LDF, but it was to remain self-contained and largely detached from the public policy arena. One of the few non-lawyers who played a part in the LDF campaign was Hugo Bedau who had been a leading participant in the successful Oregan campaign. The adoption of an abolitionist agenda by the LDF was a quantum leap but, as Bedau has commented, it was 'pending a completion of their yet unfolding and not fully defined constitutional strategy'.[44] Referring to a conference organized by LDF in New York in 1967, Bedau remarked that confronting the death penalty was largely an 'equal protection' argument at that time, but it was clear that eighth amendment issues would have to be grappled with, and such a task was regarded as extremely daunting. At the conclusion of this three day conference Bedau has recalled 'my head was swimming with exciting possibilities that were going to unfold in a way that ten years earlier I could not have imagined . . . this was a calculated frontal attack that no-one had ever undertaken before . . . being part of an activity that really mattered on a national scale was something that had not happened before and I don't know that I had ever really imagined it.'[45]

In June 1972, *Furman* decided that the overwhelming majority of existing death penalty statutes were unconstitutional, but within four years this 'greatest victory' by abolitionists was revealed to be a false dawn. Procedurally correct death penalty statutes were endorsed by the Supreme Court in *Gregg v. Georgia*[46] and related cases, and in due course were enacted by more than two thirds of the states and by the federal government. As long as specified procedural requirements were satisfied, the death penalty, at least for the foreseeable future, had become constitutionally secure.

Mathiesen's abolitionist perspective provides a useful framework for reconsidering the respective struggles against the death penalty in Britain and the United States. It is evident from the preceding accounts that during 1963 signals emerged from top policy spheres in both countries. Harold Wilson, the leader of the British Labour Party, signalled that if his party won the forthcoming election, parliamentary time would be found for an abolitionist bill. The issue, of course, could be resolved only by Parliament, but the broad base of élite support for abolition across the country which had been mobilized eight years earlier was also critical. The 'Wilson signal', if it really amounted to that, gave new heart to abolitionists regardless of their party allegiances and, perhaps in particular, to members of the Conservative parliamentary party.

The 'Goldberg signal' that three Supreme Court justices were ready to consider the constitutionality of the death penalty, was more clear-cut. It was intended expressly by Goldberg to prompt public interest lawyers into action, but it also had the aim of reaching the wider public policy audience. In the event, although the dissent received coverage by the press, its impact was almost entirely confined to those lawyers intent on getting a case before the Supreme Court. This narrow reaction epitomized the damaging chasm between the public policy and litigation lines of attack on the death penalty in the United States. There were few, if any, effective networks extending across both and upon which a more coherent campaign might have been built. When the litigation campaign began in earnest in the mid-1960s, very little in the way of public policy opposition to the death penalty existed. The American League to Abolish the Death Penalty, by that time, had become a totally ineffective organization. Bedau has commented that it was clear to the lawyers at the LDF that there had to be visible public support for what they were trying to do in the courts, and 'that there needed to be a public component to the legal campaign. But the American League never went anywhere and died after *Furman*.'[47] The litigation approach, which had not existed prior to the early 1960s, was by the end of the decade clearly dominant. During the period immediately before *Furman*, lawyers (many of them associated with the LDF) enjoyed a virtual monopoly in the attack on the death penalty. One close observer has commented that 'the litigation community is almost distinct. There is some overlap but it is not enormous . . . you more or less have to deal with them as separate universes.' By this time the abolitionist movement had become 'litigation dominated . . . the Legal Defense Fund built it into a crusade - they are the crusaders, outsiders taking on all sorts of challenges at the local level . . . that legal network is at the core, and had displaced and made second-class citizens out of ordinary campaigners.'[48] The unfortunate consequence was the neglect of opposition to the death penalty at the level of public policy.

In the end, the litigation strategy was too little and too late. Even after the *Furman* decision there was no real sense of urgency. Hugo Bedau, for example, has commented that for a while he did not really detect the way in which 'the political environment that was all around us was beginning to erupt . . . maybe we had already run out of time.'[49] Although the American Civil Liberties Union (ACLU), perhaps encouraged by the 'Goldberg signal', had adopted a formal position against the death penalty in 1965, it was not until *after* the Supreme Court's *Gregg* decision and the rush by several states to re-introduce capital statutes that a concerted effort was made by ACLU to complement the LDF's litigation strategy with a public policy campaign.[50]

The first director of the ACLU capital punishment project, Henry Schwarzschild, has recalled that 'when *Gregg* came down it did two main things. It defeated the attempts to abolish the death penalty by litigating its constitutionality, and it returned the issue of the death penalty to the arena of public policy . . . The ACLU decided that since the LDF had a staff, some funding and enormous intellectual resources, including Tony Amsterdam, on the litigational side . . . (and as) the Fund isn't going to deal with anything but law cases it recognises no social reality beyond the four walls of the courthouse . . . (the ACLU would) therefore take what for the moment was the unploughed (public policy) side of that field of the death penalty.'[51] It was also at this time that Schwarzschild began putting together the National Coalition Against the Death Penalty which by 1978 was supported by some sixty multi-issue organizations.

Finally, the notion of 'positive and negative reforms', the other strand of Mathiesen's abolitionist perspective, also casts useful light upon aspects of these episodes. In particular, the British Homicide Act 1957 and the *Furman* decision by the American Supreme Court in 1972 may briefly be compared. The Homicide Act was, of course, resisted by abolitionists, but in the event, despite fears at the time, it turned out to be a 'negative' reform. The hyper-ambivalence which it generated in its wake was more than retentionists could handle, and, despite a severe hardening of attitudes on criminal policy by both main political parties during the early 1990s, the death penalty was further removed from the political agenda than at any time in British history. By contrast, it soon became evident that far from leading to abolition, *Furman* was the springboard for a search for an 'ideal of reliability'[52] in legislating for the death penalty. In Mathiesen's terminology, *Furman* can be construed as a 'positive' reform which reduced the chances of any abolitionist challenge. As Hugo Bedau cautioned: '(I)t admittedly appears that the reforms enacted during the past two decades have brought greater fairness into a death sentence system hitherto shot through with arbitrary and discriminatory use of authority. To that extent, however, these reforms rationalize every death sentence and every execution; they may have made what remains of capital punishment in the United States more, not less, acceptable.'[53]

While *Furman* sought procedural regularity, the Homicide Act indulged in the 'chimera' of defining specific categories of capital murder. The new generation of death penalty statutes in the wake of *Furman* are by no means beyond challenge on grounds of intrinsic unfairness and unreliability. As Charles Black and others have eloquently demonstrated, however by the mid-1990s a successful assault seemed more remote than ever.[54] This comparison of the Homicide Act and the *Furman* decision also underlines the uneven and often unpredictable nature of events. In Britain, abolitionists fought the Homicide Act, but this legislation probably brought abolition forward. In the United States, abolitionists applauded *Furman* but this 'greatest victory' almost certainly made abolition more unlikely.

Hugo Bedau has acknowledged the indispensable role played by moral élites, but he also has cautioned against overstating their impact. In Bedau's view, 'all those groups and individuals in and out of government in the United States who have supported efforts to end the death penalty have succeeded only in channelling a historic development that is subject to forces they can no more accelerate than others can destroy or significantly retard.'[55] Taken too far, of course, notions of historical determinism encourage apathy and inertia, and the premise of all abolitionist movements is that campaigns may make a difference to the course of events. With the death penalty in mind, Margery Fry, the British penal reformer, acknowledged these uncertainties when she remarked: 'You march round the walls of Jericho for a number of years, and they do in the end fall down, but how much this is due to your processions and trumpetings, to your meetings and pamphlets and deputations, and how much to their crumbling from internal rottenness, you will never know, nor should you too urgently ask.'[56] Perhaps Miss Fry was right.

## ENDNOTES

1. Sebastian Scheerer, 'Towards Abolitionism', *Contemporary Crises* 10 (1986), 6; see also part IV, Zbigniew Lasocik, Monika Platek and Irena Rzeplinska (eds.) *Abolitionism in History: On Another Way of Thinking* (Warsaw, International Conference on Penal Abolition, Institute of Social Prevention and Resocialization, Warsaw University, 1991), 167-188.

2. ibid., 10.

3. Thomas Mathiesen, *The Politics of Abolition* (London, Martin Robertson, 1974), 202.

4. ibid, 203 (emphasis in the original); for a good example of a 'negative reform' consider the work of Jerome Miller who as commissioner of the Massachusetts Department of Youth Services closed down the young offender institutions in the early 1970s. Miller has recalled that he took actions which questioned the premises sustaining the young offender institutions for which he was responsible. 'Even questioning them created hyper-ambivalence, weakened norms, and blurred roles. It was no recipe for smooth management, but management was not my purpose'. Jerome G. Miller, *Last One Over the Wall The Massachusetts Experiment in Closing Reform Schools* (Columbus, Ohio University Press, 1991), 90-91.

5. Thomas Mathiesen, *Prison on Trial A Critical Assessment* (London, Sage, 1990), 155.

6. Thomas Mathiesen, 'Why Prison' (Annual Lecture of the Centre for Criminology and the Social and Philosophical Study of Law, The University of Edinburgh, 23 May 1991), 13; see also op. cit. n. 5, esp. pp. 137-168. Mathiesen's exploration of the decline of the Inquisition in early seventeenth century Spain led to his instructive conclusion that 'a liberal inquisitor with support from above (thus) became instrumental in the subsequent abolition of witch burning.' ibid., 158-159. The prison population reductionist examples, which Mathiesen draws upon for his analysis, are described in Andrew Rutherford, *Prisons and the Process of Justice* (Oxford, Oxford University Press, 1986), esp. 121-151.

7. *Furman v. Georgia*, 408 U.S. 238 (1972). Although *Furman* was decided 5-4, there were nine separate judgements. Only Justices Brennan and Marshall found the death penalty to be unconstitutional under all circumstances. The centre ground was held by Justices Douglas, Stewart and White who held that existing death penalty statutes as administered were in breach of constitutional requirements, thereby opening the way to *Gregg* four years later. Among the vast literature on *Furman* is an insider's account by Justice William Brennan, which emphases the fragility of the position which he had reached, with Justice Marshall changing his mind on the constitutional arguments at some point between June 1971 and January 1972. William J. Brennan 'Constitutional Adjudication and the Death Penalty: A View from the Court', *Harvard Law Review*, 100 (1986), 313-331. For a recent appreciation of Marshall's pioneering fight against the death penalty as an advocate with the NAACP Legal Defense and Education Fund, see David I. Bruck, 'Does the Death Penalty Matter? Reflections of a Death Row Lawyer', *Reconstruction*, 3 (1991), 35-39.

8. There was a moratorium on executions from June 1967 and over five hundred persons on death rows were spared as a direct result of *Furman*. Among those who saw *Furman* as marking the end of the death penalty in the United States was Hugo Bedau, who wrote in 1974: 'Perhaps I may hazard another prediction: we will not see another execution in this century.' Hugo Bedau, *The Courts, the Constitution and Capital Punishment* (Lexington, Mass., Lexington Books, 1977), 90. Former Supreme Court Justice Arthur Goldberg, wrote in 1972 that 'it is extremely doubtful that it (the death penalty) will be legislatively revived.' Arthur J. Goldberg, 'Supreme Court Review, 1972' *Journal of Criminal Law, Criminology and Police Science*, 63 (1972), 465. Executions resumed in January 1977 when Gary Gilmore was killed by a firing squad in the Utah state prison.

9. Among the supporters of the motion was the future Labour home secretary, James Chuter Ede. He was a retentionist during the period he was home secretary, but, as noted below, thereafter reverted to his abolitionist position.

10. James B. Christoph, *Capital Punishment and British Politics The British Movement to Abolish the Death Penalty 1947-57* (London, George Allen and Unwin, 1962), 38.

11. CM (47) *89th Conclusions,* quoted in Lord Windlesham, *Responses to Crime Volume 2 Penal Policy in the Making* (Oxford, Oxford University Press), 58-59. Windlesham also mentions the estimate by the historian Keith Morgan that within the Labour Cabinet there was a majority in the Cabinet of 11-5 in favour of retaining the death penalty.

12. Sydney Silverman (1895-1968) was on the left of the Labour Party and might not have seemed ideally suited to leading a cross-party attack on the death penalty in the House of Commons (a solicitor by training, he was an M. P. from 1935 until his death). James Christoph commented that perhaps the main problem for the Conservative abolitionists, 'was to convince their followers to accept the overall leadership of Sydney Silverman. To swallow this leadership was no easy thing for any Conservative, for among Government backbenchers Silverman had gained a singular reputation as a vitriolic and effective Tory-baiter. It was a measure of Silverman's skill and self-restraint on this issue, and of the dedication to their cause of the small band of Conservative abolitionists, that this obstacle was successfully overcome . . .' op. cit. n. 10, p. 142. For Silverman's own account of the parliamentary struggle against capital punishment up to 1956, see his Afterword in Arthur Koestler, *Reflections on Hanging* (New York, Macmillan, 1957), 205-214.

13. *Report of the Royal Commission on Capital Punishment, 1949-1953* Cmd. 8932 (London, H.M.S.O. 1953), 214.

14. Timothy Evans was hanged in March 1950 after the home secretary, James Chuter Ede (who had been an abolitionist before the War) refused to grant a reprieve. This execution did not, however, received much attention until the arrest and subsequent trial of the serial murderer John Reginald Halliday Christie, who had been the leading Crown witness against Evans. Contemporary accounts include, Michael Eddowes, *The Man on your Conscience: An Investigation of the Evans Murder Trial* (London, Cassell, 1955), and Ludovic Kennedy, *Ten Rillington Place* (London, Victor Gollancz, 1961). The Evans case was one of a handful of *causes célèbres* which did much to shape, and gain wider support for, the abolitionist campaign of the period.

15. Terence Morris, *Crime and Criminal Justice since 1945* (Oxford, Blackwell, 1989), 83. The third case which did much to galvanise the nation was the hanging in 1953 of nineteen year old Derek Bentley who was under police arrest at the moment when his sixteen year old accomplice shot and killed a police officer.

16. The National Campaign for the Abolition of Capital Punishment was successful in recruiting a very distinguished array of some seventy leading personalities onto its Committee of Honour. The Campaign was chaired by the publisher, Victor Gollancz and among the members of the executive committee was Gerald Gardiner and Arthur Koestler, both of whom wrote influential books on the topic. See, Gerald Gardiner, *Capital Punishment as a Deterrent: and the Alternative* (London, Gollancz, 1956); and Arthur Koestler, *Reflections On Hanging* (London, Macmillan, 1956; and New York, Macmillan, 1957, with a preface by Edmond Cahn).

17. For a useful account of the inequities produced by the Homicide Act 1957, see J. E. Hall Williams 'Developments since the Homicide Act 1957', Appendix in Elizabeth Orman Tuttle, *The Crusade against Capital Punishment in Great Britain* (London, Stevens, 1961), 149-165.

18. Enid Huws Jones, *Margery Fry The Essential Amateur* (York, William Sessions, 1990), 236. The author recalls Leon Radzinowicz, who had been a member of the Royal Commission on Capital Punishment, making a similar point to his students at Cambridge in 1961.

19. Sir Ernest Gowers in remarks to Louis Blom-Cooper and Terence Morris, op. cit. n. 15, p. 81. The Royal Commission, after a thorough review of the problems arising from degrees of murder, including international experience, concluded 'with regret that the object of our quest is chimerical and that it must be abandoned'. op. cit. n. 13, 189.

Gowers had himself made an important contribution to the abolitionist literature, see Sir Ernest Gowers, *Life For A Life? The Problem Of Capital Punishment* (London, Chatto and Windus, 1956).

20. R. A. Butler, *The Art of the Possible* (London, Hamish Hamilton, 1971), 202.

21. Tony Benn, *Out of the Wilderness: Diaries 1963-67* (London , Hutchinson, 1987), 36. Benn added that 'this is very close to Gerald Gardiner' s heart and was almost an invitation for him to join the Government.' When Labour won the general election in October 1964, Gardiner became the Lord Chancellor.

22. At the time, the Labour Government had an overall majority of three in the House of Commons.

23. op. cit. n. 11, p. 89.

24. Philip English Mackey, (ed). *Voices Against Death; American Opposition to Capital Punishment, 1787-1975* (New York, Burt Franklin, 1976). The earlier reform eras identified by Mackey were 1833-53 and 1895-1917.

25. In May 1966 a Gallup survey showed, for the first time, more Americans against rather than in favour of the death penalty for murder. This poll found 47 percent of respondents against the death penalty, 42 percent in favour and 11 percent undecided. However, within thirteen months opinion had begun its sharp swing in the other direction. As Robert M Bohm notes, the watershed year for long-term trends is 1966 which marked the end of a thirteen year nonlinear decline and the beginning of a twenty year nonlinear increase in support of the death penalty. Between 1953-1966 support for the death penalty decreased 28 percentage points, whereas between 1966-85 support increased by 33 percentage points. Robert M. Bohm, *The Death Penalty in America: Current Research* (Cincinnati, Ohio, Anderson Publishing, 1991, 117).

26. Herbert L. Cobin, 'Abolition and Restoration of the Death Penalty in Delaware' in Hugo Adam Bedau (ed.) *The Death Penalty in America* (Chicago, Aldine, 1967), 359-373.

27. Hugo Adam Bedau, *Death is Different Studies in the Morality, Law and Politics of Capital Punishment* (Boston University Press, 1987), 155-163.

28. These states were Vermont, New York and New Mexico. In 1972, and prior to the *Furman* decision on 29 June, the state supreme courts in New Jersey and California abolished the death penalty. The states which had already abolished the death penalty were Michigan (1846), Rhode Island

(1852), Wisconsin (1853), Maine (1853), Minnesota (1911), Alaska (1957) and Hawaii (1957). See, William J. Bowers *Legal Homicide Death as Punishment in America, 1964-1982* (Boston, Northeastern University Press, 1984), 9.

29. Thurgood Marshall, who was leading counsel in the landmark *Brown v. Board of Education* (1954), was appointed by President Johnson to be Solicitor General in 1965 and two years later was elevated to the Supreme Court.

30. Michael Meltsner, *Cruel and Unusual: the Supreme Court and Capital Punishment* (New York, Random House, 1973), 79. Meltsner was lawyer with the LDF during this period and this insider's account of the litigation line of attack on the death penalty up to *Furman* is an indispensable source.

31. Jack Greenberg and Jack Himmelstein, 'Varieties of Attack on the Death Penalty', *Crime and Delinquency,* 15 (1969), 114-115.

32. Arthur J. Goldberg, 'The Death Penalty and the Supreme Court', *Arizona Law Review,* 15 (1973), 360. Goldberg left the Supreme Court in 1965 to become U.S. Ambassador to the United Nations. In 1970 Goldberg and Dershowitz wrote a joint article in which they argued that the Supreme Court should declare the death penalty to be in violation of the eighth amendment. Arthur J. Goldberg and Alan M. Dershowitz, 'Declaring the Death Penalty Unconstitutional', *Harvard Law Review,* 83 (1970), 1773-1819.

33. Alan M. Dershowitz, *Best Counsel* (New York, Random House, 1982), 307.

34. ibid, 308 (emphasis added).

35. op. cit. n. 32, p. 362.

36. op cit. n. 33, p. 308.

37. op. cit. n. 7, pp. 314-315 (emphasis added).

38. *Rudolph v. Alabama* 375 U.S. 889 (1963).

39. op. cit. n. 33, pp. 308-309 (emphasis added).

40. op. cit. n. 30.

41. op. cit. n. 31, p. 115.

42. ibid., 116.

43. Interview with Hugo Bedau, December 1994.

44. ibid.

45. ibid.

46. *Gregg v. Georgia* 428 U.S. 153 (1976). Justices Brennan and Marshall dissented.

47. Interview with Hugo Bedau, December 1994; it should be noted, however, that in 1968 the subcommittee of Criminal Laws and Procedures of the Senate Judiciary Committee (chairman, Senator Philip A. Hart) held hearings on the death penalty. See especially the statement to the subcommittee by Attorney General Ramsey Clark, 2 July 1968.

48. Interview with William J. Bowers, January 1993.

49. Interview with Hugo Bedau, December 1994.

50. The ACLU did, however, publish Hugo Adam Bedau, *The Case Against Capital Punishment* in 1973.

51. Interview with Henry Schwarzschild, January 1993; for a recent account of the struggle against the death penalty since *Furman* see Herbert H. Haines, *Against Capital Punishment: the Anti-Death Penalty Movement in America, 1972-1994* (New York, Oxford University Press, 1996).

52. Robert Woll, 'The Death Penalty and Federalism: Eighth Amendment Constraints on the Allocation of State Decision-making Power ', *Stanford Law Review,* 35 (1983), 806-809.

53. Hugo Adam Bedau, 'The Death Penalty in America: Yesterday and Today', *Dickinson Law Review,* 95 (1991), 767. Bedau made a somewhat similar point some years earlier, commenting that 'the very reforms in the administration of capital punishment, the hard-won results in the struggle for abolition during the last century, have paradoxically become the major obstacles to further statutory appeal. They have mitigated the rigidity and brutality of this form of punishment to a point where the average citizen no longer regards it as an affront to his moral sensibilities. As a consequence, he has no strong motive to press for further reduction, much less complete abolition of the death penalty.' Hugo Adam Bedau, 'General Introduction' in Hugo Adam Bedau (ed.) *The Death Penalty in America* (Chicago, Aldine, 1967), 14-15. This argument has, for example, been

applied to the ending of public executions in Britain in 1868. V.A.C. Gatrell has written that this legislation marked a 'civilizing' but not 'a humane moment in British history, a civilizing process may redeploy, sanitize, and camouflage disciplinary and other violence without necessarily diminishing it . . . As MPs knew, abolishing public executions ensured that capital punishment for the worst of crimes would continue, its deterrent horror enhanced through its invisibility. Total abolitionists were neatly outflanked by this manoeuvre.' V. A. C. Gatrell, *The Hanging Tree Execution and the English People 1770-1868* (Oxford, Oxford University Press, 1994), 590, 610.

54. Charles L. Black, Jnr., *Capital Punishment The Inevitability of Caprice and Mistake* Second edition (New York and London, W.W. Norton, 1978).

55. op. cit. n. 27, p. 154; For an earlier version, see Hugo Adam Bedau, 'The Death Penalty in the United States: Imposed Law and the Role of Moral Elites' in Sandra B. Burman and Barbara Harrell-Bond (eds.), *The Imposition of Law* (New York, Academic Press, 1979), 45-68.

56. Margery Fry, BBC radio interview broadcast on 12 May 1957, cited op. cit. n. 18, p. 236.

# Index

285

# Transforming Criminal Policy

Andrew Rutherford                                    ISBN 1 872 870 31 7

TRANSFORMING CRIMINAL POLICY is the first work in the series. Other volumes (to be issued at a rate of four to six each year) address key issues for criminal policy in the United Kingdom and across the world. This initial volume is written by the series editor **Andrew Rutherford,** author of *Prisons and the Process Justice, Growing Out of Crime: The New Era* and *Criminal Justice and the Pursuit of Decency.*

TRANSFORMING CRIMINAL POLICY explores what the subtitle calls 'Spheres of Influence in the USA, The Netherlands and England and Wales during the 1980s', focusing on the activities of three strategically placed individuals: James Q. Wilson, Dato Steenhuis and David Faulkner.

Whilst the policy-making process cannot be determined by referenda, it is too important to be left exclusively to experts. In a central argument the author insists on the need for an integrated criminal policy as a means of protecting those values which are fundamental to a liberal democracy. A way forward is outlined which seeks to overcome 'narrow and compartmentalised ways of thinking about crime and what to do about it'. These ideas will be of interest to people across the whole arena of criminal policy - and of particular interest to those practitioners and students of criminology or criminal justice who reject tidy or simplistic solutions and the often seductive impact of populist agenda.

*160 pages. Direct mail price £16 plus £1.50 p&p (UK only. Postage abroad charged at cost).*

From

## WATERSIDE PRESS

Domum Road Winchester SO23 9NN
Telephone or Fax 01962 855567

Criminal Policy Series readers may also be interested in an earlier Waterside Press publication:

# Relational Justice
## Repairing the Breach

Edited by Jonathan Burnside and Nicola Baker

Foreword by Lord Woolf

In the light of widespread disillusionment with measures to tackle crime, *Relational Justice* takes up a neglected theme at the heart of justice: the need to tackle relationships damaged by crime, particularly those between victims and offenders.

Thirteen authors come together to explore this theme bringing personal, professional or academic perspectives to the argument. The essays challenge current thinking about criminal justice and are designed to encourage debate on the values underlying penal theory and practice.

The *Relational Justice* reform dynamic will be of interest to all people who are concerned about crime and responses too it.

'There could not be a more appropriate time to publish this extremely important book': Lord Woolf

ISBN 1 872 870 22 8 *Direct mail price: £10 plus £1.50 p&p (UK only. Postage abroad charged at cost).*

## Some further titles from Waterside Press

**Growing Out of Crime** The New Era  Andrew Rutherford  A classic and challenging work about young offenders and their progress towards adulthood. (Second reprint) ISBN 1 872 870 06 6. £12.

**Criminal Justice and the Pursuit of Decency** Andrew Rutherford
'By reminding us that, without "good men and women" committed to humanising penal practice, criminal justice can so easily sink into apathy and pointless represssion, Andrew Rutherford has sounded both a warning and a note of optimism.' : *Sunday Telegraph*. ISBN 1 872 870 21 X. £12.50.

**Criminal Classes** Offenders at School  Angela Devlin  As featured by the BBC and in *The Guardian*, this book examines for the first time in detail the links between educational failure and offending. ISBN 1 872 870 30 9. £16.

Introduction to the **Criminal Justice Process**  Bryan Gibson Paul Cavadino  'Rarely, if ever, has this complex process been described with such comprehensiveness and clarity, total lack of jargon and in a mere 160 pages': *Justice of the Peace*. ISBN 1 872 870 09 0. £12.

Introduction to the **Magistrates' Court**  Bryan Gibson  The second edition of this popular work. A clear and comprehensive outline in twelve concise chapters - plus a *Glossary of Words, Phrases and Abbreviations* (750 entries). ISBN 1 872 870 15 5. £10.

Introduction to the **Probation Service**  Anthony Osler  An illuminating overview, including a brief history and a survey of modern-day duties, responsibilities and issues. ISBN 1 872 870 19 8. £10.

**The Sentence of the Court** A Handbook for Magistrates  Michael Watkins, Winston Gordon and Anthony Jeffries. Consultant Dr David Thomas. Foreword by Lord Taylor, Lord Chief Justice.  Created under the auspices of the Justices' Clerks' Society, the handbook has been supplied to every magistrate in areas such as Inner London, Manchester, Bristol and Newcastle. This invaluable guide for *all* practitioners contains a simple but effective outline of magistrates' sentencing powers. ISBN 1 872 870 25 2. £10.

Order direct from WATERSIDE PRESS, Domum Road, Winchester, SO23 9NN. Tel or Fax 01962 855567. The direct mail price is given above. **Important:** please add £1.50 per volume for p&p to a maximum of £6 (UK only. Postage abroad is charged at cost). Cheques should be made payable to 'Waterside Press'. If requested, we can invoice organizations for two or more books.